Note t

The titles in the GMB series of *Doing Business wi* of the 10 countries that joined the European Ur ...ay 2004 were first published in hard copy over the 18 months preceding entry.

Since publication, there have been changes in the law and regulatory environment in each country, both in the period up to accession as countries strove to complete the harmonization of their systems with the EU's *acquis communataire* body of legislation and directives and during the 18 months since. In some countries there have been changes in the taxation regimes or in accounting regulations. Change has occurred in political environments too, following parliamentary elections or in the balance of coalition governments.

The economic climate of some states has been affected by the continuing malaise of the EU15 economies. Six of the EU10 (Cyprus, Estonia, Latvia, Lithuania, Malta and Slovakia) have entered the EU exchange rate mechanism 2, the eurozone's ante-chamber and ... ct to ... ed in ... ly en ... or la...

... s, wh ... e re ... re ta ... of re...

... rs pu ... al su...

... e inc ... 5, 2.6

... d ... r

Doing Business with the CZECH REPUBLIC

THE WORLD HEALTH SERVICE
commitment
As the world's largest expatriate health insurer, we're committed to providing the highest quality service to our members. With over 27 years experience and a global network spanning 190 countries, you can rely on us to be there for your overseas employees, wherever they may be.
BUPA International - trust us to care.
Manchester
Official Health Partner
www.bupa-intl.com
+44 (0) 1273 208200
DBG1/07

GLOBAL MARKET BRIEFINGS

Doing Business with the CZECH REPUBLIC

CONSULTANT EDITORS:

JONATHAN REUVID AND MARAT TERTEROV

IN ASSOCIATION WITH:

BANK AUSTRIA CREDITANSTALT

CMS CAMERON MCKENNA

COFACE

CZECHINVEST

DELOITTE & TOUCHE

MERCHANT INTERNATIONAL GROUP

GMB

Publishers' note

First published 2003 updated in 2005

Book ISBN 1 9050 5021 6 E-book ISBN 1905050550

British Library Cataloguing in Publication Data

A CIP record for this book is available from the British Library

Čermák Hořejš Myslil

(Lawyers and patent attorneys)

Národní 32

110 00 PraGUE 1

Czech Republic

Telephone: (+420) 2 96 167 111

Telefax: (+420) 2 24 94 67 24

E-mail: intelprop@apk.cz

Senior partner: Dr Karel Čermák

Number of lawyers: 15

Fields of activity

Intellectual property law (patents, trade marks, utility models, industrial designs, copyright), competition law, real property, antimonopoly law, arbitration, commercial, investments, corporate, mergers and acquisitions and litigation.

Language spoken

Czech, English, German, French, Russian, Swedish.

Firm Profile

Čermák Hořejš Myslil counts among the leading intellectual property practices in the Czech Republic. It has a large expertise in all kinds of intellectual property matters, including patents, trade marks, utility models, industrial designs, copyright, in IP litigation and in related fields, such as unfair competition, pharmaceuticals, technical standards, domain names and other intellectual property aspects of the Internet etc. Its clients include a number of the world's leading multinational corporations as well as same of the leaders of the Czech economy.

Another major area of practice of the firm is commercial and corporate law, with a special forms on litigation, arbitration and other kinds of dispute resolution, merges & acquisitions, antitrust, bankruptcy, real estate, investment and international commercial transactions.

Through its Slovak associates Bušová Ursínyová Bušo, the firm provides all kinds of legal services in Slovakia, in particular in intellectual property and business law matters.

At present, the law and patent office has fifteen lawyers, five in-house patent attorneys and more than fifty members of administrative staff, including qualified translators in all major languages and technical experts. It also regularly collaborates with approximately one hundred outside consultants from various fields of technology and law. Languages spoken are Czech, Slovak, English, German, French and Swedish.

Contents

Service Industries

PART FIVE: CASE STUDIES

PART SIX: APPENDICES

Foreword

Czech Republic consolidates lead in foreign direct investment

The Czech Republic is lead recipient of foreign direct investment (FDI) in Central Europe per capita, and FDI inflows as a percentage of GDP—at an average of more than 10 per cent per year since 1999—have been among the highest in the world. Moreover, the country is sustaining its high rate of foreign investment, despite the global decline in the flow of foreign direct investment in 2001 and the significant reduction in neighbouring Poland.

The €1.5 billion investment by Toyota Peugeot Citroën Automobile in a state-of-the-art car plant in Kolin, where the ground-breaking ceremony was attended by the respective company presidents in the spring of 2002, clearly underpinned the flow of investment and represented a major vote of confidence in the Czech Republic.

The prognosis over the next five years is that the annual flow for foreign direct investment, currently circa €5 billion, will gradually decrease along with the number of new jobs created. However, this will be offset by a significant increase in higher value-added projects particularly within the sphere of strategic services. Analysts can already witness the 'flight to quality' in the Czech Republic, which no longer depends on lower labour costs for competitive advantage.

Already, 54 per cent of the cumulative flow of foreign direct investment (since 1992) is in the service sector, which also accounted for 68 per cent of the flow in 2000. Given the feature-rich telecommunications infrastructure, high intellectual capital, excellent German and English linguistic skills and an investment climate conducive to growth, the Czech Government decided to fully capitalise on these inherent strengths by preparing an incentives scheme for strategic services investors. Essentially, the aim of the incentives programme is to bridge any competitive gap between the Czech Republic and successful recipients of high value-added service sector investments, particularly in Western Europe.

The strength of the educational system and the pace of productivity increases hold the key to sustaining economic growth and enhancing living standards. In terms of productivity, many investors, particularly within the automotive sectors, achieve German levels of productivity in little more than two years from start-up, and when it comes to intellectual capital the Czech Republic excels.

The country has one of the highest outputs of science and engineering graduates in the world as a percentage of total degrees awarded. Prague's CVUT is the largest technical university in Europe, with 17,000 students, and throughout the Czech Republic there are around 50,000 technological university students out of a student population of circa 75,000 producing around 6,000 computer science related graduates per year.

CzechInvest, the Foreign Investment Agency, acts on behalf of the Ministry of Industry and Trade to promote the country as an investment location and, most importantly, to demonstrate to potential investors why their needs can be more competitively satisfied in the Czech Republic than in any other country in Europe. The Agency appreciates that the investor is driven by the need to better serve customers while enhancing cost efficiencies and productivity. And this sharp customer focus has been reflected by CzechInvest winning the coveted 'European Investment Promotion Agency of the Year' for two consecutive years.

For foreign investors wishing to source locally, CzechInvest also facilitates this process by raising the profile of over 1,000 competent Czech suppliers within the Agency's suppliers database that can be accessed via the website (www.czechinvest.org). Initially focusing on the electronics sector, the database, which has a broad regional spread, will soon include Czech firms operating within the precision engineering, aerospace and health care sectors.

To broaden the choice of locations in the Czech Republic CzechInvest instigated an Industrial Zone initiative which has created over 50 zones, bringing, in the process, 1,700 hectares of suitable land on to the market. And to encourage existing investors to put down deeper roots, CzechInvest's Aftercare Service aims to strengthen the links and anchor the ends of the value chains that have already been established in the Czech Republic—particularly within the automotive, electronics and precision engineering sectors.

Given the importance of current and accurate information, in relation to all the factors impacting on the investment appraisal process, this particular publication is aimed at providing most, if not all, of the pertinent data that investors seek in order to quantify the very considerable benefits from starting and expanding business in the Czech Republic.

Martin John
Chief Executive, CzechInvest
marketing@czechinvest.org

List of Contributors

ABN AMRO Bank is a prominent banking group, AA rated by Standard & Poor's and Aa2 by Moody's. The Bank has over 3,400 branches and a staff of some 110,000 in more than 60 countries. With the total assets of €597.4 billion (as per 2001), ABN AMRO ranks eighth in Europe and seventeenth in the world based on tier 1 capital. ABN AMRO entered the Czech market in 1991 and the Bank focuses there on providing high quality services in the fields of corporate and investment banking for select corporate, institutional and public sector clients. Two subsidiaries of ABN AMRO Group are also present on the Czech market—ABN AMRO Asset Management and ABN AMRO Pension Fund.

Aon Czech Republic Ltd is one of the leading insurance brokers companies on the Czech insurance market. It is part of Aon world-wide network of 550 offices in 120 countries. Aon Czech Republic provides the service to both the international and local clients. The company specializes in the insurance of industrial and other large risks. It has offices in Prague, Brno and Olomouc. The company has specialists in construction insurance, fire protection, claims handling, customs bonds, car fleet insurance, employee benefits, etc. Mr. Petr Knebl is the Managing Director and Mrs. Jitka Bendova is the main international contact.

The Bank Austria Creditanstalt Group is responsible for the markets in Central and Eastern Europe within the HVB Group, Europe's third largest banking group. Bank Austria Creditanstalt is Austria's largest commercial bank and one of the leading banking groups in the East. This is reflected in a comprehensive network of banking subsidiaries, representative offices and other financial services companies.

Within the HVB Group the Economics Department of Bank Austria Creditanstalt is competent for the entire macro and microeconomic research for Austria and the CEE region. In fulfilling these tasks, the department coordinates the data provided by and made available to the economic research units of the Group's CEE subsidiaries. It is also the EU competence centre for lobbying and for questions on eastward enlargement.

BT Ignite is the European arm of BT Group Plc, providing solutions to large multinational companies in the area of managed information and communication technology (ICT) services. BT Ignite builds on its world wide connectivity, broad-band, e-commerce, outsourcing and system integration capabilities. In the Central and Eastern European region, BT Ignite, in addition to its traditional telco operator role, is a partner to over 500 large enterprises and carriers in shaping the ICT infrastructure according to their business strategy.

Tomas Studenik (25) is a BT Ignite Solutions consultant working with large corporate clients to look for innovative ways of doing business using information and communication technology. His focus is on business process reengineering in the field of customer relationship management.

CA IB is one of the leading investment banks in CEE with its head office located in Vienna complemented by a product centre in London. CA IB Securities offers a wide range of services in the area of investment banking and is the market maker in equity and capital markets in the Czech Republic. It has an experienced professional staff. Its know-how, thorough understanding of business development and legal environment, contacts within the Czech professional community and state authorities, guarantee the highest standard of professionalism. Michal Srb is an Associate in the Research Department and is responsible for monitoring macroeconomic development in the Czech Republic as well as monitoring Czech banking, the oil and refinery sector and Czech construction sector. Martina Lambert is PR Manager, responsible for the development of effective marketing strategies and applying a broad spectrum of communication tools to build awareness of CA IB. She is also in charge of internal and external communication and providing support to Corporate Finance and Sales Team.

CA IB Financial Advisors is a major player and a prominent leading adviser in the area of international merges and acquisitions (M&A) as well as in consultancy services during privatization, primary equity issues and global certificates of deposit, which it is able to place either straight on the market or into the hands of private investors. Pavel Dedek is Assistant Director, Corporate Finance, and has worked on numerous transactions in several sectors, in particular energy, banking and utilities. He is an expert in valuations and due diligence. Bohdan Malaniuk is Director, Corporate Finance, and is responsible for overall M&A transaction execution. He has closed several transactions in the banking, food and drinks and finance sectors and advised VSŽ Košice (the largest steel mill in Slovakia) on the sale of its non-core asset, Czech football club and Champions League participant Sparta Prague. Filip Otruba is Director, Corporate Finance, and is responsible for M&A project management. He has closed many transactions in the Internet and TMT (telecommunications, media, technology) sector and led numerous transactions searching for strategic investors and advising clients mainly from developed markets investing in the Czech Republic.

CMS Cameron McKenna has been advising clients in the Czech Republic since 1991. Its Prague office is established as a General Commercial Partnership (v.o.s.) and is able to provide local experience combined with a full range of legal services to both domestic and international corporate clients, financial institutions and central and local government.

The office has been at the forefront of developing the regulatory environment, working closely with the Czech ministries on energy regulation, and the construction and planning laws. The office has been involved with many of the larger privatizations in the industrial, energy and banking sectors over the past five years, in both the Czech and Slovak republics.

The Prague office is staffed by both Czech and international lawyers, a number of which are recognized as leaders in their field. The resident legal team consists of some 20 partners and associate lawyers.

CzechInvest is an autonomous agency set up by the Ministry of Industry & Trade in 1992 charged with promoting and facilitating the inflow of direct investment to the Czech Republic. The agency currently focuses solely on manufacturing sector investment but there are plans to expand this to include service sector projects in the areas of shared services, call centres, software development, R&D, design centres and advanced distribution centres.

Deloitte & Touche Central Europe spans 17 countries and has 27 offices, but it operates as one cohesive entity.

In 1997 we integrated our national practices to form Deloitte & Touche Central Europe because we realized that to best serve our clients we needed to be able to share our knowledge and our manpower throughout the whole of our geography. Our integration has allowed us to manage regionally and deliver locally, adding value to our services and allowing them to be performed in the most efficient manner.

In becoming one firm, we positioned ourselves as the professional services firm to beat. Deloitte & Touche Central Europe has the expertise and the cultural diversity that is necessary to provide world-class services in the 21st century.

In addition to all the resources we have to draw on within Central Europe, we also have the expertise of our global organization, Deloitte Touche Tohmatsu. As part of Deloitte Touche Tohmatsu, our clients are given the same high level of services that we provide, anywhere in the world.

DTZ are one of the world's leading commercial real estate consultancies—with 125 offices in 33 countries—together with partners CY Leung & Co and Edmund Tie & Co in the Asia Pacific and AEW Capital Management in the US. The Prague office is part of DTZ CEE, which includes six other offices in Budapest, Vienna, Warsaw, Moscow, Kiev and St. Petersburg.

Omar Sattar, MRICS, is Joint Managing Director of DTZ Prague. Since joining the Prague office in 1997 he has been in charge of all valuation instructions and investment sales/purchases.

Egon Zehnder International specializes in assessing and recruiting business leaders with outstanding track records who will create competitive advantage and sustainable value. The worldwide success of the firm has been built on its insights into the people dynamics of corporations and their leadership requirements at the highest levels. Lubomir Ochotnicky is a consultant at the Prague office. He was formerly Managing Director at Scala Slovakia s.r.o., Bratislava.

Healey and Baker is an international partnership providing international real estate consultancy and agency advice. The company was established in London in 1820. It specialises in all types of commercial property, providing advice to investors, developers and occupiers. This advice includes: strategic advice, lease/portfolio administration, master planning, transaction management and implementation, valuation and asset management.

Healey and Baker operates throughout Europe, the Middle East and Africa and, as part of Cushman and Wakefield, delivers a global service through 10,800 staff in 156 offices in 50 countries.

Healey and Baker Czech Republic was established in Prague in 1993 and is situated in the centre of the City. The office has 32 employees with dedicated professional and specialised teams for all commercial sectors. Its clients include both national and international companies such as Ford, GE Capital, CS First Boston, DePfa, Rodamco, 3M, TriStannifer, ING Real Estate, Tesco, Bristish Airways, Walt Disney and Bat'a.

Ian Hutchins is International Corporate Affairs Manager at Tesco PLC. Based in the UK, he support teams in each country to manage press and government relations. Prior to joining Tesco he worked for Shell Chemical Europe in a commercial role based in Warsaw, Poland. Before joining Shell he studied Russian and East European History at the School of Slavonic & East European Studies, University of London, and undertook postgraduate research at the University of Gdansk (Poland). He is a fluent Polish speaker.

The PP Agency s.r.o. is one of the Czech Republic's few publishers of economic information focusing on the interests of foreign readers—busi nessmen, managers, investors. In this area, the PP Agency's publishing strategy is geared to providing economic information in its bi-monthly journal, *Czech Business and Trade,* appearing in five language versions, in its English language publication, *Doing Business in the Czech Republic* and the information server www.doingbusiness.cz.

Seddons is a multi-disciplinary legal practice with offices in London and Prague serving international and Czech clients in both the UK and the Czech Republic. The firm has been involved in the former Czechoslovakia since 1992, initially acting for foreign clients wishing to set up subsidiaries or branches to invest, to trade or to conduct other activities in the Czech Republic. It now has a highly developed general practice in Prague and provides advice primarily on corporate/commercial, property, employment and litigation matters.

Jan Grozdanovic LLB is a Partner in Seddons admitted to practice both in England (as a solicitor) and the Czech Republic (as an advocate) with a special responsibility for the firm's Czech practice. Barbara Stankevova is a Junior Associate at the Prague office, specializing in intellectual property law.

Oliver Schmitt, Dipl.-Kfm is the Managing Partner of Teamconsult, Czech Republic. A graduate of the University of Economics, Passau, he was Regional Manager of HVB Bank Czech Republic and a member of the Board of Directors of Transfinance and the Supervisory Board of Allianz penzijni fond until joining Teamconsult in 1999.

Skanska Property Czech Republic, s.r.o., is a member of Skanska group. Skanska is one of the largest companies in the world in construction-related services and project development. Skanska has operations in some 60 countries.

Since 1997 Skanska Property Czech Republic s.r.o, real estate developer, has been operating in the Czech Republic. Skanska is further represented by IPS Skanska a.s., which is the largest construction company on the Czech market with a number of successfully completed construction projects.

Skanska Property has finalized a new commercial project—Bredovský dvur—situated in the centre of Prague and is currently developing two new commercial schemes: Vysocanská brána, Prague 9 and Budejovická Alej. Next to these office projects Skanska has two new retail projects—Retail Park in Cestlice and Retail Park in Cerný Most, which are the first retail schemes for Skanska Property in the Czech Republic and also in Central Europe.

Anders Hall is the managing director of Skanska Property Czech Republic, s.r.o. and Ludek Schmidt is the head of project development.

Kevin R Smith is Managing Director of AWS Structured Finance Ltd. AWS acts as an adviser to companies on most financing and accounting matters including raising trade and project finance, debt and equity but has particular expertise in Central and Eastern Europe and the Former Soviet Union. Kevin Smith can be contacted on 01892 667891 or by email at kevin.r.smith@awsconsult.co.uk and more information can be found at www.awsconsult.co.uk

Technology Park Brno is a low density development providing modern business premises for technology companies in a business park environment adjacent to the Technical University of Brno. The park is intended to provide a total of 190,000m^2 of mixed commercial accommodation for office, research and light industry, together with associated retail, leisure and services facilities. Strategically located at the very heart of Europe the City of Brno provides excellent location advantages for modern businesses operating within the existing European Community and the progressive economies of Central and Eastern Europe.

Roderick Barker, General Manager of Technology Park Brno, joined the P&O Group in October 1994 as a development manager responsible for overseas projects in Portugal, Spain and the Czech Republic within the international property portfolio of Bovis. A Member of the Royal Institution of Chartered Surveyors, Mr Barker is seconded to the joint venture company as General Manager and has completed four and a half years in the post based at the Technology Park in Brno.

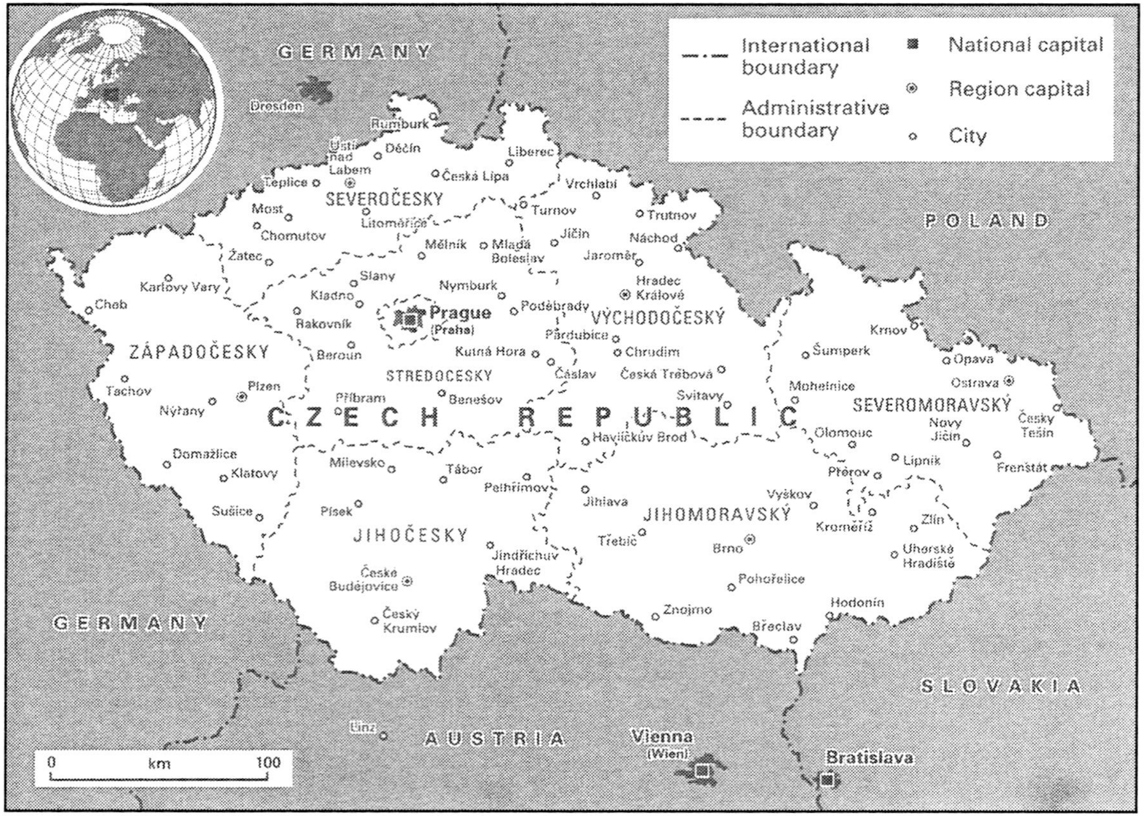

Map 1: The Czech Republic and its neighbours

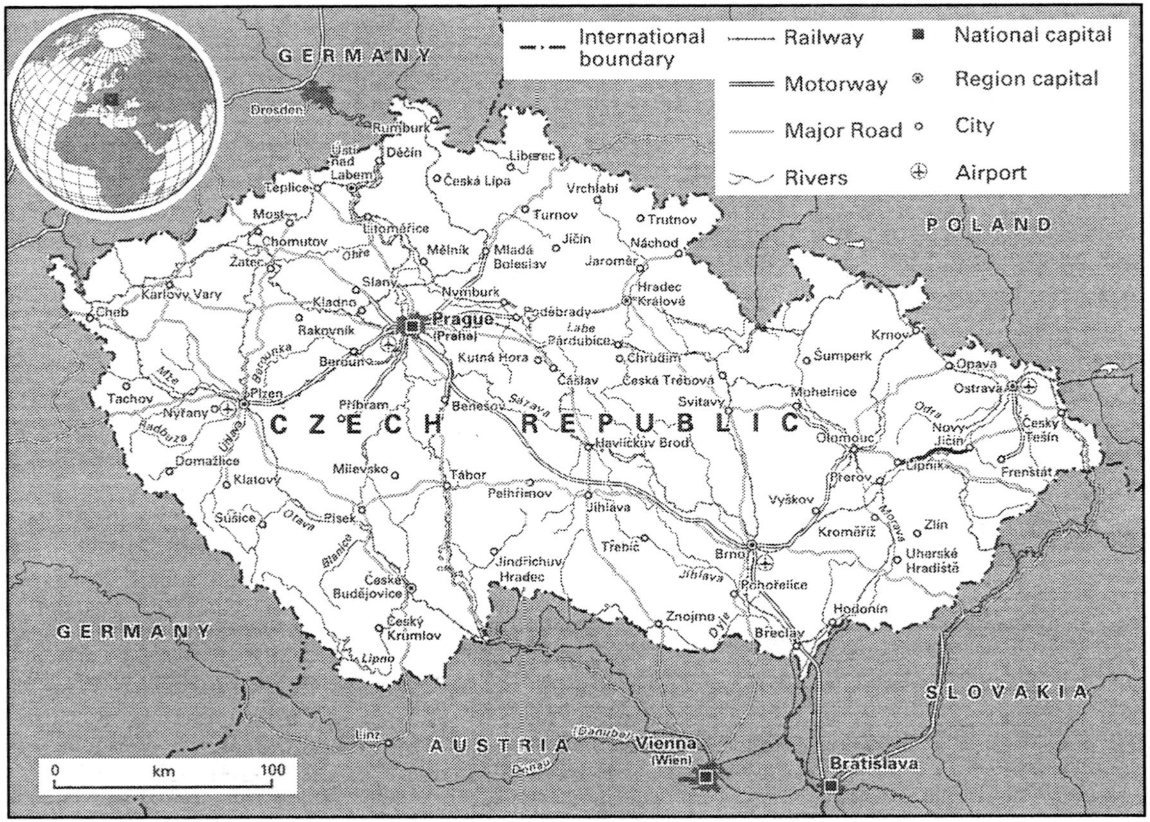

Map 2: The infrastructure of the Czech Republic

Introduction

As one of the first former East European states to commit to the transformation process into democratic government and a market economy the Czech Republic has remained in the forefront of inward investor attention and foreign trade since the early 1990s.

From the outset, Czechoslovakia and then the Czech Republic, following the agreed division into separate Czech and Slovakia states, set its sights on achieving rapid integration, both economically and politically, in the European Union (EU). The initial Europe Agreement between the EU and the Czech Republic, signed in 1993, came into force in 1995 and was followed swiftly by official accession negotiations beginning on 31 March 1993. Today, together with Hungary and Poland, the Czech Republic leads the first wave of accession candidates scheduled for EU membership by 2005.

Economic progress has been impressive but not without vicissitudes. In the early years of independence, the Czech Republic achieved rapid growth accompanied by high employment and low inflation. Foreign trade multiplied more than two and a half times between 1992 and 1996. However, the strains of high development activity and delayed reforms contributed to crises in the banking and other industries and the economy tumbled into a lengthy recession. As a result, between 1997 and 1999 the average growth rate of the Czech economy fell behind those of other CEE countries in transition. From this experience a broad consensus among Czech politicians emerged for a painful reform process of which the major elements have been: continuing restructuring and privatization of the state-owned banks and the industrial sector, incentive packages for foreign investors involving substantial tax relief, especially in the subsidized industrial parks, capital market legislation creating an independent regulatory authority and more rapid decision-making processes by the authorities. All of these developments are featured in *Doing Business with the Czech Republic;* most of the measures were necessary preconditions for EU accession.

As a result of this sustained reform programme the growth of the Czech economy resumed in 2000 and has continued during the more recent period of economic slowdown in the Western European economies.

The upturn in the economy and the reasonably good track record of the centre-left coalition in power up to June 2002 have encouraged Western business to invest strongly in the Czech Republic. Since 1998, foreign investment inflows have run at an average of 7 per cent of Czech GDP (approximately €4 billion) each year with about 80 per cent from EU countries up to the end of 2000. Aside from the economic potential, plus-points for investment in the Czech Republic include its solid infrastructure, its well-educated workforce and inherent manufacturing skills. Already in pole position among the EU accession candidates, the Czech automotive industry has now achieved a predominant status following the €1 billion joint venture investment announced by Toyota and PSA Peugeot Citroën earlier this year.

The outcome of the June 2002 election was another coalition government with the ruling Social Democrats, who have been in power since 1998, supported by a two-party block of Christian Democrats and free-market liberals under a new prime minister, Mr Vladimir Spidla. Since there is unanimity among all leading parties on EU accession issues, no significant changes are anticipated in the direction of economic and foreign policy. However, it is less clear whether labour market reform, now a pressing issue, will be addressed as a priority. Other issues affecting business on which it is hoped that the new Czech government will focus are the remaining deficiencies in the legal system and bureaucratic bottlenecks in administration.

This new edition of *Doing Business with the Czech Republic* is the first in a new series of Kogan Page titles focused on the leading EU accession candidates and other selected countries of Central and Eastern Europe. For foreign firms that have taken the decision to engage in changing growth markets a working knowledge of the legal system, the regulatory framework, taxation and audit and accountancy regimes is a necessary condition for avoiding the pitfalls that can destroy an investment or frustrate market entry initiatives. A thorough understanding of general economic and business conditions and of the specific industries in which a market entrant intends to do business are also an important aid to successful engagement.

Part One of this book provides overviews and commentary on the Czech economy and business environment; Part Two is devoted to the legal structure and business regulations and Part Three to finance, accountancy and taxation including capital markets and privatization. Together, these three sections provide recommended reading for all those who have taken the decision in principle to enter the market and are engaged in the evaluation of ways and means.

In Part Four key industries and markets are analysed individually by leading participants and practitioners and these chapters are intended to give practical insight to the newcomer. The two case studies that follow record the market entry experience of a leading international retailer and the management experience of the British development partner in the Brno industrial park.

The book is complemented by a series of Appendices providing contact lists of government agencies, business associations and facilitators in the Czech Republic from whom further information and assistance may be sought.

Acknowledgements

Our principal knowledge partners who have provided most of the source content for Parts One to Three, and the opening paragraphs of this introduction, are Bank Austria Creditanstalt, and the Prague offices of CMS Cameron McKenna and Deloitte & Touche and Coface. Without their involvement this book in its new form would not have been possible and the contributions of individual authors are gratefully acknowledged. All four are participating in further titles in the series and will be providing a continuing flow of updates and material for revisions to these texts.

We are also obliged equally to the individual authors of the chapters in Part Four and of the case histories, who have given generously of their time to provide authoritative insight to the industries that they represent or of which they have direct experience in the Czech Republic.

Finally, we offer our thanks to the Czech Agency for Foreign Investment (CzechInvest) for its endorsement of *Doing Business with the Czech Republic* and for the provision of editorial material; to the PP Agency, Prague for its major editorial contribution; and to Trade Partners UK for its support and encouragement.

Jonathan Reuvid and Marat Terterov
London, June 2002

Part One

The Economy and the Business Environment

1.1

Economic Performance and Outlook[1]

Economic growth in the Czech Republic slowed during 2001, from 3.8 per cent in the first half of the year to 3.2 per cent in the final quarter. However, with an average annual growth rate of 3.6 per cent, the Czech economy performed far better than the Euro zone (0.6 per cent) and was among the top-performing accession candidates. Indeed, among the Central and Eastern European (CEE-5) candidates, only Hungary with GDP real growth of 3.8 per cent was stronger in 2001.

The vigorous domestic economy was the major factor in this growth. Domestic demand rose by 5.6 per cent, the highest rate of growth since 1996, although nearly one-third of it was attributable to the building up of stocks. Bank Austria Creditanstalt (Bank Austria) has forecast a noticeable decrease in the growth rate in the first quarter of 2002 as a result of three factors:

- wage increases in the public sector did not take effect until March;
- stock reduction is probable and will diminish growth;
- exports are unlikely to provide any stimuli.

In subsequent quarters, the growth rate is forecast to rise steadily, reaching 3.1 per cent by mid-year. The slower rate of growth for the year as a whole, as compared with the previous year, will be largely due to a decline in investment growth to 5 per cent following 7 per cent in 2001. Nevertheless, investments will still constitute the most dynamic component of growth in domestic demand.

Private consumption will rise by 3.6 per cent again. The cyclical upturn in the Euro zone will accelerate the rate of export growth; however, the strong Czech crown (CZK) will have a potentially dampening effect while also increasing the demand for imports. No noticeable boost to growth

[1] This chapter is made up primarily of content from the *Investment Guide for the Czech Republic,* edited by Kurt Fesselhofer (Bank Austria Creditanstalt Economics Department) and the review of the Czech Republic by Alexander Tscherteu in the Bank Austria Creditanstalt 'CEE Report 2/2002' and 3/2002.

from foreign trade is expected until 2003, causing the growth rate that year to rise to 3.8 per cent. By comparison, *The Economist* poll is currently forecasting GDP growth for the Euro zone at 1.3 per cent for 2002 and 2.9 per cent for 2003.

The growth in Czech industrial output is expected to fall in 2002 to 4.5 per cent from its 2001 peak of 6.9 per cent, although in February it remained at the 5.8 per cent level in contrast to the Euro zone's decline of 3.3 per cent.

Stable current account

The Czech current account deficit in 2001 amounted to about CZK100 billion or 4.6 per cent of GDP compared with deficits of 2.2 per cent for Hungary and 4.0 per cent for Poland. In absolute terms, the Czech deficit is slightly worse than the previous year, when the deficit was CZK91 billion. However, in GDP terms, the deficit remained nearly unchanged.

The trade deficit in 2001 at €3503 million was smaller than in 2000 (€3555 million) despite the difference in growth rates between the Czech Republic and its major trading partners. The trade gap narrowed from minus 6.5 per cent of GDP in 2000 to minus 5.5 per cent in 2001, in large part due to the favourable trend in raw material prices. The sharp decline in the oil price in 2001 substantially decreased the chronic deficit with the CIS countries. At the same time, Czech exports to the European Union grew at a higher nominal rate (11 per cent) than imports from the European Union (9 per cent). Here the country reaped the fruits of the massive investments that Europeans have made in the Czech economy.

The favourable trend in the trade balance continued in the first months of 2002. In fact, the sustained positive trend in import prices enabled the country to achieve a monthly trade surplus for only the second time in the last three years. This strong start to the year, Bank Austria expects is not to be repeated in the subsequent months of the year. The recovery in the Euro zone in 2002 will gain in momentum and benefit the Czech export industry, but export growth will be curbed by the sharp rise in the value of the Czech crown. As the global economy gets back on its feet, raw material prices will rise, as is already occurring with the oil price. This, in turn, will result in an increased demand for imports. However, altogether the trade deficit is thus forecast to end up in the region of €2900 million, €600 million lower than in 2001. Although the more favourable trade balance will benefit the current account deficit, lowering it from 4.6 per cent in 2001 to 3.8

per cent in 2002, the deficit for Hungary is forecast to be less in GDP terms, at 3.5 per cent and that for Poland at 4.0 per cent to be slightly above this level.

New record in direct investment

Opposite the current account deficit for 2001 was a surplus in the balance of capital transactions of 7.1 per cent of GDP. As detailed in Chapter 1.5, Foreign Direct Investment, this was due to the massive inflow of foreign direct investment (FDI) and reflects a new record for FDI of €5.4 billion. The record will be broken again this year when FDI totalling some €8.2 billion, or 11.0 per cent of GDP, is expected to flow into the Czech economy.

Currency value

In 2001, the value of the Czech crown in relation to the euro rose by approximately 9 per cent in real terms. This process began to pick up speed near the end of the year and then accelerated further in the first months of 2002. Although the Czech National Bank (CNB) favours a gradual upward valuation of the Czech crown in real terms, it intervenes if it feels that adjustment is occurring too quickly. Such was the case here.

Accordingly, the CNB intervened, first verbally and then by buying foreign currency to curb the upward trend, but had only short-term success in doing so. In November 2001 and January 2002, it reduced key interest rates several times by a total of 125 basis points to counteract the restrictive monetary climate created by the strong Czech crown. This was followed at the end of April by a further cut of 50 basis points. The fundamental cause of the upward valuation is the constant massive influx of foreign capital in the form of direct investment. Privatization proceeds are not converted on the market into Czech crowns but are kept intermediately at the CNB. However, this procedure is not possible in the case of greenfield investments. The strong currency is a drag on growth in 2002 and will thus also have a negative effect on foreign trade. In addition, it will cause a marked decline in prices.

Lower inflation

In February 2002, the strong upward valuation of the Czech crown coupled with lower raw material prices led to the first year-to-year decline in producer prices in three years. In the months ahead, Bank Austria expects the falling producer prices and the strong currency to begin to have a positive effect on consumer prices. The moderate increase in food prices in the first two months of the year also had a dampening effect on consumer prices. In anticipation of the June elections, the ruling Czech Social Democrats (CSSD) also managed to push through an 8 per cent reduction in gas prices for private households. All things considered, the inflation rate should therefore be far below 3 per cent from mid-2002 onwards and not rise above 3 per cent again until the last quarter. The average rate of inflation for 2002 is forecast to be 2.9 per cent after 4.7 per cent in 2001. By comparison, in its 'East-West Report 3/2002', Bank Austria forecasts declines in consumer price inflation for Hungary from 9.2 per cent to 6.0 per cent and for Poland from 5.5 per cent to 3.0 per cent, while the current *Economist* poll predicts 1.9 per cent for the Euro zone.

Economic outlook

Structural reform

The reforms carried out since 1997 in the Czech Republic have helped to create an institutional framework meeting the requirements of a functioning market economy. Modified capital market legislation plus changes in commercial law and in bankruptcy proceedings will help to prevent a repeat in the future of developments of the kind that led to the currency crisis in 1997 and that were partly responsible for the low productivity growth during that period. In addition, the now completed restructuring and privatization of the banking industry along with the resulting stricter lending guidelines have made lenders more selective in granting loans, ushering in what at times has been a painful restructuring, both in the real estate and in the financial sectors. The cumulative effect of these changes in the regulatory environment has been strong inflow of FDI in recent years and far higher productivity growth.

A continuation of the efforts in all these areas should help to accelerate the rate at which the Czech Republic is closing the prosperity gap between it and Western European countries.

Short-term economic outlook

With anticipated growth in 2002 of 3.1 per cent, the Czech Republic is expected to come through the current global economic weakness relatively unscathed. Private consumption is on the rise after the three-year recession from 1997 to 1999, and gross fixed capital formation remains strong thanks to the continuing inflow of FDI. Along with these factors, the quite expansive fiscal and monetary policy now in place is certain to play a decisive role in overcoming the effects of global economic weakness. At the start of 2002, the real interest rate in the Czech Republic was less than one per cent; the Czech Ministry of Finance forecasts a budget deficit of about 9 per cent (excluding privatization proceeds) for 2002 as a whole. Although the current state of the recently reorganized banking sector limits the effect of monetary policy to lending and a large part of government spending is earmarked for servicing past costs incurred in the reorganization of these banks, the government and the CNB have both used whatever leeway they have had to the maximum. From 2003 onwards, the structural reform of government finances, recently called for by the European Central Bank (ECB), the International Monetary Fund (IMF) and the Organization for Economic Cooperation and Development (OECD), and the return to a more balanced interest rate structure will cost the country some of the growth it will gain this year and next from the policy being pursued.

Medium-term economic outlook

In the medium term, the development of the country will be shaped primarily by the ongoing process of integration into the European Union and its effects. Given the opportunities offered by the transfer of technological know-how, the Czech Republic will most likely have a higher rate of productivity growth in the long term than its key trade partners (the European Union). This trend is a desirable one and necessary to narrow the prosperity gap between the Czech Republic and member countries of the European Union.

Economically, this catch-up process could have one of two possible consequences: either the inflation rate in the Czech Republic will be higher than that of its key trade partners or the value of the Czech crown will appreciate in nominal terms. The second effect is prevailing at the moment. Whatever happens, the two possibilities signify an appreciation of the national currency in real terms, which should roughly equal the productivity differential to the European Union and the relative size of the service sector. The CNB's medium-term target for the inflation rate, at 3 +/- 1 per cent by December 2005, is about 1.5 per cent above that of the ECB. Should Czech productivity growth exceed that of the European Union by more than 1.5 per cent, a gradual nominal appreciation of the Czech crown in relation to the euro may be expected.

This presents no problem as long as the exchange rate of the Czech crown is left free to float. However, after accession to the European Union, the Czech Republic will be expected to meet the Maastricht criteria and sooner or later accede to the Exchange Rate Mechanism 2 (ERM2), which demands that the central rate against the euro be fixed in a fluctuation band of +/- 15 per cent. Prospects for real growth will suffer if the Czech Republic tries simultaneously to meet the ERM2 exchange rate requirements and to achieve the low inflation rate required prior to introduction of the single currency. A possible way out of this problem would be for the European Union to recognize differences in productivity growth when determining acceptable inflation rates for the Czech Republic.

In domestic politics, labour market reform is an increasingly pressing issue. If the country fails to tackle the problem of unemployment, which has risen sharply since 1996, and that of long-term unemployment, which has accelerated even faster, there is a danger that the current high level of unemployment, forecast to climb back to 8.7 per cent by the end of 2003, could become structurally fixed.

As in all countries with an age structure like that of the Czech Republic, the country will face the long-term task of reforming the health care and pension system to ensure financing and the quality of the system in the long term.[2]

[2] A table of selected indicators of the Czech Republic's economic performance from 1998 and recent Bank Austria Creditanstalt's forecasts for 2002/2003 is included in Chapter 1.4, Business Risk Assessment.

ONLINE UPDATES - 27 May 2005

Economic progress and outlook (Chap. 1.1)

Czech Republic selected indicators

Czech Republic - Selected Indicators

	2001	2002	2003	2004	2005	2006
Change from previous year in %					*Forecast*	
GDP (real)	2.6	1.5	3.2	4.4	4.8	4.2
Industrial output (real)	6.8	4.8	5.8	9.5	6.0	6.0
Gross fixed capital formation (real)	5.4	3.4	4.7	7.6	2.0	5.0
Consumer prices (yearly average)	4.7	1.8	0.1	2.8	1.9	2.9
Unemployment (yearly average)	8.5	9.2	9.9	10.2	9.7	9.3
Budget balance (ESA 95, in % of GDP)	-5.9	-6.8	-12.5	-3.0	-3.5	-5.0
in EUR mn						
Merchandise exports	37,267	40,701	43,110	53,715	62,390	70,950
Merchandise imports	40,690	43,014	45,305	54,415	61,350	69,260
Current account	-3,654	-4,426	-5,050	-4,492	-2,640	-3,190
Current account (in % of GDP)	-5.4	-5.6	-6.3	-5.2	-2.7	-3.0
FDI (inflow, net)	6,114	8,791	1,682	3,156	6,790	3,620
Gross foreign debt (end of period)	25,368	25,738	27,599	33,258	36,800	40,000
Gross foreign debt (in % of GDP)	36.7	36.4	38.3	38.6	37.4	37.3
Import cover (in months)	4.1	6.0	5.5	4.4	4.0	3.5
Average exchange rate: CZK/EUR	34.07	30.8	31.8	31.9	29.9	29.1
Average exchange rate: CZK/USD	38.0	32.6	28.1	25.6	23.8	23.1

Sources: Bank Austria Creditanstalt Economics Department, CNB

Following installation of the new cabinet of Prime Minister Jiri Paroubek, political stability has improved but no firm policies are likely before the next election, possibly as far away as 2006.

The positive economic development of 2004 appears to be continuing with strong industrial output forecast for 2005/06 at around 6 per cent and exports continuing to increase strongly. GDP growth of 3.7 per cent to 3.8 per cent is forecast with some confidence. The slowing of inflation has already enabled the central bank to lower the prime interest rate twice in 2005—at the end of January and on 1 April—each time by 25 basis points.

EU factors may be less positive than recently with the weak economies of the Czech's neighbours, particularly Germany. The price of oil is certainly a negative, although the cost impact is somewhat offset by the strong currency.

As a percentage of GDP, the budget deficit shrank encouragingly in 2004 but is expected to climb back to 4.5 per cent in 2005 before shading down in 2006.

The trade deficit will soon begin to be impacted favourably from the TCPA vehicle factory opened recently and the foreign trade balance will turn positive in coming years. In the short term, although the current account deficit balance may increase, as a percentage of GDP, the deficit will continue to diminish steadily, hopefully to 4.5 per cent in 2006.

April 2005, Bank Austria Creditanstalt CEE Report 2- 2005

1.2

Progress Report on EU Accession[1]

EU enlargement in context

The programme of EU enlargement under way at the start of the 21st century is a major challenge for the European Union. There is an opportunity now for all the countries of the European continent to grow closer together by peaceful means by forming a political and economic union in which democratic rights are respected and the economy functions according to the principles of a market economy. The prospects of EU integration require accession candidates to adopt a type of market economy arising from the tradition of Western Europe, and not the tradition of the United States or Japan. This consolidation signifies a strengthening of the socio-economic ideals of the European continent.

The negotiation process launched in 1998 began with six countries and was later expanded to include six more. In December 2000, the European Commission announced that it expected the most advanced applicant countries, including the Czech Republic, to finish negotiations by the end of 2002 and committed itself to make the European Union ready for enlargement by the beginning of 2003. With the exception of Bulgaria and Romania, the process is nearing completion; in October 2002, the EU will publish progress reports in which it will announce the candidates that have met the accession criteria and would thus be ready politically, economically and administratively to accede to the European Union in 2004.

No new dates or topics for the current enlargement negotiations were introduced at the Laeken Summit in mid-December 2001. However, the meeting did serve to confirm 2004 as the year in which the first few Central and Eastern European (CEE) countries are to join the European Union, when their representatives will be elected to the European Parliament.

---

[1] The content of this chapter is a consolidation of papers by Marianne Kager and Bernhard Sinhuber of the Bank Austria Creditanstalt Economics Department in their 'East-West Report 1/2002'.

The Accession Partnerships and their operation

The European Union makes available some €3 billion annually to ensure that the appropriate flanking measures accompany the accession process. This substantial financial assistance is intended to be used for drawing up tailor-made plans to assist the countries in preparing for accession. However, the actual investments required of the candidates are many times greater.

The budgetary basis for the EU programme is 'Agenda 2000', which sets the financial framework for the European Union for the period 2000–2006. Accession Partnerships are drawn up annually for each accession candidate to define its short-, medium- and long-term goals, which also include the major financial assistance being granted, so that they are the core element of European assistance for enlargement.

Each Accession Partnership is supplemented by a National Programme for the Adoption of the Acquis (NPAA), produced by the accession candidate, in which the concrete actions they plan to take to achieve the goals set down in the Accession Partnership are stated. On this basis, the EU signs what is known as a Financial Memorandum every year with each individual accession candidate. The Financial Memorandum contains the projects and programmes that are to be co-funded by the European Union.

Following accession to the European Union, assistance thereafter will be based on European regional policy directives and regulations, and the programmes of the Structured Funds and the Cohesion Fund will apply from the negotiated accession dates.

Presumably, most accession regimes will be classified as 'Objective 1' regions (regions whose development is lagging behind). At present, some 70 per cent of European assistance goes to Objective 1 regions. Therefore, unless the European Union decides to exceed greatly the budget fixed for the period up to 2006, the successful accession candidates will initially receive only a certain percentage of the possible funding assistance. Sufficient assurance must also be given that each country has adequate administrative capacity to implement the European assistance policy and to monitor the use of resources efficiently.

EU budgetary issues

The European Commission's plan has diverged from Agenda 2000 in two respects: the first countries will join the European Union in 2004 at the very earliest (instead of 2002) and the number of first wave accessions is now assumed to be 10 instead of the original six.

While adhering to the financial framework, the European Union may consider reducing the costs of accession still further. In the EU budget, obligations towards accession candidates are set at €10.8 billion (2004) and will increase to €13.4 billion (2005) and €16 billion (2006). Specific provisions have been earmarked within the overall budget for agriculture, possibly the most divisive issue in accession negotiations, structural policy and 'internal policies' such as nuclear safety.

In the case of agriculture, the allocation to market measures of the Common Agricultural Policy (CAP) is €516 million. The issue of direct payments has still to be decided. In its draft report, following discussion at the Berlin summit, the European Commission foresees a two-phase model according to which direct payments will be gradually increased until they match the level of support that is generally applicable to all EU member states in 2013. A second area in the chapter on agriculture concerns rural development in relation to managing the effects of the CAP. The financial resources assigned to this area would amount to €1532 million in 2004, rising to €1781 million by 2006. One-third of these funds could be provided through the Cohesion Fund with the advantage that the co-financing by the European Union would amount to 85 per cent instead of 80 per cent.

Structural policy is the second major expense area. The subsidies granted to the new member states will be massive compared to their per capita GDP, which is low by EU standards. The European Commission proposes that funds amounting to €7067 million be made available to the new member states in 2004, increasing to €8150 million in 2005 and €10,350 million in 2006.

A further area of support is the building of institutions, referred to above, but these funds will be reduced after accession. A total of about €1 billion is currently being made available, mostly under the Phare programme, to the candidate countries for the development of their administrative systems and for taking over the Acquis Communautaire.

The overall financial framework for enlargement for the period 2004 to 2006 is summarized in Table 1.2.1.

Table 1.2.1 Financial framework for enlargement 2004–2006 (€million, 1999 prices)

	2004	*2005*	*2006*
Commitment appropriations			
Agriculture	2048	3596	3933
Structural actions	7067	8150	10,350
Internal policies	1176	1056	1071
Administration	503	558	612
Total commitment appropriations	10,794	13,400	15,966
Total commitment appropriations (Berlin 1999 scenario)	11,610	14,200	16,760
Payment appropriations (enlargement)	5686	10,493	11,840
Payment appropriations (Berlin 1999 scenario)	8890	11,440	14,220

Scenario: accession of 10 new member states in 2004
Source: European Commission

Difficult negotiation issues

Agriculture

The number of people employed in the agricultural sector and the relevant share of GDP is much higher in the candidate countries than in the European Union. However, the employment percentage is lowest in the Czech Republic (4.8 per cent) in contrast to Poland, where agricultural employment is highest at 25.7 per cent.

Contributory factors in the significance of the agricultural sector in the CEE have been motives such as self-sufficiency in food production and the high subsidies received by the sector generally in the region. Whatever the reasons, the impact of the CAP will be considerable.

In common with other CEE countries, unemployment in the Czech Republic has not fallen since 2000 although GDP is growing strongly. Agriculture is just one of the sectors where increased productivity has impeded progress in reducing unemployment.

Direct payments

Among the measures agreed at the 1999 Berlin summit for the reform of the CAP was the reduction of intervention prices with the objective of moving from price subsidies to direct payment. The lowering of intervention prices, which reduces income, was offset by higher direct payments. As the agricultural prices in the candidate countries in the CEE are also partly below the intervention prices, this measure would amount to an additional price subsidy. The efforts of recent years to establish a competitive agricultural system in the CEE, which were supported by the European Union, would be countered or at least delayed from a prompt and complete outcome by taking over the system of direct payments. Not only would the present structure become more inflexible, new tensions would also result as incomes in the agricultural sector would rise to well above those of an industrial worker. For this reason, the European Commission is calling for a plan that is to be implemented gradually by stages.

Progress of negotiations

By 11 June 2002, out of the 31 chapters the Czech Republic had closed 25, Hungary 24, Cyprus 28, and Slovenia provisionally 27 chapters. Of the remaining countries striving for accession in 2004, Malta had closed 27, Poland 25, Estonia 26, Lithuania 28, Latvia 27 and Slovakia 26, Bulgaria 20 and Romania 11.

Reviewing past progress, the Czech Republic applied for EU membership in 1996 and started negotiations in March 1999. By December 1999, the country had presented position papers on 29 chapters; it was the first to close the key and difficult chapter on the free movement of goods. Following the European Commission's 1999 accession progress report, which criticized it for slow harmonization, the Czech government accelerated the country's adoption of EU-compatible legislation. A record number of laws were passed in 1999 and 2000 and the EU's November 2000 annual progress report stated that the Czech Republic had achieved excellent improvements, giving the country a broadly favourable assessment of readiness for accession. In February 2001, the Czech government registered further advances towards EU harmonization by withdrawing requests for transition periods in several areas such as energy sector liberalization, tax rates harmonization and implementation of several environmental protection regulations.

Accession in 2004 is an ambitious undertaking, both for the approved candidate countries and for the present EU member states. For example, the achievement of a common negotiating position on agriculture has been hampered by the elections in France and Germany, which have made the realization of a consensus more difficult.

In October 2002, the European Commission's next annual progress report must confirm that the accession candidates have fulfilled the Copenhagen criteria. When the negotiations have finally been concluded, the European Parliament, the parliaments of the current 15 member states and the parliaments of the new member states must approve the negotiation results.

The negative outcome of the Irish referendum on the Treaty of Nice, a prerequisite for EU enlargement, is an obstacle that has yet to be overcome, although the return to power of Bertie Ahern with an increased endorsement in Ireland's May elections might signal a change in public mood on this issue.

Issues concerning the divided island of Cyprus could also lead to further delays in the final stages of negotiations. So far, the European Commission has been prepared to consider Cyprus as a candidate for accession only as a single political entity. The financial framework now presented provides for additional funds for Northern Cyprus.

With the opening of the chapters on agriculture, structural policy and financial and budgetary provisions, the accession negotiations have entered a decisive phase, since these chapters also deal with funding. The diverse positions of the individual candidate countries are becoming more apparent as the respective parties try to exploit sensitive negotiating issues for their own domestic political purposes.

At present, in all accession candidate countries, there is a larger group of people in favour of membership than against—46 per cent versus 9 per cent in the case of the Czech Republic at the last count. Only if the European Union and the respective accession candidates fail to reach an understanding quickly on these outstanding issues will the question regarding the necessity of membership assume significance.

Under the Spanish presidency of the European Union, the schedule calls for the conclusion of negotiations by the end of 2002, which will require considerable sensitivity above the technical considerations. However, even if the negotiations drag on into the first few months of 2003, it is reasonable to assume that eastward enlargement will have reached a point of no return.

1.3

Foreign Investment Regime

CMS Cameron McKenna

Introduction

The investment climate in the Czech Republic has developed dramatically and positively since the Velvet Revolution of 1989. The government has tried to create an environment that not only accommodates but also encourages foreign investment. It has passed commercial legislation to ensure, in effect, a level playing field for both domestic and foreign investors; indeed, the Commercial Code of 1991 repealed many of the laws hindering foreign investment. Not only are foreigners not discriminated against under the Commercial Code, but they are also not obliged to acquire official authorization when establishing a company.

Structure

Membership of the Organization for Economic Cooperation and Development (OECD) largely came about as a result of the Foreign Exchange Act (1995). The immediate result of this Act is that the Czech crown (CZK) became fully convertible on the current account of the trade balance.

The transformation of the commercial legislation heralded new opportunities for foreign companies seeking to hold a majority interest in domestic companies. Prior to 1989, the joint-venture law explicitly stated that the Czech partner should enjoy at least a minimal amount of the shareholding. This was amended to allow foreign investors to either establish or invest in a company where the whole of the issued capital is exclusively their own.

Foreign investors also have the option to open a branch office in the

Czech Republic as a separate legal entity. It is not necessary to form a subsidiary company.

Since coming into force on 1 October 1995, the Foreign Exchange Act has had significant implications for the success of foreign investments in the country, as well as boosting the Czech economy.

The Investment Incentives Act (2000) allows for companies to apply for various benefits, after satisfying certain conditions set out in the Act, such as:

- reduced income tax;
- restructuring and development subsidies for municipalities;
- subsidies for the creation of new working places;
- subsidies for re-qualification programmes;
- limited conveyance of land and other real property estates.

Practice

In general, foreign investors favour the joint-stock company or the limited liability company structure for their investments, since these structures tend to be the most suitable for practical business needs. However, mechanisms also exist for general commercial or limited partnerships and cooperatives.

The influence of the Czech Ministry of Finance has diminished and the majority of joint ventures may be established without the need for official approval. The only exception to this relaxation of control concerns joint ventures involving state enterprises. However, licences are obligatory for both domestic and foreign entrepreneurs in areas such as banking and insurance.

The privatization of state enterprises provided a tremendous opportunity for foreign investors to invest their expertise and capital into privatized state joint-stock companies. However, since this process is now drawing to a close, foreign investors have turned towards the Prague Stock Exchange, which was re-opened in 1993. Indeed, there should be further, growing foreign interest in this area since the capital markets are now regulated properly.

There is also an alternative stock exchange system (the so-called 'RM system'), which auctions securities on a continual basis. A US-style Securities Exchange Commission (Commission for Securities) commenced operations in April 1998 in order to develop and protect the Czech capital market. The Commission's activities are wide ranging; the following are a few of the most important:

- The Commission has authority to regulate the securities market (supervisory function, authority to withdraw securities and trading) and also controls the fulfilment of obligations set out in the Commercial Code.
- The Commission administers the Securities Act, the Act on Protection of Economic Competition and other relevant laws (particularly, various notification obligations).
- The Commission issues legal opinions and partially cooperates with the Czech National Bank (CNB) and the Ministry of Finance on the regulation of the banking sector.

Foreign exchange non-residents can now convert their Czech crown income to convertible currencies without penalty. Hence, there is now no obligation for sole traders or branch offices to obtain a licence from the CNB authorizing them to make their foreign currency payments in Czech crowns.

Foreign exchange residents can now also take advantage of easier access to foreign currency since they are no longer obliged to obtain a CNB licence or to place their foreign currency in domestic banks. The result is that they can open foreign exchange accounts in the domestic market as well as providing financial services for non-residents.

However, any undertakings that are made to non-residents, as well as investments or accounts abroad, are monitored and regulated by the Foreign Exchange Act and must be reported to the relevant state authorities.

Other positive changes introduced by the Foreign Exchange Act include the ability of local businesses to take loans from non-residents in foreign currencies and the ability of Czech companies to issue debentures abroad.

According to subsequent legislation, there is a notification duty on only some dealings with foreign currencies applicable to Czech residents and foreign residents living in the Czech Republic.

Essentials

Adequate protection has been a key issue for potential foreign investors in all former communist states and its non-existence has often been a most powerful disincentive. Although the constitution protects against expropriation, there are also bilateral investment protection agreements between the Czech Republic, the United States, European Union and most other OECD countries.

Within the Commercial Code, there are provisions which declare that foreign entities may run a business under the same conditions as Czech entities, and a foreign legal entity is permitted to run a business from the moment of entering its subsidiary (or branch office) in the Commercial Register. Hence, there are particular laws that allow for a withdrawal of certain proprietary rights; naturally, freely transferable and convertible compensation must be paid should such an eventuality occur.

Since 1989, great strides have been made to encourage foreign investment into the Czech Republic, and these have been largely welcomed by the international business community. Excluding the employee stock and 'voucher' schemes, almost all the privatization schemes have sought the investment of foreign capital. Privatizations are now drawing to a close and there has been substantial foreign interest in the Prague Stock Exchange. This interest should increase farther upon the completion of the process of reform including the introduction of a monitoring watchdog with responsibility for ensuring that dealings in the marketplace become more transparent.

One of the most important goals of the Czech Republic's foreign affairs policy is to join the European Union. The country is closing several chapters a year while dealing with the European Union in order to reconcile national law with the Acquis Communitaire. As a result, a growing number of legislative acts transforming EU law into national rules (eg the new Act on Protection of Economic Competition (2000)) are reproducing almost the exact wording of European law.

The Czech Republic has become an attractive place for foreign investment and in order to compete with neighbouring countries such as Poland and Hungary should continue to develop so as to secure more attention from the prudent investor.

Concerns

If there is an obstacle to foreign investment it probably lies in the rather different business culture of the Czech Republic, its slowly developing justice system and, in certain cases, the influence of local lobbyists who use different forms of competition, some of which may be unacceptable to many foreign companies.

The main area of government intransigence concerns the sale of real estate to foreign investors. Traditionally, the Czechs have been loath to sell their land to outsiders since they feel that their sovereignty is threatened. Foreign nationals are only able to lease property or buy land upon establishment of a Czech company.

Previously, the tax on land for a non-domestically financed purchase was set at the world market rate, and this was several times higher than its domestic value. Although real estate values are now uniform, the scarcity of property (both residential and commercial) ensures that prices remain at a premium, particularly since construction is often hampered by an arduous and sometimes arbitrary procedure for planning permission.

ONLINE UPDATES - 26 Ma 2005

Foreign investment regime (Chap.1.3)

Restrictions on foreign investment

Following completion of the major privatization programmes and with many of the remaining state-owned enterprises of interest now in the hands of the National Property Fund, most types of foreign investment do not require special government approval, including ventures that are 100 per cent foreign-owned and operated, involving a Czech co-operative founded after 1 July 1988, or involving a local partner that is either a legal person or a local company in which all the partners are foreign persons or Czech legal persons. No distinction is made between wholly foreign-owned direct investment and joint ventures linking foreign and domestic companies.

Exceptions to this freedom remain in:

- defence or national security;
- banking.

Acquiring even one share in a Czech Bank requires prior approval from the Czech National Bank (usually given within 30 days). The minimum capital requirement for new banks is CZK500 million and the acquisition of more than 10 per cent of a bank by a Czech legal or physical entity requires central bank approval.

Any sale of state assets in the Czech Republic must be conducted by competitive, public tender. Negotiations tend to be long and slow requiring much patience.

Cautions

Foreign investors are strongly advised to:

- read the Commercial Code thoroughly to decide which type of organization is most suitable before setting up a company;
- verify ownership of the target company and its assets, particularly any real estate involved in the acquisition;
- determine in advance the actions necessary to secure building and related permits;
- conduct an environmental audit of prospective production sites. Clean-up costs on polluted industrial land can often be deducted from the purchase price of property;
- register any company that you intend to use as the acquisition vehicle in good time. The cost is CZK1,200 and the procedure straightforward but court backlogs may extend the process from 30 days to three months.

July 2004, Deloitte Touche Tohmatsu, Prague

Investment incentives

Effective May 2004, the following amendments were introduced:

- The minimum limit in the value of investment to qualify for investment incentives was reduced from EUR11 million (CZK350 million) to EUR6.3 million (CZK200 million). In districts with the highest unemployment rates a lower limit was set of EUR3.2 million (CZK100 million).
- The incentives package may now include reimbursement for the cost of employees' training; other forms of incentive (eg income tax relief, subsidies to create new jobs, etc) remain.
- The maximum terms for benefits from investment incentives granted for expansion of established businesses was extended from five to 10 years.
- To gain entitlement to the incentives, foreign investors are obliged to keep their investments in the country for at least five years.
- Power to define the permitted level of state aid granted to particular investors was transferred to the Czech Ministry of Industry and Trade from the Czech Anti-Monopoly office.

The amendments apply to investments after 1 May 2004. Those investors who had already entered the Czech market may benefit from the new rules relating to reimbursement of staff training costs. They should also consider opportunities for gaining incentives for the expansion or modernization of their current operations.

Incentives may take the form of:

- income tax relief;
- job-creation and training and retraining grants;
- industrial property (infrastructure) or the transfer of land owned by the Czech Republic at a discounted price.

In line with relevant EU legislation, investment subsidies can be provided to any industrial sector, other than certain 'sensitive sectors' such as, synthetic fibres, shipbuilding, the motor industry, transport, coal mining, etc. Outside these sectors, the European Commission should not need to approve any project individually.

March 2004, CMS Cameron McKenna

1.4

Business Risk Assessment

Coface analysis

Coface

Strengths

- The Czech Republic's progressive integration into Western organizations works in favour of stability and continuity in the country's political and economic choices.
- The modernization and restructuring efforts undertaken, as well as the increase in investments, are helping to improve the competitiveness of exports.
- The country is potentially strong in manufacturing.
- With an external debt level remaining moderate, the Czech authorities maintain a satisfactory financial room for manoeuvre.

Weaknesses

- The public finances deficit, which is already widened by the completion of a costly banking sector restructuring and is also likely to be burdened with the weight of welfare expenditures, might prove rather unsustainable.
- The level of activity is dependent on that in the country's main trading partners (Germany, Italy, Slovakia).
- The economy is suffering from insufficient industrial restructuring.
- The government's weak political base may slow down the pace of these structural reforms necessary to adjust the fiscal accounts and to overhaul the social welfare system as well as the manufacturing sector.

Risk assessment

- Czech economic growth is expected to remain sustained, despite a deteriorating international economic environment, and will be driven, as a substitute, by buoyant domestic demand and, notably, investments.

- The main macroeconomic problem comes from the size of the twin deficits: the consolidated fiscal deficit, which is aggravating mainly because of a costly banking sector restructuring, although for the time being its financing is easily secured by privatization revenues; and the external accounts deficit, which is deteriorating due to the economic slowdown in the European Union and a robust domestic demand—even if it will be broadly covered by foreign direct investment (FDI) flows and although the external debt is moderate, the high level of the short-term debt creates a factor of vulnerability.
- After the parliamentary elections in June 2002, the next government's likely fragility might affect the momentum of the essential structural reforms, even if a policy of economic reform and public finances restoring should be carried on.

Economic data

Bank Austria Creditanstalt

Table 1.4.1 Czech Republic—selected indicators

	1998	*1999*	*2000*	*2001*	*2002*	*2003*
					Forecast	
Change from previous year (%)						
GDP (real)	-1.2	-0.4	2.9	3.6	3.1	3.8
Industrial output (real)	1.6	-3.1	5.1	6.8	4.5	6.5
Gross fixed capital formation (real)	-3.9	-5.5	5.2	7.0	5.0	6.0
Consumer prices (yearly average)	10.7	2.1	3.9	4.7	2.9	3.6
Unemployment (yearly average)	6.0	8.6	9.0	8.4	8.8	8.7
Budget balance (% of GDP)	-2.9	-3.4	-4.3	-5.7	-7.5	-4.5
€million						
Merchandise exports	23,557	24,620	31,411	37,237	42,100	44,600
Merchandise imports	25,840	26,403	34,966	40,740	45,000	48,100
Current account	-1193	-1469	-2568	-2963	-2800	-3300
Current account (% of GDP)	-2.4	-3.0	-4.5	-4.6	-3.8	-4.0
FDI (inflow, net)	3434	3941	3870	5387	8200	6500

Table 1.4.1 continued

	1998	*1999*	*2000*	*2001*	*2002*	*2003*
Gross foreign debt (end of period)	21,497	21,199	22,360	25,446	27,100	28,000
Gross foreign debt (% of GDP)	43.2	42.6	39.6	39.7	36.0	34.1
Import cover (months)	4.4	4.5	4.2	4.1	4.0	3.4
Average exchange rate: CZK/€	36.2	36.9	35.7	34.1	30.8	30.3
Average exchange rate: CZK/US$	32.2	34.6	38.6	38.0	33.7	31.4

Sources: WIIW, CNB, Bank Austria Creditanstalt Economics Department 'CEE Report 3/2002'

Conditions of access to the market

Coface

Means of entry

There are no quotas or tariffs impeding imports of industrial products from the European Union. Negotiations with the European Commission targeting mutual concessions on farm products have been underway since March 2000. The current level of customs duties is 11 per cent on agricultural products emanating from the European Union.

The progressive liberalization of capital flows is proceeding in the framework of the admission procedure. SWIFT transfers are becoming increasingly commonplace. Creditworthiness information is obtainable but of questionable reliability.

Attitude towards foreign investors

The authorities have adopted a resolute policy to foster foreign investment, particularly via the CzechInvest investment promotion agency. National and foreign investors receive identical treatment. Furthermore, a new law on investment incentives came into force in May 2000. Formerly limited to start-up investments, it now also applies to companies expanding or modernizing existing operations for the purposes of setting up new production facilities. The minimum investment has dropped to CZK350 million €10.2 million) and, in high-unemployment regions, to CZK175 million (€5.1 million). Newly created entities enjoy a 10-year corporate tax holiday while existing entities enjoy a five-year partial exemption. The new law also provides other forms of support targeting job creation, training and infrastructure development.

Furthermore, there is progressive modernizing of commercial law and adoption of an auction law that guarantees greater security and effectiveness for creditors. However, the judicial implementation of these changes remains perfectible and decisions linked to bankruptcy procedures can take time.

Access to land or other fixed-asset ownership remains prohibited to foreign individuals and necessitates creation of a locally registered company.

The Labour Code amendment voted in 2001 established a standard 40-hour working week with a minimum of four weeks holiday. Restrictions also apply to overtime. In addition, trade unions should be consulted regarding collective redundancies.

Foreign exchange regulations

The Czech crown is fully convertible. The current exchange rate system is a dirty (or managed) float.

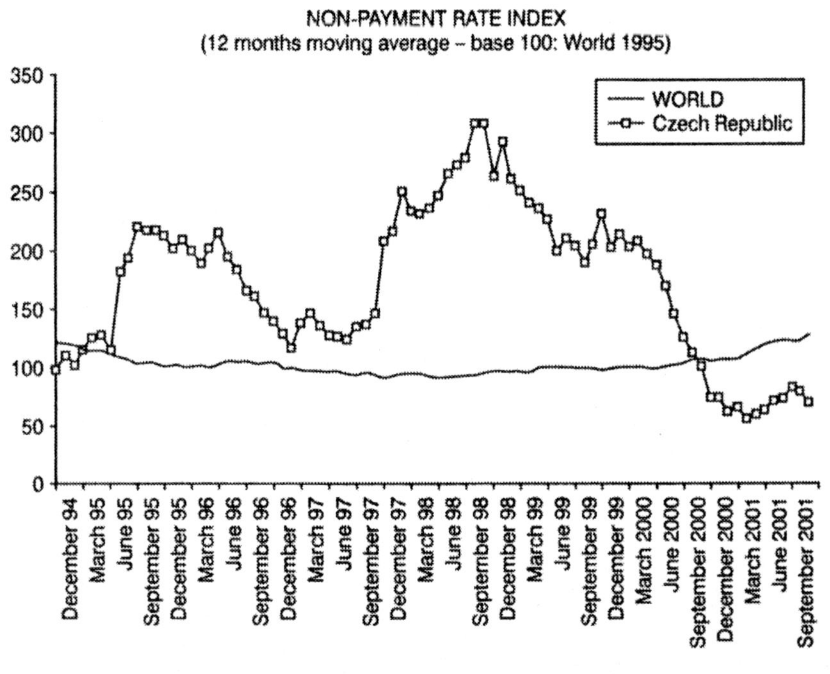

Figure 1.4.1 Non-payment rate index

Business opportunity

Coface

Opportunity scope

■ Population 10.3 million inhabitants	■ GDP 53,111 million US dollars

Breakdown of internal demand (GDP+imports)	%
■ Private consumption	32
■ Public spending	12
■ Investment	17

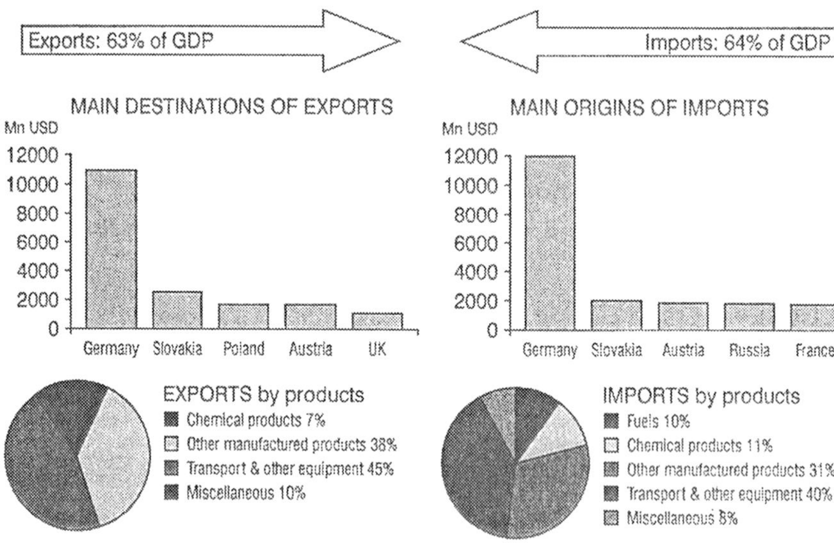

Standard of living/purchasing power

Indicators	*Czech Republic*	*Regional average*	*DC average*
GNP per capita (PPP dollars)	12,840	7689	6010
GNP per capita	5020	3229	3899
Human development index	0.844	0.794	0.697
Wealthiest 10% share of national income	22	25	32
Urban population percentage	75	62	59
Percentage under 15 years old	17	20	32
Number of telephones per 1,000 inhabitants	371	275	148
Number of computers per 1,000 inhabitants	107	81	53

Business threats

MIG Corporate Intelligence

Introduction

The centre-right coalition currently in power in the Czech Republic, despite being split, has a reasonably good track record. The economy is easing itself out of three years of recession, thanks to increased domestic productivity and healthy foreign investment. Eighty per cent of enterprises are now in private hands.

The Czech government is an uneasy alliance, which explains the ideological splits. However, the elections due in June 2002 will be significant. The next government will take the country into the European Union. One sticking point to Czech membership remains Prague's treatment of the Roma minority, their low standard of living and their human rights.

Second Quarter 2002 Grey Area Dynamics™ Rating (GAD): 52.5
(Europe & FSU benchmark GAD Rating: 58.5)

Fighting index	Low
Crime levels	Medium to High
Bureaucracy	Medium to High
Cultural integration	Low
Religious extremism	Low

Practice

Crime levels

Czech police have recorded a rapid growth in criminal activities with an extremist subtext. There has been an increase in the number of people prosecuted in connection with political extremism.

There is some concern among the authorities with regard to the activities of groups such as the Patriotic Front, the Patriotic League and the National Front of Castists. Intelligence reports claim that the groups have undergone qualitative changes and are trying to broaden their base of appeal.

Organized crime groups (OCGs) remain active. Recent reports reveal that they are exploiting opportunities in the fields of toxic substances and waste storing, exploiting gaps in Czech environmental protection legislation.

There has also been a shift in the activities of OCGs in the Czech Republic, primarily the Russian mafia, from drug trafficking to legitimate business. OCGs are gaining influence in strategic sectors of the economy and investing in property. Since their businesses are legal, it is difficult for foreign investors to ascertain if a Czech partner or distributor has indirect links to an OCG.

White-collar crimes continue to impact on business operations.

Bureaucratic overburdening

The Czech bureaucracy is often subject to heavy lobbying from established groups. This can lead to blackmail and extortion. The Czechs are signatories to the OECD's charter on anti-corruption of public officials in international business transactions. However, its implementation in the Czech business sphere is another matter.

Legal safeguards

An inadequate legal framework is among the biggest obstacles that the foreign investor faces in the Czech Republic. Businessmen lack faith in the ability of the judiciary and enforcement agencies to implement and enforce property rights, shareholder rights and contracts.

Essentials

With elections due in summer 2002, political considerations will dominate the Energy Regulatory Office's (ERU) decisions on the extent of energy prices to be liberalized later in the year. The ERU has given in to pressure and is to liberalize the gas market at a slower pace than originally stated in the Energy Act. This is a worrying development from the perspective of the foreign investor.

Following some ill-advised reforms in the mid-1990s, the Czech economy appears to have recovered from a three-year recession. Despite the global downturn, Czech consumers have increased their spending. GDP growth in 2002 is expected to reach 4 per cent.

The banking sector, rescued by foreign investors and a few judicious state bailouts, is in the midst of a restructuring. Banks are guarded against lending excessively to domestic firms that are attempting to finance IT upgrades in order to prevent a repeat crisis.

The European Union's annual report on accession issued in November 2001 criticized the tendency for non-transparent public tenders, the failure to adopt a Civil Service Act and slow progress in implementing judicial reform and fighting economic crime. There are an estimated 150,000 commercial cases awaiting trial in the courts.

In addition, several Western companies cite difficulties in getting paid promptly as a disincentive to investing in the Czech Republic.

Concerns

High corporate leverage can be a problem. Incumbent enterprise directors and others with vested interests put pressure on the government concerning investors' business plans. Labour regulations can also get in the way of an investor's rationalization plans as trade unions seek to safeguard jobs. The bankruptcy law is inadequate, so investors can come up against obstacles to shutting down a distressed asset.

Bureaucrats with the power to make decisions pertaining to an investment are known to seek additional payment for their services. However, the occurrence of bribery is not as widespread in the Czech Republic as in other transitional former communist countries.

Despite its shortcomings, the Czech Republic is among the favourite destinations for FDI in the European emerging markets. The authorities have shown willing. The introduction of a package of incentives, including tax breaks and grants for job creation, have encouraged the enterprising businessman. However, it can take months of bureaucratic delays to see the specified benefits realized.

Foreign direct investment would need to be prepared to take the rough with the smooth when investing in the Czech Republic.

ONLINE UPDATES - 26 May 2005

Business risk assessment (Chap.1.4)

Overview

The dynamism of firmer growth in 2004 should persist throughout 2005, although forecasts could suffer from the continuing weak performance of EU economies, notably that of Germany. Loss of competitiveness due to exchange rate appreciation is also possible.

Although reduced, the current account deficit remains relatively large, partly as a result of the repatriation of earnings by foreign-owned companies. External financing needs have remained low in relation to export revenues. Further privatization is likely to boost foreign direct investment inflows.

Coface rating: A2

Strengths

- Work productivity has been increasing sharply.
- Highest levels of FDI per capita in Central Europe.
- Foreign exchange reserves remain at comfortable levels.
- Moderate foreign debt burden.
- Economic stability strengthened by EU accession.

Weaknesses

- Public sector deficit increased by banking sector restructuring costs.
- Dependency on economic fortunes of main trading partners.
- Large current account deficit reflects increased earnings paid to foreign investors.

May 2005, Coface

1.5

Foreign Direct Investment (FDI)[1]

Foreign direct investment (FDI) has been a key element in the economic development of the Czech Republic, and formerly Czechoslovakia, since 1990, with more than US$25 billion recorded up to the end of 2001. Since 1998, when a package of favourable investment incentives was introduced, FDI has been the main driver of continuing growth with a massive inflow of FDI into both greenfield and brownfield projects. The Czech Republic has become one of foreign investors' favourite targets in Central and Eastern European (CEE) countries and among transition economies.

Performance since 1998

In each of the past four years, the Czech Republic has run a current account deficit increasing from 2.4 per cent of GDP in 1998 to 4.7 per cent in 2000 and 2001. However, FDI net inflows have offset the foreign exchange deficits and in 2001 the surplus in the balance of capital transactions amounted to 7.1 per cent of GDP, thanks to a new record FDI of almost €5.4 billion.

This inflow is increasingly made up of greenfield investments. The more than €1 billion being invested by Toyota and PSA Peugeot Citroën is only the tip of the Czech Republic's investment iceberg. The advantages of this trend are that the economy can count on a constant inflow of investment even after privatization is finished from 2003 onwards, and that this influx can continue to help provide debt-free cover for the current account deficit. The disadvantage is that a constant inflow of foreign currency into the country exerts growing pressure for an upward valuation of the Czech crown.

The proceeds from privatization of major state-owned enterprises have been a significant factor in maintaining the inflow, and the rousing

[1] The content for this chapter is drawn from publications of the Bank Austria Creditanstalt Economics Department and fact sheets published by CzechInvest (the Czech Agency for Foreign Investment).

success of several major projects, of which VW's acquisition of Skoda is the prime example, have been particularly important. Based on the success of ventures such as this, manufacturers in the supply chain have also decided to set up operations in the Czech Republic, leading to the formation of clusters, which, like the cluster of automotive component businesses in the Stredoceský region, have acted as magnets for further investment.

As might be expected, Western European companies predominate among the regional composition of inward investors. At the end of 2000, more than 80 per cent of the stock of foreign capital invested in the Czech Republic had come from EU countries, of which the three largest sources were the same countries that had led the way in investment throughout the 1990s: Germany, the Netherlands and Austria. The relative shares of the three leaders together with France and Switzerland are illustrated in Figure 1.5.1.

A more detailed account of country contributions to FDI is given in the upper half of Table 1.5.1. In the period 1990–2000, the FDI contributions of Britain and the United States amounted to just 4.5 per cent and 4.6 per cent respectively, compared to Germany (25.6 per cent), the Netherlands (28.9 per cent) and Austria (12.4 per cent).

FDI is also analysed by major industrial sector in Figure 1.5.2 and in greater detail by manufacturing and services sectors in the lower half of Table 1.5.1.

Over the period 1990–2000, while trade and repairs accounted for 20.9 per cent, finance and insurance represented 19.5 per cent, and real estate and other business services 12.5 per cent of FDI. Automotive production was the only manufacturing sector to attract more than 10 per cent of overall FDI. Other significant manufacturing

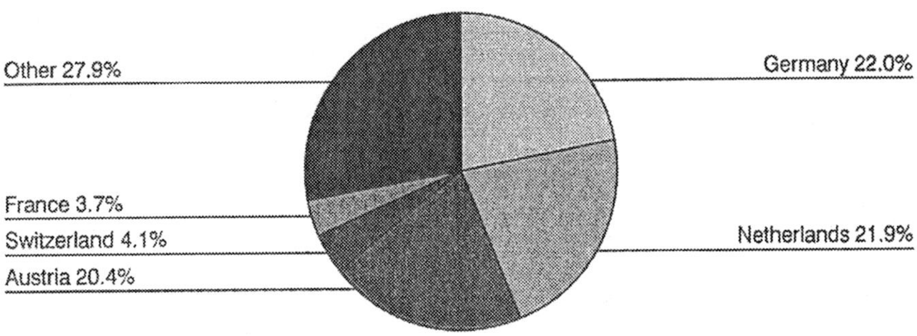

Figure 1.5.1 FDI by country, end 2000

Table 1.5.1 FDI inflow into the Czech Republic by country and sector

Country	*1999* *Million USD*	%	*2000* *Million USD*	%	*1990–2000* *Million USD*	%	*3Q 2001* *Million USD*	%
Netherlands	1,130.8	17.9	1,005.8	21.9	6,392.5	28.9	700.85	24.0
Germany	1,299.7	20.6	1,010.6	22.0	5,677.6	25.6	1,025.89	36.0
Austria	833.3	13.2	937.8	20.4	2,715.5	12.3	137.32	5.0
USA	580.8	9.2	208.0	4.5	1,388.4	6.3	232.47	8.0
Great Britain	104.2	1.6	130.3	2.8	1,018.0	4.6	40.94	1.5
Belgium	1,377.7	21.8	113.0	2.5	985.8	4.5	20.57	1.0
France	232.3	3.6	172.4	3.7	946.2	4.2	257.95	9.0
Switzerland	353.8	5.6	187.1	4.1	574.6	2.6	118.35	4.0
Sweden	126.7	2.0	128.9	2.8	386.6	1.7	41.64	1.5
Others	284.7	4.5	701.2	15.3	2,062.0	9.3	297.32	10.0
TOTAL	**6,324.0**	**100.0**	**4,595.1**	**100.0**	**22,147.2**	**100.0**	**2,873.30**	**100.0**
Sector								
Manufacturing—total	**2,008.1**	**31.8**	**1,582.8**	**34.4**	**8,369.5**	**37.8**	**872.57**	**30.37**
Production of non-metallic mineral products	315.2	5.0	152.6	3.3	1,620.5	7.3	53.30	2.00
Production of motor vehicles	199.2	3.1	471.1	10.3	1,365.6	6.2	37.42	1.00
Production of food products and beverages	359.2	5.7	186.2	4.1	1,311.8	5.9	18.71	0.70
Petroleum, chemical and rubber products	394.4	6.2	74.9	1.6	788.0	3.6	64.82	2.35
Production of electrical machinery and apparatus	59.2	0.9	116.7	2.5	603.1	2.7	17.57	0.60
Consumer electronics, computers	87.2	1.4	38.0	0.8	125.2	0.6	244.88	9.00
Others	593.7	9.5	543.3	11.8	2,555.3	11.5	435.87	15.00
Services—total	**4,060.5**	**64.2**	**2,978.0**	**64.9**	**13,634.1**	**61.6**	**1,962.10**	**68.28**
Trade and repairs	1,274.2	20.1	960.3	20.9	3,730.9	16.8	603.07	21.00
Financial intermediation and insurance	1,505.1	23.8	898.2	19.5	3,546.6	16.0	150.19	5.00
Transport and telecommunications	196.7	3.1	205.1	4.5	2,347.0	10.6	705.88	25.00
Real estate and other business activities	421.0	6.7	271.8	5.9	1,569.4	7.1	238.64	8.00
Electricity, gas and water	333.2	5.3	204.2	4.4	1,551.4	7.0	203.75	7.00
Others	330.3	5.2	438.4	9.7	888.8	4.1	60.57	2.00
Farming and mining	**255.4**	**4.0**	**34.3**	**0.7**	**143.6**	**0.6**	**34.50**	**1.35**
TOTAL	**6,324.0**	**100.0**	**4,595.1**	**100.0**	**22,147.2**	**100.0**	**2,317.40**	**100.00**

Source: The Czech National Bank, 2001

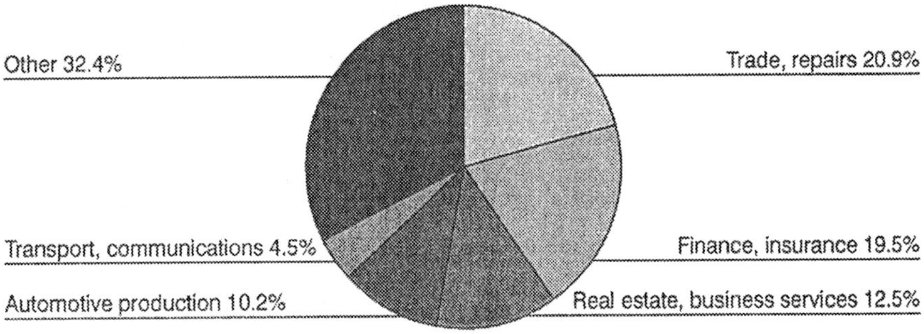

Figure 1.5.2 FDI by sector, end 2000
Source: Austrian Federal Ministry for Economic Affairs and Labour

manufacturing sectors include food products and beverages (4.1 per cent), non-metallic mineral products (3.3 per cent) and electrical machinery and apparatus (2.5 per cent).

Foreign-backed manufacturing experience

For each year since 1997, CzechInvest has sponsored an annual independent survey of foreign-backed manufacturers. The most recent survey revealed that more than 1200 foreign manufacturing companies now have subsidiaries in the Czech Republic, among which nearly every famous multinational is represented. The following conclusions were reached in respect of growth, expansion and job creation:

- Thirty per cent of firms intend to expand production in a new location in the Czech Republic by the end of 2002, and 76 per cent in their existing Czech location. This optimistic outlook confirms the findings of the 1999 survey when 91 per cent of firms reported that they had already reinvested within the Czech Republic since the start of initial production, with almost two-thirds reinvesting more than the value of their start-up investment.
- Collectively, these firms expected to employ 14 per cent more people at the start of 2001 than they did in December 1999. The survey indicated a long-term annual net job creation rate in the period 1998–2000 of 6 per cent. The automotive sector alone, of which 70 per cent is foreign-owned, is estimated to employ 140,000 and makes up 13 per cent of national exports. The joint

Citroën plant at Kolín will employ a farther 3000 and create another 7000 indirect jobs.

- Seventy-nine per cent of respondents indicated that they are actively planning to increase their staff levels in the future.

The previous survey reported that foreign-backed firms had experienced strong operational benefits:

- Forty-four per cent of firms anticipated that they would reduce their absenteeism rate in 2000 compared to the previous year.
- Forty-nine per cent of firms expected to decrease the rate of staff turnover.
- The Czech supply base is consistently able to support incoming investors. Fifty-seven per cent of firms indicated that they were currently able to increase their local content.
- The firms surveyed reported strong export growth, with 69 per cent expecting to increase the proportion of their revenues earned by exports, 45 per cent to increase the number of countries to which they export and 90 per cent to increase their total revenues and the value of revenues accounted for by exports.
- Foreign-backed firms have committed themselves to achieving international quality assurance standards. Seventy-one per cent of surveyed firms have already achieved ISO 9000, 901,14000 or 14001 qualification and less than 5 per cent stated that they did not have and had no plans to gain some kind of quality rating.
- Bureaucratic problems are receding. In both the 1998 and 1999 surveys more firms reported improvements, rather than worsening conditions, in dealing with tax and labour offices and with their local municipal offices. However, as Chapter 1.4, Business Risk Assessment, makes clear, the impact of bureaucracy is still a significant constraining factor on doing business in the Czech Republic.

The 1999 survey included questions on the organization and management of workforces that were not repeated in the next survey. Nevertheless, the findings were encouraging:

- Foreign-backed firms had successfully introduced continuous production in their Czech subsidiaries, with 26 per cent claiming seven days a week and 16 per cent six days a week operations. Continuous production (24/7) was reported by 49 per cent of the firms surveyed.
- No union problems were reported, with 61 per cent of foreign manufacturers operating non-union plants.

- R&D activity in Czech subsidiaries is at healthy levels. In 1999, 21 per cent of firms surveyed reported that they were engaged in 'significant R&D', with the ratio rising to 40 per cent when external subcontractors were included. Eleven per cent of firms had already patented results of their research, of which all but one had incorporated their research into exportable products.

As at the last quarter of 2001, the following positive achievements of foreign-backed manufacturers were listed by CzechInvest:

- between sixty-five and seventy per cent of all manufactured exports;
- employment of approximately 300,000 people. Firms supported by FDI with workforces of more than 100 employ more than 25 per cent of the total Czech manufacturing workforce employed in that segment;
- creation of an estimated 15,000–25,000 new jobs during the next 12 months, subject to economic conditions;
- underpinning of an estimated 10,000 Czech suppliers in the manufacturing and service sectors and a minimum of 600,000 jobs in local supplier companies, approximately 12 per cent of the total Czech labour force in employment.

Foreign investment climate

Since 1998, the Czech Republic has been a favourite target for foreign investors in Central and Eastern Europe. Contributory factors to this trend have been the incentive package for foreign investors passed in 1998 and the market's growing expectations of positive effects from EU accession. As a result, net FDI inflows have grown from €3.4 billion in 1998 to €3.9 billion in each of 1999 and 2000, and to €5.4 billion in 2001. The forecast for 2002, which includes the proceeds from two major privatizations, is for record FDI of €8.4 billion before falling back to a more sustainable €4.2 billion in 2003. The new investment to be committed in 2002 of some €7.8 billion is estimated to represent 11.5 per cent of GDP.

The parliamentary elections in June 2002 are imminent, with the ruling Czech Social Democrats (CSSD) and the Civic Democratic Party (ODS) in close contention. The ODS was slightly in the lead during the spring. The Coalition of Four (Ctyrkoalice) was the strongest political force in the country at the end of 1991, but became fragmented in early February when it decided against joint candidacy due to the heavy debt of the Civic Democratic Alliance (ODA). Therefore, the two

Table 1.5.2 Major foreign investors in the manufacturing sector

Company	*Country*	*Sector*	*Activities in the Czech Republic*
ABB	Sweden	Engineering	4000 employees
AVX (Kyocera)	United States, Japan	Electronics	Over 4000 employees
Boeing	United States	Aerospace	Manufacturing and R&D
Celestica	Canada	Electronics	2 manufacturing plants
Continental	Germany	Automotive	3 manufacturing plants
Flextronics	United States, Singapore	Electronics	Nearly 2000 employees
Foxconn	Taiwan	Electronics	Over 1000 employees
Glaverbel	Belgium, Japan	Glass	8 manufacturing plants
IrisBus	France, Italy	Automotive	Renault/Iveco joint venture
Matsushita	Japan	Electronics	5 investments
Magna	Canada	Automotive	4 manufacturing plants
On Semi-conductor	United States	Electronics	Former Motorola subsidiary
Philips	The Netherlands	Electronics	US$624 million invested
Procter & Gamble	United States	Consumer goods	Over 750 employees
Siemens	Germany	Engineering	9 plants/11,000 employees
Toyota/PSA	Japan, France	Automotive	€1.5 billion investment/ 10,000 jobs
Tyco	United States	Automotive	Over 1200 employees
Unilever UK	The Netherlands	Consumer goods	Over US$100 million invested
Visteon (Ford)	United States	Automotive	Nearly 4000 employees
Volkswagen	Germany	Automotive	Skoda Auto: 22,000 employees

Source: CzechInvest, September 2001

remaining parties running joint candidates, the Democratic Union (DEU) and the Christian Democratic Union/Czech People's Party (KDU-CSL), were seriously weakened and fell to third place in the polls. Throughout, the Communist Party (KCSM) has maintained fourth position, with some 25 per cent of the vote. The outcome of the election should make little difference to prospects for foreign investors since all three of the top-ranking political groupings are clearly committed to EU accession and reject a coalition with the Communists.

Looking in more detail at the underlying factors that are a continuing encouragement to inward investment, the following advantages may be identified:

Non-discrimination

Under Czech law, foreign and domestic entities are treated identically in all areas from protection of property rights to investment incentives. The government does not screen any foreign investment projects, with the exception of the defence and banking sectors. (The latter is now largely in the hands of multinational banking groups.)

As an OECD member, the Czech Republic is committed not to discriminate against foreign investors in privatization sales, with the same exceptions.

Investment protection

The Czech Republic is a member of the Multilateral Investment Guarantee Agency (MIGA), an international organization for protection of investment belonging to the World Bank-IMF group. The country has signed a number of bilateral international treaties, including agreements for the avoidance of double taxation, which support and protect foreign investments—for example, with the United States, Germany, United Kingdom, France, Austria, Switzerland, Italy, Belgium, Luxembourg, Netherlands, Finland, Norway and Denmark.

Protection of property rights

The Czech Republic is a signatory to the Bern, Paris and Universal Copyright Conventions (see Chapter 2.6, Intellectual Property). The property of a foreign person or entity may be expropriated in the Czech Republic only on public interest grounds that cannot be satisfied by other means, only through an Act of Parliament and with full compensation at market value. No expropriation of the property of a foreign investor has taken place since 1989.

Repatriation of profits

No limitations exist concerning the distribution and expatriation of profits by Czech subsidiaries to their foreign parent companies, other than the obligation of joint-stock and limited liability companies to generate a mandatory reserve fund and pay withholding taxes (see Chapter 3.2, Accountancy and Audit, and Chapter 3.3, Business Taxation).

Double taxation treaties cover taxes on dividends, interest and royalties. Actual rates of withholding tax are determined by the individual treaty and range from 0 to 15 per cent.

Competitive labour rates

The Czech Republic has an extremely competitive labour potential in terms of education and training, particularly in manufacturing—for example, its unit labour costs are about 30 per cent only of those in Austria.

FDI outlook

The association agreements concluded in the course of EU accession negotiations have led to the creation of a free trade zone for manufactured goods and have ensured that foreign investors have been able to utilize the country's cost advantages for producing goods for the EU market. As a result, the Czech Republic had the highest level of total FDI per capita of any CEE country in 2001, at more than US$2400.

The Czech Republic will continue to benefit in the future from the market's expectations of positive effects from EU accession. For one thing, the last trade barriers will fall in sectors previously excluded from the association agreements, such as steel, textiles and agriculture. For another, the further implementation of the Acquis Communautaire will result in a successive approximation of legal regulations to those of the European Union. This harmonization process will, in turn, eliminate one of the biggest existing shortcomings—the lack of effective bankruptcy proceedings. Furthermore, legal certainty will be further increased by the planned availability of€250 million under the Phare programme to train administrative authorities so that EU law and regulations are effectively implemented.

Finally, the accession will eliminate the last restrictions to the free movement of capital and will make the Czech Republic eligible for further EU assistance, which will stimulate new investment projects. When the country adopts the euro as its currency, any remaining vestiges of foreign exchange risk will disappear. Accession to the European Union will in no way detract from the advantages for manufacturing facilities of productivity growth coupled with low production costs which investors in the Czech Republic enjoy.

ONLINE UPDATES - 27 May 2005

Foreign direct investment (Chap. 1.5)

The net inflow of foreign direct investment (FDI) regained momentum in 2004, recovering from EUR2,086 million in 2003 to EUR3,595 million in 2004. A further increase to EUR5,450 is forecast for 2005 before falling back to EUR3,720. The higher levels of FDI recorded in the period of major privatizations are most unlikely to be repeated.

Investors from the EU are the dominant source of FDI, accounting for 85 per cent of the total stock of foreign capital accumulated up to year-end 2002. The league table for total FDI inflows of approximately EUR37 billion in the period 1993–2002 stood at :

- Germany: 31.3 per cent;
- Netherlands: 18.4 per cent;
- Austria: 10.2 per cent;
- France: 8.4 per cent;
- USA: 6.9 per cent;
- Belgium: 5.3 per cent;
- UK: 4.5 per cent;
- Switzerland: 3.9 per cent;
- Other: 11.1 per cent.

Over the same period FDI inflows by sector were recorded as:

- Transport, communications: 21.2 per cent;
- Financial intermediaries: 19.9 per cent;
- Trade, restaurants and hotels: 12.3 per cent;
- Machine building, automotive: 11.5 per cent;

- Real estate, businesses services: 7.2 per cent;
- Electricity, as and water supply: 5.5 per cent;
- Food industry: 4.7 per cent;
- Other: 13.6 per cent.

Changes to investment incentives and grants are covered in Updates to Chap. 3.3 – business taxation.

April 2005, Bank Austria Creditanstalt CEE Report 2- 2005, Investment Guide Czech Republic 2004.

1.6

Foreign Trade[1]

Jonathan Reuvid

Evolution of foreign trade since 1990

The reorientation of the Czech Republic's economy following the Velvet Revolution of 1989 encouraged the combined and then individual Czech and Slovak governments to build up trade relations with the European Union as quickly as possible. By 1993, trade with the European Union accounted for 49.4 per cent of all merchandise exports; in 2000, the proportion of exports had risen to 68.6 per cent while the share of exports to Central and Eastern European (CEE) countries had declined to 19.1 per cent from 27.1 per cent over the same period. In parallel, the share of imports from the European Union in 2000 was 61.9 per cent.

While the nominal growth of exports in Czech crowns from CZK385 billion in 1993 to CZK1121 billion in 2000 was nearly three-fold, nominal GDP less than doubled. However, in US dollars, exports and GDP growth were more in line, as Table 1.6.1 demonstrates. During the same period, merchandise imports in US dollars more than doubled and, except for 1993 after inclusion of trade in commercial services, the Czech Republic maintained a deficit on current account. The deficit for 2000 was US$1816 million.

The dynamic pace of growth in exports was not only a function of rapid reorientation with Western Europe, but also the substantial inflows of foreign direct investment (FDI) into the establishment of manufacturing plants to produce goods for Western markets (see Chapter 1.3, Foreign Investment Regime). Not only has the foreign exchange inflow from investment helped to offset current account deficits, but it

[1] Content for the Czech customs system section is derived from CzechInvest Fact Sheet No. 16, 'Customs System', September 2001.

Table 1.6.1 Czech Republic exports and imports, 1992–2000 (US$ million)

	Exports			Imports		
	Merchandise	*Commercial services*	*Total trade*	*Merchandise*	*Commercial services*	*Total trade*
1992	12,170	—	12,170	12,880	—	12,880
1993	24,465	4679	19,144	14,615	3701	18,316
1994	16,205	5120	21,325	17,425	4685	22,110
1995	21,655	6638	28,293	25,625	4860	30,125
1996	21,905	8071	29,976	27,715	6198	33,913
1997	22,775	7033	39,808	27,165	5305	32,470
1998	26,350	7366	33,716	28,790	5665	34,455
1999	26,240	6808	33,048	28,075	5750	33,825
2000	29,000	7119	36,119	32,180	5755	37,935

Source: WTO international trade statistics, 2001

has also generated a strong base from which the Czech Republic can hope to establish a current account surplus in the future.

Trade partners

The predominance of Czech foreign trade with the European Union and CEE countries is emphasized in Table 1.6.2, which logs exports and imports with global regions and groupings in recent years. In addition, Table 1.6.2 breaks down foreign trade into the basic WTO product elements of agriculture, mining and manufactures.

Table 1.6.2 also highlights the predominance of manufactures in the composition of the country's foreign trade.

In terms of the Czech Republic's significance in world trade, its merchandise trade represent one half of one per cent of the global total, with rankings of 39 and 36 respectively among exporting and importing countries. In commercial services, the Czech Republic ranks 35 among exporters and 40 among importers with a similar percentage of the global total. While world trade in merchandise is growing at 12 per cent and 6 per cent in commercial services annually, the growth in Czech foreign trade is about one percentage point less.

The Czech Republic's trade within CEE countries, the Baltic States and the CIS combined remains significant, representing 10.7 per cent of exports and 13.3 per cent of imports in 2000. Both exports to and imports from these markets are closely similar in value to those of

Table 1.6.2 Czech Republic merchandise exports and imports worldwide, % total merchandise trade

	Exports			*Imports*		
	1998	*1999*	*2000*	*1998*	*1999*	*2000*
Total merchandise (US$ million)	26.350	26.240	29.000	28.790	28,075	32,180
	%	%	%	%	%	%
North America	2.5	2.7	3.0	4.1	4.4	4.7
Latin America	0.7	0.5	0.6	0.8	0.7	0.9
Western Europe	68.4	73.3	72.8	66.6	67.6	65.6
European Union	64.2	69.2	68.6	63.3	64.2	61.9
CEE/Baltic States/CIS	24.0	19.5	19.1	18.9	17.4	19.4
CEE	19.2	16.4	15.9	12.2	11.4	11.3
Russian Federation	2.5	1.4	1.3	5.5	4.8	6.4
Africa	0.7	0.6	0.5	0.6	0.6	0.7
Middle East	1.3	1.3	1.3	0.4	0.4	0.3
Asia	2.1	2.9	2.6	7.1	7.3	7.4
Major product groups						
Agriculture	7.2	6.7	6.6	8.6	7.8	7.0
Mining	5.1	4.7	4.9	10.3	9.8	13.3
Manufactures	89.3	88.1	88.1	81.0	82.3	79.7

Source: WTO international trade statistics, 2001

Hungary. Poland's relative shares are rather more at 11.7 per cent of exports and 20.3 per cent of imports.

Composition of Czech foreign trade

The changed composition of the Czech Republic's exported goods over the period 1993–2000 is shown in Figures 1.6.1 and 1.6.2. The biggest change has been in the machinery and transport equipment sector, where its share of exported goods has risen from 27.6 per cent to 44.5 per cent.

A more detailed analysis of manufactured goods exported and imported is provided in Tables 1.6.3 and 1.6.4, which are based on WTO statistics and product definitions.

Comparing Table 1.6.3 with Table 1.6.4 it is apparent that, although the Czech Republic is a net importer of merchandise, its trade in manufactures is approximately in balance. Within the manufacturing sector, machinery and transport equipment—the largest product group—is also almost in balance, and automotive products, textiles and clothing exports exceed imports. Of the product groups analysed in these tables,

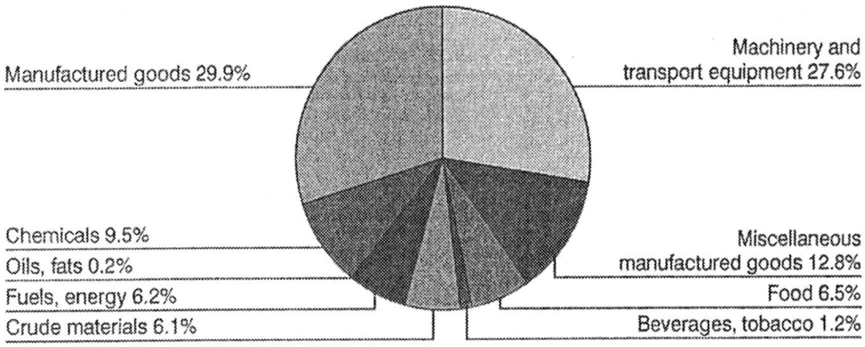

Source: Vienna Institute for International Economic Studies (WIIW), Bank Austria Creditanstalt Economics Department

Figure 1.6.1 Structure of exported goods in 1993 (SITC)

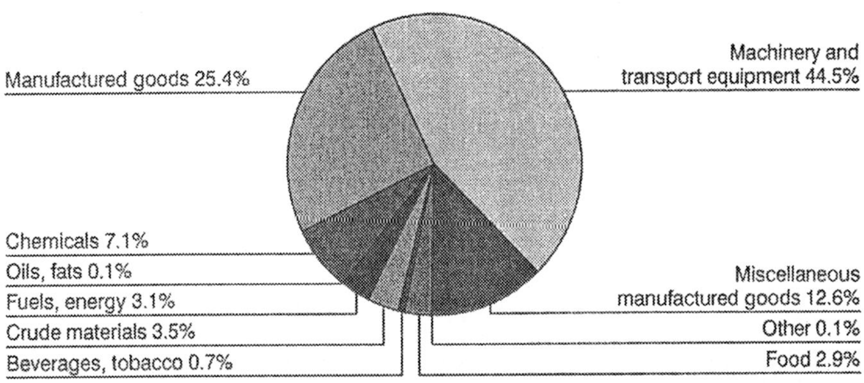

Source: Vienna Institute for International Economic Studies (WIIW), Bank Austria Creditanstalt Economics Department

Figure 1.6.2 Structure of exported goods in 2000 (SITC)

product groups analysed in these tables, only office machines and telecoms equipment are in deficit. In 2000, steel exports to both the European Union and the United States rose strongly, totalling US$723 million.

Czech customs system

The Czech foreign trade regime is strongly liberal and rates highly in the 'World Economic Forum Global Competitiveness Report

Table 1.6.3 Czech exports in selected product groups

	1995	*1998*	*1999*	*2000*	*% total merchandise trade 2000*
		(US$ million)			
Exports					
Machinery & transport equipment	6585	10,874	11,336	12,892	44.5
Automotive products	1,532	3752	4036	4662	16.1
Office machines & telecoms equipment	488	682	676	1282	4.4
Textiles	1342	1136	1072	1218	4.2
Clothing	523	705	655	634	2.2
Total manufactures	18,000	23,000	23,120	25,550	88.1
Total merchandise	21,655	26,350	26,240	29,000	100.0

Table 1.6.4 Czech imports in selected product groups

	1995	*1998*	*1999*	*2000*	*% total merchandise trade 2000*
		(US$ million)			
Imports					
Machinery & transport Equipment	9363	11,353	11,335	12,906	40.0
Automotive products	1472	2225	2326	2592	8.0
Office machines & telecoms equipment	11,962	2011	2146	3079	9.5
Textiles	935	1122	1095	1203	3.7
Clothing	460	438	425	425	1.3
Total manufactures	19,820	23,320	23,100	25,640	79.5
Total merchandise	25,265	28,790	28,075	32,180	100.0

Czech Republic is a founder member of GATT and the WTO and has additional trade agreements with the European Union, the European Free Trade Area (EFTA) countries, the eight Central European Free Trade Agreement (CEFTA) countries and other selected individual countries including Estonia, Latvia, Lithuania, Turkey and Israel. Since 1993, when the former Czechoslovakia was divided, there has been a customs union with Slovakia.

Goods originating in these countries are subject to preferential rates of customs duty.

Manufactured goods are usually zero-rated.

Customs procedures

Recent amendments to the Czech Customs Act (No. 13/1993), which was based on EU rules, has harmonized customs legislation further with EU standards. There are 14 regional Customs Directorates under the authority of the General Directorate of Customs and at least one local Customs Office in each of the 77 districts. Customs clearings may be handled by the consignee direct or through an appointed representative.

Unless the customs office grants the importer permission to use the simplified customs procedures described below, customs clearance is carried out at the local customs office. Although a computerized declaration processing system is being introduced, importers must also provide a hard-copy declaration within 30 days.

The customs office assesses and collects import customs duty, VAT, excise taxes and other applicable charges. The importer pays a fee for each shipment into the customs office's bank account or presents a guarantee certificate. Commercial banks, insurance companies or other entities approved by the customs authorities may act as guarantors.

Simplified customs procedures

Companies that export or import goods frequently may be allowed to use simplified procedures:

- An approved exporter may provide a simplified Proof of Preferential Origin for exports.
- An approved consignee may declare imported goods on its premises rather than in the customs office.
- An approved consignor may declare exported goods on its premises rather than in the customs office.

The Customs Act and a government decree stipulate the conditions for obtaining permission to use simplified customs procedures, and local customs offices issue permissions. Applicants are required to show a clean customs history of several months and to keep sufficient records of all movements of goods.

Inward processing regime (IPR)

Goods that are imported into the Czech Republic for processing and re-export are subject to IPR, which may be used anywhere in the country and has two forms:

- The Suspension System, which allows a company to import goods without paying customs duty.
- The Drawback System, which allows goods to be released into free circulation, with the remission or repayment of import duties and VAT imposed on them if they are processed and re-exported.

The respective customs office that approves the IPR, perhaps for an unlimited period, defines the conditions under which it may be used including specification of the period in which processed products must be exported.

Importers are required by the customs office to supply a security bond or a guarantee certificate to support their undertaking that goods granted the IPR status will not be released into free circulation without payment of customs duty and other charges. Companies with a sufficiently long, clean customs history may be relieved of this obligation.

The outward processing regime (OPR), also specified in the Customs Act, is a corollary to the IPR and applies to goods that are exported from the Czech Republic to undergo processing abroad and subsequent re-import.

1.7

Regions of the Czech Republic

The Czech Republic is divided into 14 regions (Higher Territorial Self-governing Units, Vyssi Uzemnespravni Celky, VUSC), which came into effect on 1 January 2000. The new regions have been subdivided into 77 districts (Okres). The central national government continues to transfer selected competencies to the devolved self-governing regional councils. The geographical disposition of the 14 regions is shown in Map 1.7.1

The following is a brief description of the main features of each region taken from Bank Austria Creditanstalt's *Investment Guide for the Czech Republic,* February 2002.

Map 1.7.1

Regional overview

Praha (1.2 million inhabitants)

The capital city is also the economic centre of the country. Somewhat more than 10 per cent of the total population lives here and generates about 20 per cent of total GDP. The Ruzyne Airport and eight universities provide an appropriate infrastructure. Unemployment is far below the national average while the wage level is far above it. The fastest-growing sectors are services in general and financial services, wholesale/retail trade and telecoms in particular.

Středočeský

The region around Prague benefits from its proximity to the centre. Skoda Auto, the largest manufacturer and leading exporter in the Czech Republic, and its various suppliers provide a majority of the jobs in the region. Commuters into the capital also ensure that this region has several districts with some of the lowest unemployment rates in the country.

Budějovický

Despite its rural character, Budějovický (Southern Bohemia) has the fifth-highest per capita GDP of the 14 regions in the Czech Republic. In recent years, its peripheral location directly bordering Austria and Germany has attracted mechanical engineering and food processing companies in addition to the region's key sectors of agriculture, wood processing and textiles.

Plzeňský

Bordering on the German Land of Bavaria, Plzenský links Prague with the German autobahn system via the D5. The first and most successful industrial park in the Czech Republic was established here in 1990 and has attracted largely automotive supply businesses. In 2000, some 70 per cent of the region's net product was generated in manufacturing as opposed to 50 per cent in 1990.

Karlovarský

Besides the R6 express highway linking its key cities to Germany, this westernmost region in the Czech Republic also has an international airport in the regional capital of Karlovy Vary (Carlsbad), but it currently serves only one foreign destination. The region is rich in natural resources, which explains why mining and power production account for such a large percentage of the net product generated in the region.

Ústecký

This region bordering on the Saxony Land of Germany has the highest unemployment rate in the country despite various efforts such as investments in a new motorway (D8) or the founding of a university in Ústí nad Labem in 1991. The region was very hard hit by economic restructuring due to its one-sided dependency on mining and heavy industry. As a result, huge government subsidies are being put into projects aimed at attracting new business to Ústecký.

Liberecký

Bordering on Poland and Germany and located just a one-hour drive from Prague, this region also benefits from its proximity to the Skoda Auto production plants. Many supplier businesses, eg Varta, Peguform and Johnson Controls, have settled in the region, giving Liberecký the highest percentage of industrial workers in the country—some 45 per cent.

Královéhradecký

Královéhradecký has a poorly developed transportation infrastructure, with construction only now starting on the D11 from Prague to Poland and no international airports in the region. It has therefore not benefited from the investment boom in the same way as other regions have. Královéhradecký has a rural character with about 7 per cent of the workforce engaged in agriculture. Although this has kept the unemployment rate below the national average, wages are likewise about 10 per cent below the national average, indicating the lack of economic dynamism here.

Pardubický

With its central location, Pardubický is a key transportation hub. An international airport and the Berlin-Prague-Vienna railway line also provide it with a good transportation infrastructure even though it has no motorway. The D11 currently being built and a planned river port on the Labe (German: Elbe), which flows towards Hamburg) will further improve this infrastructure.

Jihlavský

Located halfway between the key cities of Prague and Brno, Jihlavský benefits from its proximity to these two centres and to Austria. In November 2001, the German mechanical engineering group Bosch Diesel chose Jihlavský as the location for a new plant. The investment totalling some US$ 200 million will create about 1400 new jobs.

Brněnský

Bordering on the Slovak Republic and Austria, Brnenský is one of the most populous regions in the country with more than 1 million inhabitants. Its capital city is Brno, the country's second-largest city. Two railway lines (Berlin-Prague-Vienna and Warsaw-Ostrava-Vienna) converge in Brno, which also has an international airport. The country's first high-tech park was established here and has attracted companies such as IBM and Silicon Graphics.

Olomoucký

The region of Olomoucký borders Poland and has been selected as a business location by major electronics companies such as Phillips, Siemens and Epcos. Nonetheless, the region's unemployment rate is above the national average because its key sectors, food and textiles, were particularly hard hit by economic restructuring.

Zlínský

Bordering on Slovakia, Zlínský has a relatively high percentage of industrial workers (40 per cent of the industrial workforce). Traditional key sectors are shoe and leather production and the rubber and textile industries. Despite the relatively high level of unemployment in Zlínský, one thing that the region has going for it is that it has the largest number of new business start-ups in the country.

Ostravský

Mining and heavy industry dominate in this easternmost region of the Czech Republic. Owing to the crisis in these sectors, the unemployment rate in Ostravský is second only to Ústecký. Although several Western companies such as Siemens, Danone, Ford and Shimano have been persuaded to open branches here, unemployment will remain high in the years ahead as a result of the ongoing consolidation in the steel and mining industries. The completion of the D47 by 2005 is one of the Czech government's largest road construction projects.

Regional Development Agencies (RDAs)

The Ministry for Regional Development has established a Regional Development Agency (RDA) in each region to support entrepreneurial activities. The RDAs can provide region-specific information, contacts with and introductions to local businesses, as well as guiding the investor through the local government structure.

CzechInvest is represented at each office of the RDA and is supported by additional representatives in some of the larger cities.

Regional economic data

Table 1.7.1 Basic data on the regions

Region	*Regional Capital (01/2001)*	*Area (km^2) (01/2001)*	*Population (03/2000)*	*Labour force*	*Unemployment rate (%)*	*GDP per capita**
Praha	Prague	496	1,184,723	640,686	3.5	21,927
Central Bohemia (Středočeský)	Kladno	11014	1,112,181	557,197	7.1	9,085
South Bohemia (Budějovický)	Cesky Budejovický	10056	625,900	316,113	6.2	10,709
Plzeňský	Plzenský	7561	551,532	284,254	6.7	11,749
Karlovarský	Karlovy Vary	3314	304,705	216,125	6.4	10,398
Ústecký	Usti nad Labem	5335	826,984	413,229	16.6	10,822
Laberecký	Liberecký	3163	428,978	217,515	6.6	9,944
Královéhradecký	Hradec Kralove	4758	551,304	280,984	6.1	10,333
Pardubický	Pardubický	4518	508,429	330,238	6.3	10,236

Table 1.7.1 continued

Region	*Regional Capital (01/2001)*	*Area (km²) (01/2001)*	*Population (03/2000)*	*Labour force*	*Unemployment rate (%)*	*GDP per capita**
Vysochina (Jihlavský)	Jihlava	6925	521,162`	260,615	7.8	9,436
South Moravia (Brně nský)	Brno	7066	1,136,823	573,898	9.8	10,956
Olomoucký	Olomoucký	5139	641,582	312,734	12.8	9,806
Zlínský	Zlínský	3964	597,970	292,233	8.6	10,182
Ostravský	Ostravský	5554	1,280,533	625,723	15.5	11,172
Total		78,864	10,272,806	5,209,637	9.1	11,761

Source: Czech Statistical Office
* Average GDP per capita, 1995–1997 PPS (purchasing power standard)

Part Two

The Legal Structure and Business Regulation

2.1

Legal Framework

CMS Cameron McKenna

Introduction

The roots of the Czech Republic's legal system are similar to those of the rest of Continental Europe. On independence in 1918, the Czech Republic inherited the laws of the Austro-Hungarian Empire, which had been subject to complete codification. The key differences between a codified civil law system and a system based on common law (eg that of the United Kingdom, United States or Australia) are:

- Judges are asked to interpret the law in a purposive way (ie codes are drafted in broad conceptual terms and the courts will use them as a basis to accommodate novel situations).
- The role of judges is to interpret the text of statutes in relation to the facts of specific individual cases. Unlike judges in common law jurisdictions, they are unable to create new law.

After the establishment of the Czech Republic on 1 January 1993, the new state adopted the legislation of the former Czech and Slovak Republic into its internal legal system.

Structure

The system of Czech law is based on its internal conformity and consistency—that is, the legal system cannot contain any contradictory rules. The legal norms are classed in two principal subsystems:

- material and procedural law;
- public and private law.

The Czech legal system is a unified system of primary and secondary law. The primary laws are laws voted by parliament while the secondary laws are laws originally drafted by the government, ministries or other central administrative authorities of the State and by local governments.

Practice

Primary laws are voted by parliament on the basis of a proposal put forward, most frequently by the government or by a group of deputies. The following are examples of primary laws:

- constitutional acts amending the constitution;
- ordinary laws;
- legislative measures taken by the senate (under section 33 of the constitution).

Secondary laws are drafted and enacted by the government, ministries and other central state authorities or by local government on the basis of a delegation of legislative power. Secondary laws may not enlarge rights and obligations set forth in the primary laws; neither may they enlarge the scope of penalties set forth by the primary laws.

The following courts are found in the Czech Republic:

- district courts;
- regional (municipal) courts;
- superior courts;
- supreme court and constitutional court.

Unless special legislation provides otherwise, the courts usually have a civil agenda and a penal agenda. Special administrative senates operate in the superior courts reviewing decisions by ministries and other central state authorities.

The government has the constitutional power to issue decrees to implement any act duly voted on by parliament in the legislative process prescribed by the constitution. In this sense, the government decides on the implementation of some acts itself.

The government may be empowered by an act voted on by parliament to issue its decree to help the implementation of specific laws. For instance, the Labour Code instructs the government to issue a decree specifying the level of the minimum wage in the Czech Republic.

Any ministry or a central state administration authority, such as the Czech National Bank (CNB) and territorial self-governing units (regions) in the Czech Republic, is authorized to issue a decree to implement an act dealing with matters falling within the competence of the given ministry or the central state authority. If the decree itself does not provide otherwise, such a ministerial decree becomes binding on the day of its publication.

Plenary sessions of the regional or district governments vote on such regulations and they can be issued with the following conditions:

- there is an explicit authorization in the ordinary law to issue such regulation;
- the regulation cannot exceed the substance regulated by primary law;
- the regulation is published.

With the exception of the constitutional court, decisions of courts taken in the first instance are always subject to an appeal to a higher court within the judicial system. Courts are the only legal bodies authorized to officially interpret the law in a binding way.

Essentials

Material law sets forth a number of individual rights and obligations. Procedural law formally sets out in what way (ie by which process) material rights can be implemented and how natural persons and legal entities may behave in the legal process; it also establishes the formal way by which obligations may be enforced.

Public law regulates relations between entities that are in a mutual relation of subordination, or relations between the State and natural persons and legal entities. Within this relationship, the State issues orders and prohibitions to which natural persons and legal entities must adhere and out of which they cannot contract.

Included in the branches of public law are constitutional or state law, financial law, administrative law, penal law, international and public law.

Private law regulates relations between private entities that are in a mutual relation of equality and, where a contract is freely entered into on the basis of law, constitutes a fundamental principle to govern mutual relations between contractual parties.

The basis of private law is civil law and includes commercial law, labour law, family law and international private law.

Individual branches of both public and private law are further subdivided. Thus, for example, patent law is a special area of civil law, trademark law or bills of exchange and promissory notes law are part of commercial law, and tax law is a special area of financial law. There are also mixed branches involving both public and private law—for example, social security law, environmental law and energy law.

There is a difference between governmental decrees as a general legal standard, which become the applicable legal standard, and governmental decisions, which become binding only internally for individual members of the Cabinet.

ONLINE UPDATES - 26 May 2005

Legal framework (Chap.2.1)

The Energy Act

Right to choose natural gas supplier

- From 1 January 2005, all end customers whose 2003 annual gas consumption exceeded 15 million m^3 and all licensed energy producers who burn natural gas.
- From 1 January 2006, all commercial and industrial end customers.
- From 1 January 2007, all end customers.

Unbundling in the gas market

- From 1 January 2006, transmission system operators may not engage in any activities unconnected with transmission, storage or distribution.
- From 1 January 2007, the same restriction will apply to distribution system operators.

Unbundling in the electricity market

- From 1 January 2005, transmission system operators must not engage in any activities unconnected with transmission.
- From 1 January 2007, distribution system operators must not engage in any activities unconnected with distribution.

February 2005, CMS Cameron McKenna

Czech law on e-commerce

On 7 September 2004, a new law came into force implementing those parts of the EU Directive 200/31/ED on e-commerce not introduced previously into Czech law. Failure to comply with the new laws is punishable by a fine of up to EUR300,000.

November 2004, CMS Cameron McKenna

Competition law

Amendment No. 340/2004 Coll. to the Czech ct No. 143/2001 Coll. on the Protection of competition took effect from 2 June 2004. The major changes were :

- The national competition law (R 1/2003 and R 139/2004) only applies now if a transaction has no Community dimension.
- *Merger control.* New thresholds for notification to the Competition Authority were set at:
  - combined turnover of more that EUR48 million or more and a turnover of EUR7 million or more by each of at least two undertakings involved in the Czech Republic;
  - turnover of EUR48 million by one participant in a merger, or by the target of share purchases or by the seller of assets, or by one partner in a joint venture; and
  - the worldwide turnover of at least one other undertaking involved is EUR48 million.
- *Anticompetitive agreements.* The system of individual exemptions is cancelled. Exemptions are now applicable only if the entity fulfils conditions set directly by law. 'De minimis' percentages have been increased from five to 10 per cent (for horizontal agreements) and from 10 to 15 pr cent (for vertical agreements).

July 2004, CMS C ameron McKenna

Public procurement

A new Act, No. 40/2004 Coll., has been adopted on public procurement. The Act, which transposes certain regulations issued by the European Council, Parliament and Commission into Czech national law, defines:

- New thresholds – CZK2 million (EUR65,000 approx.) basic and new 'above a certain limit' category ranging from EUR130,000 to EUR 5 million.

- Three types of public procurement – supplies, services and construction works.
- Four types of tender – open tender, closed tender, negotiation proceedings including publishing and negotiation proceedings excluding publishing.
- Basic criteria for the evaluation of offers – economic advantage and price.

The new Act also governs public tenders organized by public authorities and private persons where the public procurement is funded by more than 50 per cent from public budgets. The Act also regulates the procedural aspects of public procurement and expressly states that any actions in contradiction to or in circumvention of the law, or made in bad faith are invalid.

May 2004, CMS Cameron McKenna

2.2

Privatization and the Legal Environment for Reform

CMS Cameron McKenna

Introduction

A substantial amount of state assets were privatized in the period to 1996 through two voucher privatization schemes. The schemes were popular with the general public but, as most people had little experience of investment instruments of any sort, it was not surprising that they entrusted most of their entitlements to investment funds. Since many investment funds were owned or administered by state-owned banks, in this way 'privatized' companies found their way back into the indirect ownership of the State.

All the major banks have now been privatized and this process, as well as changes to the law, has resulted in the banks divesting themselves of large ownership stakes in non-banking-related companies.

After 1996, the privatization process slowed, but began again in earnest in 2000, including the sale of the Ceska Sporitelna, a.s., the main retail bank, to the Austrian Erste Bank. One of the driving forces behind the relaunched privatization process was the finance minister, Pavel Mertlik, who resigned in April 2001. His replacement, Jiri Rusnok, pledged to continue the privatization process.

The most important sectors of the economy yet to be privatized are energy, steel and telecommunications.

Structure

Privatization now consists of case-by-case sales. The legal structure of such sales is well established. In general, state-owned assets are transferred into the ownership of the National Property Fund, a body that is under the control of the Czech government.

The National Property Fund then administers these assets until such time as a decision is made to sell them. For example, as the owner of shares in companies it will exercise normal shareholder rights such as voting at general meetings.

However, the National Property Fund does not have the ability to decide on how assets are to be privatized. It simply implements decisions made by the minister of finance or the government.

Practice

If there is likely to be interest in a company to be privatized from more than one potential buyer, a competitive tender may be organized:

- Typically, four tenders are short-listed on the basis of indicative bids.
- After a due diligence period, the tender companies are required to submit binding bids.
- Negotiations are then conducted in parallel with two tender companies.
- On the basis of the results of the negotiations, the government's strategic advisers make a recommendation to the government as to which tender should succeed.
- The company is then privatized on the basis of a government resolution.

Essentials

The government does not like giving guarantees and indemnities in respect of assets that it wishes to privatize, instead preferring a clean break from its past period of ownership. Unless the tender company is in a very strong position (eg as a result of being the only tender company), requests for government commitments going forward will harm the tender company's bid.

The government is willing to listen to genuine concerns about specific problems discovered in due diligence, but generally will ask that the tender company takes them into account when making its bid.

Concerns

If the shares in the company to be privatized are traded on a public stock exchange, the privatization of the National Property Fund's shares in the company could give rise to a duty on the part of the purchaser to make a public offer to other shareholders to purchase their shares. The Commercial Code of 1991 exempts purchasers in privatizations from this requirement, but for the purchaser to enjoy this exemption it is important that the government privatization resolution is appropriately worded.

The law permits the National Property Fund to hold a 'golden share' in companies. This permits the fund to enjoy special voting rights at general meetings. In general, this means that the fund enjoys a veto over certain key decisions.

The National Property Fund is aware that this practice is usually unacceptable to foreign investors and consequently the golden share is now rarely proposed when assets to be privatized are likely to be of interest to foreign investors. However, if there is any suggestion of continuing state influence in the privatized company, investors need to clarify at an early stage what the intentions of the government are in this respect.

2.3

Alternative Corporate Structures

CMS Cameron McKenna

Introduction

Any foreign person (natural or legal) may engage in business activities in the Czech Republic under the same conditions and to the same extent as Czech nationals. According to the Commercial Code of 1991, a foreign person may found and participate in a Czech legal entity and has the same rights and duties as a Czech national.

Structure

A foreign national may:

- set up a branch office in the Czech Republic;
- found/acquire a Czech legal entity;
- participate in the business of a Czech business entity in the form of a so-called 'silent partnership';
- set up an association.

Branch office

A branch office is not a separate legal entity; however, it must be registered in the Commercial Register.

Czech legal entity

Czech law recognizes the following legal entities that are allowed to perform business activities as their main activity:

- general partnership (v.o.s.);
- limited partnership (k.s.);
- limited liability company (s.r.o.);

- joint-stock company (a.s.);
- cooperative;
- association of legal entities.

General partnership (v.o.s.)

A general partnership (v.o.s.) is a company founded by two or more partners (individuals or legal entities). All partners of the company are fully liable for the liabilities of the company.

Limited partnership (k.s.)

A limited partnership (k.s.) is a company founded by two or more partners (individuals or legal entities). One or more partners of the company will be fully liable for the liabilities of the company (fully liable partners) and one or more partners will be liable only up to the amount of their unpaid registered contributions (limited liable partners).

Another significant difference between the two classes of partner is that each fully liable partner of the company is a statutory representative of the company, whereas limited liable partners are not entitled to manage the company.

Limited liability company (s.r.o.)

A limited liability company may be founded by one or more natural or legal persons.

Unless it is agreed otherwise, each partner has a participation interest in the company according to the amount of his contribution to the registered capital of the company. Each member's liability is limited to the amount of the subscription in full for his allotted shareholding.

Joint-stock company (a.s.)

A joint-stock company (a.s.) is the company type with the highest level of mandatory regulation of its internal affairs (eg corporate changes, decision-making etc) and external matters (eg legal actions, restrictions for legal actions) by the Commercial Code. Only a joint-stock company may be publicly traded on the securities market.

One or more legal persons or at least two natural persons may found a joint-stock company. A joint-stock company cannot be founded by only one natural person. However, over time, one natural person may concentrate all the shares of the company into his ownership.

Cooperative company

A cooperative must have at least five founding members. Members of the cooperative may be liable for the liabilities of the cooperative only up to three times their membership fee, if such liability is approved by a resolution of the general assembly of the cooperative.

The minimum registered capital of a cooperative is CZK 50,000, provided always that at least 50 per cent is paid up by members prior to registration in the Commercial Register.

Association of legal entities

An association of legal entities is a special purpose vehicle (for the protection of interests or other specific purpose) founded only by legal entities according to the terms of a formal foundation agreement. Members of the association are not liable for the liabilities of the association.

Practice

General partnership (v.o.s)

Unless agreed otherwise, each individual partner of the general partnership (v.o.s.) is a statutory representative of the company. All partners are entitled to manage the company unless one or more partners are appointed to manage the company in the association agreement.

Limited partnership (k.s.)

The limited partnership (k.s.) has no formalized bodies. Each limited liability partner must pay at least CZK 5,000 to the registered capital of the company. Fully limited partners are not obliged to pay any registered capital.

Limited liability company (s.r.o.)

Executive director(s) or partner(s) with 10 per cent and higher participation interest(s) must call a general meeting of members at least once a year. Each member has a voting entitlement corresponding to his participation interest. The quorum for a general meeting must be at least 50 per cent.

Profits of the company, which are declared for distribution, are distributed according to the participation interests of members.

The statutory governing body of the company is/are the executive director(s). The executive director(s) is/are appointed by the general meeting.

The company may create a supervisory board.

Joint-stock company (a.s.)

The registered capital of a joint-stock company (a.s.) is divided into shares. The shares may be bearer shares (freely transferable) or registered shares whose transfer is limited by the approval of the statutory body of the company. The shares may be materialized (physically printed) or immaterialized (registered at the Securities Centre).

Each share represents an equal voting right, an equal right to distributed dividends and equal right for liquidation payments in the case of dissolution of the company.

A general meeting of shareholders must be called at least once a year by the board of directors. A meeting of shareholders may also be called in certain conditions by the supervisory board or shareholder(s) with at least 3 per cent of shares. For operational decisions, the consent of a simple majority of attending shareholders is required.

The company must appoint a supervisory board of at least three members elected by the general meeting of shareholders.

The board of executive directors is the statutory body of the company. The directors are appointed by the general meeting or by the supervisory board.

Cooperative company

A cooperative has to create the following bodies: general assembly, presidium and controlling committee. The presidium and controlling committee are not mandatory if the cooperative has less than 50 members. Unless agreed otherwise, each member has one vote at the general assembly.

Association of legal entities

An association of legal entities may create its bodies and adopt other internal rules according to its articles of association. Unless it is agreed otherwise, the profit is distributed equally among members.

Essentials

Branch office

There may be accounting and tax advantages in establishing a branch office instead of a company, particularly if the branch is to conduct a great deal of business on behalf of the company to which it is attached.

Persons who are statutory bodies of companies must be Czech residents. Business enterprises may also be represented by a proxy (prokurista). The proxy must be appointed by a statutory representative(s) or the general meeting of partners and must also be a Czech resident.

General partnership (v.o.s.)

A general partnership (v.o.s) has no formalized bodies. No registered capital is required. Profits are distributed equally among the partners.

Limited partnership (k.s.)

Unless agreed otherwise, fully liable partners are entitled to receive half of the profit (distributed equally among them) and limited liability partners are entitled to receive half of the profit (distributed according to the amount of their contributions to the registered capital).

Limited liability company (s.r.o.)

One natural person cannot be a partner of more than three limited liability companies with a single partner.

Partners of the limited liability company are liable for the company's liabilities only up to the aggregate amount of their unpaid contributions to the registered capital.

Joint-stock company (a.s.)

Shareholders are not liable for the company's liabilities. Profit of the company, if declared for distribution, must be distributed equally for each share.

Cooperative company

The cooperative must create a so-called 'non-divisible fund' in an amount corresponding to at least 10 per cent of the registered capital and must be subsidized by at least 10 per cent of the annual profit until it represents 50 per cent of the registered capital. The cooperative may merge only with another cooperative. However, it may be transformed into any type of company.

Concerns

Branch office

There is a risk is that the 'mother' company may be held liable for all liabilities of the branch office and the authority of the director of the branch office to act on behalf of the company towards third parties cannot be limited.

General partnership (v.o.s.)

A general partnership (v.o.s.) may only merge with a limited partnership subject to the condition that all the partners of the limited partnership become unlimited partners of the general partnership or all the partners of the successor general partnership become fully liable partners of the successor limited partnership.

Limited partnership (k.s.)

A limited partnership (k.s.) may merge only with a general partnership subject to the condition that all the partners of the limited partnership become unlimited partners of the successor general partnership or all the partners of the general partnership become fully liable partners of the successor limited partnership.

Limited liability company (s.r.o.)

The limited liability company (s.r.o.) may merge only with another limited liability company or with a joint-stock company.

Joint-stock company (a.s.)

The joint-stock company (a.s.) may merge only with another joint-stock company or with a limited liability company.

ONLINE UPDATES - 27 May 2005

Alternative corporate structures (Chap. 2.3)

Company formation

The procedures for setting up a company in the Czech Republic will be simplified, subject to pending approval by Parliament to the Commercial Code and Civil Procedure Code. Key changes include:

- a standard form and documentation required for registration issued by the Ministry of Justice;
- in the first year after the amendment comes into force, all applications to register a company at the Commercial Register will be decided by the court within 10 days from receipt of complete set of documents and court fee. After the first year, all applications will be dealt with in five days;

- all applications for registration (or amendment) that are not decided within the requisite period are deemed to be approved with effect from the following day;
- from 1 January 2007 an electronic version of the Commercial Register will be maintained.

April 2005, CMS Cameron McKenna

Amendments to Czech Commercial Code

Important amendments to the Commercial Code that came into force from 1 May 2004 include:

- simplified procedure for registration of company branch offices seated in the EU into the Czech Commercial Register;
- mandatory public offers in joint stock companies apply to shares in a Czech joint-stock company that are traded on any securities market in the EU or EFTA;
- the decisive date for the payment of dividends on book-entered shares is the day of the general meting at which such dividend distribution is decided;
- for non-book-entered shares, a general meeting may decide on another decisive day for payment of dividends from the day of the meting to the maturity date of the dividends.

Most other changes to the Commercial Code to harmonize with EU directives were adopted in 2003.

May 2004, CMS Cameron McKenna

2.4

Agency Agreements, Distributorships and Franchising

CMS Cameron McKenna

Introduction

In EU commercial law, the legal difference between agents and distributors is clear-cut. An agent finds customers or suppliers for his principal, but the contract for the supply of the goods or services is between the principal and the customer or supplier. In a distributorship, the distributor finds customers for the supplier's goods, but those goods become the property of the distributor in one transaction before they are passed on to the final customer in a second separate transaction.

Both these forms of intermediary also exist in the Czech Republic. However, the Czech Republic also has a third variant, the commission agent's contract, which combines features of both the agency agreement and the distributorship agreement.

The main advantage to the commission agent arrangement is that although no obligations fall on the principal as a result of the commission agent's relationships with third parties, the principal can enforce the obligations of third parties if the commission agent is unable to do so.

Structure

Agency

The Commercial Code of 1991 differentiates between 'commercial representation' and 'brokerage contracts'. Brokerage contracts are usually only applicable to one-off transactions; most firms and companies doing business in the Czech Republic require commercial representation based upon a formal contract applicable to multiple transactions over a period of time.

Distributorship

There are no particular provisions of the Commercial Code that are distributorship specific. The provisions of the Code that apply to distributorships are generally those that apply to the sale and purchase of goods generally, and most of them can be varied by agreement between the parties.

Franchising

The concept of franchising is understood in the Czech Republic but there are no particular franchise-specific laws. The legal situation is very similar to EU laws that apply to the franchise and depend upon the form of franchise chosen.

Practice

Agency

There are a number of provisions in the Commercial Code that apply to commercial representatives, but, provided that the commercial representation agreement is suitably drafted, most can be avoided if both parties so require.

Franchising

The most common form of franchising in the Czech Republic is a combination of a distributorship and the licence of a package of intellectual property (IP) rights: know-how, goodwill, business methods and trade secrets.

The parties are generally free to choose whichever form of IP licence they wish, although any anti-competitive restrictions in the IP licence may need to be submitted to the Authority for Economic Competition. It is advisable to draft the licence so that it adheres to EU competition law as this often makes it easier to persuade the Authority to accept the provisions concerned and ensures that it will remain valid when the Czech Republic accedes to the European Union.

Essentials

Agency

Provisions introduced into the Commercial Code, which came into effect on 1 January 2001, incorporate many of the provisions of the European Union's Commercial Agents Directive.

The Directive applies both to future agency relationships as well as those in existence at the time the directive was implemented. Consequently, the Commercial Code now provides for compensation or indemnity payments on termination of all current agency agreements.

Distributorship

Many of the restrictive provisions in distributorship agreements familiar to suppliers in Western Europe will require the approval of the Authority for Economic Competition. The Authority usually makes its decisions on a case-by-case basis. In general, however, the Authority accepts distributorship agreements which conform to EU competition law.

Franchising

It is customary for the franchisor's trademarks to be used by the franchisee. In such cases, the franchisee must be registered at the Czech Intellectual Property Office (IPO) as the registered user of the franchisor's trademarks. Unless the franchisor has its trademarks internationally registered under the Madrid Agreement of 1891, the franchisor's trademarks must also be registered at the Czech IPO.

Concerns

Agency

A number of provisions in the Commercial Code are mandatory. In particular, if the principal terminates the representation contract after more than one year, the principal is still obliged to pay commission to the commercial representative for customers that the representative has obtained.

Many principals have found that their ability to terminate agency relationships is now constrained by the fact that a substantial sum of money is payable to the agents on termination and it is generally not possible for the parties to derogate from these provisions to the agents' disadvantage.

Distributorship

Typically, distributorship agreements provide for some trading restrictions on the distributor, particularly with regard to the distributor's ability to handle competing products or to distribute the supplier's products outside of the territory (geographical area) allotted to the distributor. In the Czech Republic, such restrictions raise issues under the Act on Protection of Economic Competition. The new competition regulation now more clearly defines the exception from restrictions on distributorship or other vertical agreements. In general terms, the statutory instrument of the competition act allows for agreements where the supplier has not more than 30 per cent of the market share or, alternatively, the buyer has not more than 30 per cent of the market share, in case the agreement includes obligation for exclusive supply. Restrictions on the exception following the EC legislation apply.

Franchising

The inadequacies of the courts should make a franchisor wary about appointing a head-franchisee who will contract with sub franchisees. Franchisors may be well advised to contract directly with each franchisee individually.

A head-franchisee will effectively control the network and outlets will be leased to himself or his franchisees. If the head-franchisee decides to switch allegiance to another franchisor, the original franchisor's remedies would be limited, even if the head-franchisee were to act in flagrant breach of contract.

Cases of this nature usually take at least three years for a first-instance decision, and it is also extremely difficult to obtain injunctions from Czech judges. In the meantime, the original franchisor's outlets could have disappeared from public view.

ONLINE UPDATES - 27 May 2005

Agency agreements, distributorships and franchising (Chap. 2.4)

Act on Insurance Agents and Insurance Appraisers

Act No. 38/2004 Coll., effective from 1 January 2005, provides new regulation for the activities of insurance agents and insurance appraisers. The performance of an agency activity in the insurance sector and activity of independent insurance appraisers is now qualified as business activity requiring the registration of the person engaged in this activity.

The Act sets forth conditions of registration with the State Insurance and Additional Pension Insurance Supervision Authority which maintains a register of insurance agents and appraisers. It also specifies requirement concerning professional ability and integrity.

March 2004, Deloitte, Prague

2.5

Employment Law

CMS Cameron McKenna

Introduction

The Czech Labour Code grants to employees rights that have significant implications for employers. The Labour Code has recently been substantially amended mainly in order to harmonize Czech law with that of the European Union in anticipation of accession in 2004.

Structure

The laws regulating employment in the Czech Republic tend to be complex, detailed and rigid.

The Labour Code leaves little scope for employees and employers to negotiate their own arrangements, except in cases where the employer is foreign and the employee(s) Czech or vice versa. In such circumstances, generally the employment relationship can be governed by foreign law, and the Labour Code plays a minor role.

The laws regulating social security contributions are equally inflexible. However, it should be remembered that in many respects the laws are typical of the Continental European Civil Code tradition and are comparable, for example, with many of the laws operating in Germany and France.

Although there are other methods for establishing an employment relationship, a written employment contract is certainly the most common method adopted.

Practice

It is very difficult to assign work to an employee who is not covered by a contract of employment. Therefore, when defining the type of work to be performed by the employee, the employer should ensure that a clear, precise and adequately flexible definition is produced and that all potential activities are covered.

Provided that the potential employee is 15 years or older and has completed the requisite school education required by law, he or she is in a position to conclude an employment contract for either a definite or an indefinite period of time.

Either party may want to include a clause allowing for a probationary period of up to three months, which would allow immediate termination of the contract without penalty during that period.

The employment contract must stipulate a working week not exceeding 40 hours in a format that affords employees at least a 30-minute break every four and a half hours and at least a 12-hour rest period between shifts.

Employees can also refuse to work more than eight hours per week and 150 hours per year of overtime unless they are employed in the energy, telecommunications or transportation sectors or are involved in 24-hour operations.

Essentials

Currently, the minimum wage is set at CZK5700 per month, which, like all wages, is normally paid in arrears at the end of each month. Employees can demand payment in cash.

The Labour Code entitles employees to four weeks' holiday per year. Should an employee not take up his full entitlement, the remaining days are carried over to the following year.

The employer also needs to be aware of the relevant regulations encompassing medical insurance and social security contributions. A total of 34 per cent of the employee's gross salary must be set aside for these purposes, of which 9 per cent is for medical insurance and 25 per cent for social security.

For medical insurance, the total contribution is set at 13.5 per cent of gross salary, towards which an employee contributes 4.5 per cent and the employer pays 9 per cent.

All employees must be registered at the local social security administration office and the relevant medical insurance company should also be informed.

Concerns

Should an employee suffer an accident, the employer is held liable unless it was caused by the employee's own negligence, in which case he or she can be penalized by up to four and a half months' salary.

In addition to occupational illnesses, the employer is obliged to insure against liability for accidents. The employee is entitled to compensation for medical costs, pain and suffering and loss of earnings. Material damage is also covered.

Termination of contract

Contracts of employment may be terminated by mutual agreement or by giving due notice.

Mutual agreement

The agreement of the parties must be in writing, specifying the cause and date of termination.

Serving notice

The employee is much less restricted by law than the employer as regards the necessary grounds for serving notice. In effect, the employee does not need to give any reason at all for wanting to leave.

However, the employer can only dismiss an employee if one of the grounds in the Labour Code applies, such as:

- medically certified ill health;
- restructuring the focus of the business activities;
- inadequate work performance;
- serious breach of work discipline after a warning;
- inability to meet the standards required by the Labour Law regulations.

The employer may also be obliged to place the employee in a different position within the organization. Alternatively, if the employee is made redundant as a result of restructuring the business and there is no possibility of transfer to another job, the employer may be obliged to assist the employee's attempt to find further appropriate employment. In any case, the employee can claim severance pay.

The notice period lasts two months commencing on the first day of the month following the month when the notice was served. However, should the employee be made redundant, the period of notice is extended to three months.

ONLINE UPDATES - 27 May 2005

Employment law (Chap.2.5)

Amendments to Labour Code

The Labour Code Amendments, published 1 March 2004 under No. 46/2004 Coll., came into immediate effect. The main am was to remove various forms of discrimination in labour law relationships in compliance with EU legislation.

The amendments also include:

- Modified provisions to allow for the inclusion of non-competition arrangements (Maximum of one year) in contracts of employment. If a non-compete clause is included, the employer is obliged to pay the employee financial compensation equal to salary prior to the termination of employment.
- The concept of fixed term employments is included. Conrats may be agreed or extended by agreement for a maximum period of two years from date of first employment.

March 2004, MS Cameron McKenna

2.6

Intellectual Property

CMS Cameron McKenna

Introduction

Czech intellectual property law and its principles are based on the Continental law concepts of copyright and industrial property rights. Works that are subject to copyright do not need to be registered. However, industrial property rights are only protected if they are registered at the Industrial Property Office (IPO), unless they are protected under an international industrial property convention.

Many aspects of the regulations laid down by Czech intellectual property law are compatible with the current EU standards. However, the protections of IP rights against infringement still do not meet the common standards used by the European Union.

Foreign companies conducting business in the Czech Republic need to protect intellectual property rights when they are using Czech companies, individuals as employees, independent contractors, distributors or users during the creation, modification and distribution of their products and services.

Structure

Copyright

Any work that is the unique result of the creative activity of an author and is expressed in an objective appearance may be subject to copyright under the Act on Copyright and on Rights Similar to Copyright No. 121/2000 Coll. This Act also provides rights similar to those of authors' copyright, such as the rights of performing artists, producers of audiovisual recordings and publishers etc. Copyright protection is not based on registration in the Czech Republic.

Trademarks

Trademarks are governed by the Act on Trademarks No. 137/1995 Coll., as amended. Registration in the Trademark Register maintained by the IPO is required for protection. However, the registered trademark is protected from the date when the application for registration was filed at the IPO (priority date).

Inventions and innovations

Patents for inventions are governed by the Act on Inventions and Innovations No. 527/1990 Coll., as amended. An invention is protected if a patent is granted by the IPO. Patents are registered by the IPO in the Register of Patents. Innovations are not subject to registration by the IPO.

Biotech inventions

Biotech inventions are also subject to patents under the Act on Protection of Biotechnological Inventions No. 206/2000 Coll.

Industrial designs

Designs used for an industrial product which are new and unique may be protected as industrial designs under the provisions of the Act on Industrial Designs No. 207/2000 Coll.

Licensing intellectual property rights

Licence agreements in respect of industrial property rights (eg inventions, industrial designs, trademark, industrial designs etc) are generally governed by the provisions of the Czech Commercial Code No. 513/1991 Coll, as amended. Special types of licence agreements are provided for in the Act on Copyright and on Rights Similar to Copyright No. 121/2000 Coll. for the licensing of works that are subject to copyright.

Licences for industrial designs must comply with licensing provisions in the Act on Industrial Designs No. 207/2000 Coll. in addition to the requirements of the Commercial Code.

There are other intellectual property rights, such as utility models or the country of origin markings, which are protected in the Czech Republic. Although 'know-how' is not protected as having special legal rights, it may enjoy protection as a part of a commercial secret under the Commercial Code.

Practice

Copyright

The following works are subject to copyright: literal, artistic and scientific works, in particular works of music, drama and photography, audiovisual work, cinematographic work, architectural work and also computer programmes and databases.

Only the author can be the individual who created the work. There are two types of rights arising from Czech copyright protection:

- author's moral rights;
- author's economic rights (mostly the right to use the authorship work).

None of these rights are transferable to third parties; however, an author may grant a licence in respect of economic rights. Copyright generally lasts during the life of an author and 70 years after his death. In the case of databases, copyright protection lasts 15 years from the creation of a database.

Trademarks

Trademarks are protected for use within set classes of goods and services according to the Nice classification. Trademark protection lasts 10 years and is renewable. However, the IPO can delete a trademark from the Trademark Register if its owner or licensee has not used it in the Czech Republic for five years.

Inventions and innovations

Patents are granted for inventions that are new, are of a technical nature and have practical industrial applications. A patent is granted for 20 years from the date on which the application for granting a patent was filed. Patents are not granted to inventions contradictory to common interests, medical diagnostic methods or newly developed plant varieties or animal breeds.

Biotech inventions

Biotech inventions that may be subject to patents are:

- biological substances isolated from a natural environment and produced via technical process;
- a microbiological or technical process or product other than animal or plant which was created as a result of such process.

Industrial designs

Any product design, which is new and unique, may be protected as an industrial design if registered in the Register of Industrial Designs maintained by the IPO. An industrial design is protected for five years from the priority date and the protection period is renewable up to 25 years.

Essentials

Copyright

Unless otherwise agreed, if an author created the work as an employee within the course of his employment, the employer is entitled to exercise the author's economic right. The employer would need to obtain the employee's consent before licensing the work to third parties.

Trademarks

Protection for a trademark in the Czech Republic can be claimed from the priority date of a trademark registration in any member state of the Paris Convention on the Protection of Industrial Property Rights or member state of the WTO.

A trademark licence agreement and assignment of the trademark to a third party is effective towards third parties upon its registration in the Register of Trademarks maintained by the IPO. Czech law also allows the pledging of a trademark and grants the trademark owner the right to ask the Czech customs office not to release commercial goods into the Czech market where the markings of such goods infringe the rights of the trademark owner.

Inventions and innovations

The inventor or his legal successor is entitled to the patent. If an inventor created an invention as an employee within his employment tasks, unless otherwise agreed, rights to the patent are passed to the employer.

The employee as the inventor is entitled to appropriate remuneration, which is based upon the technical and economic importance of an invention and the benefit acquired from it. Additional remuneration may be payable if, in the future, the benefits acquired by an employer are disproportionate to the original remuneration.

Biotech inventions

Biotech inventions patent registration is identical to the proceedings used for patenting inventions.

Industrial designs

The creator of an industrial design is the owner of it. Unless otherwise agreed, if a creator produces a design as an employee within the course of his employment, the right to the industrial design passes to the employer.

The employee, as the creator, is entitled to remuneration based upon similar principles to those used to calculate remuneration in relation to inventions.

Licensing intellectual property rights

In order to be valid, the licensing of copyright must be concluded in writing. Registration of a licence by the IPO is required for certain industrial property rights, such as a trademark licence, to make the licence effective towards third parties.

In the case of copyright work, exclusive or non-exclusive licences may be granted to third parties and no registration of the licence is required.

If an exclusive licence is granted to the copyright owner, he is not permitted to grant the licence to any other third party and is obliged not to perform the economic rights himself which the licence covers.

A licence may be limited for specific types of use of copyright work. Exclusive or non-exclusive licences may also be granted in respect of industrial designs

Concerns

Intellectual property rights holders now have certain recourse within customs proceedings, which allows them to observe and sometimes block the export or import of infringing copies; however, due to the lengthy and costly Czech court procedures, the enforceability and effectiveness of protection in practice remains insufficient.

ONLINE UPDATES - 26 May 2005

Intellectual property (Chap.2.6)

New Trademark Act

At the beginning of 2004, the Czech Parliament adopted a new Trademark Actthat updates the previous act of 1995 and harmonizes Czech trademark law with EU law. The new Act became effective from 1 April 2004 (1 May 2004 in respet of Community Trademarks provisions). The major changes are:

- introduction of the concept of the Community Trademark in full compliance with Regulation EC 40/94;
- lack of good faith is expressly stated as a possible ground for refusal of registration and a reason for prohibition of usage;
- a generally known (unregistered) trademark enables its proprietor to ban its use for similar or identical goods or services only;
- the concept of a trademark enjoying good reputation is introduced, enabling its proprietor to also ban its use for goods or services that are not similar to those in respect of which the trademark is registered;
- more detailed regulation concerning the deletion of trademarks from the Register of Trademarks: the concepts of invalidity, revocation and surrender are introduced.

February 2004, CMS Cameron McKenna

2.7

Dispute Resolution

CMS Cameron McKenna

Introduction

However well an agreement starts out, be it a share acquisition or a joint venture, there is always the chance that the parties are going to come to a standstill or deadlock where they cannot reach an agreement. This chapter looks at how these situations can be dealt with when you are doing business in the Czech Republic.

Structure

In the Czech Republic, as in all Western European countries, there are two main ways to deal with a dispute: litigation and arbitration.

Litigation is the default mechanism for most contracts. If the contract does not set out a dispute resolution mechanism and the parties cannot agree one, the dispute will end up in court. In most countries, this can be expensive and time consuming—and the Czech Republic is no exception.

In 1994, the Czech government introduced a new Arbitration Act, which made wide-ranging changes aimed at helping to secure inward foreign investment by providing an internationally acceptable system for commercial dispute resolutions.

The legislation allows for ad hoc arbitration or arbitration conducted by one of the three permanent courts of arbitration, of which the main one is the arbitration court attached to the Economic Chamber of the Czech Republic and the Agricultural Chamber of the Czech Republic. The arbitration court is based in Prague, but has a number of regional offices throughout the country.

Each court has a list of the Czech arbitrators who can be called upon to arbiter proceedings. It is also possible to use foreign arbitrators, if the parties so wish, provided that they are qualified in their home country.

Practice

Court proceedings in the Czech Republic will normally take place in public, even if this goes against the wishes of the parties.

It is possible, and advisable, for an agreement to be governed by a legal system where there is an established procedure for dealing with commercial disputes. However, if both parties to the agreement are Czech entities, which include Czech subsidiaries of foreign companies, Czech law prevails.

Arbitration gives the parties the benefit of being able to choose arbitrators whom they believe will be able to understand technical detail or other relevant information.

Arbitration cannot be undertaken without the written consent of the parties, which can be given either before or after the dispute arises. Coming to a compromise on arbitration after the dispute has arisen may be as complex as coming to an agreement on the dispute itself. Such problems may be reduced, if not eliminated, by writing arbitration procedures into the original commercial contract.

When the parties agree on arbitration, it is possible for them to decide where it will be held. Most foreign companies investing and working in the Czech Republic seem to rely on recognized neutral arbitration venues such as London, Vienna or Geneva.

The Czech Republic is a signatory to the 1958 New York Convention on the recognition and enforcement for foreign arbitral awards. This means that international arbitration awards can be enforced in the Czech Republic, in stark contrast to the international litigation situation.

Essentials

Litigation

An automatic right to appeal on a point of law or fact is available to litigants in every case and this can increase the length of the proceedings.

Unless there is a bilateral treaty between the Czech Republic and another state (as between the Czech Republic and certain Eastern European states) or unless there is a mutuality of principle duly respected between the Czech Republic and a foreign country, foreign countries' court judgements are not recognized and are unenforceable in the Czech Republic.

The process is under way for the Czech Republic to become a party to the Lugano Treaty on recognition and enforcement of foreign courts' judgements among the European countries.

As with other jurisdictions, litigation in the Czech Republic should only be used as a last resort.

Arbitration

The process of arbitration itself is confidential, with the arbitrators owing a duty of confidentiality to the parties. Unlike proceedings in litigation cases, arbitration takes place in private, thereby allowing confidential information to remain so.

Once a decision has been reached, the arbitrators will confirm it in writing and then produce a written opinion giving the grounds for the arbitral award, unless the parties dispense with this requirement.

Unlike litigation, there is no automatic appeal, so unless the parties have expressly retained the option of later submission of their dispute to the courts of litigation, the arbitral award becomes final and binding.

Alternative dispute resolution (ADR)

In addition, mediation is a new process gaining ground for alternative dispute resolutions (ADR). ADR aims to encourage parties to settle and normally costs a fraction of the cost of litigation and arbitration.

The parties can agree to use ADR in a similar way to international arbitration.

The court of arbitration offers a conciliation service, which is about half the cost of arbitration and might be more appropriate in certain situations.

An arbitration clause in the original agreement can save time, money and further disputes. Arbitration in most situations is preferable to litigation, particularly within the Czech Republic

Concerns

The process of litigation in the Czech Republic has advanced. However, due to the shortage of experienced judges and a large backlog of cases, it can take years to obtain a first-instance judgment.

Judges also lack the specialist knowledge that can be obtained by choosing one's own arbitrator, as they may not know the intricacies of a particular sector.

Although the government has clamped down on corruption in the court system, it can still be found. Corruption within the judiciary can lead to longer trials or the appointment of judges biased towards one party.

ONLINE UPDATES - 26 May 2005

Dispute resolution (Chap.2.7)

New default interest rates

On 28 April 2005, a government decree prescribing a new rate of default interest came into force applying to defaults occurring after that date under agreements made pursuant to the Czech Civil Code or (unless the parties agree otherwise) pursuant to the Commercial Code.

The new default interest rate is the Czech National Bank (CNB) repo rate plus seven points applicable on the more recent of the previous 1 January or 1 July. Creditors are therefore obliged to monitor the actual amount of default interest twice a year.

May 2005, CMS Cameron McKenna

Tighter conditions for preliminary injunctions

Under an amendment to the Czech Civil Procedural Code, effective 1 April 2005, a preliminary injunction will not be granted unless a plaintiff deposits CZK50,000 (CZK100,000 in commercial cases) with the court as collateral for any compensation arising. The collateral is not required for labour matters, claims for damage to health and cases where the defendant is exempt from court fees.

The amendment also requires a plaintiff to compensate the defendant for any loss suffered as a result of a preliminary injunction if the plaintiff's action fails, provided that the defendant's claim for compensation is submitted to the court within six months after the injunction comes to end.

April 2005, CMS Cameron McKenna

The EU Mediation Atlas'

The first comprehensive guide to mediation throughout the EU, *The EU Mediation Atlas*, a joint venture between CMS Cameron McKenna and CEDR was published in October 2004. Written by CMS Cameron McKenna solicitor Jayne Singer, the book's publication coincides with the EC's adoption of a Directive for harmonizing mediation in civil and commercial disputes across the EU.

October 2004, CMS Cameron McKenna

Part Three

Finance, Accountancy and Taxation

3.1

Financial Services Sector

Kevin R Smith, Managing Director, AWS Structured Finance Ltd

Introduction

As with any sector in an emerging economy, the financial services sector has undergone massive change in recent years and this change is far from over. In the early 1990s, the Czech Republic was widely applauded for the rapid way in which it introduced privatization and the international banking community lined up to provide medium-term loans to Czech banks at extremely attractive rates.

Unfortunately, the voucher privatization scheme totally failed to achieve the two main benefits of privatization—namely, the introduction of external investment and external expertise. This might not have been so much of a problem if the banking sector had been privatized, but it was one of the few sectors that remained in government hands. As a consequence, banks did not act as commercial institutions but continued to make loans that were misused and had no real prospect of ever being repaid. These failures in turn undermined the whole of the Czech banking sector and influenced many aspects of the general financial services sector. The cost to the government in cleaning up the banks' balance sheets and trying to turn the sector around has been massive.

There is a common misconception that the Czech currency (crown, CZK) is in some form restricted. This is not the case as the Czech crown has been fully convertible for some years.

Banks

The Czech banking sector has some 40 banks, although just four hold 60 per cent of banking assets in the country. All four of the main Czech banks have now been privatized, with the last one, Komercni Banca, becoming privately owned in 2001. All four banks were sold to international bank groups from Austria, Belgium and France. Foreign banks (as opposed to foreign-owned local banks) hold approximately 15 per cent of total banking assets.

As in other countries of this region, many of the banks are competing in the same sector and the majority of foreign banks initially focused on foreign companies operating in the Czech Republic and the larger local corporates. Competition has been fierce, particularly in the larger corporate sector, and has resulted in a number of the banks now looking at smaller corporates and the retail sector. It is this competitiveness and the 'over-banked' situation in the Czech Republic that is the driving force behind the change of focus, but some consolidation is the result of the mergers and acquisitions of the parent banks on a global or regional scale. Nevertheless, due to the level of historic bad debts and other factors, there has been a considerable credit squeeze in recent times, although this should ease in the future.

The level of bad debts continues to be a drag on the economy as a whole, despite the fact that most have been transferred to Konsolidacni Banca (the state-owned 'bad' bank). Konsolidacni is in the process of selling off large portfolios of debt, with the first such sale only achieving 7 per cent of face value, underlining the seriousness of the problem.

Overall, the banking sector is both well developed and sophisticated and offers the majority of products and services that would be expected in any developed market economy. Telephone banking is widely available and Internet banking is being introduced by many banks.

One part of the banking sector that has yet to make much progress is the provision of residential mortgages. There is no doubt that this market will become very important in the future but, due to factors such as legislation which makes it difficult for the lender to repossess the property when necessary, the continued existence of subsidized rents (which will be phased out shortly) and the lack of long-term loans, it will be some while before any major development is seen. It is unlikely that this part of the banking sector will develop as quickly as in some neighbouring countries.

Demand for commercial mortgages is high, however, being driven primarily by foreign companies investing in factory and office accommodation for their own operations. Foreign banks are the largest providers of commercial mortgages, while Czech banks predominate in the provision of residential loans, although a number of foreign banks are beginning to take more interest having regard to the ultimate potential of the market.

While most sectors of the banking market are fully catered for, there has been a rapid expansion recently in a number of niche areas. The market for home-collected credit in the Czech Republic was created by a British company only within the last few years but has grown very rapidly and is expected to continue to do so for the foreseeable future. A similar pattern has emerged recently in the provision of consumer credit provided in-store at the point of sale. While this type of credit had actually been available for many years in the Czech Republic (even in the Soviet era), it has been transformed in recent years and continues to expand.

Financing trade and projects

Approximately 90 per cent of all trade in the European Union is conducted on an open account basis, although many companies have some form of credit insurance. Trade with the Czech Republic has not as yet reached this level, but already some 70 per cent of trade is conducted on this basis.

Over the years, there have been many successful projects financed on a non-recourse project finance basis. These have been structured both with and without assistance from the British Export Credit Guarantee Department (ECGD) and other export credit agencies. In recent times, the ECGD has changed its policy on financing projects in the region in order to secure more business and this means that projects that were previously unable to obtain cover can now do so. Perhaps the most important change is that, in many cases, the ECGD no longer needs a government guarantee but will accept municipality or large local corporate risk.

The trend towards financing major projects by way of partnerships established between central and/or local government and private companies has not been ignored by the Czechs. While the Czech Republic is far from being the leader in the region in this form of project finance, there is growing recognition of the impact that PPPs can have in developing infrastructure such as roads, rail, water treatment plants and many other large projects. Again, actual progress on this front has been slower than in neighbouring countries, but it is expected that momentum will start to build shortly.

Typically, laws need to change and attitudes and ideas need to become more flexible in order to make these projects happen.

However, PPPs offer the most realistic way to finance the many projects required and, as this becomes more widely understood, the number of PPP projects in the country will increase dramatically. As Britain and British-based firms are world leaders in this type of finance, the development of this sector in the Czech Republic should be regarded as offering many opportunities in the future.

Investment funds

A small number of investment funds and providers of private equity have been active in the Czech Republic for many years, although their role is made much more difficult by the limitations on exit strategy which result from the inadequacies of the stock exchange described below. Some 10 or more funds exist and, in an effort to promote the sector, the European Bank for Reconstruction and Development (EBRD) has invested in most of them. In very simple terms, the preferred scenario for a fund is to invest between US$2 million and US$5 million in a joint venture company with a local partner and a foreign strategic investor. Clearly, this is an over-simplification and, for the right project, both smaller and much larger funds can be found and any commercially sound project can, in theory, attract funds.

A number of the locally based funds are effectively subsidiaries of the more global funds or linked to banks. As the market continues to mature and stabilize, the growing demand for this type of funding is being met by the creation of new funds and the expansion of existing ones. The sector remains difficult given the constraints in which it operates, but steady growth is expected to continue.

Insurance

Life insurance is underdeveloped as is the private pensions industry. In 1998, life insurance premiums represented some 1 per cent of GDP compared with an EU average of over 4 per cent, although sales of life insurance policies are now growing more rapidly than other forms of insurance.

The development of private pensions in the Czech Republic has lagged behind other countries in the region. As with every country, there is an urgent need to move away from the provision of pure state systems but the Czech government is the only one to have rejected the implementation of the second pillar, ie mandatory contributions to a private pension fund. This decision will act as a brake on the whole sector, although a growing number of Czechs are making voluntary contributions as they can see that the state system will not be able to be sustained in the current form. As the situation becomes ever more urgent, the 'new' government (after elections in June 2002) will undoubtedly have to re-visit this problem.

The non-life and general insurance sector is, in general, reasonably well developed—but with a number of particular aspects. There are now over 40 insurance companies present, although the market is still dominated by Ceská Pojist'ovna and other Czech companies.

Many of the more sophisticated products are still not generally available in the Czech Republic, even by the foreign companies that offer such products in other countries. This is largely due to the attitude towards making claims and the difficulty that the insurance companies have in verifying and adjusting claims. However, the level of competition continues to push back the boundaries.

The provision of third-party motor insurance has provoked much interest recently as this type of insurance is legally required and was opened to competition from January 2001.

Legal

Part Two of this book is dedicated to legal issues, but given the impact of legislation on doing business in the financial services sector a brief outline is appropriate here.

Perhaps the legal sector, or more correctly the law, has undergone more change than any other sector. Most of the large international law firms are present and many have been instrumental in adapting old legislation and writing new laws. As the Czech economy moves ever closer to a market-driven economy, the need for change in legislation to allow the economy to expand and foreign companies to invest and trade in a safe environment becomes ever greater. The scope and depth of these changes has increased significantly as EU membership beckons. One recent example is the provision of a large EU grant to improve bankruptcy legislation.

It is true that many of the laws are not directly comparable with UK or EU legislation, but much progress has been made. However, implementing new legislation is only one aspect of changing laws. It is widely recognized that the interpretation of new laws can be questionable in the Czech Republic and it is also generally recognized that corruption undermines the system as a whole. In addition, the judicial system is lacking in experience, although this will of course improve over time.

Accountancy

One of the requirements for any company wishing to raise debt or equity funding, trade finance, or establish any form of partnership with a foreign party, has been the need to produce accounts to international accounting standards. Czech accounts are often not very transparent, rather brief and open to misinterpretation and, as such, are not very reliable.

All the large foreign accountancy firms are present and the trend towards international accounting standards continues to move down towards ever-smaller companies. However, as all companies are required to produce accounts conforming to Czech standards, many companies must now produce two sets of accounts.

Accountancy and audit issues are addressed in Chapter 3.2.

Prague Stock Exchange

The Prague Stock Exchange is very illiquid, which impacts on many other aspects of the financial services sector. For example, it is not an attractive home for insurance and pension fund assets, does not encourage long-term savings (thus reducing the possibilities of providing long-term loans), and is not able to act as a provider of fresh capital to fund the growth of local companies. For many historic reasons, the Prague Stock Exchange is among the worst of all the poor, illiquid stock exchanges in the region.

There is a cooperation agreement in place with the London Stock Exchange and four Czech companies are listed in London.

Corporate governance

The way in which business is conducted, the transparency of transactions and relationships, minority shareholder rights and general financial management are some of the main concerns behind corporate governance. As with many aspects of the financial services sector in the Czech Republic, much has been done but more needs to be done—and in this respect a significant amount more.

Much effort is now being put into addressing many aspects of corporate governance, with the Securities Exchange Commission and other similar bodies both working together and in cooperation with external advisers.

Despite these advances, some rather questionable actions continue to be taken throughout the country and, regrettably, many of these seem to be at a government level. It is arguable whether matters have deteriorated in the Czech Republic, but as conditions improve elsewhere the difficulties there are certainly becoming more apparent.

Regulation

The banking sector is regulated by the Czech National Bank (CNB), which also has a duty to set interest rates and control inflation. Regrettably, the Czech government is trying to reduce the level of independence currently enjoyed by the CNB.

The pensions sector is supervised by the Ministry of Finance and the Ministry of Labour and Social Affairs, while the pension fund sector is supervised by the Securities Exchange Commission. The Prague Stock Exchange and other capital markets are also supervised by the Securities Exchange Commission.

Regulation and supervision of the various parts of the financial services sector is generally regarded as being relatively good and continues to improve, although it is recognized that the lack of experienced professionals is a limiting factor. However, it is most important that the government resists any temptation to interfere, as this will only be detrimental.

Summary

The financial services sector has been totally transformed over the last decade. While mistakes have been made and there is still much to be done, the progress made has nevertheless been remarkable and many of the past mistakes are now being recognized and rectified.

3.2

Accountancy and Audit

Deloitte & Touche

Introduction

A new accounting system was introduced into the Czech Republic on 1 January 1993, when the Law on Accounting came into effect. The law represents a fundamental change from the accounting principles used during the communist era, which were designed to generate information for statistical and tax collection purposes only.

The law draws heavily on EU standards, in addition to implementing a chart of accounts modelled on the French system. However, there are still differences between the Czech and EU accounting systems.

Structure

The Law on Accounting allows the Ministry of Finance to prescribe mandatory formats for accounts. These are known as the 'chart of accounts'. Five separate formats exist for the following types of business:

- entrepreneurs (the majority of businesses), within which there are various categories;
- banks;
- insurance companies;
- municipalities and institutions which are financed by the state budget;
- non-profit-making organizations, political parties, civic associations and other similar bodies.

Statutory audits are required by:

- all joint-stock companies;
- limited liability companies (if they meet special requirements);
- limited partnerships (if they meet special requirements);

- unlimited partnerships (if they meet special requirements);
- cooperatives (if they meet special requirements);
- individuals (entrepreneurs) using double-entry bookkeeping (if they meet special requirements);
- foreign entities doing business in the Czech Republic (if they meet special requirements).

These entities are not required to have a statutory audit in their first year.

Practice

In general, assets should be recorded at acquisition/purchase value. Fixed assets are shown at either cost or replacement cost and intangibles at the lower of development cost or replacement value. Assets are written off over their useful economic lives as determined by the entity. Prescribed depreciation rates are applied only for tax purposes.

Stock is valued at the acquisition costs.

Audits are governed by both the Law on Auditors and auditing guidelines issued by the Chamber of Auditors. These guidelines are essentially adapted translations of international accounting standards. As a result, a properly conducted Czech statutory audit should not differ significantly from one performed in accordance with international standards.

Essentials

However, Czech accounting standards differ from international accounting standards in a number of ways, including:

- 'Last in, first out' (LIFO) valuation of stock is forbidden, but direct cost valuation is permitted.
- Long-term construction, manufacturing and services contracts must be accounted for under the completed contract method or as provided for in the contract. The 'percentage of completion' method is not permitted.
- Unrealized foreign exchange gains or losses on currency transactions are not recognized as income/expenses.
- All leases are treated as operating leases except for leases of major segments of a business, which must be capitalized.

- Deferred taxation is only required for depreciation and amortization differences in consolidated accounts.
- The effect of any change in accounting policy must be reflected in the accounts of the year in which the change occurred.
- There are no regulations governing accounting for derivatives.
- Investment funds should not record unrealized revaluation gains and losses arising from their portfolios in the income statement, but should record them on the balance sheet as part of capital in a specific revaluation account.

The year end financial statements consist of a balance sheet, a profit and loss account and notes, including a cash flow statement.

The notes must contain information to assess the entity's assets, liabilities, financial position and results. The required information includes the accounting principles, valuation methods and depreciation rates used in the period.

The balance sheet and income statement must be prepared on pre-printed forms and the Ministry of Finance specifies the content of the notes in detail.

Changes in accounting policy or methods of estimation can only be adopted at the beginning of an accounting period. The effect of any changes must be reflected in the year of change—prior year adjustments are not permitted. The reasons for any change and the effect on financial statements must be stated in the notes.

The offset of assets and liabilities, or income and expenditure, is only possible if specifically permitted by the Ministry of Finance.

The financial statements and the company's tax return must be submitted to the local tax authority by 31 March following the calendar year end. The deadline is extended to 30 June for companies that must be audited or have their tax returns signed by a registered tax adviser.

Audited entities must prepare an annual report, including condensed financial statements with notes, the auditor's opinion and a comment on the business's past and projected future performance and financial position. This is a public document and should be made widely available.

Consolidated accounts must be prepared by any company that owns more than 20 per cent of another company or where one company effectively controls the other, regardless of its equity holding.

Consolidated companies must adopt uniform and consistent accounting policies for the purposes of consolidation.

Concerns

No specific penalties apply for failure to comply with disclosure requirements, although the following can be imposed in certain circumstances:

- 3 per cent out of the total balance-sheet value;
- eventually 6 per cent of the total balance-sheet value – depending on the seriousness of the breach.

ONLINE UPDATES - 27 May 2005

Audit and accountancy (Chap. 3.2)

Czech Accounting Standards

The full version of amendment to the Czech Accounting Standards for financial institutions, insurance companies, health insurance companies and accounting units, which are not primarily engaged in business activities, was published on 31 December 2004. The amendment replaced the version published one year earlier under No.49 in the Financial Bulletin No. 11-12/1/2003.

One of the most important changes is the amendment of Czech Accounting Standard No. 108 (Securities), introducing the definition of securities valued at fair value and setting out the accounting treatment for fair value changes in respect of particular types of securities.

February 2005, Deloitte, Prague

Statutory changes for 2004

The major changes under the Amended Accounting Act published in the Collection of Laws of the Czech Republic No.145/2003 are:

Choice of fiscal year

In circumstances where an entity opts to use a fiscal year that differs from the calendar year, it is no longer required to seek approval from the relevant tax authorities.

Revised limits for the obligation to consolidate

Entities are obliged to consolidate if two of the following criteria are met for the two previous years:

- the average recalculated number of employees is 'more than 250';
- gross assets are in excess of CZK350 million; or
- total net turnover for the year exceeds CZK700 million.

Changes in the annual report

The requirement to report balances for the previous two comparative periods has been removed, eliminating the need for reporting entities to disclose figures for three periods.

3.3

Business Taxation

Deloitte & Touche

Introduction

The Czech government recognizes that foreign investment is essential to the development of the economy. Foreigners are allowed to carry on business activities in the Czech Republic under the same conditions and in the same way as Czech nationals, and foreign investments are protected by Czech law and investment protection treaties, if concluded.

Structure

The following forms of business organization can be established in the Czech Republic:

- joint-stock company;
- limited liability company;
- unlimited partnership;
- limited partnership;
- cooperative.

A foreign investor may operate through a branch or may establish a Czech entity.

It is not possible to register a representative office in the Czech Republic; an office performing that function would be registered as a branch.

Enterprises with foreign participation are often referred to colloquially as 'joint ventures', although they are not recognized as such in law.

Partners in an unlimited partnership are subject to personal income tax. General partners in a limited partnership are taxed with respect to their individual shares of profit and are subject to personal income tax. The profit of limited partners is subject to corporate income tax. Unless a different division of profits is stipulated in the

on regulated markets of the EU and regulated markets that require the application of other internationally accepted standards (eg US GAAP) must conform in certain respects by 2007.

- Entities that issue securities as above must (and other entities reporting on a consolidated basis may) prepare consolidated financial statements and annual reports under IFRS.

January 2004, Deloitte, Prague

Refined definition of accruals

In recording an accounting transaction relating to assets or liabilities, the entity needs to apply the '3-2-1 rule' as follows:

- If the economic substance, amount and period of the transaction is known, the transaction is an accrual.
- If the economic substance and period of the transaction is known, the transaction is an estimated balance.
- If the economic substance of the transaction only is known, it is a provision.

Changes in the notes: the financial statements of trading companies for the year ended 31 December 2004

Regulation 500/2002 Coll. was updated to reflect new requirements in respect of disclosures about due social security payables, contributions to the government's employment policy, the amounts of due public health insurance payables and tax arrears.

Amendments were also made to the requirements for reporting information about fair value measurement, relating largely to more detailed information about individual types of derivatives.

There was a new requirement to disclose the balance of receivables held for trading and measured at fair value.

Exemption from the audit obligation for companies in bankruptcy

Reporting entities are not required to have their financial statements audited during the course of bankruptcy proceedings over a period of 36 successive calendar months, beginning on the fist day of the month following the day when the bankruptcy was declared.

May 2004, Deloitte, Prague

Application of International Financial Reporting Standards

The amended Accounting Act, which took effect from 2004 and was published in the Collection of Laws No. 158/2003, introduced the following requirements to observe International Financial Reporting Standards (IFRS):

- Entities, which are trading companies and issue securities admitted to public trading on regulated securities markets of EU member states, (the Prague Stock Exchange and the RMS system in the case of the Czech Republic) must use IFRS as modified by the European Communities' law in maintaining their accounts and preparing their financial statements, at the latest by 2005.
- Companies whose equity securities are admitted to public trading

partnership agreement, profit is distributed equally among the partners.

Resident entities

An entity is regarded as resident if its legal seat is registered or it has a place of effective management in the Czech Republic (the relevant tax treaty should be taken into consideration).

Resident entities are subject to corporate income tax on their worldwide income. Capital gains are included in the tax base for corporate income tax purposes. Foreign-source business income is included in the corporate income tax base.

Tax losses may be carried forward for seven years. No carry-back of tax losses is allowed.

Tax losses from securities trading are deductible only to the extent of revenue from securities trading and interest income on debentures, and may be carried forward for only three years.

Non-resident entities

A legal entity with its legal seat and its place of effective management outside the Czech Republic is subject to tax on Czech-source income only.

Various types of income are deemed to have their source in the Czech Republic, such as income derived from business carried on through a permanent establishment in the Czech Republic. In general, technical or consulting services performed in the Czech Republic are regarded as Czech-source income.

The domestic definition of a permanent establishment expressly includes a building site or construction or assembly project if it exists for more than six months, or provision of services if they are provided for more than six months in a 12-month period.

When a tax treaty applies, the treaty definition of permanent establishment should take precedence over the definition provided by Czech legislation.

Practice

Taxable income

Taxable income is determined by taking the accounting profit and making the adjustments required by the tax law.

The standard rate of corporate income tax for both resident and non-resident entities is 31 per cent of taxable income and 15 per cent in the case of resident investment funds and pension funds.

Inventory valuation

Purchased inventory is valued at its acquisition price (market value including related acquisition costs) using the 'first in, first out' (FIFO) method, weighted average valuation method or fixed storage valuation method. Inventory produced by the business itself is valued at the direct and related indirect cost incurred to produce it.

Interest income

Interest income is generally included in the corporate income tax base. However, the 15 per cent withholding tax that is applied to interest on deposits is treated as an advance payment towards the entity's total tax liability.

Depreciation

Tax depreciation is generally treated as a tax-deductible expense, using the straight-line or the accelerated method of depreciation, both of which are permitted under the Czech Income Taxes Act.

Starting from the 1999 taxable period, the depreciable lives of assets were shortened. For depreciation purposes, assets are divided into five categories, for which the prescribed periods of depreciation are:

- Computers, software and certain motor vehicles: 4 years.
- Licences, industrial rights and most plant and equipment: 6 years.
- Patent rights and industrial plant and equipment: 12 years.
- Pipelines, wooden buildings and equipment providing energy: 20 years.
- Other buildings: 30 years.

Allowable business expenses and deductions

Expenses incurred to generate, ensure and maintain income are generally treated as tax deductible.

Neither directors' nor representatives' remuneration is tax deductible. Remuneration paid to gainfully employed members of staff and the workforce is generally deductible.

Interest

In general, loan interest is deductible, provided that thin capitalization rules are not infringed and other conditions stipulated by Czech tax law are met. A debt-to-equity ratio of four-to-one is allowable for loans from related parties. Interest on debt exceeding this ratio is not deductible.

Bad debts

A deduction for the writing-off of bad debts is allowed up to a certain percentage depending on the age of the debts. Special rules apply to banks and insurance companies.

Investment incentives

Investment incentives are available to high-tech manufacturing investments exceeding approximately US$10 million (approximately US$5 should be own equity); US$3 million for investments in districts where the unemployment rate is at least 50 per cent higher than the average for the previous half year (1/2 should be covered by own equity).

Newly formed companies and new joint ventures are eligible for the following incentives:

- Income tax relief within the period of 10 consecutive years provided that the specific claim conditions of the Czech Income Tax Act are met.
- Subsidies to municipalities for:
  - technical facilities on the site where production should be located;
  - transfer of plots owned by the Czech Republic.
- Financial support for the creation of new employment opportunities.
- Financial support for re-qualification of employees.

Taxation of non-resident legal entities

The rules for computing taxable profits of non-resident legal entities are generally the same as for resident entities, and the corporate tax rate of 31 per cent applies equally.

In certain circumstances, the taxable profits of a Czech branch of a foreign entity are determined by allocating a portion of the profits of the foreign entity to the Czech branch. If a non-trading branch is unable to determine its profit or can document that its profit is not an accurate allocation of true income, the tax authorities and the taxpayer may negotiate a special method of assessing the tax base (eg a percentage of all costs).

Various categories of Czech-source income are subject to with-holding taxes.

Withholding taxes

Non-Czech source income from capital assets might be taxed at a separate tax rate of 15 per cent instead of including it in the general annual tax base. Generally no expenses can be deducted from non-Czech source income which is subject to a separate tax rate.

Some income is not included in the general individual annual tax base subject to the progressive tax rates or is not subject to separate tax rates. Such income is subject to withholding tax at various rates (obviously, the relevant tax treaty should be followed, if concluded):

- at 25 per cent on royalties paid to non-residents;
- at 20 per cent on income from non-Czech-source winnings in lotteries, bets and similar gains, winnings from advertising contests and prizes in public contests and sports competitions;
- at 15 per cent on dividends (and other yields from securities or partnerships) from limited liability companies, limited partnerships, profit shares from silent partnerships, interest from deposit certificates and bonds paid by a Czech resident entity to resident and non-resident individuals;
- at 15 per cent on income received by individuals from interest and other yields from savings, deposit accounts and certificates, which are not designed for business activities;
- at 10 per cent on incomes of up to CZK3000 from contributions to Czech newspapers, magazines, television or radio.

Corporate assessments and payments

A taxpayer must submit an annual tax return on or before the end of the third month (31 March) in the year following the tax year. However, if the return is submitted by an authorized tax adviser, or if the taxpayer is legally obliged to have its financial statements verified by an independent auditor, the due filing date is extended to the end of the sixth month (30 June) in the year following the tax year.

Advance payments of tax must generally be made unless the last known tax liability did not exceed CZK 30,000. The following scale applies:

Last known tax liability	Advances
CZK30,000-CZK150,000	2 of 40%
CZK150,000-CZK10 million	4 of 25%

Any outstanding annual tax liability must be paid within the time allowed for the submission of the return.

Tax may be assessed or additionally assessed normally no later than three years after the end of the tax period during which the duty to file a tax return or declaration arose, or during which a tax liability arose without a concurrent duty to file a tax return or declaration. In special cases the term can be prolonged. Taxpayers have one month from the issue of a notice of assessment in which to file an appeal. The appeal may be passed to a directorate, whose decision is final.

Other taxes and employers' contributions

The rates of other significant national taxes and employers' contributions are:

	Standard rate
VAT	
most goods	22 per cent
most foodstuffs and services	5 per cent
financial, insurance, educational and health care services	exempt
exports (with right to recover VAT on related inputs)	exempt
Employers' social security contributions	
health insurance fund	9 per cent of total payroll
social security fund	26 per cent of total payroll
Employees' contributions	
health insurance fund	4.5 per cent of their wages
social security fund	8 per cent of their wages
Self-employed social security contributions	
(based on 35 per cent of net income up to CZK486,000)	
health insurance fund	13.5 per cent
social security (excluding sickness insurance)	29.6 per cent

Land tax	
agricultural land according to use	variable
other land according to area and type	variable
Buildings—floor space and usage	variable
Real estate transfer tax (based on the higher of the value as determined by the Decree on Valuation of Buildings and Land or the transfer price)	5 per cent

Miscellaneous taxes are levied as duties on fuel and lubricants, alcohol and spirits, beer, wine and tobacco products or as road tax on owners of motor vehicles used for business activities in the Czech Republic, including owners of motor vehicles registered abroad who use their vehicles in the Czech Republic.

The Czech Republic also levies local taxes/fees including a tax on recreational facilities and a tax on the use of public grounds.

Essentials

Tax considerations for groups

No provision exists for group consolidation of profits or losses for tax purposes. Transfer pricing provisions apply when the contract price of a transaction between either associated or unassociated persons differs from the usual market price. Special treatment is given for the interest.

The profits of a branch are subject only to corporate income tax. By contrast, the distributions of a subsidiary are subject to withholding tax at 15 per cent, subject to relief provided by the terms of an applicable tax treaty. Under certain circumstances, the subsidiary may deduct from its tax liability an amount corresponding to one half of the tax withheld from dividends paid in the tax period.

Corporate assessments and withholding tax

The tax year is the calendar year or the economic year. Tax is basically self-assessed. Taxpayers calculate their own liabilities and claim any exemptions and reliefs on annual tax returns. Income subject to final withholding tax is excluded.

The withholding tax rates may be reduced under the double taxation treaties that the Czech Republic has negotiated. A number of these treaties were negotiated by the former Czechoslovakia; however, most treaty partners have formally agreed to continue to apply the treaties to the successor states or are doing so in practice.

VAT

VAT is payable on all sales of goods and services and on the importation of goods and is based on the price of goods and services including duties.

VAT legislation is slowly being amended to remove differences between the VAT systems in the Czech Republic and the European Union. Under certain circumstances, non-resident persons may obtain refunds of Czech VAT.

Employers' deductions

Employers must calculate and withhold tax from monthly salaries and wages. If a foreign employer employs personnel for more than 183 days and does not have a permanent establishment (with the exception of commercial, technical and other consulting services and of foreign diplomatic missions in the country), it is generally obliged to withhold and remit Czech tax from the employees' income.

Foreign nationals

Foreign nationals may be employed on the same basis as Czech nationals, provided that they have the necessary visa and work permits.

Resident individuals are subject to Czech personal income tax on their worldwide income and gains. Non-resident individuals are subject to tax on income and gains derived from Czech sources only. An individual is regarded as resident if his permanent residence or usual domicile is in the Czech Republic, which is judged to be the case if he is present in the country for at least 183 days in 12 consecutive months (naturally, the relevant tax treaty should be considered).

Concerns

If a tax loss is deducted by a resident entity, the possibility of granting a tax exemption shall be excluded.

The previous ten-to-one debt-to-equity ratio for tax-deductible interest on loans from unrelated foreign companies was eliminated from 1 January 1998.

The Czech Republic continues to observe the multilateral treaties concluded by Czechoslovakia and members of the former Council for Mutual Economic Assistance (COMECON), which provide for the exemption of dividends, interest and royalties from taxation in the source country. Some other members have decided not to reciprocate or have since signed treaties with the Czech Republic, which supersede the COMECON treaties. The COMECON treaties now mostly apply only to Azerbaijan, Kyrgyzstan and Tajikistan.

Tax assessments may be extended from three to ten years after the end of the tax period to which they relate. However, if a taxpayer is entitled to the deduction of a tax loss or part thereof in periods subsequent to the tax period when the tax loss occurred, the review period may be extended up to a maximum of 17 years.

If an investment incentive is granted in the form of tax relief, the period within which the tax authority may impose additional taxes is extended to 15 years from the end of the calendar year in which the right to the tax relief was claimed.

Old Czechoslovak bilateral agreements on social security, not previously enforced, are now being enforced and new agreements are being concluded; thus, more careful consideration should be given to social security for expatriates.

The Czech Republic does not levy business licence or trade taxes, but administration and court fees are levied on those registering a business or independent activities.

ONLINE UPDATES - 27 May 2005

Business taxation (Chap. 3.3)

Current taxation

The September 2003 package of fiscal reforms, effective 1 January 2004, amended the Income Taxes Act (Act No. 596/92 Coll), easing corporate tax rates for both resident and non-resident entities from 31 per cent to:

- 28 per cent in 2004;
- 26 per cent in 2005;
- 24 per cent in 2006

The logic behind the reduced rates was to encourage companies to decide that it is better to pay the lower rates instead of risking tax evasion penalties and that tax revenues would actually increase. Tax evasion devices have included under-reporting of income, paying expatriate employees in their own countries and artificially high transfer prices to reduce local income. Investigation and enforcement are improving.

Investment incentives

Investment incentives that were approved in 1998 and amended in 1999, 2000 and 2004, including tax holidays, continue to provide relief on a case-by-case basis.

Depreciation

All tangible assets with a value of more than CZK40,000 and a usage of more than one year are depreciated for tax purposes. A sixth depreciation category of tangible assets was introduced in September 2003 increasing the period of depreciation for certain buildings including hotels and similar accommodation, administrative buildings, department stores, underground shopping centres and buildings for social and cultural purposes from 30 to 50 years.

At the same time, a ceiling of CZK900,000 was set on the cumulative tax depreciation charges of passenger cars, and depreciation of intangible assets with an acquisition cost of more than CZK60,000 was re-introduced for purchases after 31 December 2003. Generally, intangible assets are depreciated on a straight-line basis over the period of contracted use. In the absence of a contract for a definite period, the depreciation for software is four years, for incorporation expenses five years and six years for all other intangible assets.

Loss relief

Under the amended Czech Income Taxes Act, companies are generally able to carry forward their tax losses incurred in a taxable period beginning 2004 or since over five subsequent years. Tax losses incurred earlier are still governed by the unamended provisions of the Income Taxes Act and may be carried forwarded and credited against future profits for up to seven years.

At the same time, the available period for carrying back tax loses was reduced from seven years to five.

Withholding taxes

For countries where there are no double-tax treaties, the withholding tax on dividends is 15 per cent, on interest income from zero to 15 per cent and 25 per cent on royalties. Where double-tax treaties apply, the withholding tax rates vary from zero to 15 per cent on dividends, zero to 12.5 per cent on interest and zero to 15 per cent on royalties. There are no restrictions on profits repatriation.

VAT

On accession to the EU, the system of VAT was changed extensively to comply with the common EU VAT system. New taxation mechanisms apply for transactions in the EU (reverse charge, self-assessment, etc). Imported goods are assessed at the same rates as domestic goods and the export of goods to non-EU countries is an exempt supply.

The standard rate of VAT set for most goods and services is 19 per cent (formerly 22 per cent) with a reduced five per cent rate for specified supplies (eg food, books, medical supplies, etc).

Companies located in the Czech Republic with a turnover exceeding CZK1 million for 12 months are obliged to register for VAT. Some specific transactions may create an immediate obligation to register.

Changes to other taxes

Estate transfer tax

Under a law approved by parliament in December 2003, the real estate transfer tax was reduced from five per cent to three per cent, based on the higher of an official valuation of the property and the purchase price. Exemptions of transfer tax for contributions of real estate to the registered capital of commercial companies and in mergers were cancelled by the same amendment.

Road tax

Amendment No. 102/2004 to Sb. to the Road Tax Act increased the period in which the tax rate reduction for commercial vehicles that met emission standards is effective :

- The 60 per cent reduction for vehicles meeting Euro 2 limits applies until 31 Deember 2005.
- The 66 per cent reduction for vehicles meeting Euro 3 limits applies until 31 December 2006.

Update: July 2004, Deloitte Touche Tohmatsu, Prague

3.4

Financial Support and Finance Facilities from the European Union[1]

Bank Austria Creditanstalt

Much of the international project financing which has been applied to enterprises in the Czech Republic originates from the European Bank for Reconstruction and Development (EBRD), established in 1991, and the European Investment Bank (EIB), which is the financing institution of the European Union. The EBRD is dedicated to promoting the transition to an open market economy and to encouraging private and entrepreneurial activities in all those countries of Central and Eastern Europe and the Commonwealth of Independent States (CIS) which have committed themselves to the principles of multi-party democracy and pluralism, as well as a market economy. The main types of EBRD financing for private sector enterprises are loans, equity investments and guarantees.

The EIB and its operation

By contrast, the EIB finances projects that are consistent with EU objectives, such as the promotion of SMEs, environmental protection, improvements of transportation and telecom infrastructures, and involves sums over €25 million at open market rates in the form of individual loan arrangements. The EIB funds project costs up to a maximum of 50 per cent and the balance must be raised through equity capital and commercial bank loans or other EU assistance

---

[1] The text of this chapter is derived from Bank Austria Creditanstalt's *Investment Guide for the Czech Republic,* published in February 2002. Contacts in the Bank Austria Creditanstalt Group specializing in each of the types of fund and finance facility referred to in the chapter are listed in Appendix 3.

schemes. Since the EIB enjoys AAA credit rating it is able to refinance its loans on global capital markets. For smaller projects, the EIB extends loans to banks subject to the condition that these banks will grant loans to project applicants.

For those CEE countries, such as the Czech Republic, which are EU accession applicants, EIB activities are coordinated with the Phare and ISPA programmes described below and with EBRD financing arrangements. Under a new financing scheme for CEE countries, the EIB has made available a total of €8.7 billion for the period 2000–2007. In addition, a 'pre-accession facility' was renewed and a total of €8.5 billion earmarked for the period 2000–2003.

EU financial support for accession candidates

In order to address the unique challenge of EU enlargement, the European Commission has set itself the goal of providing a comprehensive finance plan to help the 10 accession candidates (Bulgaria, Czech Republic, Estonia, Hungary, Latvia, Lithuania, Poland, Romania, Slovak Republic and Slovenia) to prepare for accession. This EU support is being provided through three programmes from 2000 to 2006: Phare, ISPA and SAPARD. The European Commission is allocating a total budget of approximately €3 billion annually to fund these three initiatives.

Phare programme

Through an annual budget of €1.5 billion, the European Commission gives non-repayable grants under the Phare programme to support goals set in the Accession Partnerships to prepare candidates for EU accession. Phare has as its two main priorities:

- Investment support (70 per cent of Phare budget) to help the accession candidates adapt their infrastructure and enterprises and bring them up to EU standards.
- Institution building (30 per cent of the Phare budget). Efforts to develop and strengthen institutions and administrative bodies are to be intensified by 'twinning' and 'technical support' so that the candidate is equipped to adopt and implement the EU legal system and has the administrative resources to accomplish this task.

Since the signing of the Accession Partnerships in 1998, Phare has been fundamentally realigned and no longer includes programmes for the environment, transportation infrastructure and agriculture—sectors that are covered through separate programmes. The programmes are no longer based on demand from the individual countries but exclusively on the needs arising from the forthcoming accession.

A number of needs-oriented programmes have been created for each accession candidate, based on the Accession Partnership and the ensuing Financing Memorandum. The European Commission has set up a separate page covering the currently valid programmes for each country and sector on its website http://europa.eu.int/phare-cgi/plsql/prog.search). The page for the Czech Republic gives short descriptions of about 40 programmes and cross references to contact details.

Like ISPA and SAPARD, the Phare programme is implemented in a decentralized manner, whereby the recipient countries are responsible for programme execution. In most projects funded by Phare, international tendering procedures are employed to determine the companies that are to carry out the projects. Forecasted tenders are published by the EC office for external programmes, the Europe-Aid Cooperation Office, at http://europa.eu.int/comm/eropeaid/cgi/frame12.pl.

Companies and experts wishing to participate in public tenders should first enter their names in the General Consultant Register, which serves as the central database for the European Commission. They can then signal their interest in a project, on the basis of information provided on the Internet, by sending a 'letter of interest' and, if selected for the shortlist, can participate in the actual public tender.

National programmes

A large part of Phare funds goes to national programmes negotiated between the European Commission and the accession candidates on the basis of the Accession Partnerships. These programmes also include schemes promoting cross-border cooperation with neighbouring countries and, in the case of the Czech Republic, include programmes with Austria, Germany, Poland and Slovakia.

Individual projects are derived from the national programmes; before a project is launched, a final report is prepared which contains key statements and information on the project. Information on each project can be obtained from the EC Delegation in Prague.

Multi-beneficiary programmes

Most of the remaining Phare funds go to horizontal and crossborder initiatives tailored not to a single country, as with the national programmes, but to promoting a given sector or topic. The programmes apply equally to all accession candidates and are administered by the European Commission in cooperation with the countries involved.

The number of these programmes, which are categorized by area and subject matter and do not always provide assistance tailored to accession, will be steadily reduced by the European Commission as a part of its realignment of Phare. An overview and descriptions of the existing programmes can be found at http://europa.eu.int/comm/enlargement/pas/phare/programmes/multi-bene/index/htm.

Opening up of EU programmes to the accession candidate

Apart from EU assistance earmarked for specific countries, EU member states also benefit from a number of sectoral programmes open equally to all. Since 1998, successive steps have been taken to open up these programmes to the accession candidates as well. So long as an accession candidate has applied for participation in a given programme and the EU Council has passed a relevant resolution, the accession candidate and the business undertakings in that country can participate in the regularly announced public tenders and submit projects. An overview of the EU programmes in which the Czech Republic is a participant is presented at http://europa.eu.int/comm/enlargement/pas/ocp_index.htm

ISPA

Since the beginning of 2000, an annual €1040 million in structural assistance has been made available to accession candidates through the Instrument for Structured Policies for Pre-Accession (ISPA). These funds are directed to three main areas:

- Environment. To bring the accession candidates up to EU environmental standards. In this context, ISPA promotes investments in those areas where meeting the EU standards entails heavy costs, ie drinking water supply, waste-water treatment and air pollution, and solid-waste management.
- Transport. Where the goal is to improve the mobility of people and the transport of goods by investing in transport infrastructure. Fundamental to these efforts is the development of the Trans-European Networks (TENs).

- Technical assistance. A small part of the budget will be used to fund feasibility studies and project management. (There is also a Phare programme providing assistance for such studies.)

Projects should involve a minimum investment of €5 million and are to be proposed by the applicant countries within the framework of their national implementation programmes (NPAA) and then approved by the European Union. Financial assistance can cover up to 75 per cent of project costs, and in special cases up to 85 per cent. Co-financing arrangements can be entered into with international finance institutions (IFIs) or with commercial banks. The European Commission is responsible for selecting and monitoring projects. Provision is made for annual assistance of between €57 million and €83 million for the Czech Republic. Companies planning to carry out projects in the accession candidate countries with Phare or ISPA assistance are advised to contact the office administering the relevant programme at an early stage to discuss potential inclusion of their project. A list of contacts for ISPA and the Phare Address Book are available from Bank Austria Creditanstalt's EU advisory team.

Further information on the ISPA programme and projects is available at http://europa.eu.int/comm/regional_policy/activity/ispa/sector_en.htm

SAPARD

The Special Accession Programme for Agriculture and Rural Development (SAPARD), which came into effect from the beginning of 2000, is intended to promote sustainable rural development, resolve the problems related to the long-term adaptation of the agricultural sector and rural areas, and support the accession candidate countries in adopting and implementing the Acquis Communitaire, the entire body of European law, in the area of the Common Agricultural Policy (CAP) and related measures. However, the priorities vary considerably from country to country in respect of the programmes for which assistance is granted. Over €500 million is made available annually under SAPARD to the candidate countries, of which the Czech Republic receives €22 million annually.

The SAPARD programme is also based on the principles of decentralized management. As a first step, the individual countries signed a Multi-annual Financing Agreement with the European Union as a master agreement for the priorities to be financed under

SAPARD. On the basis of the master agreement, an Annual Financing Agreement is then signed each year, determining the amount to be committed for the year. In each country, a SAPARD Agency has been set up, which is responsible for the implementation of the SAPARD programme.

The maximum project size for which support may be granted under the SAPARD programme varies from country to country. SAPARD funds, in the form of non-repayable grants, cover up to a maximum of 50 per cent of the project costs, and the remaining funds have to be raised by the beneficiary from its own resources, bank loans, government loans or other sources.

SAPARD differs from other external aid programmes of the European Commission in that the projects must be filed directly with the local SAPARD Agency. SAPARD funds are granted to enterprises, individuals and, in certain cases, government agencies in the agricultural sector in the candidate countries.

EU SME Finance Facility Phase II (SME FF)

In 1999, the European Commission launched a regional finance facility for the 10 applicant countries. The Commission administers the programme in cooperation with the EBRD, the EIB and the Council of Europe Development Bank (CEB) or Kreditanstalt für Wiederaufbau (KfW). The facility is funded from Phare resources.

The essential purpose of the programme is to facilitate long-term lending to SMEs by local financial institutions (banks and equity funds) in the applicant countries. Support to the intermediaries is provided in two ways:

- The 'traditional' lending procedure, through the so-called 'Loan and Guarantee Window' in which technical assistance, performance bonuses, exchange risk hedging, incentives for small value loans and the assumption of costs of special loan guarantees are offered.
- The so-called 'Equity Window', where the EBRD makes available equity capital and management support.

In either 'Window', the local SMEs as final borrowers have to meet certain minimum local and national standards in the areas of environmental protection, security and health protection. The lending banks are contractually obliged to apply the assistance granted to them exclusively to measures promoting SMEs and to provide information on individual financings to the institutions administering the programme and the European Commission on request.

In 2001, HVB Bank Czech Republic, a.s. (http://www.hvb.cz), a member of the Bank Austria Creditanstalt Group, signed agreements with the EIB and with KfW for refinancing lines covering a total of €185 million to be used by SMEs and also for infrastructure projects of territorial authorities, PPPs and companies active in promoting the interests of communities. These refinancing lines are a pre-condition for participation in the 'Loan Window' of the EU SME Finance Facility. HVB Czech Republic is negotiating participation in this programme.

SME Finance Facility arrangements currently exist in the Czech Republic with the following institutions:

- Ceska Sporitelna, a.s. http://www.csas.cz).
- Ceskomoravska Zarueni a Rozvojova Banka, a.s./Czech-Moravian Guarantee and Development Bank http://www.cmzrb.cz).
- In the Equity Window with GIMV Czech and Slovak SME Fund/GIMV Czech Partners Management Company B.V. c/o E1CZ, s.r.o. (http://www.gimv.be).

3.5

Capital Markets

Michal Srb and Martina Lambert, CA IB Securities, Prague

History and structure of the stock market

The Stock Exchange Law was approved in December 1992 (Act No. 214/1992) and the Prague Stock Exchange (PSE) started trading on 6 April 1993. The PSE is based on electronic trading and members are connected through an online communications system. As of 31 December 2001, there were 44 members of the PSE of which only Czech legal bodies can be members. The PSE currently operates both a market-making system for most liquid stocks and an order-driven system for other stocks. The PSE is a joint-stock company authorized to organize the offer and demand for various kinds of securities: shares, debentures, bonds and share certificates. Derivatives are also traded.

Settlement of the trades executed on the PSE is organized by the PSE's daughter company, UNIVYC. This company guarantees the DvP principle through their online links to the Central Depository of the Securities and Clearing Centre of the Czech National Bank (CNB).

The PSE has set itself a primary single target: to help in bringing the Czech capital environment as close as possible to advanced standardized markets. Since 1997, when it abandoned some 1301 illiquid issues, the PSE has striven to strengthen the functionality of Czech capital markets. In 1999, the SPAD system (system for the support of trading in stock and obligations), introduced by the PSE in May 1998, increased the transparency of trading in shares and participation certificates.

An off-exchange market organizer in the Czech Republic, called the RM system, is a joint-stock company organizing the offer of and demand for securities, and off-exchange deals. It was created primarily for the millions of individual shareholders arising from voucher privatization. Investors can buy and sell shares at over 100 outlets in the Czech Republic, which are connected to a central computer and pricing mechanism. It is an order-driven system and all trades are settled immediately. Volumes were substantially lower than on the PSE. As its activities are based on a user principle, no limitations exist in accessing the market. Any individual or company, Czech or foreign, can utilize the services provided by the RM system. The activities of the RM system have been authorized by the Czech capital markets regulator—the Czech Securities Commission. The Commission is headquartered in Prague. The trading system holds to the 'over-the-counter principle'. This market is directly accessible to dealers in securities and individual entrepreneurs as well as investors and is focused on both direct and block deals.

The main market index, PX50, has ceased to be a reasonable mirror of the market in last few years, as it is hard to find 50 companies on the market which are traded at least once a month. The index is therefore often influenced by old prices of the companies with zero trading volume. The PX-D, originally created as the basis of Index Futures Contracts, is now a more reasonable index. This index represents only those companies traded on SPAD, a fully price-transparent system. SPAD is based on exploitation of the function performed by market-makers. A market-maker (MM) is a PSE member that has made an official contract with the PSE to act as an MM for selected issues. Neither the number of MMs per issue nor number of issues per MM is limited.

Derivatives trading market

The derivatives trading system of the PSE is a fully automated trading system based on standard principles used on all international markets. This system consists of several modules (trading, settlement, surveillance and dealer's modules) and, as an entity, has been integrated into the existing trading and settlement environment of the PSE, which enables all data flows to be progressed in real time.

At the end of 2000, the Presidium of the Securities Commission decided to prepare and take individual steps leading to the creation and implementation of an organized derivatives market in the Czech Republic. The major rules were set for granting licences to trade in derivatives: licences will be granted by the Securities Commission to traders who demonstrate that they are sufficiently well organized and technically equipped and will meet the capital adequacy requirements standards.

Several legal changes were also made during 2001. On 17 December 2001, the Securities Commission granted permission to settle derivatives trades concluded at the PSE to the company UNIVYC.

The Securities Commission is focused on preparations for entry into the European Union, adapting its rules and regulations as well as its procedures. One of the Commission's main goals is to implement EU standards.

Market structure

Trading system

The basic trading system of the PSE is the market-making segment called SPAD. The seven most liquid equity issues are traded through this system. Those seven issues represent 92 per cent of the total trading volume of the PSE. The chances of increasing the number of the shares on SPAD from the stocks traded on other segments is very low, as other stocks have substantially lower liquidity.

There are strict rules for the MMs on SPAD. All MMs (usually 5–10 on every issue) have to quote from the opening to the end of the business day with at least one quote on each side of the market. The size of the lot and the maximum spread of the quotation are defined by the Trading Committee of the PSE. All members of the PSE, including all MMs, can trade anytime at the best quotation(s). Market-makers have to input a new quotation within a specified period of time (currently three minutes) after they were forced to trade at their old quotation. Odd lots, bigger amounts, but also standard-size transactions can be executed via telephone between members of the PSE. However, the trade should always be within the best spread and has to be registered within three minutes on the SPAD screen. The trade then becomes visible for all members and information agencies. The system is very efficient and has been running without any major problems since May 1998.

Issues not traded in SPAD are traded either by fixing or continued matching of the orders. However, this system does not have sufficient liquidity to execute institutional orders. Over-the-counter transactions are registered on the PSE as a 'block transaction'.

The market is open from 9.30am until 4pm daily. A list of the principal brokers and other important PSE contacts is included at the close of this chapter.

Market size

The market size of the PSE, in terms of the number of equity listings and their market value, is shown in Table 3.5.1. The market capitalization at the end of 2001 of the 20 largest companies on the PSE is shown in Table 3.5.2, together with the relevant tracking system and market segment to which each belongs.

Trading volume

The total value of equity trading (shares and unit trusts) fell by 51 per cent from CZK264,145.30 million in 2000 to CZK128,799.10 million in 2001. The total number of shares traded on PSE decreased by 27 per cent from 822,909.87 million shares in 2000 to 596,188.00 million shares in 2001. Despite this negative, decreasing trend, in 2001 the share of trades closed out on the fully price-transparent system (SPAD) reached a level of 91.6 per cent. Trading volumes for each of the years 1995–2001 are given in Table 3.5.3 and the shares most actively traded during 2001 in Table 3.5.4.

Table 3.5.1 Number of listings and market value

Year end	*No. of all companies listed on PSE*	*Market capitalization (CZK million) Main, secondary and free market*	*No. of mpanies listed on main secondary markets*	*Market capitalization (CZK million) Main & secondary markets*
1995	1,716	478.6	68	275.98
1996	1,670	539.2	96	423.57
1997	320	495.6	103	408.20
1998	304	416.2	106	348.61
1999	195	479.6	89	416.77
2000	151	442.9	65	376.90
2001	102	340.2	53	296.75

Source: Prague Stock Exchange

Table 3.5.2 Market capitalization of the 20 largest listed companies, PSE, end 2001

Rank	*Security name*	*Market capitalization (mil.Kè)*	*Trading system*	*Market*
1	Český Telecom	85,233.0	Spad	Main market
2	ČEZ	45,910.5	Spad	Main market
3	Česká spoř itelna	41,743.9	Spad	Main market
4	Komerč ní Banka	39,378.2	Spad	Main market
5	Philip Morris Čr	15,851.2	Spad	Free market
6	Č Radiokomunikace	10,771.0	Spad	Secondary market
7	Unipetrol	8167.3	Spad	Main market
8	Česká Pojištovna	5882.9	Fixing	Secondary market
9	Jihomor Energet	4147.6	Fixing	Secondary market
10	Pražská Energetika	3917.6	Fixing	Secondary market
11	Pražská Tepláren	3801.1	Fixing	Secondary market
12	Jihomor Plynáren	3207.5	Fixing	Secondary market
13	Semor Energetika	2830.0	Fixing	Secondary market
14	Semor Plynárenská	2542.6	Fixing	Secondary market
15	Středoč Energet	2481.8	Fixing	Secondary market
16	Živnostenská Banka	2326.3	Fixing	Secondary market
17	Severoč Energet	2259.2	Fixing	Secondary market
18	Severoč Doly	2153.6	Fixing	Secondary market
19	Pražská Plynáren	2031.8	Fixing	Secondary market
20	Moravské Naft.Doly	2018.1	Fixing	Secondary market

Source: Prague Stock Exchange

Table 3.5.3 Trading volume and value, PSE, end 2001

Year	*Total (shares+unit trusts)*		*Shares only*	
	Value (CZK mil.)	*Volume (mil. pcs)*	*Value (CZK mil.)*	*Volume (mil. pcs)*
1995	125,642.70	164,156.80	124,902.90	158,919.00
1996	249,935.30	326,322.90	246,989.60	305,783.00
1997	246,301.90	311,652.70	241,897.70	294,956.00
1998	172,594.00	428,733.80	169,213.60	415,589.00
1999	163,456.70	772,630.00	160,862.10	765,795.00
2000	264,145.30	822,909.87	261,672.50	821,124.00
2001	128,799.10	596,188.00	128,754.20	546,494.00

Source: Prague Stock Exchange

Table 3.5.4 Most actively traded shares, PSE, end 2001

Rank	*Security name*	*Value (CZK mil.)*	*Cumulative share on the market (%)*
1	Český Telecom	36,574.32	28.4
2	Komerč ní banka	30,645.48	52.2
3	ČEZ	19,577.30	67.4
4	Česká spoř itelna	11,136.73	81.6
5	Ceske Radiokomunikace	11,136.73	90.3
6	Unipetrol	4746.66	93.9
7	Philip Morris CR	4359.73	97.3
8	1.If Živnobanka	811.74	98.0
9	Stavoy silnic a zeleznic	707.43	98.5
10	P.I.F.	246.52	98.7

Source: Prague Stock Exchange

Investors in the equity capital market

Investors on the PSE can be divided into three major groups:

- Foreign institutional.
- Domestic institutional.
- Domestic retail.

Foreign institutional

Foreign institutional investors remain the major driving force of the market. It is rather difficult to estimate the volume of the transactions executed by this investor group, but CA IB's estimation is around 60 per cent.

Domestic institutional

There are two kinds of domestic institutional investor. They can be divided simply into 'old' and 'new'. The old investors are the privatization funds, which are going (or went) public and whose exposure to PSE issues is falling dramatically as they focus more on the world equity markets. In total, there is CZK89 billion invested in CZK-denominated domestic funds, but only around 10 per cent are in equities, of which the majority are in foreign equities. There was massive disinvestment in recent years; between 1993 and 1995 those funds were invested basically 100 per cent in domestic equities.

The new investors are asset management companies, managing assets for pension funds, insurers, municipalities, foundations, corporates and guarantee funds as well as for private individuals. The value of the assets under management is estimated to be CZK100 billion, of which the domestic equity proportion is estimated at 5–10 per cent.

CA IB estimates that the share of the volume traded by domestic institutional investors is 35 per cent.

Domestic retail

This basic group of investors was almost non-existent a few years ago. Although almost 80 per cent of the adult population held, or still hold, shares from voucher privatization, only a small number have bought any shares on the market during recent years. Retail clients have an extremely negative view of capital markets, due to the lack of regulation in the early 1990s. The most problematic areas were minority shareholder protection, the obligatory buy-out rules, asset striping of corporates and some funds, and the negative publicity in the local press which resulted. This attitude has been slowly changing over the last two years; furthermore, some e-broking activities have also been introduced. However, the share of retail in market volume remains very low and is estimated by CA IB at 5 per cent.

Regulations affecting foreign investors

The current legislation and regulations relating to capital markets are being reviewed in order to converge Czech legislation progressively with that of the European Union.

Laws and directives

The following laws and directives relate to Czech capital markets:

- Securities Commission Act No. 15/1998 Coll., as the regulatory authority for the capital market, as subsequently amended;
- Stock Exchange Act No. 214/1992 Coll., as subsequently amended;
- Securities Act No. 591/1992 Coll., as subsequently amended;

- Investment Companies and Investment Funds Act No. 248/1992 Coll., as subsequently amended;
- Administration of Taxes Act No. 337/1992 Coll., as amended;
- Czech National Bank Act No. 6/1993 Coll., as subsequently amended;
- Commercial Code Act No. 513/1991 Coll., as subsequently amended;
- Accounting Act No. 563/1991 Coll., as subsequently amended;
- Bankruptcy and Composition Act No. 328/1991 Coll., as subsequently amended;
- Labour Code No. 65/1965 Coll., as subsequently amended;
- Income Taxes Act No. 586/1992 Coll., as subsequently amended;
- Trades Licensing Act No. 455/1991 Coll., as subsequently amended;
- Foreign Exchange Act No. 219/1995 Coll., as subsequently amended;
- Act on Private International Law No. 97/1963 Coll., as subsequently amended;
- Investment Incentives Act No. 72/2000 Coll., as subsequently amended;
- Employment Act No. 1/1991 Coll., as subsequently amended;
- Act on Foreigners' Stay and Residence in the Czech Republic No. 326/1999 Coll., as subsequently amended;
- Rules of the PSE;
- Banking Act No. 21/1992 Coll., as amended;
- Money Laundering Act No. 61/1996 Coll., as amended;
- Bonds Act No. 530/1990 Coll., as amended;
- Bills of Exchange and Cheques Act No. 191/1950 Coll., as amended;
- Insurance Act No. 393/1999 Coll., as amended;
- Civil Code No. 40/1964 Coll., as amended.

The Securities Act

The Securities Act, approved by the Czech parliament, stipulates the fundamental rules for activities in capital markets by investors, market organizers, brokers and dealers, and issuers as well as clearing and settlement bodies and registrars.

The Act also specifies contractual relationships applicable to securities. The basic conditions for the establishment, activities and duties of the organizer of off-exchange securities trading are defined from the RM system point of view.

Legal and regulatory framework

The situation of the Czech market has improved dramatically in the last two years. While from 1993 until 1997 the Czech market was considered to be 'the wild east', now almost standard regulations are in place. The Securities Commission has been in existence since 1998, there are strict rules about minority shareholders buyouts, transparency of the trading system has improved and the information duties of companies are supervised by the PSE. However, there is one very non-standard feature in the Czech market system. There is no nominee ownership principle in place, so that all securities have to be registered to the owner's account in the Central Depository (SCP). The SCP therefore holds millions of accounts. This system is the residue of voucher privatization and is quite an important bottleneck for market development. However, some foreign custodians hold nominee accounts for their international clients. A new securities law is under preparation and it should address this problem.

Initial public offering (IPO)

The new issues market has not developed yet, but there are a number of signs that the situation should improve in the future as there have been a number of market defects to remedy.

The main reason for the current sorry state in comparison to neighbouring countries is the way in which privatization was conducted in the Czech Republic. Initially the voucher privatization, and more recently the government's preference for direct sales to strategic investors over equity offerings, eliminated a number of possible IPO candidates. Another important factor affecting IPOs was the unpropitious legal framework making any share capital increase an arduous exercise with a long and uncertain timetable (in particular the need for two capital increase entries into Companies Register and the difficulty of trading with claims on shares already subscribed and paid for, but not yet issued). Fortunately, this difficulty has been removed by the last amendment to the Commercial Code, which sets the exact deadlines for the recording of capital increases as well as enabling an issue of tradable securities (depository receipts) immediately upon payment of the full subscription price.

However, with difficult trading conditions on equity markets elsewhere as well as in the Czech Republic, no issuer has taken advantage of the improved legislation and there is some time to wait for IPO activity to take off.

Czech Capital Market Association (AKAT)

The Czech Capital Market Association (AKAT) was founded in Prague on 19 May 2000 to contribute to the reform of Czech capital markets. The Association is a mutual interest association of legal entities, leading brokerage houses and foreign banks. The main objective of its activities is to achieve, by means of development, standardization and popularization of the capital market in the Czech Republic, the creation of a capital market compatible with the EU capital markets environment. In order to achieve its objective, the Association holds lectures, seminars and conferences, publishes studies, legal opinions, and ethical standards, participates in raising comments on parliamentary bills and decrees related to capital markets, and supports education on the subject of capital markets. An Association ethical committee and 10 working sections are focused on capital markets, investment banking, brokerage, sales and trading, asset management, collective investment and law regulations. The Association currently consists of 45 professional members and partners.

Guarantee Fund of Securities Dealers

A new Guarantee Fund of Securities Dealers was founded in March 2001 in order to enhance investor safety and protect and compensate clients of bankrupt brokerage houses in the Czech Republic. In accordance with the amended Securities Act, the Guarantee Fund is a legal entity but not a government fund. However, due to the imperfect definition of the Securities Act, the Guarantee Fund is still not functioning to its potential in terms of covering financial needs.

Listing and reporting requirements

Listing requirements

Securities are traded in three markets of the PSE: main, secondary and free. The main and secondary markets, the so-called listed markets', have emerged from the original listed market. Since 30 September 1999, it has been also possible to trade securities in the so-called 'new market', which constitutes an organic segment of the secondary market. The new market is intended to allow companies with high growth potential to raise the financial resources needed for the implementation of their projects through the PSE. However, no company has yet been listed on the new market. In order to be able to list a security issue, it is necessary that such issue is fully repaid, marketable without any limitation and that the following requirements for individual exchange markets are met:

Main market

Sufficient liquidity is also a listing requirement for an issue applicable to the main market. Liquidity criteria are set by the Exchange Listing Committee, which publishes all of its decisions well in advance of such a decision entering into effect. Specific listing requirements are:

- a minimum public issue of CZK200 million;
- a minimum of 20 per cent of the overall issue to be issued via a public offer;
- prior existence of the company for at least two years.

Secondary market

Listing requirements include:

- a minimum amount issued of CZK100 million;
- a minimum of 15 per cent of the shares made available via a public offer;
- prior existence of the company for at least two years.

The Stock Exchange Quotation Committee makes decisions regarding the registration of securities in the free market.

New market

The PSE has adopted the objective of focusing on trading in small and medium-sized companies. Any issue released by a company whose shares are already traded in the main, secondary or free markets of the PSE is ineligible for listing in the new market. The purpose of the new market is to enable companies, with shorter histories but with strong business prospects, to acquire financial resources to exploit further growth and innovations in a capital market through public subscription.

The basic listing requirements for the new market are:

- a minimum registered capital of CZK210 million;
- a minimum of 15 per cent of the shares made via a public offer,
- a minimum market capitalization for issue of CZK20 million;
- prior existence of the company for at least one year.

Companies are introduced to the new market by a PSE member, known as a 'patron', who is to serve as a guarantor to the investment community that the company has satisfied all the prerequisites, meets the parameters necessary for admission to the new market and is therefore ready to trade on the PSE. The patron's name will guarantee that the company floated on the PSE has good long-term prospects, which should awake investors' interest in buying the company's shares. Based on the relevant application, the patron is appointed by the Exchange Listing Committee and then entered in the Register of Patrons. The patron also exercises supervision over the issuer's compliance with disclosure duties, not only before admission of an issue to the new market but also throughout the time that the issue is listed on the new market—usually a period of two years, unless the Committee rules otherwise. As in the case of issues on the main and secondary markets, the issuer's financial results must be published on a quarterly basis.

The following is a list of accredited patrons:

- EPIC Securities, a.s.; http://www.epic.cz
- Patria Finance, a.s.; http://www.patria.cz
- Baader Securities, a.s.; http://www.baader.cz
- CA IB Securities, a.s.; http://www.ca-ib.cz

Reporting requirements

Submissions

Under PSE regulations, companies listed on the main and secondary markets must provide the PSE periodically with economic and financial data, including a quarterly profit and loss statement, an audited financial statement, an annual report, and any other information that may be required by the PSE.

Brokers

All PSE members have to report periodically to the PSE about their trading activities and transactions. All transactions with securities traded on SPAD are reported immediately, while transactions with securities outside SPAD are to be reported on the same day only. The SCP publishes a summary of all transfers executed in the market, but without categorizing different deals (all the various types of transactions are mixed together in the daily summary).

Research

Trading reports are available through Reuters, Bloomberg and via the Internet. Many investment banks regularly publish excellent research reports on the Czech Republic, including CA IB Securities, CS First Boston, ING Bank, Patria Finance, Merrill Lynch and Wood Securities.

Most of the useful information such as statistical data, online data, details about trading, securities, members of the PSE, legislation and financial results can be also found on the PSE's web pages. These professionally designed web pages provide users with all necessary updated details concerning the Czech equity capital market and also offer many links to related bodies and subjects in connection with the market.

Summary information

Market capitalization (main and secondary market, end 2000): US$8.13 billion
Market liquidity ratio* (end 2000): 41.8 per cent
Market capitalization as a percentage of nominal GDP (local currency, end 2000): 14.3 per cent (est)
Number of domestic/foreign companies listed (end 2000): 53/0
Market P/E (end 2000): 7.5
Market value as a percentage of nominal GDP (end 2001): 15.8 per cent
MSCI Index (change in US$ terms, 2000): (4.3) per cent
Prime interest rate (three-month Pribor, end 2000): 4.62 per cent
Long-term (three-year) bond yield (end 2000): 6.03 per cent
Budget deficit as a percentage of nominal GDP (est 2000): (3.3) per cent
Annual increase in money (M2) supply (end 2000): 11.8 per cent (est)
Inflation rate (2000): 4.7 per cent
US$ exchange rate (end 1999): CZK36.47

* Total share turnover (full year)/total market capitalization (year end) of main and secondary market.

Developments in equity markets in 2001

During 2001, the PSE experienced several up and downs. Nevertheless, by the end of December, the broad-based market index, PX50, had fallen 17.5 per cent from the beginning of the year, while

Table 3.5.5 Year end share price index, price/earnings ratios and yields

Year	*PX50 index*	*P/E*	*Div. yield (%)**
1995	425.9	10.4	1.88
1996	539.6	12.7	1.43
1997	495.3	13.7	1.51
1998	394.2	14.3	1.47
1999	489.7	15.9	0.62
2000	478.5	16.7	0.59
2001	394.6	7.5	6.69

Source: Prague Stock Exchange

*Note: Dividend yield has very poor explanatory value as only a few companies are paying out reasonable dividends

the blue-chip index, PX-D, fell even more by 22 per cent. The main reason behind the steeper fall was a substantial decline in the share prices of Česke Radiokomunikace and Český Telecom. A notable rally of Philip Morris CR shares and banking stocks was not able to offset the negative performance of the telecom companies' shares. In the first quarter of the year, PSE market development was under the influence of other exchanges around the world. It changed in the second quarter when local corporate events became the main driver. As a result of applying the new PSE regulatory rules, according to which non-liquid stocks must be delisted, the number of traded shares and unit trusts declined from 151 to 102 during 2001. This should contribute to overall concentration and better transparency in the local market. The SPAD trading system remained the dominant market segment and even strengthened its position with 96.3 per cent of the total annual equity trading volume (US$3.4 billion) being conducted there, having achieved a share of 92 per cent in 2000. The market capitalization of the seven biggest and most liquid stocks traded in SPAD was CZK284.4 billion (US$7.8 billion) at the end of December 2001, representing 84.1 per cent of the market capitalization of the whole equity market.

Privatization was among the major driving forces in 2001. The State completed the privatization of Česke Radiokomunikace, Komerč ní Banka and Unipetrol. While the sale of Komerč ní Banka was very good for the price that peaked in June at 30.9 per cent above the January level before the contract was announced, the Ceske Radiokomunikace deal was not so positive as it involved a split of the company's activities causing several uncertainties. In addition, the share price also fell due to the two declared dividends totalling CZK430 per share. Except for the dividend, the Unipetrol privatization followed the Česke Radiokomunikace pattern closely and was also not so positive. There are two large privatization deals pending: ČEZ and Český Telecom.

Principal PSE brokers

Baader Securities, a.s.
28. ř íjna 3,110 00, Prague 1
Tel: +420 2/2010 8200; Fax: +420 2/267 751
http://www.baader.cz

CA IB Securities, a.s.
nám. Kinských 2/602, 150 00, Prague 5
Tel: +420 2/5701 6222; Fax: +420 2/5701 6550
http:/www.ca-ib.cz

Credit Suisse First Boston, a.s.
Staromě stské nám. 15,110 01, Prague 1
Tel: +420 2/2108 3111; Fax: +420 2/2108 3444
http://www.csfb.com ÿÿwww.csfb.com

Česká Spoř itelna, a.s.
Václavské nám. 16,110 00, Prague 1
Tel: +420 2/2440 2228–30; Fax. +420 2/2440 2246
http://www.csas.cz

FIO Burzovní Společ nost, a.s.
Rybná 14,110 05, Prague 1
Tel: +420 2/2184 4020; Fax: +420 2/2184 4022
http://http://www.fio.cz

ING Bank N.V., Organizač ní Složka
Pobře žní 3, 186 00, Prague 8
Tel: +420 2/2320 000; +420 2/2320 026
http://www.ingbpb.com

Patria Finance, a.s.
Škrétova 12,120 00, Prague 2
Tel: +420 2/2141 4211; Fax: +420 2/2142 4204
http://www.patria.cz ÿÿwww.patria.cz

Raiffeisen Capital Investment
Václavské, nám. 1,100 00, Prague 1
Tel: +420 2/2440 7806; Fax: +420 2/2440 7806
http://www.rci.cz

Wood & Company, s.r.o.
Martinská 4,110 00, Prague 1
Tel: +420 2/2422 7731; Fax: +420 2/2422 7759
http://www.wood.com

Other important contacts

Prague Stock Exchange
Rybná 14,110 00 Prague 1
Tel: +420 2/2183 2126; Fax: +420 2/2183 3031
http://www.pse.cz

Czech Securities Commission
PO Box 208 Washingtonova 7, 111 21 Prague 1
Tel: +420 2/2109 6111; Fax:+420 2/2421 2879
http://www.sec.cz

RM system
Podvinný mlýn 6,190 00 Prague 9
Tel: +420 2/6619 8111; Fax: +420 2/6619 8607
http://www.rmsystem.cz

UNIVYC
Rybná 14,110 05, Prague 1
Tel: +420 2/2183 2803; Fax: +420 2/2183 3008
http://www.pse.cz/univyc/

3.6

Mergers and Acquisitions

Filip Otruba, Bohdan Malaniuk, Pavel Dedek and Martina Lambert, Corporate Finance, CA IB Financial Advisers

M&A market, 1997–2001

In comparison to other markets in the Central and Eastern European (CEE) geographical region, the Czech market is rather small. However, in M&A activity, the Czech Republic is a key and mature market which is able to attract a large number of investments. Today, almost all large privatization transactions where the State was selling its strategic stakes in key companies have been completed. The privatization of the banking sector was finalized with the sale of Komerč ní Banka to the French Société, Genérale in 2001. However, sales of Český Telecom, Unipetrol and Transgas have not yet been completed. There are only few state-owned companies remaining, such as the Czech Post, Airport, EEZ and Czech railways.

The Czech M&A market has developed significantly since 1997, reflecting the maturing of the market economy in the Czech Republic. A continuous development of domestic transactions is a healthy sign of a growing competitiveness in the Czech market, a maturing corporate outlook and investor confidence. The amount of foreign direct investment (FDI) invested in the Czech Republic since 1997 has confirmed the growing investor confidence (see Table 3.6.1). M&A is no longer an imported phenomenon and has become an indigenous part of corporate culture in the Czech Republic. Another major factor affecting the Czech M&A climate—market transparency—has also increased every year. The number of transactions with disclosed price has increased significantly in the last few years (see Table 3.6.2). The offered price was announced in 35 per cent of cases, in comparison with 28 per cent in 1999, 10 per cent in 1998 and 13 per cent in 1997.

Transaction values

The Czech Republic has been able to attract large and important investments in acquisitions: in 1998, the total value of M&A transaction investments in the Czech Republic was US$748 million; in 1999 US$2.5 billion; in 2000, US$3 billion; and in 2001, US$2.3 billion. Excluding transactions in excess of US$100 million, the average deal size in the Czech Republic shows a consistent decrease, reflecting the increasing proportion of domestic deals, which on average are smaller than cross-border transactions (source: PWC and CA IB analyses).

Domestic and cross-border transactions[1]

In 1997–1998, the number of domestic deals increased significantly faster than cross-border transactions, as factors such as industry consolidation started to gain importance relative to inward

Table 3.6.1 FDI 1997–2001

	1997	*1998*	*1999*	*2000*	*2001*
Net FDI (US$ billion)	3.59	6.23	4.48	4.94	4.82

Table 3.6.2 Disclosed price transactions 1997–2000

	No. of transactions	*Average deal size (US$ million)*	*Average deal size, excl. deals in excess of US$100 million*	*Disclosure rate (%)*
1997	67	64	22	13
1998	77	33	17	10
1999	203	52	15	28
2000	224	31	12	35

Source: PricewaterhouseCoopers

[1]A domestic transaction is where a Czech registered entity is involved in a transaction with another Czech entity. It is classified as a domestic transaction regardless of how that transaction is funded.

A cross-border transaction involves a Czech registered entity and a foreign registered entity, including both outward and inward investment.

ment. The number of cross-border transactions grew and represented largely inward investment. The most active investors into the Czech Republic were the United States, Germany, the United Kingdom and, later, Japan.

The Czech Republic holds second place in the CEE region as a result of transactions successfully closed out in 1999, with a value totalling US$2.5 billion (1998: US$748 million). Moreover, during 2000, the transparency of transactions had dramatically increased. The rate of successfully closed-out cross-border transactions (Czech entity plus foreign entity) was 81 per cent in 1999, 61 per cent in 2000 and 83 per cent in 2001 (see Figure 3.6.1).

Most active sectors

The most active sectors for foreign investments were and still are:

- TMT (telecommunication, media and technology);
- IT;
- banking and financial services;
- manufacturing and food processing industry (food and beverages);
- retail.

TMT sector

In 2001, the most significant and largest transaction in the Czech Republic with a value of US$185 million was successfully closed out in telecommunications. Bivideon BV, a joint-venture between Deutsche Bank and TFC (formerly Tele Danmark and one of the largest providers of communication solutions in Europe) acquired a

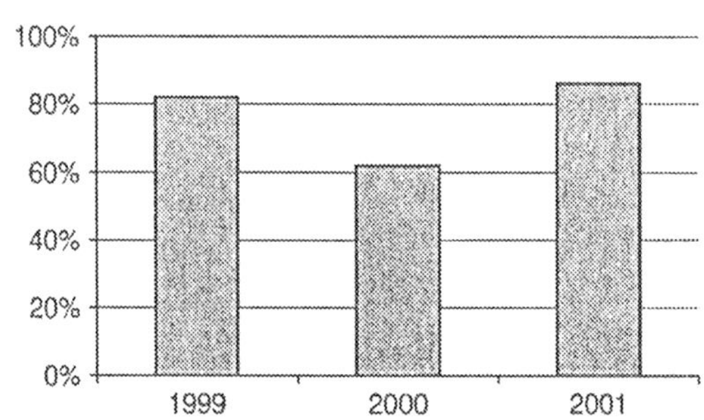

Figure 3.6.1 Rate of successfully closed cross-border transactions, 1999–2001

51 per cent stake in Ceske Radiokomunikace. CA IB acted as an adviser in the transaction on behalf of Bivideon.

Many important acquisitions and changes in ownership took place during 2000: CA IB advised Telekom Austria AG on the acquisition of 100 per cent equity interest in Czech On Line, the largest Czech Internet service provider (ISP); Contactel acquired a commercial network, CESNET, to the value of US$20.3 million; Irish e-Tel acquired 35 per cent in Globix Communications Ltd and become its 100 per cent owner; Advent acquired a majority stake in the ISP SkyNet. Previously, in 1999, Sun Microsystems had acquired NetBeans Czech Republic.

IT sector

There was a shift in IT sector activity during 1999–2000. While the actual number of deals grew, the transaction values were relatively small compared to deals in other industries. CA IB was the adviser in the most significant IT transactions, in which a Czech company found a strategic investor. In 2000, CA IB advised Infinity, a major Czech IT systems integrator and two leading Czech Internet portals, ATLAS.CZ and SEZNAM.CZ.

Banking sector

All large Czech banks have been privatized and sold to strategic partners: in 2001, Komercní Banka was sold to the French Société Genérate; in 2000, the State sold Ceska Sporitelna to Austrian Erste Bank for US$253.7 million; and in 1999, a 66 per cent state stake in CSOB was sold to the Belgian KBC Bank. CA IB advised KBC during this transaction, which had a value of US$1.1 billion. This transaction was the largest M&A transaction in 1998 and the second largest transaction ever contemplated in the Czech Republic.

Food and beverage sector

The food and beverage sector started with a restructuring after privatization. The impetus for restructuring was the change of export market orientation and the growing power of retail chains. The continuing consolidation in the food and beverage sector seems to be a general trend. For example, a significant event in the brewery sector was the acquisition in 1999 of Pilsner Urquell Breweries by South African Breweries (SAB) for US$629 million.

Energy and utilities

In 1990, energy distribution was separated from energy generation and transmission. Later, in the first half of the 1990s, the minority stakes in EEZ, the country biggest state-owned energy company, regional distribution companies (RDCs), gas distribution companies (GDCs) and combined heat and power companies (CHPs) were privatized in a coupon privatization. In the second half of the 1990s, the minority stakes in RDCs and GDCs were concentrated in the hands of strategic investors such as E.ON, RWE, Ruhrgas, Wintershal and VNG.

In the period 1997–2000, CA IB advised the German utility MEAG, part of the RWE Group, on its acquisition of a blocking minority stake in the Northern Bohemian RDC. During the second half of the 1990s, other major independent power producers and combined heat and power companies were also acquired by strategic investors through a number of transactions with municipalities, investment funds, and among strategic investors themselves. Investors operating in the Czech power market include International Power, Horizon, Dalkia, Cinergy and MVV.

In 2001, the Czech government decided on a complete privatization of the electricity and gas supply sector. It succeeded only in gas and signed a contract with RWE (€4.1 billion) and which is currently waiting for anti-monopoly approval. CA IB advised E.ON on a bid for the State's stake in Transgas and its gas supply branch. In the electricity sector, investors did not fulfil the criteria set by the Czech government. The government decided that EEZ would acquire the regional distribution companies from the State in exchange for the transmission grid.

In the water and sewage sector, a number of transactions were executed with investors such as Vivendi, Suez Lyonnaise des Eaux and Anglian Water. CA IB advised Suez Lyonnaise des Eaux on a bid to purchase a majority stake in Severoceske vodovody a kanalizace. The transaction with the highest profile was the sale of a majority stake in the Prague water works (PVK) to Vivendi (CZK 6 billion). CA IB advised International Water on its bid for PVK.

Industrial and manufacturing sector

In the late 1990s, M&A activity in the industrial manufacturing sector grew, reflecting the consolidation of a number of sub-sectors, notably automotive, among, for example, suppliers to Skoda Volkswagen. M&A in 2000 was kicked off by the privatization of a 30 per cent stake in Skoda, the largest Czech car producer and manufacturer, to Volkswagen.

Among examples of deals in this sector, other transactions from 2000 can be mentioned, such as the Skanska acquisition of a 66.6 per cent stake in IPS, the largest Czech construction company, for

US$556.2 million, followed shortly thereafter by Metrostav. In 1999, Veletržní financní sold its 47.24 per cent stake in the Zbrojovka company, a Czech producer of weapons and munitions. In each of the last two deals CA IB acted as an adviser.

Activities in this sector were also driven by domestic investment funds in the Czech Republic (mostly set up during the voucher privatization process), which were forced by changes in legislation to divest their significant stakes in industrial companies. Examples of divestment transactions, in each of which CA IB acted as an adviser, were: Ateso, a Czech car components producer; Metrostav, the third biggest Czech construction company; Juta, a Czech producer and distributor of materials for building and agricultural industry; followed by the privatization and sale of state-owned strategic stakes in Czech companies such as EKD Holding, Škoda Plzee and Poldi Kladno.

Factors driving transactions

Consolidation

During the privatization era, a number of industries have entered a period of consolidation, as evidenced by a secondary wave of private sector transactions between parties in the same industry, including those buying out joint venture partners. Consolidation has been driven largely by increased competition, often following inward investment into the industry, which has forced companies to seek larger market shares and economies of scale. This process has been facilitated by improved access to capital as described below, which made it easier for stronger companies to buy up their weaker competitors.

Tighter bank financing controls

The banking sector has tightened control over borrowing. Increased emphasis has been placed on monitoring loan performance and exposure risks. This tightening has forced some companies and conglomerates to sell off non-core businesses. Škoda Plzen's sale of its subsidiary, Can, to Schmalbach Lubeca AG in 1998 in the Czech Republic is an example of such a transaction. In 2001, CSOB, owned by the Belgian KBC Bank, took over a failed Czech bank, IPB. CSOB bought IPB's assets from the appointed administrator shortly after IPB's collapse on 16 June 2001.

Access to capital

A significant increase in the numbers of domestic transactions is in part due to the improvement in access to capital, available in the form of venture capital, public offerings or banking facilities for successful, growing companies. The increased financial discipline of the banking sector is not affecting these companies adversely—in fact, the increased competition among capital providers is resulting in more favourable financing terms.

Development and position of advisers

In 1999, the M&A market in the Czech Republic was split into 'players and audience'. The main players active in the market are the large North American and European investment banks, due to their size and profitability, together with investment banks focused on the CEE region, such as CA IB. The latter have a very strong position in the Czech Republic due to their know-how, thorough understanding of business development and the legal environment, contacts within the Czech professional community and the state authorities. This expertise guarantees the highest standard of professionalism. Major players in investment banking are identified in Figure 3.6.2.

Market development

Privatization of the major industries and sectors is almost complete. The closing of Czech privatization and consolidation in most industry sectors will have a significant impact on the M&A market and its development. There will be fewer transactions with a smaller average value concluded in the future and therefore the large North American and West European global investment banks are more likely to leave the Czech market. The market will be divided among regional investments banks and boutiques. Some of the current advisers will also leave due to the consolidation of advisory services in the Czech Republic.

The remaining advisers will focus their activities on advising venture capital funds or large global companies during divestitures and the restructuring of their assets in cross-border or outward investments.

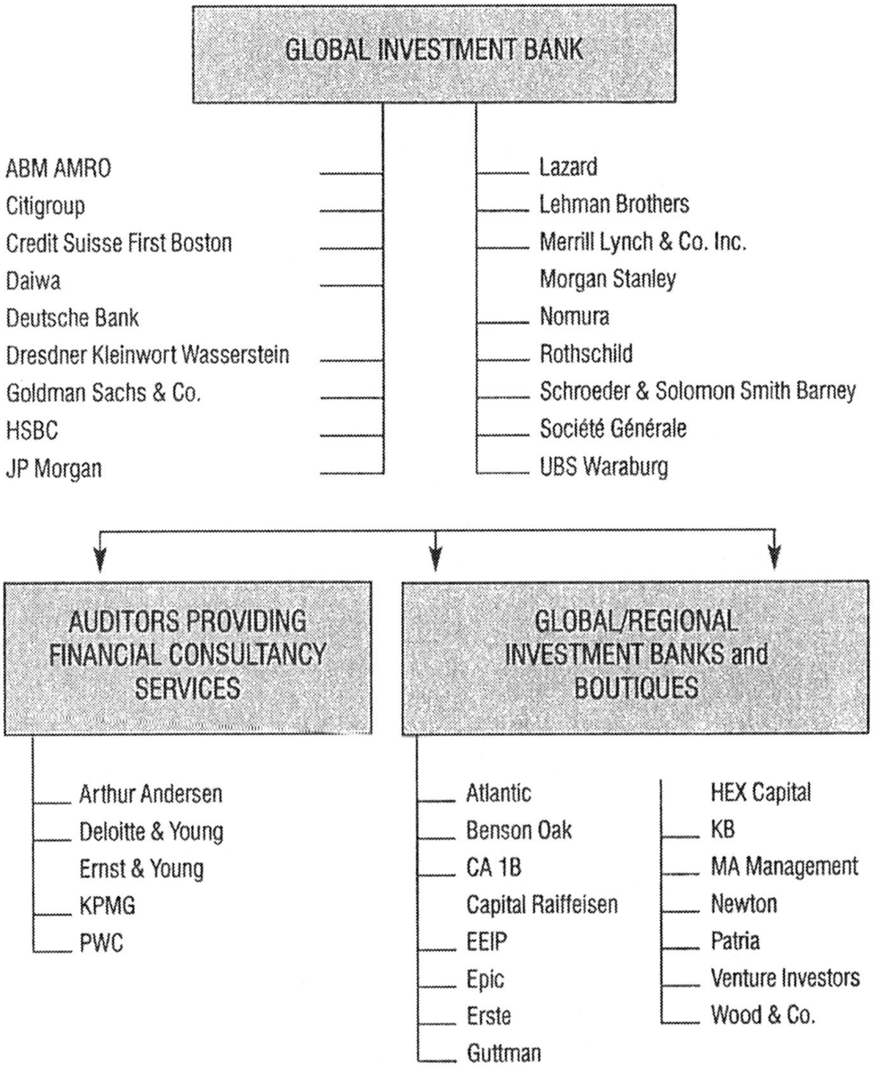

Figure 3.6.2 Major players in investment banking

3.7

Privatization: A Progress Report

Jiri Hrbacek, Head of Corporate Finance, ABN Amro, Prague Branch

Year end summary (2001/2002)

While 2001 was important because of the completion of the privatization of the Czech banking sector, the main feature of early 2002 was the privatization of the gas and chemical industries.

The government completed the process of privatization of the Czech banking sector by selling its 60 per cent share in Komercní Banka to Société Générale for CZK1.186 billion. The privatization of Ceské Radiokomunikace was also completed in the second half of 2001. The government decided to privatize the company by selling it directly to Bivideon BV, based on the results of the September 2001 tender. Bivideon BV paid CZK6.8 billion for a 51 per cent shareholding. As the key transaction settlement conditions of approval by each of the Office for Protection of Economic Competition and the European Commission were met, the privatization of Ceské Radiokomunikace was completed in November 2001.

The privatization of Karlovarská Becherovka, a.s. was completed in the same period. Altogether, 59 per cent of the company's shares were sold to SALB, s.r.o. for CZK1.377 billion. The government decided to use the income generated by the privatization of Karlovarská Becherovka, a. s. towards funding the pension, health and employment insurance programmes.

The final stage of privatization of Ceská Pojiščovna was also completed before the end of 2001 with the financial group PPF, a. s. buying a 30.25 per cent shareholding for CZK3.871 billion.

Electricity and gas sectors

In August 2001, the government appointed its consultants for the privatization of the electricity and gas sectors; also in the same month, potential strategic investors were invited to express their interest in buying the state shares in each of these industries. Subsequently, the government decided to sell the gas companies to German-based RWE Gas and to postpone the privatization of the electricity sector.

The companies interested in the privatization of CEZ (electricity company), the transmission system and the state shares in six distribution companies were Electrabel s.a., EDF International, a consortium of Enel SpA and Iberdrola SA and a consortium of NRG Energy Inc. and International Power plc. The government was supposed to select a new strategic owner by the end of 2001. However, as many experts predicted, the price offered for the companies to be privatized did not reach the level expected by the government by reason of the strict and constraining contractual conditions imposed on the potential investor. The selected candidates were invited by the government to increase their bids, but none of them were prepared to pay the CZK200 billion price targeted by the government. As a result, the government decided to cancel the tender.

In contrast, the government selection of the new strategic owner for the gas sector before the end of 2001 signalled the biggest privatization transaction in Central and Eastern Europe that year. The state shareholding of 97 per cent in Transgas, a. s. and the state shareholdings in eight regional gas distribution companies were sold to RWE Gas AG for €4.1 billion, a price which exceeded the government's expectations. Through successful privatization, the Czech government expected to receive adequate income for the state budget and also wanted to secure the competitiveness and stability of the gas sector, to create a liberalized gas market in compliance with the EU principles, to achieve optimum prices of gas for end users and to ensure reliable and effective supplies of natural gas.

A good starting point for the selection of the strategic owner of the Czech gas sector was the fact that altogether nine highly reputable, well-established and trustworthy gas companies wished to be involved in the privatization of the industry, including DUKE Energy, E.ON Energie AG, Edison Gas SpA, Gas Invest a.s., the consortium of Gaz de France, Ruhrgas AG and Snam SpA and the consortium of RWE Gas AG and Wintershall AG. ABN AMRO, the financial adviser to the National Property Fund and the Czech government, recommended RWE Gas AG to be the tender winner on the basis that it offered the highest price for the state shares and accepted the government's contractual conditions ensuring stability, successful growth and competitiveness of the companies to be privatized. In December 2001, the government confirmed that RWE's bid was the best and the purchase agreement was signed in January 2002. The transaction is subject to approval by the Office for Protection of Economic Competition (of the Czech Republic). If the transaction is approved by the Czech anti-monopoly office, it will become the biggest gas industry privatization transaction in the 'Emerging Europe' region to date.

Chemical and petrochemical industries

The Czech chemical and petrochemical industries were scheduled for privatization at the same time as the privatization of the electricity and gas sectors. In privatizing the chemical sector, the government again set numerous constraining conditions.

Altogether, nine companies showed preliminary interest in the privatization of the 62.99 per cent state shareholding in Unipetrol, a. s. in late 2001. The following companies were put on a shortlist and invited to take part in an in-depth audit: the consortia of Agip, Conoco and Shell; MOL with TVK; ÖMV with Agrofert Holding and Rotch Energy. Binding bids were then presented by the British-based Rotch Energy, the Austrian-Czech-Hungarian consortium MOL, TVK, ÖMV and the company Agrofert. The government decided to sell 62.99 per cent of Unipetrol, a. s. shares to Agrofert Holding, a. s. for €361 million and the agreement for the sale of the state shareholding in Unipetrol, a. s. was signed in February 2002.

Ceský Telecom

In November 2001, the Czech government decided to sell at least 51.1 per cent of the state shares in Ceský Telecom, a.s., which provides services to 3.84 million clients and whose net profits in 2001 totalled CZK 6.1 billion. The shareholding to be sold was supposed to be made up either exclusively by shares held by the National Property Fund or partly by shares held by the National Property Fund and partly by shares held by TelSource NV, depending on a TelSource NV decision to be taken in compliance with the

Cooperation Agreement made by the National property Fund, TelSource NV, KPN Telecom BV and Swisscom AG in June 2001. If TelSource NV decided to take part in the tender through its shares, the shareholding made up by the shares held by the National Property Fund and TelSource NV would reach as much as 78.1 per cent.

During stage one of the tender, the National Property Fund received letters of interest from eight potential investors including consortia. Having evaluated preliminary bids, the Coordination Committee for Privatization decided to invite seven potential investors to the next stage. In February 2002, the due diligence process commenced, during which the candidates could visit data locations, attend presentations by company management and meetings dealing with the agreement on the purchase of shares. In the second half of April, the Czech government held negotiations with two consortia—the Deutsche Bank group, Danish-based operator TDC and the Blackstone Group on the one side and the alliance of Swisscom, CVS Capital Partners and Spectrum Equity Partners on the other. The finance minister, Jiri Rusnok, stated that at that stage the bids presented by both candidates were about 5–10 per cent above the market price for the 51 per cent package of shares. In late March 2001, the market capitalization of Ceský Telecom was about CZK108 billion, so that the price of the state package plus a 10 per cent bonus would be about CZK60 billion. At the end of the tender process, the government negotiated only with the Deutsche Bank group, TDC and the Blackstone Group consortium. The consortium's bid ended at CZK55 billion, which did not meet the expectations of the government. Therefore, on 29 April 2002, the government decided to postpone the privatization of Ceský Telecom.

The postponed privatizations of the telecommunications and electricity sectors are expected to be completed during 2003.

Part Four

Key Sectors of Industry and Business

4.1

Metallurgy and Metalworking Production[1]

Vladimir Toman, Chairman of the Ferrous Metallurgy Strategic Development Department and Josef Klofac, Metal Materials Department, Ministry of Industry and Trade of the Czech Republic[1]

Introduction and historical overview

The production of iron and steel in today's Czech Republic has a long tradition dating back several centuries. The majority of production companies currently operating in the ferrous metallurgy branch were established as long ago as the 1850s. Until 1989, metallurgical companies delivered most of their production (particularly steel seamless tubes) as payment for oil and natural gas supplies from the Soviet Union and as an equivalent for the deliveries of other goods from different countries. After 1989, this market disappeared for metallurgical companies and it was therefore necessary to turn to other, more demanding markets. It was inevitable that these markets would have to face not only new delivery conditions but also the consequences of stipulated antidumping measures coming from the European Union (gradually applied on seamless tubes, thick metal plates, foundry pig-iron etc).

The biggest inter-annual steel production decrease was reached in 1991, but since then the production volume measured as a representative amount of raw steel production volume has succeeded in maintaining the branch as a whole at an annual production level of

[1] The content for this chapter was supplied by the PP Agency in Prague.

between 6.2 million and 6.5 million tonnes. The overall decline in steel production was 40 per cent as measured against 1989, with the drop occurring over a two-year period—although there was no serious restructuring taking place either in metallurgical production as a whole or within individual companies. With regard to general indicators, the annual share in the 1990s of the ferrous metallurgy branch can be characterized as 1.4 per cent-2.4 per cent of GDP, 5 per cent of total industrial production, and 4 per cent of the economically active workforce in industry.

Reforming the metallurgy sector

In 1990–1991, a comprehensive restructuring study of the ferrous metallurgy branch was undertaken. The study took into account the experience of the implementation of similar programmes by several EU countries and established several basic premises for future development of the industry in the Czech Republic, including:

- realization of the restructuring of the companies in combination with considerable modernization of the production basis and ecologizing of production;
- achieving production parameters according to the limits of the European Union, which were valid in the ecological area at that time;

Table 4.1.1 Basic metallurgy production in the Czech Republic, 1989–1998 ('000 tonnes per year)

	1989	*1990*	*1991*	*1992*	*1993*	*1994*	*1995*	*1996*	*1997*	*1998*
Pig-iron	6369	6106	5317	5086	4655	5267	5274	4898	5195	4981
Raw steel in metallurgy	10,223	9698	7597	7082	6543	6845	6749	6259	6496	6220
Raw steel in the Czech Republic—total	10,723	10,098	7964	7322	6776	7085	7184	6509	9750	6498
Rolled material	8166	7752	6200	5796	5503	5811	5975	5585	5777	5400

Note: Production of steel in ferrous metallurgical companies with respect to the Czech Republic on an annual basis is 300,000 to 500, 000 higher.

Table 4.1.2 Basic metallurgical production in the Czech Republic, 1989–1998 (%). 1989 is taken as the base year, at 100 per cent

	1989	*1990*	*1991*	*1992*	*1993*	*1994*	*1995*	*1996*	*1997*	*1998*
Pig-iron	100	94.56	83.13	79.52	72.77	82.34	82.46	76.58	81.22	77.87
Raw steel in the Czech Republic—total	100	94.86	74.31	69.27	64.00	66.96	66.01	61.22	63.54	60.84
Rolled material	100	94.93	75.92	70.64	67.39	71.16	70.60	68.39	70.74	66.13

- achieving such productivity of labour which could be compared with the competitive companies in the metallurgical branch in Europe and in the world as well;
- entering into the privatization process effectively and hence operating companies which were modernized in such a way.

It was considered necessary within the Czech Republic for the State to have considerable involvement in the programme if it were to be realized successfully. The proposed programme was changed by government decision in 1992, which meant that the companies would first have to be privatized and that it should be the new private owners themselves who would perform the restructuring and ecologization. Furthermore, the companies should search for their own strategic partners. However, considering the given privatization parameters, it proved very difficult for the companies to perform the entire process of restructuring on their own while maintaining optimal deadlines.

Priority trends for further development of metallurgical companies were defined in virtue of the chosen approach towards the restructuring of metallurgical companies:

- privatization of the companies;
- change of organizational structure in the metallurgical companies (the independence of non-productive activities, besides that of the metallurgical companies);
- certification of production (in order to provide supplies for the advanced markets), including certificates in accordance with the ISO 14000 standards;
- construction of ZPO (machinery for flow steel casting) in order to achieve the largest possible production volume of steel cast in ZPO—as far as the objective conditions were concerned, its share should reach 90 per cent–95 per cent;
- discontinuance of steel production in Siemens-Martin furnaces;
- ecologization of production in all areas, with the emphasis on environmental areas;
- concentration of production on new and modernized production aggregates and discontinuance of obsolete and economically ineffective aggregates.

Results of the implementation of individual trends of the development

All metallurgical companies in the Czech Republic have either been privatized or are undergoing the process, with the exception of Nova Hut, a.s. (in which the State has kept a 49 per cent share) and Vitkovice, a.s. (in which the State has kept a 67 per cent share). The government is still considering the divestiture of state equity in these companies. During the 1990s, five production facilities for flow steel casting (ZPO) with total annual capacity of 5.1 million tonnes were put into operation. Another was added in 1999, with a capacity of 0.9 million tonnes. The total volume of steel casting reached 6.3 million tonnes per year by early 2000. The construction of the aforementioned six ZPOs required investments of approximately CZK7.5 billion (US$250 million).

During the 1990s, the modernization programme of ferrous metallurgy, excluding the aforementioned ZPO programme, included the following individual technological stages of production:

- General refurbishment of four blast furnaces. Consequently, this enabled discontinuance of the operation of the blast furnace company Vitkovice, a.s., in Ostrava in September 1998 (which included three blast furnaces, agglomeration zones and coking plants), which also carried with it indispensable ecological objectives. The capacity of operating blast furnaces amounts to 5.1 million tonnes per year.
- Reconstructions and modernization of coke batteries in the companies Nova Hut, a.s. in Ostrava and Trinecke Zelezarny (Trinec Ironworks), a.s. in Trinec; two coking batteries were closed down.
- Reconstruction of all currently operating agglomerations in order to meet the requirements of the Act on the Environment.
- In the sphere of raw steel production, there was a reduction in capacity from 10.3 million tonnes in 1989 to 8.4 million tonnes by the end of the 1990s. During the stated period, there was a considerable reduction of annual capacities in Siemens-Martin furnaces, from 1.775 million tonnes to 1.20 million tonnes and a moderate decrease in the capacity of electrical arc furnaces; a major increase in the oxygen converter capacity was achieved. The total number of functioning steel aggregates in the field of ferrous metallurgy had decreased by the end of the 1990s to half of the total of 1989.

- In the production of rolled materials, there was a slight reduction in the number of operating rolling tracks, from 39 to 35, and the annual production volume was cut back from 9.5 million tonnes in 1989 to 8.9 million tones in 1999.
- In the Czech Republic, steel production by oxygen processes represents the major share of total steel production—at approximately 88 per cent—whereas the share of electrical processes in total steel production reached 10.5 per cent in the late 1990s, which represents approximately one-third of the level of surrounding countries.
- The workforce in the ferrous metallurgy branch fell from approximately 128,000 to 59,000. Some employees left the industry as a result of reorganization in the various companies, and others due to the drop in production and to implementation of new technologies. The process of separation of non-productive activities is not yet fully complete, however, and it is due to this development that it is not possible to consider the value of the indicator 'steel production per worker per year' as satisfactory. The latter indicator was obtained by simply dividing total steel production by the number of employees. The real productivity, based on the actual number of workers engaged directly in production, is approximately 70 per cent higher than the value obtained in the process of simple arithmetical division of the two numerical statistics.
- The ecologizing of metallurgical production was qualified by the high level of finances that were invested in the emissions reduction programme. Furthermore, three productive companies have already received ecological certificates in accordance with ISO 14000 standards.

Main objectives for the future

The basic trends for the development of the production basis in the ferrous metallurgical branch can be expressed in the following way:

- to complete the ZPO programme in order to achieve the aimed-for share of the steel cast through ZPOs, which is 90–95 per cent of total production volume;
- to increase the use of scrap iron and scrap steel as important secondary materials;
- to further concentrate the production of rolled material in the modernized aggregates;

- after an analysis of BAT (best available technologies) requirements has been performed, to suggest a plan for their fulfilment in individual technological stages while respecting the conditions of the economics of metallurgical production;
- to achieve the level of today's advanced countries in the metallurgical branch in steel production volume per worker.

Introduction to metalworking production in the Czech Republic

Metalworking production in the Czech Republic is characterized by an above-average growth in labour productivity and exports. Currently, the metalworking industry provides finishing to more sophisticated machinery and equipment for the sectors of investment, general and transport engineering and for the electrical industry, and belongs among the follow-up sectors in the metallurgical industry. The tradition and inventiveness of the people of the Czech Republic enabled bridging over the transformation period and successful continuation in the development of the sector. After a decline in production of the metalworking industry at the beginning of the economic transformation in the early 1990s, an upturn took place as of 1994 and the metalworking production sector is currently witnessing positive development trends, as is indicated by the overall data.

Industry structure

The metalworking industry is characterized by a relatively high diversification of products manufactured by a considerable number of domestic producers (there are 1600 companies registered in the metalworking industry). The product range and the production activity of the sector are represented by the branches of Section 28 of the NACE coding:

28.1 Metal structures represent a typical supplementary product used in the construction industry as an important element of bridge structures and various building structures. In engineering production, metal structures are an important part of investment units. Czech firms supplied metal structures at home and abroad as long ago as the 19th century. The production is provided by more than 200 firms.

28.2 Reservoirs, tanks and containers represent a simple type of engineering production with low added value following up from the Czech metallurgical industry. The nature of this production, which does not require (in particular for the manufacture of reservoirs and containers) any large investments, is reflected in the number of firms doing business in the sector. Concerned is a single piece or final type of production. The development of this sector directly depends on the situation in the government's investment construction policy.
28.3 Steam boilers. This is one of the essential sectors of Czech investment engineering, with long and ongoing tradition based on experience, high-quality research and development background and experienced design firms. The final stage is provided by engineering and assembly firms carrying out deliveries of power industry investment units at home as well as abroad. The production in this sector in the case of complete investment units is characterized by a high share of national labour. Diversification in the sector is the lowest for the whole of the metalworking industry.
28.4 Forging, stamping and other types of forming. This is, in fact, an in-between stage of metalworking production to prepare semi-finished products for subsequent finishing, further processing or use as components. Forging has a long tradition in the Czech Republic.
28.5 Surface finishing of metals is a sector common to all engineering firms since the resultant quality and the lifespan of any engineering product depends on the quality of surface finishing.
28.6 Cutlery, tools and ironmongery. The sector includes tools for manual handicraft, for forming and working various materials and for other purposes. The sector is characterized by the largest diversification. Its production is registered in more than 550 organizations.
28.7 Other metal products include primarily products of metallurgical secondary production originating from a developed metallurgical base and comprised mainly of manufacture of drawn wires, wire products, connecting material, chains and springs.

Position of the metalworking industry within the processing industry

During the late 1990s, the metalworking industry was contributing almost 8 per cent of total sales of products and services for the processing industry as a whole and 8.6 per cent to total added value and 9.6 per cent in the overall workforce. A major advantage of the metalworking industry is that it is virtually non-dependent on imports of raw materials. A major part of raw materials is comprised of steel from Czech manufacturers. The producer-customer chains with steelworks in production of sophisticated products have been retained, eg semi-finished products from Trinecke Zelezarny, a.s. (Trinec Ironworks) are processed by wire drawing in ZDB, a.s., in Bohumin. This applies similarly to semi-finished products from non-ferrous metals: copper and aluminium.

Main features of the metalworking industry

Between 1990 and 1994, essential changes took place in the structure of the production base of the metalworking industry, primarily leading to a significant decline in production. The country's good trading positions on the eastern markets were taken by competitors, which used the ignorance of newly established Czech producers and exporters and pushed them out of the markets. The substitutive exports to the European Union and other markets only partially and gradually compensated for the decline in sales.

The conversion of the armament industry also brought about a reduced demand for metalworking. As a result of the privatization process, many firms lost their bonds with the sales and supplier network. Many firms had difficulty finding an optimal ownership structure and some firms became subject to mere speculations. Those firms that found a real owner, whether domestic or foreign, began to restructure their production and look for new customers. Success soon arrived and between 1995 and 1998 production began to grow and exports were redirected to the EU countries.

All main industrial firms were privatized primarily into joint-stock companies or limited liability companies. The share of the State in this sector is currently below one per cent. The structure of the production base by company size, shares of size groups on total sales, added value and number of employees in 1997 is shown in Table 4.1.3.

Main economic indicators

The sales for products and services in nominal prices developed positively. A high growth rate of production was returned in tools, cutlery and ironmongery. Total sales in the metalworking industry have doubled since 1994. Furthermore, up to 1995, positive trends in the metalworking industry were attained by reduction of the workforce.

Table 4.1.3 Production description in 1997 by size groups—NACE 28 (CZK million)

Persons per company	0–9	10–49	50–249	250–999	over 1000
Sales for products and services	20,009	27,831	33,905	24,337	9692
Added value	4573	7766	9096	7759	2807
Number of employees	22,614	29,542	41,647	31,148	10,413

Source: Czech Statistical Office, calculation by the Ministry of Industry and Trade

Since then, the number of employees has grown along with the rise in labour productivity. The metalworking industry has been affected by the change in foreign trade orientation from the former COMECON countries, which formerly absorbed most of the production, to newly acquired markets. The strongest foreign trade orientation is currently towards Germany, Slovakia and Austria. The traditional markets of the former COMECON countries and developing countries should be constantly observed by producers with respect to the possibilities of recovering these customers. Throughout the monitored period, the metalworking industry returned a positive balance of foreign trade.

International comparison and competitiveness

The metalworking industry has been gradually restructured to increase its competitiveness. At the same time, in order to survive, it has had to change its orientation from the originally simple eastern markets to developed western customers. The execution of this step has been successful and at present the largest share of exports is directed to the European Union. Due to the recovery of these markets, further growth may be expected and exports to EU countries are continuing to grow. Products coming from the metalworking production sector in the Czech Republic are, for the most part, competitive and of good quality, which can be maintained in the future only through research and development.

Conclusion

Metalworking production, as the basic building brick in the processing industry, has a positive development trend and a jump in its growth by 12–16 per cent is expected upon the accession of the Czech Republic to the European Union. This assumption is based largely on access to a larger market and removal of trade barriers for products that are otherwise competitive. The level of national self-sufficiency has been practically constant at around 70 per cent. This proves that the Czech Republic can successfully withstand foreign competition on the domestic market.

4.2

Oil and Gas Industry[1]

Miloš Podrazil, General Manager, Czech Association of the Petroleum Industry and Trade; and Trade Partners UK

Introduction to the petroleum industry

Since 1990, the petroleum industry and accompanying trade in the Czech Republic has undergone a process of restructuring and privatization, culminating in the entry of international oil companies into the refineries at Litvínov and Kralupy—merged into a single entity, Česká Rafinérská, Litvínov joint-stock company—and also the breaking up of the monopoly of the former Benzina state enterprise in fuels and lubricants distribution. The oil refineries at Kolín and Pardubice were privatized simultaneously into the legal form of joint-stock companies. The Ostramo state enterprise refinery, which processed used lubricating oils, was privatized by a direct sale. These changes had a positive effect on the organizational, technical and economic level of the refinery industry and trade. The oil products market underwent a process of consistent liberalization, during which large international oil companies made a vigorous push into business in the Czech Republic's marketplace. As a result, the limited domestic market became an object of their competitive struggles. This situation was reflected in the increasing share of imported foreign products on the domestic market and the growing number of foreign companies' service stations.

In the late 1990s, imports accounted for 50 per cent of total sales of the chief commodities. At that point, foreign distributing companies held a 26 per cent share in the network of public petrol stations. This was due to the low competitiveness of domestic refineries, which lacked an efficient oil cracking operation and, as a result, also effectiveness in the processing of oil into demand products.

[1] The first section of this chapter was supplied by the PP Agency, Prague.

Talks with international oil companies

In September 1994, the government agreed to open talks with international oil companies (IOCs) on their entry into the amalgamated refineries of Litvínov and Kaučuk. The IOCs were comprised of the British-Dutch Shell complex, US Conoco, Italian Petroli and, originally, Total. The government also agreed to create a new organizational structure enabling the former fragmented entities to form a refinery and petrochemical unit that was both competitive and financially strong. In essence, the new organization was to create a structure of the holding type (Unipetrol joint-stock company), with the chief producers and distributors in the Czech Republic's refinery and oil industry becoming its subsidiaries. It was also decided to establish the Česká Rafinérská (ČR) joint-stock company from the refinery divisions of the Chemopetrol joint-stock company (Litvínov refinery) and Kaučuk joint-stock company (Kralupy refinery). At the time, the foreign companies refused to enter the Chemopetrol and Kaučuk petrochemical companies as a singular entity.

The setting up of ČR, a.s. and the successful finding of a strategic partner created conditions for the Czech refinery industry to be competitive and to further develop, and thus ensure raw material sources for the petrochemical and agrochemical sectors. The signing of final contracts by Unipetrol, a.s., Chemopetrol, a.s., Kaucuk, a.s. and ČR, a.s. and the Czech government (Ministry of Trade and Industry) with the IOCs (Shell Overseas Investments, Conoco Energy Company, AGIP Petroli International) on their entry into the ČR joint-stock company (the two largest domestic refineries) in November 1995 completed the second stage of the restructuring and privatization of the refinery industry.

The Czech Republic expected this process to effectively launch the long-prepared modernization of the refineries, in order to help strengthen their strategic trade stability, bring know-how, consolidate their position on the domestic market and support their expansion into neighbouring markets. By subsequently increasing basic assets of ČR by US$173 million, the foreign investors gained 19 per cent of the company's stock. In the new joint operation (ČR, a.s.), the companies have been independent entities, each holding 16.3 per cent of the stock. The remainder (ie 51 per cent of the shares) is owned by the Unipetrol joint-stock company of Kralupy nad Vltavou.

Privatization of Benzina state enterprise

The former Benzina state enterprise was privatized in two stages. In the first, about 180 service stations were sold to private Czech entities within the programme known as small businesses privatization while another 40 went into private hands either on the basis of competitive privatization projects or in restitution claims. In the second stage of privatization, the Benzina state enterprise was transformed into two joint-stock companies. One was Benzina Praha, which today operates 339 petrol stations as its main line of business. The other was Čepro, Praha. This joint-stock company operates a network of pipelines and fuel terminals, protects stocks of fuels and lubricants for the state material stocks, and is involved in wholesaling. The company also operates a small local network of petrol stations situated close to the terminals. The reduced Benzina state enterprise continued as the owner of the property still remaining to be privatized (primarily service stations and some warehouses) and also assumed the obligations of the former state enterprise. The quick and complete privatization of the remaining petrol stations was considered a priority.

Involvement of the National Property Fund

After the split of the Czech and Slovak Federal Republic, a new joint-stock company, Petrotrans, Kralupy nad Vltavou came into being on 1 January 1993 to take over the operation of the Czech section of the Friendship (Druzhba) oil pipeline from the Transpetrol, Bratislava joint-stock company. Subsequently, Petrotrans merged with Chemopetrol-IKL Ltd, which was constructing the Ingolstadt-Kralupy-Litvínov (IKL) oil pipeline. The company changed its name to MERO-ČR, a.s. The merged company constructed the MERO-IKL oil pipeline, putting it into operation in 1996, at a total cost of CZK14 billion, which was provided mostly by the National Property Fund (FNM).

The new oil pipeline eliminated the dependence of Czech refineries on one source and enabled them to buy crude oil at a desired quality and optimum commercial terms. The project can be evaluated as one of the most important steps taken by the Czech government since the beginning of the economic transformation. For strategic reasons, the MERO, Kralupy nad Vltavou and Čepro, Praha joint-stock companies are 100 per cent owned by the FNM

ČR. A major share of the stock of Paramo, Pardubice has remained the property of the FNM ČR, although it is possible that it will be privatized in the future. A majority share of the Koramo, Kolín joint-stock company was sold to Chemapol Group, a.s., with a smaller part going to banks. In addition, the FNM ČR has retained a 26 per cent stake in the company.

In 1997, ČR, a.s. shareholders took the important decision to modernize the Litvínov refinery, and subsequently also the one in Kralupy. A visbreaking unit was installed in Litvínov and put into operation at the end of 1999. An oil-cracking unit—with a fluid catalytic cracking process currently under construction at the Kralupy refinery—was scheduled to start operating during 2001. Once the cracking unit is put into operation, the fuel yield from oil will be significantly raised to the level of state-of-the-art European refineries. This will increase the economic efficiency of oil processing in the Czech Republic and substantially strengthen the competitiveness of ČR, a.s. on the domestic as well as Central European markets.

Recent trends in privatization and restructuring in the petroleum sector

The Czech government recently adopted important decisions on the restructuring and privatization of the remaining parts of a number of oil companies. First of all, it chose the winner of a tender to determine the assignee in the privatization of a 70.87 per cent stake in Paramo a.s.and Unipetrol a.s., Kralupy nad Vltavou enterprises. The approved offer guarantees continuation of oil processing in the existing range and volume of products, modernization and technology development for the production of lubricating oils and asphalts, achieving synergetic effects from product linkage with the ČR joint-stock company, and improving the level of distribution capacities.

The government also dealt with, and approved, the position of the Čepro, Praha joint-stock company in guaranteeing the State's interests in oil products. According to the appertaining resolution, the government agreed to preserve the present structure of the company, with 100 per cent of the stock remaining in the hands of the FNM ČR. The government also dealt with the Unipetrol, Kralupy nad Vltavou joint-stock company and approved a blueprint for the restructuring and privatization of the refineries and petrochemical industry of the Czech Republic.

Items which have yet to be privatized in the Czech refinery industry and trade include about 180 service stations, which are operated by what remains of the Benzina state enterprise, now in control of an almost 5.5 per cent share of the domestic fuels market. In 1997, the government adopted a resolution on declaring a public tender to sell these stations. However, the tender was unsuccessful, and since then no new decision has been made on the privatization of this property. A 26 per cent share of the stock remains to be privatized in the Koramo, Kolín joint-stock company, an oil refinery that does not process crude. Instead, semi-finished products from the Litvínov refinery are supplied as the raw material for production of lubricating oils. No decision has been taken to complete the privatization of this company either. To some extent, the situation is influenced by the fact that a majority share of the stock is tied up in the a.s. Chemapol Group bankruptcy estate.

Adoption of European standards

In 2000, the Czech Republic became a member of the International Energy Agency. The granting of full membership was largely due to the adoption of legislation on setting up and maintaining strategic stocks of oil and oil products, and also the country's quick response to the requirement for providing statistical data on the oil market. Domestic producers follow the trends of EU countries with regard to the quality and range of refinery products. The sale of leaded petrol for cars was prohibited as of 1 January 2001. Petrol and diesel oil meeting quality indicators according to Directive 98/70/EC, and fuel oils corresponding to the provisions of Directive 99/32/EC, all of which are made in the Czech Republic, will be marketed from 1 January 2003.

A process of network concentration has been underway in the sector of distribution companies and petrol station operators, which will continue with high intensity for three to four years. In tandem, the number of stations, their facilities and services will be stabilized at levels corresponding to European standards. Decisive positions will be held by strong foreign trademark companies and a.s. Benzina. As a result of these changes and developments, oil supplies to domestic refineries have been diversified since 1996, and in addition the capacity of the MERO-IKL and Friendship pipelines is sufficient for domestic oil consumption, including in the long term.

Concluding comments on the oil industry and refinery products

The refinery products market is a branch with good prospects in the Czech Republic. The analyses worked out justify the assumption of a rise in demand for fuels in road and air transport, and for petrochemical raw materials. The growth trend will depend on the economic situation and the purchasing power of the population. Amid this, changes in ownership rights, which can hardly be predicted, are possible in the existing ownership structure of shares in private companies. Share transfers are limited to some degree by the contract between the State, Unipetrol and the foreign owners in the Česká Rafinérská joint-stock company. Significant share transfers within a.s. Unipetrol, in which FNM ČR has a 63 per cent holding, will also be subject to government endorsement.

The oil industry and accompanying trade in the Czech Republic is and will continue to be subject to strong competitive pressure from foreign refineries (Slovnaft Bratislava, Austria's OMV Schwechat and the German refineries in Leuna and Ingolstadt). The industry's position in this competitive environment will be strengthened by completing the modernization of the Kralupy refinery (construction of a fluid catalytic cracking unit), by taking advantage of synergy between domestic producers and distribution companies, by rationalization of the service station network, and by optimum trade policies. By the time of the Czech Republic's admission to the European Union, domestic producers will have no substantial problems in adapting to the EU countries' standards of business conditions in the oil industry. The range and quality of fuels meets European standards. With regard to the expected growth in the consumption of fuels and semi-finished petrochemical products, the prospects of the oil industry and trade in the Czech Republic are favourable in the medium term.

Gas industry

In the same way as the petroleum industry, and discussed in the previous section, the gas sector in the Czech Republic was restructured in the early 1990s. This led to the creation of Transgas, responsible for importing, transiting and supplying gas to distribution companies and storage. Responsibility for distribution was given to eight regional distribution companies. Transgas is also responsible for transiting gas primarily from Russia into Western markets via the Czech Republic. The Czech government is planning to privatize a majority stake of the fully state-owned Transgas and all of the regional distribution companies, in which foreign shareholders have stakes of varying sizes. It is expected that this will coincide with privatization of the electricity sector. As a preliminary step, Transgas has recently been turned into a joint-stock company.

Imports

Gas is imported primarily from Russia and Norway. In 1999, some 9.2 billion cubic metres of gas was imported to be sold in the Czech Republic. This supply was dominated by Russian exports from Gazprom/Gazexport. Imports from Norway were provided by Statoil, Norsk Hyrdo, Saga Petroleum and Total Norge. A small amount of gas was imported from Wintershall, Germany. Transgas has entered into long-term contracts with Russian and Norwegian suppliers for gas imports. A 15-year 'take or pay' contract with Gazprom/Gazexport commits the company to import a set volume of gas each year. The volume imported is re-calculated annually based on economic factors. A separate contract with the Norwegian consortium agrees that Transgas will import 53 billion cubic metres of gas over 20 years from 1997.

Transmission

Transgas is also responsible for transiting gas from Russia into Western Europe. In 1999, Transgas had contractual responsibility to transit some 54 billion cubic metres of gas across the Czech Republic. In 1999, Transgas signed a long-term transit agreement with Gazprom/Gazexport. Building on an existing contract, Transgas guarantee that transit gas levels will be maintained at 28 billion cubic metres annually until 2008 and a volume of at least 13 billion cubic metres will be maintained until 2020 with an option to increase this further. Transgas also has transit agreements with Verbundnetz Leipzig, Wintershall Kassel and Ruhrgas Essen. Gas imported for sale within the Czech Republic is transited through domestic pipelines to the gas distribution companies and into underground gas storage facilities.

Distribution

Since 1990, eight regional distribution companies (RDCs) have held responsibility for gas distribution. The RDCs cover the same regions as the electricity distribution companies (see Table 4.2.1) and are monopoly suppliers in their individual areas. All the distributors rely on Transgas for gas supplies.

Table 4.2.1 Regional gas distribution companies

SouthBohemia	Jihoceska Plynarenska
South Moravia	Jihomoravska Plynarenska
Prague	Prazska Plynarenska
North Bohemia	Severoceska Plynarenska
North Moravia	Severomoravska Plynarenska
Central Bohemia	Stredoceska Plynarenska
East Bohemia	Vychodoceska Plynarenska
West Bohemia	Zapadoceska Plynarenska

In the early 1990s, the RDCs were partially privatized (see Table 4.2.2).

Table 4.2.2 Typical ownership of an RDC, early 1990s

The State (NPF)	46%–48%
Municipalities	34%
Employees	1%–2%
Privatized	17%–19%

Source: CA IB

Strategic investors have since acquired the majority of the privatized stakes and now hold minority stakes in each company of up to 20 per cent. Municipal shares are not tradable. However, strategic investors have managed to purchase the voting and other rights attached to these shares. In some cases, investors have paid high premiums. The complexity of some of these transactions makes it difficult to give an accurate and true picture of the ownership for some RDCs. In 1998, Transgas acquired small stakes in seven of the RDCs to effectively restore state control in six of the eight RDCs. Prazska Plynarenska and Jihoceska Plynarenska are effectively already privatized.

Storage

Transgas is responsible for gas storage in the Czech Republic. Gas is stored to:

- balance supply with demand in the winter months. Natural gas consumption ranges from circa 8 million cubic metres per day on non-working days in the summer to more than 65 million cubic metres per day on a cold (-12°C) working day in the winter;
- secure natural gas supplies in case of limitations on imports or problems with the transportation systems.

Transgas owns the following underground storage facilities (Table 4.2.3):

Table 4.2.3 Gas storage facilities in the Czech Republic

Maximum storage capacity	(million cubic metres)
Dolni Dunajovice	695
Tvrdonice	488
Stramberk	420
Loboice	145
Haje	48

Source: 1999 Transgas Annual Report

Apart from the smallest site at Haje (in southern Prague), all of these facilities are located in the south or west of the country.

Demand

In 1999, demand for gas was 9.39 billion cubic metres. This represented a one per cent increase on 1998. Demand for gas grew markedly between 1995 and 1997.

Pricing

Household gas prices are cross-subsidized primarily by transit prices, and not through industry as in the electricity sector. The government's Energy Policy is committed to tackling this problem to

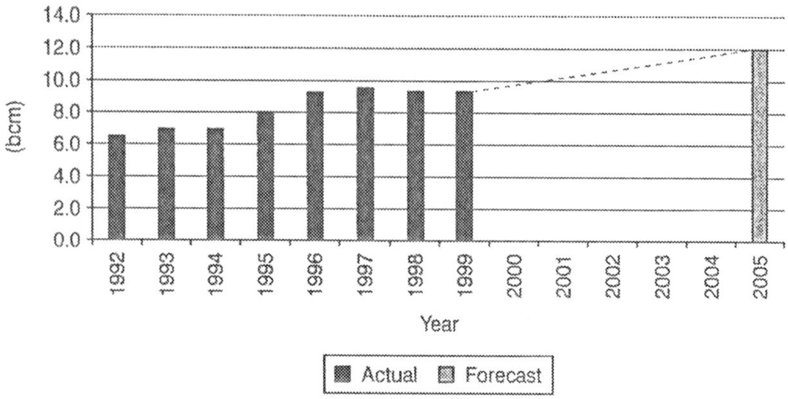

Figure 4.2.1 Gas demand in the Czech republic

to conform to EU regulations, and the cross subsidies are scheduled to be removed by 2002, with increases of 10 per cent and 5 per cent having been scheduled for 2001 and 2002 respectively. However, given that general elections are due in 2002, the government is likely to show restraint in pushing through any unpopular price increases.

Privatization

The government has advocated its commitment towards privatizing the gas industry in the first half of 2002. The main features of the privatization programme in the sector are likely to be the offering of a 50 per cent stake in Transgas, a 34 per cent stake in the six state-controlled RDCs, and an option to purchase an additional 1 per cent–16 per cent stake in the RDCs. This would involve matching the best offer submitted for these stakes. Minority shareholders in the RDCs to be sold are expected to protest against this approach. Bidders are expected to include Rhurgas (Germany) and Gazprom (Russia).

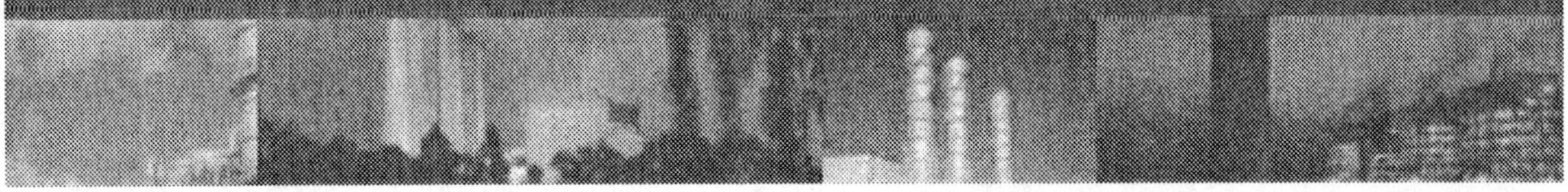

4.3

Construction Sector[1]

Milan Veverka, President of the Association of Building Entrepreneurs; and Jirí žemlička, Economist

Market composition and development

The construction sector has been operating in an environment of open competition for 10 years. From judging its potential and chances in 2000, it should now be noted that the sector has fully coped with privatization, price and wage liberalization, and companies have assumed full responsibility for their business. In technical standard, aesthetic appearance, service life, speed of construction and guarantees, the Czech Republic is very close to the European Union. In price terms, however, the Czech Republic rates far lower. Some 18,000 certified engineers and constructors form a high-quality pool of human capital that is weaker in apprentices but fairly strong in skilled labour. The construction sector maintains about a 7 per cent share of GDP; its output amounts to more than CZK210 billion, production of materials to CZK50 billion. The number of employees is approximately 200,000, and if workers with their own trade licences are included it exceeds 390,000. Another 40,000–50,000 work in the production of materials, and about 30,000 in design.

By 1996, construction output in the Czech Republic was growing by several per cent per year—8 per cent in 1994, 8 per cent in 1995 and 4.8 per cent in 1996. Since 1997, however, production in the sector has steadily declined—first by 4 per cent, then by 7 per cent in 1998 and 6.5 per cent in 1999. This was accompanied by a 35,000–40,000 decrease in the number of employees, the loss of complete units, and the disintegration and liquidation of companies. The productivity of labour stayed ahead of average wages up until

[1] This chapter was supplied by the PP Agency, Prague.

1998. In the first half of 1999, this ratio also collapsed, although the balance was regained at the end of the year. Labour costs went down from 18 per cent to 14 per cent. The price increase of building work slowed down from 12 per cent to 4 per cent, but still covered inflation.

Thus, what factors have led to this situation? Certainly they are not on the offer side. On a European scale this sector is competitive. Nor are the causes in over-sized capacities. A comparison with EU countries shows that per capita construction work in the Czech Republic is substantially lower—not to mention the high saturation of these countries with construction parts. Per capita construction output in the European Union amounts to €2000, in the Czech Republic to €500. Thus, what remains is demand. Its decline was the result of a decline in GDP and the ensuing ill-considered restrictive policy of the government, which reduced investments at a rate that exceeded the GDP decline. The drop in overall demand also resulted in lower private investments.

Development of the industry

During the next four years or so, the construction industry in the Czech Republic is expected to expand significantly, mostly through investments into the domestic market, but also through the participation of Czech construction companies in projects abroad. Some of the main industry bodies that will be influencing the development of the construction industry in the Czech Republic include the Association of Construction Entrepreneurs (SPS), which has become a partner to the government in the process of influencing legislation and taking other measures to the benefit of the building trade. According to the SPS, the potential of the construction industry in the Czech Republic is represented by the following investment estimates, which are planned for the sector in the coming years:

- CZK300 billion in housing construction, increasing by CZK30 billion annually.
- CZK400 billion in delayed maintenance and modernization.
- CZK330 billion in ecology, according to an EU audit.
- CZK450 billion in the construction of transport routes.
- CZK190 billion in road and railway repairs.
- CZK400 billion in other public investments.
- An estimated CZK80 billion annually in industrial construction. However, this forecast is difficult in respect to private investment.

> The industrial sector is seeking a new structure. New investments will go parallel with the phasing out of old operations. Only a small part will be fit for reconstruction and emphasis will be given mostly to new industrial projects.

The SPS has suggested that in order for these ambitious investment projects to be realized, some of the following strategic factors will have to be taken seriously into account:

- launching faster growth of investment and/or capital expenditures than of overall expenditures in the state budget and public budgets;
- the annual volumes of construction output should rise from the present level of CZK210 billion to CZK280 billion–CZK300 billion in constant prices at the end of the period;
- introducing four-year budget outlooks of the government and launching 6-to-12-year strategic concepts of the Czech Republic as the basis for projected investments;
- pressing the government to make overall economic growth the priority of its economic policy and monetary concepts, and to solve the issues of deficit, inflation and taxation in the longer term;
- in housing construction completing 50,000 flats by 2003;
- seeing the Housing Fund and the Transport Fund filled from state resources;
- achieving massive state participation in housing repairs, particularly of pre-fab blocks, from 2000;
- achieving an increase in state spending on housing construction from the present 0.75 per cent to 2 per cent–3 per cent of GDP;
- preserving the framework of the law on investment incentives as a prerequisite for an influx of foreign capital exceeding US$4 billion annually;
- further increasing support from the state budget for SMEs;
- paying increased attention to the preparation of projects eligible for financing from EU funds.

Towards improvement in the economic framework for the construction industry

In order for the construction industry to realize more comprehensive levels of efficiency, however, the SPS has recommended that the government adopt some of the following policy measures:

- further reducing the taxation of legal and natural entities below 30 per cent in the course of four years;
- increasing profitability to a minimum of 3.5 per cent of the average proceeds in the sector;
- balancing claims and liabilities;
- endeavouring that productivity grows faster than wages;
- improving the structure of assets and liabilities to strengthen companies' own resources;
- enabling companies to create reserve funds;
- achieving a more advantageous depreciation of investments;
- achieving accelerated write-offs of unmanageable debts.

EU accession and the construction sector in the Czech Republic

As the Czech Republic nears entry into the European Union, the competitiveness of construction companies in the domestic market will no longer be measured within the framework of that domestic market, but ultimately by the standards set by the European Union. However, the expansion of the market in the next few years does not mean that orders for Czech companies will expand in the same proportion, since EU entry will provide both an opportunity and a risk for the Czech construction sector. Changing its competitiveness and harmonizing norms and legislation are inevitable if the industry is to make good use of this chance.

Regulatory environment

The Building Act: conditions for the construction of new facilities

According to current legislation, foreign firms wishing to become engaged in entrepreneurial activities in the Czech Republic may, among other things, gain landed property through the construction of suitable production or marketing facilities, depending on the production process or the form of business organization they choose. In this respect, investing capital in the Czech Republic is governed by Act No. 50/1976 on Physical Planning and Building Rules, referred to as 'the Building Act'. The Building Act has been supplemented and amended many times. The latest major amendment was made in 2000, with most of the new provisions coming into effect on 1 January 2001.

The Building Act sets out and defines the main rules for capital construction, including the fact that all work carried out in connection with capital construction must be in agreement with the aims and tasks of physical planning. Physical plans outline systematically and comprehensively the functional use of land, set out the principles of their organization and coordinate the construction and other activities influencing regional development. It further creates prerequisites for ensuring lasting harmony between all natural, social and cultural values in the region, particularly as regards care for the environment and the protection of its basic components: land, water and the atmosphere.

Preparation of physical plans

Physical plans are prepared by municipalities, district offices, regional offices, the Ministry for Regional Development and the Ministry of Defence, each drawing on its own specialized knowledge. The plans take the form of:

- Physical plans for large areas setting out the arrangement and limits of the region concerned, defining important development surfaces, main transport corridors and technical infrastructures, as well as regional ecological stability systems. They are plans covering several municipalities or districts.
- Physical plans for communities, setting out town-planning concepts, solving admissible, inadmissible, possibly conditional functional uses of land and its arrangement, determining the basic regulation of the area and demarcating the boundaries of municipal land suitable for construction. They are prepared for individual municipalities or for several municipalities taken together, if they so wish.
- Regulatory plans setting out the use of individual plots and determining the regulatory elements for surface and spacial arrangement. If these plans for the municipalities have not been approved, the regulatory plans demarcate the boundaries of areas suitable for construction.

Placing buildings, utilizing and changing the use of land and protecting important interests in the region is only possible on the basis of the land-use decision issued by the locally appropriate building office. The parties to land-use proceedings on the placing of buildings and the use of the land are the petitioner and persons whose ownership or other rights to the land or the structures built on it, including neighbouring plots and structures on them, may be directly affected by the decision.

Land-use proceedings

Land-use proceedings open upon the written request of the petitioner, or at the instance of the building office or another body of state administration. The request must be supported by documents required by the implementing regulations of the Ministry for Regional Development No. 132/1998 or documents required by other regulations. Depending on the conditions of the localization of the structure, documents on the necessary creation of a protective zone, the effect of the structure on the environment, a document indicating the extent of the building closure, as well as documents concerning hygienic, fire-protection and work-safety conditions, conditions of the technical equipment, transport conditions, nature-protection, care for the conditions of protection of cultural monuments and farmland conditions, must be submitted to the building office as a basis for its decision. The building office also considers whether the submitted request is in accordance with the regional plans concerned. It assesses the ownership rights to the land and, in the case of broad general interest in the construction of the facility concerned in the proposed area, it considers the possibility of its expropriation.

Process of obtaining building permission

Construction work, changes to structures and their maintenance may be carried out exclusively on the basis of a building permission issued by the building office, or on the basis of a notification to the building office. In this process, the following rules apply:

- A building permission is required for structures of all types regardless of their building and technical characteristics, purpose or service life, unless otherwise provided for by the Building Act and the implementing regulations or by special regulations. A building permission is also required in the case of alterations to completed structures.
- In the case of small structures and building alterations which do not change the appearance of the structure, do not affect its supporting framework and do not change the purpose of its use, a notification to the building office is sufficient.
- Notification to the building office is required for maintenance work which might affect the stability of the structure, its fire safety or the environment, and for all maintenance work on structures which are listed buildings.

Applications for building permissions, supported by the necessary documentation, should be addressed to the building office. The builder must furnish proof that he is the owner of the plot or structure concerned, or that he has another right to the plot entitling him to erect the structure on it, make alterations to the structure or carry out maintenance work on it. In the case of building alterations, building an additional storey or carrying out maintenance work on the building, the builder may be its tenant (a corporate or natural person), provided that he has submitted, with the owner of the structure, a written contract to this effect.

Practically all investors, including foreign nationals, must apply for building permission, since as a rule their building projects exceed the size of small structures and building alterations. As the builders are obliged to submit relatively complicated documents to the building office, more detailed information may come in handy. A list of the most important documents required is as follows. Builders are requested to apply for building permissions in the case of separate structures or their alterations, sets of structures, including building site structures, separate structures of a set of structures, if after completion they are suitable for independent use; they must also apply for the relocation of technical networks conditioning the structure and for building site structures. Depending on the nature of the structure and in accordance with the Regulation of the Ministry for Regional Development No. 132/1998, implementing certain provisions of the Building Act, the applications for building permission must contain the following information:

- the builder's name and address;
- the type, purpose and location of the structure, the expected date of its completion, and in the case of an interim structure the length of its service life;
- the plot numbers and the types of the building plots, or the land to be used as a building site (eg public area) and the plot numbers of adjoining plots and structures built on them, indicating the ownership and other rights according to the land register;
- the name, address and licence of the designer of the project documentation and the way in which the structure is to be built (by contractor, by self-help);
- essential data concerning the structure, its division, technical or production equipment, future operation, and its health and environmental impacts;

- a list of the parties to the construction proceedings known to the builder, including their addresses. In the case of line structures and very extensive structures with a large number of parties, the list and addresses of the parties are not required;
- estimated cost of the structure, including technology.

The following documents are required to support the application:

- a document proving that the builder is the owner of the plot or the structure, or that he has another right to the plot or the structure entitling him to erect the structure on it or make alterations to it, or to carry out maintenance work on it;
- the construction project in two copies. If the building office is not the local council, the construction project must be submitted in three copies. If the builder is not the owner of the structure, another copy of the project document must be added:
- in the case of negotiations with the parties to the building proceedings having been held in advance, records of these negotiations, additionally also decisions, opinions, consents, assessments, and documents of other steps taken by the appropriate bodies of state administration required by special regulations, and land-use decision, if issued by a body other than the appropriate building office;
- statement by the entitled person that he will ensure the expert supervision of the construction work, and, if the builder is not qualified to carry out the expert supervision himself in case the building work is to be carried out by self-help, the statement of the person who is to carry out the expert supervision.

In the case of structures where an unconventional method of construction or an unconventional construction design is to be used, or in which unique technical equipment not comparable with other tested equipment is to be installed, and where the negative influence of the structure on the environment and human health cannot be reliably determined in advance, the building permission application must be supported by the opinion of a specialized workplace, university or expert. The Building Act further specifies what facts the project documentation supporting the application for a building permission must contain.

As part of the building proceedings, the building office examines primarily:

- whether the documents meet the conditions of the land-use decision;
- whether the documents meet the requirements concerning public interest, in particular environmental protection and the protection of health and life, and whether they meet the general technical requirements for structures serving their proper use;
- whether the structure is to be built by an authorized corporate person or a natural person engaged in business under special regulations, and whether in the case of structures and work on them, which is to be carried out by corporate persons or natural persons engaged in business under special regulations for their own use, expert management and realization of the building work has been ensured, or whether expert supervision has been guaranteed.

The building permission contains the following data:

- the builder's name and address, type and purpose of the structure or the alterations to be carried out;
- numbers of the building plots according to the land register on which the construction is permitted;
- conditions for the construction, or for the use of the structure or the removal of a structure, and the decision concerning the objections of the parties to the proceedings. By stipulating the conditions in the building permission, the building office ensures, for example, the accurate location of the structure on the plot, the protection of public interest and the observance of appropriate technical regulations. For structures of a special character it may set further conditions, such as the presentation of more detailed documentation still before the construction has begun or the submission of expert analyses.

The permission expires if construction has not begun within two years of the day on which it became effective, unless a longer period has been allowed by the building office in justified cases. Upon the builder's request, in justified cases the building office may permit an alteration to the structure before it has been completed. Before starting construction, the builder must ensure the staking-out of the position of the structure by qualified persons, according to the staking-out drawings, in agreement with the land-use decision and the building permission.

Final approval on physical structures

A completed structure or any of its parts suitable for independent use or that part of the structure to which an alteration has been made or on which maintenance work has been carried out, and in the case of a building permission having been required for such structures, may only be put into use on the basis of a final approval. The finalization of external work, mining and similar operations or work connected with them, as well as information, advertising and publicity equipment, is subject to final approval only if this has been set as a condition in the building permission.

Approval proceedings are the responsibility of the building office that has issued the building permission or a permission to carry out similar work connected with the construction. The authority to open the approval proceedings is the building office, which opens them after receiving the builder's written request. The request may also be made by the future user (operator), in which case a written agreement with the builder on the use of the structure must be submitted to the building office.

The protection of public interest and the rights and interests of corporate and natural persons protected by law, which ensue from the Building Act, regulations implementing the Act, from physical planning documentation, land-use decisions, from actual construction or the alteration of structures, is ensured by state building supervision officials, ie authorized employees of building offices and local councils, local councils which are not building offices and other bodies of state administration authorized by special regulations to supervise the erection, use and removal of structures to the extent provided for by the Building Act.

The land, the structures and the rights to them, which are necessary for building the structures, may be expropriated or the ownership rights to the structures and the land may be restricted by the decision of the building office only in cases stipulated by the law, for example:

- in the case of public utility structures complying with physical planning documentation;
- in the case of creating hygienic, safety and other protective zones and protected areas and ensuring conditions of their protection;
- in the case of the redevelopment of settlements or their betterment according to approved physical planning documentation;
- for purposes defined by special laws, such as Act No. 169/1949 on Military Districts, etc.

Expropriation is only possible if the purpose of expropriation cannot be achieved by agreement or in some other way. It may be carried out only to the necessary extent and only with compensation, in accordance with section 25 of the Commercial Code (Act No. 513/1991, as later amended) and in accordance with sections 108–116 of the Building Act (in the case of public interest which cannot be satisfied in any other way. A legal remedy may be lodged against such a decision. Compensation equivalent to the full value of the property affected by the said measures at the time of their application must be given without delay, and it must be freely transferable to a foreign country in foreign currency). The international contracts by which the Czech Republic is bound and which have been published in the Collection of Laws or in the Collection of International Contracts are not affected by the said measures.

4.4

Production of Building Materials[1]

Vaclav Knor, Head of the Building Materials Department, Ministry of Industry and Trade; and Jiří Kudrnovský

Introduction

The building materials production industry plays a specific and indispensable role in other industrial sectors in that it provides the domestic raw materials base for the building, or construction, industry. The considerable production capacity securing the self-sufficiency of the Czech building industry in the main products (brick and ceramic products, lime, cement, building stone and silicate prefabrication) was formed long ago. Despite structural deformations in some production sectors (prefabrication) and extensive growth of many production units (obsolete technology) in the pre-1989 period, the building materials production sector was more or less stabilized then and fully satisfied the needs of the building industry (with some exceptions caused by the division of production with Slovakia).

The stability and level of development of the sector allowed a relatively easy process of transformation of the majority of production firms (none of the major production units went bankrupt) and also led to considerable investments of foreign capital through the process of privatization and in later development of the industry. The involvement of foreign capital in the process of privatization made possible the necessary restructuring and modernization of the industry. This led to quality improvements, extension of the range of products and a decrease in the harmful environmental impact.

[1] This chapter was supplied by the PP Agency in Prague.

Structure of the industry

The building materials production industry in the Czech Republic consists, as a whole, of activities connected with raw materials production placed in the 'Structural Classification of Economic Activities, SCEA' scheduled in sector 'CB—other mineral resources production' in branches 141 and 142, and also in the sector of activities connected with production, which are scheduled by SCEA in sector 'DI—glass, ceramics, pottery and building materials industries' in branches 263–268. The list of activities related to building materials production is:

141—aggregate mining and processing
142—sand mining and processing
263—ceramic tiles and facing-brick production
264—brick, roof tile and construction ceramics production
265—cement, lime and gypsum production
266—cement, concrete and gypsum products production
267—natural stone processing
268—production of other non-metallic products.

Production base characteristics

The technology used by the majority of Czech building material producers in their production facilities is comparable with similar facilities in the advanced countries. The technological level improved considerably after the privatization through foreign and domestic investments.

This is particularly true for the mortar industry, where investments (after 1990) reached about CZK8 billion. These investments were concentrated in the technological reconstruction of cement and lime plants (mill room reconstruction, construction of closed cinder deposits, reconstruction of transport routes, electrostatic precipitator operation optimization etc). As a result of these investments, the technological level of cement, lime and gypsum production in the Czech Republic has reached a level comparable with leading European producers.

In the ceramics industry, the production technologies were modernized (putting highly sintered ruckling tiles into production, reorientation to large-size facings, single baking of glazed wall tiles, final product sizing and packing automatization). In the brickmaking industry the range of products for walling and roof tiles has increased considerably, the production capacity has expanded and quality has improved at the same time. Perforated, high-thermal-resistance brick block production represents a new generation in this grade of product. In the concrete production sector, the production of supporting structure elements (in particular for apartment block building, which has previously played a dominant role) has been greatly reduced, production throughout the sector has been restructured, new products have been introduced or formerly 'marginal productions' have been expanded. The range and volume of production of such small concrete products as various types of tiles, interlocking pavements, concrete pipes, shaft systems, concrete roof tiles and garden architecture materials have increased greatly.

In the sector of other mineral products, the production of mineral fibre and of products based on this fibre is dominant. The sector has a good raw material base and uses technology originating from the 1970s and 1980s when this production sector experienced a boom in the country. The decrease in demand (and growth of competition from imported products) has hit hardest the technologically obsolete stone-and-earth sector. Only about 10 per cent of plants have reached an acceptable technological level.

The production base of the stone mining and processing sectors depends to a large degree on the size and location of raw material deposits. Recently discovered deposits should last for about 150 years at the present rate of mining. Problems exist, however, with gravel-sand deposits, located in wooded areas along rivers and usually covered by fertile soil. The known gravel-sand deposits should last for about 100 years but, with the deposits lying beneath agricultural land, problems exist in opening up the deposits for mining. The presently opened deposits can last for 20–30 years.

The mining lifespan of the building material resources could be prolonged through their more rational and complex mining while the possibility of discovering new deposits within the country also remain open.

The recycling of wastes from other industrial sectors and of used building materials represent another important possible source for building material production. However, the Czech Republic is lagging considerably behind Western Europe in this field. Of the estimated total amount of building wastes in the Czech Republic (about 8–10 million tonnes), only about 10 per cent are recycled (less than a half of the EU average).

Overview of some of the main producers of building materials

Glass

Sheet glass is manufactured on two float lines of the largest central European producer, Glavebel Czech Republic in Teplice. This glass is processed in its subsidiaries, in independent firms and in the subsidiaries of other large world producers. Container glass is manufactured by Avirunion at Dubí near Teplice, and Vetropack Moravia Glass in Kyjov. Both companies are branches of important world producers. Glass for technical use is manufactured by Sklárny Kavalier in Sázava, and several smaller factories. The important manufacture of glass fibres and by-products is conducted only by Vertex in Litomyšl. Glass for television picture tubes comes from STV Glass in Valašské Meziř íč í. Utility glass is turned out mainly by small producers. The large producers include Crystalex in Nový Bor, and Sklo Bohemia in Svě tlá nad Sázavou, which manufacture soda potash glass and lead crystal glass respectively. This branch also includes illumination glass manufactured and processed by several glassworks. Other producers make raw material for artificial jewellery.

Fine ceramics

Sanitary ceramics are manufactured by two firms in three factories, the largest being Jihoč eská Keramika in Bechyně . The leader in china manufacture is the Karlovarský Porcelán group company, manufacturing under the Thun trademark in Karlovy Vary and its environs. There are also six smaller producers in the Karlovy Vary area, and Český Porcelán at Dubí. Utility and decorative ceramics are also manufactured in the Czech Republic, but are not important products.

Aggregates

The annual production of aggregates in the Czech Republic amounts to approximately 10 million cubic metres of building stone for crushing, 14.7 million cubic metres of sand and gravel sand, 12.2 million tonnes of limestone, and 3 million tonnes of china clay. The main part of the extraction is undertaken by a number of renowned European firms (Heidelberger Group, Holderbank,

Lhoist, Tarmac, Pioneer, Strabag—Bau Holding AG, Asamer—Hufnagel, Readymix, and Lasselsberger).

Ceramic tiling materials

Ceramic tiling materials are manufactured mainly by four large companies: Rakovnické Keramické Závody in Rakovník, Chlumč anské Keramické Závody in Chlumč any, Keramika Horní Bríza, and Borges in Boř ovany.

Brick products

The domestic market of burnt brick products—classical bricks and burnt roofing—is dominated by four companies: Wienerberger Cihlář ský Průmysl (WCP) in České Budě jovice, České Cihelny Josef Meindl in Stod, the Austrian concern Ziegelewerke Gleinstätten, which owns three roofing factories, and the domestic firm, Cidem Hranice.

Cement, lime, plaster

Following a number of mergers, cement is now manufactured in the Czech Republic by four companies in seven cement works: Českomoravský cement in Beroun, Cement Hranice, Cementárny a Vápenky Prachovice, and Lafarge Cement in Čížkovice. A total of 4.04 million tonnes of cement were produced in the Czech Republic in 2000. The companies Českomoravské Vápno in Mokrá, Vápenka Čertovy Schody and Vápenka Vitošov have a share of 75 per cent of the lime market in the Czech Republic. The extraction of gypsum and its processing into packed and loose plaster in the Czech Republic is in the hands of Gypstrend Koberice. There is an increase in plaster production from gypsum coming from the Pocerady and Melník power plants, used for the manufacture of plasterboard.

Ready-mixed concrete

Approximately 5.3 million cubic metres of fresh concrete were manufactured in the Czech Republic in 2000. This included some 3.5 million cubic metres of ready-mixed concrete. The largest producer of the latter is Readymix ČR, which has a share of about 25 per cent of the domestic market.

Porous concrete

Approximately 900,000 cubic metres of porous concrete were manufactured in the Czech Republic in 2000, and 85 per cent of this commodity market was in the hands of the two largest producers, YTONG Hrušovany and Hebel Chlumč any.

Prefabricated construction materials

The manufacture of prefabricated construction materials in the Czech Republic was thoroughly restructured in the 1990s. Almost all load-bearing structures for ground construction gradually became custom-made. The leading producers of prefabricated materials in the Czech Republic are Prefa Pardubice, Prefa Brno, ŽPS Uherský Ostroh, Prefa Praha, IPS Praha, and Dywidag Prefa Lysá nad Labem.

Concrete walling materials, paving, concrete roofing

Concrete walling materials account for some 7 per cent of walling materials on the domestic market. The well-known domestic manufacturers of thermal insulation moulded bricks include Betonové stavby Klatovy, Lacerta in Brandýs nad Labem, MaO Prefa Veselí nad Lužnicí, B+BC in Plzeň , and Prefa Pardubice. The largest producers of paving are Best and Presbeton. Concrete roofing is manufactured mainly by Bramac in Prague and KM Beta in Hodonín.

Fibre cement roofing

Fibre cement roofing is made of cement reinforced with fibre, and its producers in the Czech Republic are Cembrit Bohemia and Cembrit Moravia.

Plasterboard

Plaster products, which mostly serve the building industry, are plasterboards and soffits. The companies Knauf and Rigips have a dominant position on the plasterboard market in the Czech Republic. In their newly built factories, they use gypsum originating from the desulphurization of the Pocerady and Melník power plants.

Stone for rough and fine construction

A total of 132,800 cubic metres of stone for rough and fine construction were extracted in the Czech Republic in 2000. The capacities of the producers differ greatly; the medium-sized companies are Českomoravský Průmysl Kamene in Hradec Králové, Slezský Kámen in Jeseník, and Průmysl Kamene in Př íbram.

Mineral fibre insulation

Mineral fibre heat insulation materials are manufactured from domestic raw materials: fused basalt (Orsil Častolovice), glass fibres (Union Lesní Brána), and blast-furnace slag (Rockwool Prefizol Bohumín). Production totalled 3.1 million cubic metres in 2000.

Domestic demand and foreign trade

Prior to the 1990s, the building materials industry held a monopolistic position in the domestic market. In the first phase of transformation and reforms (1991–1992), when de-monopolization and privatization of the Czech economy played a decisive role, building activities were strictly limited and building material production dropped accordingly (particularly in the area of construction of apartment blocks—large panel production technology). The slump in the building industry stabilized in 1993 and during 1994–1996 some modest growth in production became typical. This trend in domestic demand for building materials continued in the late 1990s, when the Czech building industry entered another period of production decline.

Foreign trade in products from all sectors of the building material industry developed very rapidly after 1990. Before 1990, the production capacity of the majority of domestic building material industry producers was fully utilized by domestic demand. Only ceramic wall tilings, washed kaolin, cement and asbestos cement were exported. The situation in imports was similar—only products that could not be produced by domestic producers (eg white cement, gypsum etc) were imported. On the export side, growth was evident after 1990 and was caused by a drop in domestic demand due to a decrease in building activities, which made possible the rational use of domestic production capacity by Czech producers. The opening of the domestic market made possible the importation of a wide range of formerly hard-to-get products (such as gypsum plasterboards, insulating materials, refractory materials etc). Despite growing exports and imports, domestic producers still find most of their customers within the Czech Republic and thus hold a dominant position on the domestic market. Due to the limited size of the Czech building materials market, transport costs and environmental considerations, no change in this situation can be expected in the foreseeable future.

As the situation stands at present, the major part of building material trade is with EU countries. The growing volumes of exports to these countries is the result not only of the decline of the eastern markets, but also of the good and continually improving quality of Czech products (produced according to European standards), the good range of products offered and lower prices (cement, facings, concrete prefabrications etc). Imports from EU countries are used to supplement the range of products offered by the domestic market (highly clayey cement, refractory materials, facings) or as raw materials for domestic production (stone blocks, dyes, frits etc). The increased rate of imports from EU countries is the result of the growing requirements of the domestic market and the active marketing of EU producers and traders. The foreign trade balance is rising positively in favour of the Czech Republic with regards to Czech-EU trade in the industry.

International comparisons and competition

The building material production industry experienced dramatic change in the structure and size of its firms, and also in the orientation of its production towards the products currently in demand. Nearly all the production base was privatized with a more than 50 per cent share of foreign capital, which brought a great many new technologies and production methods into the industry.

The growth in domestic and foreign demand influenced the construction of new production facilities, both large and small. The current range of products is close to that in advanced countries; only a few types of product still have to be imported (eg white cement, highly clayey cement, refractory materials).

The strong raw material base for most of the production sectors and favourable wage and price trends are bases for success in competition on foreign markets. The growing exports and positive foreign trade balance bear evidence of this. The position of the building materials production industry on domestic and foreign markets, however, requires that the growth of investments and the structure of the labour force will continue. The demand for investments will give rise to growing pressure on small- and medium-sized producers, whereupon the result will be the concentration of production into several strong firms with foreign capital participation.

The building materials production industry provides about 60 per cent of materials needed in the building industry, which can be documented by statistics of material and services consumption. The development of this sector is greatly influenced by the amount and structure of investments and construction, and it also influences the structure and quality of materials used for building. Greater competitive pressures (the speed of the building process and the price of buildings) force continued innovation of the production structure. In the future, the structure of the building materials production industry will be influenced by the development of housing projects and the necessary rate of modernizations, reconstructions and building repairs.

International comparison of building materials production must start from the fact that most domestic products have reached the same level of quality as the products from top producers in Western Europe. Annual increases in exports, mainly to EU countries, have reached 15 per cent. High rates of exports in production and a highly positive foreign trade balance have been typical for the building materials industry in recent years. Liberalization of the building materials trade has reached such a level that the conditions on domestic markets are comparable to those in EU countries. Maintaining their dominant position on the domestic market has become a top priority for Czech producers in this situation. From a long-term point of view, a high rate of exports in production is undesirable due to them using non-renewable resources having a low rate of value added and a high rate of transport costs in final price etc. At the same time, the recent level of exports is determined by the necessity to utilize production capacity and thus, for many producers, exports become a life or death question.

Summary and likely future trends

The building material productions industry has maintained its position as a stable component of the national economy. In terms of international trade, it is a stabilized sector of the economy with a positive foreign trade balance in a situation where the majority of exports are oriented to advanced Western European countries. The development of the building materials production industry depends on the overall development of the Czech national economy and also of the Czech building industry, as the domestic market is decisive for the building material producers, in spite of their high exports.

Future development of the building materials production industry will be determined by the following factors and trends:

- situation on the domestic construction market, ie effective demand;
- range and quality of the domestic raw materials base;
- financial resources necessary to secure at least simple reproduction of producers' fixed assets with regard to the prices of new machinery and technology;
- haulage distances and transport facilities;
- growth in energy prices;
- growth in influence of foreign firms on the domestic market, harsher competition brought about by 'rectification' of the Czech crown exchange rate.

Growth in demand for building materials and market recovery can be expected in three to five years. This is as a result of planned railway reconstruction and the need to complete the country's motorway network. These activities will bring growth in demand for cement and for concrete products, and also for other products. The inevitable recovery of apartment block construction will also increase demand for building materials, wallings in particular, and also claddings, insulation materials and silicate prefabrication.

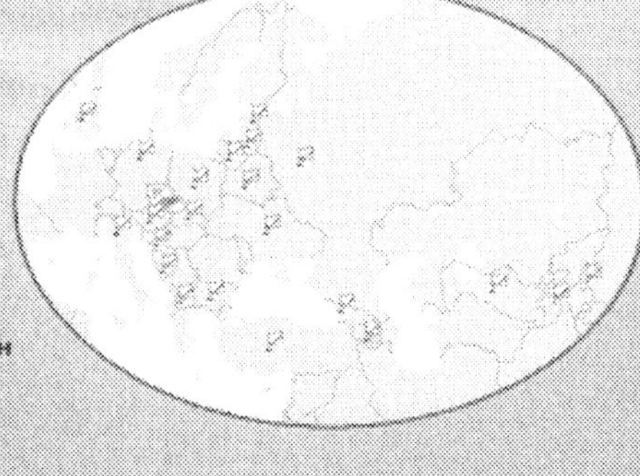

4.5

Environmental Legislation and Construction Activities

Pavel Veselý Ing., Principal Consultant, KAP Environmental Consulting and Engineering

Introduction

In general, every construction activity has an impact on the environment. The nature of the impact depends on the size and type of construction activity undertaken. For this reason, during the process of project elaboration it is necessary to assess all environmental impacts. Comparison with the relevant environmental as well as health and safety legislation is required and, if necessary, proposals for mitigating the environmental risks must be defined and implemented. The environmental impact assessment process in the Czech Republic with special focus on the construction sector is described in this chapter.

Environmental Impact Assessment (EIA)

All construction activities in the Czech Republic are governed by Act No. 109/2001 SB (the full wording of Act No.50/1976 SB as amended by several Acts) on Territorial Planning and Construction Regulations (Construction Act). Paragraphs from this Act define the necessity to conduct an impact assessment of the proposed activity on the environment. The most important paragraph is section 126 'Protection of all components of the environment and other special interests'. It defines how in special cases, which are stated in the Appendices of the Czech Environmental Act No. 100/2001 SB, the project sponsor is required to commission a more detailed environmental study, an Environmental Impact Assessment (EIA). The process of conducting this type of study is regulated by the Czech Environmental Act No. 100/2001 SB. This Act describes the necessary steps that must be undertaken and also determines the state administrative bodies that are competent in the EIA process.

In the Czech Republic, the process of preparing project documentation for a new construction activity or expanding an existing facility by 25 per cent or more consists of two phases. During the first phase, the entire EIA process must be carried out before the responsible construction office issues a territorial decision on the location of the construction.

The EIA process in the Czech Republic is an independent process and consists of several steps. The first step is to prepare a Notification Report. A private/state entity or person (hereinafter referred to as 'project sponsor') which intends to undertake a construction activity and/or install technology listed in Annex No.1 of the Czech Environmental Act No. 100/2001 SB is obliged to notify the competent authority by means of a Notification Report. The Notification Report must be structured in compliance with Annex 3 of the EIA Act and be split into eight parts. Part A will provide basic data in respect of the project sponsor. Part B will include basic information about the proposed activity, in particular: the location; characteristics; capacity; a short description of technical and/or technological solution, starting and finishing dates. Furthermore, Part B will also describe the major inputs and outputs, such as level of air emission, quantity and quality of waste water discharge, categories and amount of solid waste generated. Part C will describe the current environmental status of the area on which the activity is planned to be located. Part D will assess the impacts on population and on the environment. The main objective of Part E is to compare the proposed alternatives, if any exist. The remaining parts of the Notification Report (F, G, H) will provide some additional data such as maps, non-technical summary and also the declaration of the affected construction authority confirming that the location of activity is in compliance with land use plans.

An additional step in the EIA process is the screening procedure within which the competent environmental body (Ministry of Environment or regional authority) decides whether the project sponsor must elaborate a full EIA Study. This step must be concluded no later than 30 days after publication of the Notification Report. In the event that the Notification Report is already accompanied by an EIA Study, the closing date is extended to 45 days.

If an EIA Study must be elaborated, it must be structured in accordance with Annex No.4 of Act No. 100/2001 SB. It must provide, but in more detail, the same range of information as required for the Notification Report. In particular, it must include:

- a detailed description of the current environmental characteristics of the area potentially impacted by the planned activity;
- the identification, description and evaluation of the assumed direct and indirect impacts of the construction on each component of the environment (eg ambient air, surface and ground water, soil, rock environment, flora, fauna, human population, cultural monuments etc);
- a comparison of proposed alternative solutions (where required) and selection of the most favourable;
- the identification, description and evaluation of the potential environmental risks;
- the proposed mitigation measures and conditions which shall exclude or reduce the estimated negative impact; and
- an evaluation of the consequences should the construction not be carried out.

The EIA Study may only be elaborated by persons with a certificate of professional competence (hereinafter referred to as 'authorized persons') issued by the Czech Ministry of Environment. In addition, the Ministry also maintains the list of competent persons.

When the competent authority (Ministry of Environment or regional authority) receives the EIA Study, it shall, without delay, dispatch it to the state administrative bodies concerned and to the affected community. The second phase of the EIA procedure—publication and discussion of the EIA Study—commences from that time.

During the EIA process the competent authority is obliged to announce, within five days from receipt of the Notification Report and/or EIA Study, when and where these documents will be available for review and for taking excerpts, transcripts or copies. A public examination is conducted within the following 15 days (in the case of a Notification Report) or 30 calendar days in the case of an EIA Study. Any private person can both read the documents and submit in written form its recommendations and requirements to the competent authority.

While the state administrative bodies concerned and the affected community conduct their examinations, the competent authority ensures that an Expert Opinion is commissioned. The project sponsor pays for the Expert Opinion by depositing an agreed sum with the competent authority.

Only an authorized person can elaborate the Expert Opinion, but any qualified person who participates in the EIA Study preparation is prohibited from elaborating the Expert Opinion. It must be structured in compliance with Annex 5 of the Act and will evaluate in particular the completeness of the documentation, all opinions from the public, the affected community and the concerned state administration bodies), the completeness of all positive and negative impacts of the construction, evaluation methods applied, the completeness of input information and the alternative solutions proposed. An Expert Opinion must always contain a proposal for a statement by the competent authority. The Expert Opinion must be completed no later than 60 days after the necessary materials (EIA Study, public and other opinions) have been delivered to the Expert.

The competent authority must publish the Expert Opinion within five days from its receipt and submit it to the public, the affected communities and the state administration bodies concerned that are required to review and attach their comments to the Opinion within the next 30 days.

In cases where the competent authority receives negative comment, it is obliged to arrange a Public Discussion on the contents of the Expert Opinion and EIA Study. This discussion must take place no later than five days before the time period for obtaining comments on the Expert Opinion ends. Information about the time and place of the Public Discussion must be announced at least five days in advance.

The last step of the EIA process, which is based on the conclusions of the EIA Study, Expert Opinion and Public Discussion, is the elaboration of a Final Statement. It is elaborated by the competent authority in compliance with Annex No. 6 of Act No. 100/2001 SB and must be completed no later than 45 days after publication of the Expert Opinion. This Statement must be published and submitted to the public, the affected communities and the state administration bodies concerned within a further five days. The competent building office cannot issue a consent or measures under separate regulations without the Final Statement.

Environmental analysis

As already stated, the elaboration of the EIA Study is only required in special cases. In other cases, the Czech Construction Law No. 109/2001 SB requires the elaboration of an environmental analysis that forms an independent part of the project documentation. However, since the structure of this analysis is not strictly defined, it is suggested that all environmental impacts of the proposed construction activity are assessed. Comparisons of anticipated levels of air emission, the quality of discharged waste water, the level of noise and other factors with limits specified by Czech legislation have to be conducted and, where necessary, corrective and preventive actions must be proposed.

Conclusion

The process of assessing the impacts of construction activity on the environment is well regulated in the Czech Republic. KAP has significant experience in this area and employs four authorized persons for conducting EIA Studies and Expert Opinions. However, KAP's experience has shown that in the past some discrepancies in the EIA process existed. One of these was that some of the authorities inspect the documentation before sending it to the relevant bodies and a consequent delay of up to two weeks or more may be encountered. Nevertheless, the new Czech Environmental Act No. 100/2001 SB, which became valid on 1 January 2002, provides transparent rules for eliminating this discrepancy.

4.6

The Czech Defence Industry as a Part of Industry Policy[1]

Jiri Pisklak, Vice-President for Foreign Relations and Executive Director of AOP CR

Introduction

As a result of stabilization on the Czech political scene, several events that occurred at the beginning of 2000 may be considered as auguring well for the future, and to include the remaining parts of the Czech defence industry. Ranking high among these important circumstances is undoubtedly the Czech Republic's membership in the North Atlantic Alliance and its binding and responsible participation in allied defence planning. In this regard, parliament passed legislation which defined the relationship of the State to defence, the armed forces as a whole and uniformed military personnel.

The fact that the government included the defence industry in its industrial policy is evidence that certain issues, such as the preparedness of the country to adequate defence or the ability to ensure the security of citizens and to protect them from crises and catastrophes of all kind, have gained a firm position in Czech policy. The creation of the State Security Council and its systematic work are perhaps the most obvious sign of this change.

The Association of Defence Industry

The pressure of the harsh economic reality and the growing will to find a way out of the situation by common effort over the past two

---

[1] This chapter was supplied by the PP Agency in Prague.

years have led to important changes in the thinking and organization of companies and firms concerned with activities connected with state defence and security. The presence of the firms in the defence industry is boosted by the organizational work of the Association of Defence Industry, which, after its fourth regular general meeting held in Brno in June 2000, now unites some 101 members. Most of these are in fact corporate persons concerned with the research, development, production and sale of military material and armaments, the infrastructure and other activities connected with defence and security.

Cooperation with other specialized organizations, namely the Association of Aircraft Manufacturers, the Association of Firms for the Protection of Information and the Association of Arms and Ammunition Producers and Sellers, was initiated and has been affirmed by contract, and ways have been found to provide the defence industry with a corresponding place in the general industrial context, particularly through cooperation with the Confederation of Industry and the Association of Construction Firms.

Government policy towards the defence sector

The combination of the two trends enabled the State Security Council and later the government to make an important move, namely to prepare and adopt the document 'Principles of Cooperation of the State with the Defence Industry in the Czech Republic', with an outlook up to 2010. On 15 March 2000, the government passed Resolution No.259 setting out further conditions for the establishment of relations between the Ministry of Defence and the Association as a representative of the defence industry (together with aircraft producers). It is also a basis for a similar development involving other important ministries, such as the Ministry of Foreign Affairs, the Ministry of Industry and Trade and the Ministry of the Interior, as well as the State Administration of Material Reserves.

The fact that both parties are sincerely interested in implementing the resolution within the set time limits and on the basis of mutual consultation has resulted in the signing of the Agreement on Cooperation between the Ministry of Defence and the Association of Defence Industry. This document was signed ceremonially on 13 June 2000 by defence minister Vetchy and Association president Valousek. The preparation for similar relations with other ministries, as laid down by government resolution, was scheduled for completion by the end of 2001. This will lay a theoretical and legislative basis for relations between the defence industry and the State, which is its main and decisive customer in both domestic and international contexts.

This will further require the stability of partners and clear rules of behaviour. Naturally, one of the essential requirements is that of having a clear concept of building up the armed forces and an integrated rescue system and its elements, from which the need for armaments, outfits, provisions and the rules of procuring and tending them are derived. Equally important is the stability of the institutions of state administration. Over the past 10 years, the Czech defence industry has suffered from the continuing reorganization of the Ministry of Defence.

Possibilities for development

The Czech defence industry would certainly welcome more favourable, industrially oriented planning—in other words, planning that would take into consideration the capacity and ability of Czech research, development and production and contribute to their maintenance and development. There can be no doubt that the Czech Republic still has production branches with a good research and development base, which, after the necessary transformation, will have all the prerequisites to become part of the domestic and international industrial base for defence. It would be difficult to mention them all without a more profound study, but examples include the aircraft industry, electronics (communication technology, radar systems and equipment), small arms, ammunition and explosives, vehicles, protective equipment (masks, filters, clothes, special equipment, chemicals, etc), software for various purposes, clothes, tents and parachutes.

The Czech Republic also has very good opportunities to modernize its aircraft and military transport (including armoured vehicles). These branches should be considered in defence planning, giving an opportunity to domestic manufacturers instead of automatically accepting foreign offers. That this is possible could be seen in the case of Spain and Sweden, where a number of firms engaged in the defence industry have a clear and incontestable programme of activity for the next 10 years. In the Czech Republic, the only manufacturer in a similar situation is Aero-Vodochody.

It is likely that firms in the Czech defence industry are aware of the financial possibilities provided to them by the budget. However, there are countries where even the defence industry is earning money, through exports, helping to cover the countries' defence spending. If nothing new is produced, nothing will be exported—indeed, during 2000, for the first time in many years, the Czech Republic had to import instead of export. Usually, it is possible to export only if the system in question has been introduced and is being used in the country in which it was produced. This is not to give the impression that the industry is only making demands on the State. Czech defence firms are generally aware of the strict conditions and requirements applying to manufacturers supplying the Ministry of Defence and the Interior, and to participants in international competitions. In this sense, there has been a long-term, ongoing dialogue between the Association of Defence Industry and the Ministry of Defence about the conditions of a firm's eligibility for a particular order.

These conditions have yet to be codified, however, and the same also applies to their provability. Naturally, they will include property and ownership transparency (based on annual financial statements), technical and capacity prerequisites (references), possession of certificates of the National Security Office commensurate to the degree of the secrecy of the order, quality certificates (in particular ISO), ability to apply standardization agreements (STANAG) used in NATO and other requirements. Membership of the Association of Defence Industry as a guarantee of the seriousness of the firm is also being considered. A number of foreign customers demand such confirmation.

Cooperation between Czech and foreign firms

Making a register of suppliers is in no way discriminatory, as the registered firms should be automatically invited to take part in competitions, the same as is being done by NAMSA, the NATO maintenance and supplier agency and NC3B (the NATO agency for command and communication systems). This in no way restricts the access of other entities to information in the Commercial Gazette or on the Internet site administered by the Ministry of Defence. The Czech defence industry is finding itself in a new international context, which cannot be ignored. While in the United States and Europe strong integrated firms are forming, with a good chance of standing up to competition and being able to bear the high costs connected with the application of science, research, development and new technologies, in the Czech Republic firms are rather scattered, although a number of cooperation projects have appeared recently.

For example, AOP, together with a French partner, have launched a project to support cooperation of small and medium-sized firms, MECRADICE, in which six Czech and ten French entities are participating. It is hoped that the project will bring benefit to all participants, but it is less likely that it will succeed on the market with its own products or without cooperation or merger with stronger partners. Connected with it is, to a certain extent, the country's political orientation to US or European firms and structures, although this does not foreclose the other, including efforts at finding a suitable solution of partial interests and specificities of Central Europe. In the opinion of Czech owners and managers, the internal integration of firms may materialize on the basis of projects in which the finding of partners will be a necessity and an advantage; in other words, they do not believe in the feasibility of an artificial merger of firms.

Regrettably, only very few common projects have resulted from the numerous negotiations and visits that would lead the country into Europe. Of some help may be the recent more pronounced orientation of the Ministry of Defence and the National Armament Office to industrial structures organized by the Western European Armaments Group (WEAG) and its assistance to the defence industry in starting cooperation with the European Defence Industries Group (EDIG).

The political benefit of this approach is undeniable, but common projects and contracts are usually the result of negotiations between the industries themselves, and, notwithstanding a few exceptions, this is what we have not been able to do so far. Again, this may be connected with the Czech system of planning and the reliability of the commitments, where in some cases Czech behaviour is necessarily dissuading partners.

Ongoing state support for the industry

The Czech parliament has played an important role in supporting the sector, while a working group for the defence industry has been created by the Defence and Security Committee. The latter in particular is a good platform for the exchange of views and the examination of the situation between Czech deputies and the defence industry. Today, it has become obvious that an adequate defence industry helps towards the country's technological advance, that it creates working opportunities, brings investors into the country—the same as applies to other branches, on both a regional and national scale.

Linked to this is Czech government policy towards industrial compensation, or offset trade. The long-awaited decision on the choice of a supersonic aircraft for the Czech Air Force has to a considerable extent accelerated the country's preparations for the possibility of developing industrial offset programmes. It will be important to see into which branches of the defence industry the corresponding part of the means thus gained will be invested, so as to ensure their future on a long-term basis. This will help to ensure that they become a firm part of the future European defence industry and a driving force in Czech industry.

4.7

Engineering Sector[1]

Viktor Danielis, Director of the Department of Mechanical Engineering and Electrical Industry at the Ministry of Industry and Trade of the Czech Republic

Introduction: the engineering sector in 2001

According to an evaluation of the engineering sector in 2001, the Czech economy had not developed favourably—on the contrary, it was overcoming a recession. In 1999, GDP registered a 0.2 per cent year-on-year decline. The data for 2000 strongly hint at a more favourable turn. Gross domestic product increased by 3.1 per cent year on year and other macroeconomic indicators also developed favourably. Productivity of labour in the national economy increased, demand for investments was growing, unemployment was down (albeit moderately), and inflation was low and under control. Industry became the motor of economic recovery, with a 72 per cent share in the year-on-year increase in GDP. Industrial production went up by 5.1 per cent year on year, and the respective increases were 4.8 per cent in the manufacturing industries and 9.7 per cent in the engineering sector (as against a 6.1 per cent decline in 1999).

Revenues in the engineering sector rose by 2.5 per cent (compared to a 9.7 per cent decline in 1999), the number of employees in the sector declined by 8.2 per cent (the same as in the previous year), and productivity in industrial production went up by an interesting 19.5 per cent. In foreign trade, the category of machinery and transport equipment strengthened its dominance in the commodity structure of exports (due, among other factors, to higher exports of machinery), by 1.4 per cent to 44.4 per cent.

[1] This chapter was supplied by the PP Agency in Prague.

What is important, however, are a number of questions regarding the engineering sector. Is Sector 29 'Manufacture of machinery and equipment' to be called a sector of general engineering on the rise? Is the rise permanent?

According to NACE coding, Sector 29 is divided into seven sub-categories:

29.1 Manufacture of machinery for the generation and use of mechanical energy (combustion engines, turbines, pumps, valves, bearings).
29.2 Manufacture of machinery and equipment for general purposes (furnaces, dryers, lifting, transport, and air-conditioning equipment).
29.3 Manufacture of agricultural and forest machinery (tractors, ploughs, harvesters, milking systems, loaders).
29.4 Manufacture of machine tools (including forming and welding machines).
29.5 Manufacture of other special purpose machinery (mining, building, food, textile, printing machines).
29.6 Manufacture of weapons and ammunition.
29.7 Manufacture of household appliances (electrical and gas apparatus).

Revenues in all seven sub-categories generated from sales of their own products and services have generally been on the rise, with the one exception of manufacture of machinery for the use of mechanical energy, which has been declining in recent years. General engineering ranks fourth among the 15 sectors of the manufacturing industry, with an almost 8 per cent share of revenues. In terms of added value, its 10 per cent share ranks it third, while in the number of employees it ranks second.

Characteristic features of the production base

Around 85 per cent of the property (enterprises) in the engineering sector have been transformed into joint-stock companies (8.7 per cent have been privatized by direct sale and 3.6 per cent by public auction or public tender). The State holds (or has regained), through the Consolidation Bank or by means of subsidiaries of the National Property Fund, large shares in some engineering companies, such as Skoda Plzen or Vítkovice, which were important in the past and continue to be important today.

The present level of participation of foreign capital is more or less steady, despite the law on investment incentives, and is out of proportion to the importance and extent of the sector. A 100 per cent share of foreign capital in large organizations is infrequent. The biggest foreign investment in the sector was the launching of the construction, in February 2001, of a plant for the manufacture of needle bearings of the Torrington company in Olomoucký.

The production base of the general engineering industry is represented by more than 1000 companies. The group of companies with more than 1000 employees comprises about 30 corporations which employ 28 per cent of the workforce and are responsible for about 25 per cent of sales and 27 per cent of added value. The most efficient enterprises are currently those with 50–249 employees whose sales per employee total CZK871,000 and those enterprises with 250–999 employees in which value added per employee amounts to CZK290,000.

Besides the disintegration of the eastern markets, the decline in sales during 1990–1995 was a reflection of the fact that most Czech manufacturers were not ready to stand up adequately to the foreign competition that moved into the Czech market within a short period of time. Because the restructuring of the production base in general engineering was insufficient (as a sector, in the number of companies, financially, by cancellation or capitalization of debts, by the entry of a strategic partner, or in another way), domestic manufacturers never returned to the domestic markets. Domestic requirements for machinery and equipment continue to be met by increasing imports, a tendency which is pushing domestic manufacturers out of the market (in imports, too, the machinery and transport equipment category dominates the commodity structure list with about 41 per cent, and the proportion of machines, as against cars, is much higher than in exports). The growth in revenues in this branch since 1995 is thus mostly

Table 4.7.1 Production characteristics in 1999 according to size groups—NACE 29 (CZK million)

Persons per company	0–9	10–49	50–249	250–999	over 1000
Revenues from sale of P and S	5368.4	13079.0	38766.3	37889.1	31054.4
Value added	1072.2	4316.2	11857.1	13174.1	10999.6
Number of employees	6884	16929	44488	45372	44398

Source: Czech Statistical Office, calculations by Ministry of Industry and Trade

connected to a better placement of the output on foreign markets. It testifies to the greater financial stability of companies manufacturing competitive products.

Chief economic indicators

General engineering had been ahead of the price indices of other producers in the manufacturing industries up to 1994. The main leap in price indices in the engineering branches occurred before the end of 1992, following the price liberalization of 1991. The development of prices since 1994 is shown in Table 4.7.2.

In 2000, too, price levels grew wherever the competitiveness of engineering production went up, particularly in sections with a significant share of exports, ie in Section 29.1 'Manufacture of machinery for the generation and use of mechanical energy' and 29.4 'Manufacture of machine tools and forming machines'. Parallel to imports of consumer goods, price levels in Section 29.7 'Manufacture of household appliances' also recorded above-average increases up to 1998. Revenues from the sale of own products and services in current and constant prices grew markedly during the period 1994–1998. This applied to all branches of the sector. The recession of 1999 brought a roughly 15 per cent decline in sales for the engineering sector. The restored economic growth in 2000 increased revenues in the sector by about 8 per cent.

Table 4.7.3 shows that the development of production characteristics in the sector in 1998–2000 closely mirrored the development of the Czech economy. The permanent decline in the workforce, by 8 per

Table 4.7.2 Development of price indices of products in 1994–2000

%	*Year-on-year index*					
	95/94	*96/95*	*97/96*	*98/97*	*99/98*	*00/99*
SCP 29.1	108.9	108.8	106.9	103.3	104.6	102.6
SCP 29.2	106.6	106.4	101.6	105.2	99.8	101.8
SCP 29.3	106.6	103.3	105.8	104.5	102.4	102.5
SCP 29.4	109.9	104.9	107.0	108.2	102.3	102.4
SCP 29.5	103.6	109.0	104.0	103.7	100.7	102.2
SCP 29.6 not available						
SCP 29.7	111.1	110.2	102.7	103.8	100.4	99.6
SCP 29	106.4	107.4	104.4	104.5	101.6	102.2

Source: Czech Statistical Office, calculations by Ministry of Industry and Trade

cent annually in the given years, was due above all to the need to make the production process more efficient (to minimize costs) by cutting employee numbers in ancillary and servicing components, by outsourcing, and often even at the expense of reducing staff in the design, construction and testing facilities and elements ensuring the quality of production. The result was a growth in the productivity of labour in performance. On the other hand, purchases of external services contributed to a decline in the share of value added in production, although the decrease in the sector from 1994 to 2000 amounted only to 6 per cent.

Domestic consumption and foreign trade

With regard to domestic consumption for the engineering sector, the general trend has been one of stagnation (in constant prices the 2000 level was the same as in 1994) and the extent to which it is satisfied by domestic production is declining. Imports have been increasing, however, despite the recession of 1999, rising year on year by a total of 19.2 per cent in 2000. This means that enterprises, including engineering companies, are investing primarily in foreign production equipment.

The export trend is the only aspect which is entirely positive in the sector. Between 1995 and 2000, the exports increase index amounted to 2.03. The most dynamic, according to this indicator, were the following sections: 29.4 'Machine tools manufacture'

Table 4.7.3 Production characteristics of the sector

	1994	*1995*	*1996*	*1997*	*1998*	*1999*	*2000**
million CZK Performance							
current prices	93,494.3	106,743.1	119,055.4	138,072.2	153,721.1	127,622.3	138,783.6
1994 constant prices	93,494.3	101,903.7	105,595.2	115,195.5	121,511.2	100,809.0	107,938.8
million CZK Value added in production							
current prices	32,394.3	31,127.2	36,088.3	45,198.0	45,880.6	41,419.2	45,290.0
1994 constant prices	32,394.3	34,046.9	30,931.7	35,329.5	32,717.2	30,904.3	33,911.5
'000 CZK/worker Labour productivity in added value							
current prices	152.9	175.3	193.5	247.8	279.6	262.0	310.7
1994 constant prices	152.9	174.8	165.9	193.7	199.4	195.5	232.6
PersonsNumber of workers							
	2,111,904	94,727	186,457	182,427	164,112	158,071	145,764

* preliminary value

Source: Czech Statistical Office, calculations by Ministry of Industry and Trade

(index 2.01), 29.1 'Manufacture of machines for the generation and use of mechanical energy' (export index 2.24) and 29.2 'Manufacture of machines and equipment for general purposes' (index 2.75). The year-on-year increase in 2000 was 18.8 per cent.

The territorial division of foreign trade has altered very little, with the 10 biggest exporters (Germany, Italy, Slovakia, Austria, the United States, France, Poland, Britain, Switzerland, the Netherlands) also being (in a slightly changed order) the 10 biggest importers. Germany had the largest share in trade turnover in 2000. At the same time, Germany, together with Italy and France, accounted for the largest shares of the balance of trade.

International comparison, competitiveness and prospects

What has been said above allows for the following conclusions to be made about the Czech engineering sector in 2000:

- the Czech Republic still maintains its position as a traditional exporter of engineering products in the international market;
- the share of the sector in the domestic market is declining. The decline is occurring in all sections of general engineering;
- the export performance of the section is increasing. Czech exports to EU countries grew 3.6 times in 1994–1999;
- companies after restructuring involving products and technologies have no problem in placing them in world markets;
- a gauge of competitiveness is not just a good price (Czech machinery is particularly competitive due to price), but also the price/performance, price/quality ratios,
- the key factor in macro-indicators is maintaining a permanent growth in productivity;
- maintaining the rate of growth requires a substantial increase in the volume of investments, primarily in new technologies and machinery.

Conclusion

An answer is still owed to the question posed towards the start of this chapter: Is Sector 29, 'Manufacture of machinery and equipment' to be called a sector of general engineering on the rise? The answer needs to be conditional: 'Yes, if...'—meaning yes, if measures are taken to strengthen the growth that has started and make it a lasting and rising trend. This is a task for all those involved, beginning with the companies and not ending with the bodies of state administration.

4.8

Automotive Industry[1]

Desmond Mullan ACMA, Managing Director
Volvo Auto Czech sro

Introduction

The Czech automotive industry (encompassing the production of cars, trucks, buses, motorcycles, trailers, components, parts and vehicle accessories) represents a broad segment of the country's engineering production. Its range covers a whole spectrum of products—all types of vehicle for road transport together with related services and production activities. The environment for the industry is defined on the one hand by virtually fully privatized firms with well-defined ownership structures, and on the other by a fully liberalized domestic market with advantages for used-car importers (an import tariff of 4.7 per cent for towing vehicles imported from EU countries was only established on 1 December 1999).

The passenger car sector has established itself as a key part of the industry, and includes components and accessories. At the same time, trucks and utility vehicles have witnessed a considerable slump, both in terms of production and sales. NACE coding breaks the sector down into the following sub-sectors:

34.1 Production of double-trace motor vehicles and their engines
34.2 Car bodies, trailers and semi-trailers, and their components
34.3 Parts and accessories for motor vehicles and their components.

The Czech car industry is now represented by over 110 firms and companies, at least 80 of them being producers of accessories

[1] Some of the material for this chapter was provided by the PP Agency in Prague; Viktor Danielis, Department Head, Department of Metallurgy, Engineering and Electrotechnics, Ministry of Industry and Trade of the Czech Republic; and the Commercial Department of the British Embassy in Prague.

(Sector 34.3). Many foreign partners and a very large amount of foreign capital has entered the sector, which has had a positive influence on the otherwise complicated problems of sources of financing, research and development or ownership structure. Fully domestically owned firms also exist and prosper. The ratio of firms with foreign capital participation (or joint ventures with a foreign partner) to Czech-owned firms is closely balanced at 49 per cent to 51 per cent. The core of this sector is formed by well over 100 production firms with more than 63,000 employees. Subcontracts and semi-finished products provide employment for another 100,000 employees in related industries. Most of the firms fall into the category of 250–999 employees, but the largest share in economic results is secured by producers with over 1000 employees.

Review of automotive sales in the Czech Republic

The Czech car market has always been dominated by the domestic manufacturer, Skoda Auto. In 1993, for example, Skoda Auto had more than 75 per cent market share out of the total new car market of 86,000 cars. Since then, their share has declined as they have phased out older products and introduced more modern and 'premium' cars, such as the Octavia, Fabia and, lately, the new Skoda Superb. In 2001, Skoda Auto achieved a market share of almost 53 per cent, selling about 80,000 cars.

Imported vehicles have continued to increase over the years with major gains by Volkswagen, Renault and Peugeot, which have all reached approximately 6 per cent market share. In the premium brands of Volvo, Mercedes, BMW and Audi, all players have achieved significant growth, clearly as a result of the development of the Czech economy and subsequent improvements in personal wealth. While the country has a relatively small number of people in the 'middle-class' sector, this number is growing and should continue to grow in the coming years. Combined sales of these premium brands in 2001 represents only a 3 per cent share of the total market, which is double that compared to 1994 but still a long way to go to be a significant part of the total market.

Used car imports after an early period of rapid growth have declined substantially as local prices have stabilized and are more in line with surrounding mature countries. The Czech government has also chosen to control the number of used car imports by limiting the age of vehicles that can be imported to a maximum of five years. Ways of buying cars have also changed much in the last 10 years. Where many people bought their first car using physical cash (even carrying it to the dealership in a bag), today there are a number of sophisticated methods for purchasing and even maintaining purchased cars, such as financial and operational leasing.

The total Czech car market has exploded over the last 8–10 years. In 1993, for example, there were 86,000 new cars sold, of which 75 per cent came from Skoda. In 1997, only four years later, the market peaked at more than 171,000. After 1997, the country entered an uncertain economic period in which many of the legacies from communist times came back to haunt the country. Banking indebtedness, industrial problems, corruption and a devalued currency all added to the monetary crisis, which hit the Czech economy in May 1997. The Czech economy officially entered a recession in 1998 and the slow restructuralization of the economy resulted in the poor performance of Czech industry in 1999. Unemployment soared to 7.5 per cent in 1998 due to continued difficulties of the un-restructured industry. The unresolved major issues of the Czech economy resulted in a further increase in unemployment to 9.4 per cent in 1999. In 2000, unemployment levelled out at about 9 per cent and continued into 2001. Relatively high inflation rates in 1997 and 1998 were a direct reflection of the monetary crisis and price deregulation. The slower price deregulation and sluggish consumer confidence due to increased job insecurity and continuing economy recession resulted in a rapid decline in inflation in 1999. These factors had an immediate impact on the Czech car market, which fell to 141,000 in 1998 and has increased only by an average of 2–3 per cent per annum since then. In 2001, the market totalled 152,000 new cars, with Skoda continuing as market leader with a share of 52.6 per cent.

Consumer behaviour and the automotive market

The trend of Czech consumer expenditure shows fluctuating progress; however, the overall trend in 1997–1999 was one of growth. The spending of 'free money', ie net personal income which does not have to be used for fixed payments such as rent and food etc, and which the consumer can freely decide what to spend on, is primarily influenced by consumer satisfaction, which means the level of trust and security that citizens feel in relation to the overall economic and political situation of their own household. Index of consumer satisfaction (ICS) values, taking account of current economic conditions and expectations for the future, show a slight pessimism or general dissatisfaction (this is also a feature generally of Czech consumers). However, the ICS is increasing and results in a slight growth.

It is thus clear to see that the picture of the Czech consumer, viewed through these economic indicators, is quite positive. The volume of consumer resources is growing slightly and the allocation of spending shows a changing structure. The cost of food, clothing and shoes has been decreasing but the cost of housing has increased. One car per household remains the norm throughout the country (in 50 per cent of households). Eleven per cent of households own two cars, while 40 per cent of households have no car. The number of cars per household also depends on the number of household members. The vast majority of one-member households do not own a car, and the majority of two- and three-member households own at least one vehicle. Furthermore, the net monthly income, not surprisingly, is a major factor determining the number of cars owned: the higher the household income, the higher the number of vehicles. Thus, households within the lowest income band (less than CZK8500) mostly do not own a car, while high-earning households with income of more than CZK29,000 almost always own a car, with more than 50 per cent of them owning two or more cars.

Every fifth individual is considering buying a car. Of these, approximately 6 per cent are planning to buy a new car, and 13 per cent a used one. By comparing the actual percentage of new-car owners (4 per cent) and potential new-car buyers (6 per cent), it can be assumed that the current new-car market will continue to grow, even if not all potential buyers make a purchase. In general, the highest interest in buying a new or used car comes from the younger age group (18–29 years), probably due to significantly low car ownership. More than one-third of young people would like to buy a new car, while every second person claims that they will buy a used car, since young people usually do not have sufficient means to purchase a new one. People over 60 years of age generally show very little interest in a purchase of either a new or a used car. There is a significant decline in interest in buying a used car with the increasing age of consumers, while interest in new cars is more or less constant in the 30–59 age group.

With regard to a new-car purchase, in 50 per cent of cases the consumer's choice is confirmed as Skoda, while average interest in other brands will be opted for in 2 per cent–3 per cent of the purchases. These makes include Ford, Volkswagen, Opel, Peugeot and Renault. These brands are also strong on the used-car market, with Skoda leading the other brands.

When it comes to the factors influencing car purchase decision making, it is not surprising that price is the major factor, affecting around 65 per cent of car buyers. However, there are differences to what extent people insist on price: four out of ten consumers claim that their decision will be based 'most likely on price', while one in four would decide 'definitely with price in mind'. On the other hand, to 35 per cent of car buyers, the brand is more important when deciding: 22 per cent of consumers would 'most likely' base their decision on brand and 13 per cent would do so 'definitely'. More than half of all respondents went for the 'most likely' answers, which means that these consumers follow a multiple-factor decision-making pattern according to quality, price, perceived value, etc. Thirteen per cent of car owners have been shown to have high brand loyalty.

In the Czech Republic, spouses jointly decide about the purchase in most cases. Wives alone only decide in roughly 10 per cent of purchases, although the pattern is changing as more and more women have higher paid jobs. Women put more emphasis on price. When a woman decides alone, price is the major factor, but men are less price sensitive. When the decision is made by both partners, a compromise is often reached, albeit with a slight dominance on the man's part. Price is thus normally the decisive factor. However, it should be pointed out what price range people consider. Used-car buyers are willing to pay considerably less: 75 per cent up to CZK100,000, leaving only 25 per cent of consumers happy to buy a more expensive car. Those opting for a more expensive vehicle take into account the brand.

Car market evaluation (total market)

The total passenger car market performed extremely well in the period 1995–1997, increasing by 37 per cent (1996 against 1995) and by 11 per cent (1997 against 1996). There was a significant drop in the value of the Czech crown in the second half of 1997, which had an immediate impact on the new car sales. This decreasing trend dramatically influenced 1998 sales, showing a drop of 18 per cent. The total 1999 and 2000 passenger car performance figures are in line with macroeconomic indicators showing a slow recovery from recession. New car sales followed the economic trend, showing an increase of 4 per cent in 1999 (against 1998),

2 per cent in 2000 (against 1999) and a further 2 per cent in 2001 (against 2000). 2002 has so far shown a decrease year on year of 3 per cent in its first three months. However, in general, it is reasonable to assume continued slight growth trends in the years to come. Furthermore, this forecast is also supported by the slightly increasing trend of the consumer satisfaction index.

The small and mini segments decreased after the 1996 boom. However, sales now appear to be stable with a slightly increasing trend. This evolution is in contrast to its share of the total market, which has decreased from a level around 70 per cent in 1995 to close to 50 per cent in 2001. This indicates that other segments, ie the low-middle segment, are growing faster. The low-middle segment performs in a similar manner as the total passenger car market: sales increased during 1995–1997, there was a significant sales drop in 1998, and more recently there has been a slow recovery. The segment share of the total market has grown from its level in 1995 where it was only 17 per cent, to a level around 30 per cent despite the sales drop in 1998. It is a fair estimation that this evolution will be long term, probably caused by the improving economic situation, which allows consumers to afford small cars as private vehicles.

Sales of middle segment cars performed in the same way as the low-middle segment sales during the period 1995–1998, but the sector had still not fully recovered and continued to decrease in 2000. 2001 showed some sign of recovery in total numbers but this was only fuelled by new products—the Renault Laguna, Ford Mondeo and Volkswagen Passat. All other brands in this segment showed significant declines. The share of the total market hovers around 7 per cent–8 per cent, with a slight recovery in 2001, again due to the impact of the new products.

High and luxury segments performed the same as the total passenger car market, with sales increasing during 1995–1997, a drop in 1998 and then a slow recovery. The station-wagon share of the market continues to grow at above-average levels and is a sign that these models are no longer considered as purely utility vehicles. Increasingly, wealthy families recognize the benefits of having the space together with a luxurious brand such as Volvo. This segment represents around 3 per cent of the total market. The off-road segment has been growing constantly from 1995. Its share of the total market is in line with the growing sales trend.

The MPV segment is performing extremely well with a growing trend since the sales drop recorded during 1996. In 2001, there was a significant increase in products resulting in an explosion of sales in this area. This segment now represents 4 per cent of the total market (four times the level seen in 1995). The coupé segment reached a sales peak in 1996, but has decreased significantly since then. Current sales are the lowest in history. This segment appears to be disappearing from the Czech market despite some interesting products such as the Mercedes CLK and Volvo C70. The cabriolet segment has also reached rock bottom since a peak in 1998. This segment appears to be almost finished in the Czech Republic.

In summary, therefore, the Czech automotive market continues to evolve as the market economy develops. This market is no longer a volatile emerging market with overall giant swings from gain to loss. There are, however, marked movements between segments as consumers move from buying their first car, which is normally a used car, to their first new car and then a rapid move up the segments. The prevalence of business purchases, either as bulk purchase company cars or user-chooser purchases, is growing. The benefit of the company car is seen increasingly as a norm rather than an exception. Therefore, the evolutionary changes that were seen in other more mature markets are coming to the Czech Republic and are taking a shorter development time to be established. It is often seen that Czechs are 'skipping stages of evolution' in this area. The increased presence of international leasing companies and manufacturer-owned 'banks' will add to the ease with which consumers can fund their car purchase. Czechs are still at the early stage of fully trusting 'contract hire' or operational leasing programmes where the ownership of the car remains with the financier. However, this is only a matter of time and when that happens it is predicted that more new-car purchases will be handled in this way for corporate buyers.

The used-car business is also at a fairly immature level. However, with the focus of manufacturers and importers on the 'whole life value chain' this will also change in a short time period. There are already many pilots and developed programmes in this area, which are being launched in the market.

Foreign investment

The Czech Republic is generally considered a very attractive market for foreign investors in the car-making industry, and out of the record US$2.01 billion (CZK70 billion) foreign investments attracted into the country during 2001, 44 per cent went to the car industry. The biggest investment in the car industry in 2001 was the €1.5 billion (CZK50 billion) project announced by Toyota and PSA Peugeot Citroën, which will build a new production plant in Kolín, Central Bohemia, employing at least 2000 people. The plant will produce some 300,000 cars per year for the European market starting in 2005, raising overall car production in the Czech Republic to over 800,000 per year.

This highly substantial investment to a great degree allayed the disappointment of the Czech government in proving unable to attract a DM1 billion investment by the German car manufacturer BMW, which chose Leipzig, Germany instead of Kolín. It was also recently announced that the South Korean car manufacturer, Hyundai, was considering building a plant in the Czech Republic valued at tens of billions of Czech crowns. Hyundai's project is to be confirmed later in 2002, and the industrial zone in Nosovice, North Moravia, is one possible location that it may take.

It should be added, however, that the car industry in the Czech Republic is already host to some notable foreign investment, the most significant of which are briefly outlined below.

Denso of Japan has begun developing a plant producing components for the car industry, and will create about 1000 jobs in Liberec, North Bohemia, by 2005. The plant will specialize in the production of air conditioning. The investment is worth US$100 million (CZK6 billion) and construction started in November 2001. Continental of Germany, a producer of tyres, invested US$69.4 million (CZK5 billion) in 1999 in a new plant in Zlin, South Moravia, employing 100 people. Hella Autotechnik, a subsidiary of German concern Hella KG Hueck & Co, opened a plant for the production of lights for cars and lorries in Mohelnice, North Moravia, in September 1999, and planned to invest US$35 million (CZK22 billion). In October 2000, Mitsubishi Electric Corporation of Japan launched construction of a plant at Slany, Central Bohemia, for US$32 million (CZK1.2 billion). The plant will turn out starters and alternators and employ 270 people.

In July 1997, Showa Aluminium Corporation of Japan was the first investor attracted to Kladno, Central Bohemia. The company built a plant for the production of condensers worth US$28 million (CZK1.01 billion), creating 200 jobs. Electric Powersteering Components Europe, a joint venture of Japanese companies Mitsubishi Electric and Koyo Seiko, will cooperate in the production of steering boosters. The plant in Slany, Central Bohemia will cost CZK1 billion to build. Koito Manufacturing of Japan, producing headlamps, stated in early 2001 that it will build a production facility worth US$26.3 million (CZK1.05bn) employing 400 people in Zatec, North Bohemia.

Hayes Lemmerz Alukola, a subsidiary of Italian company Hayes Lemmerz SpA Dello, put into operation a new plant for the production of aluminium car wheels in Ostrava, North Moravia, in June 1999. The investment, worth US$25 million (CZK0.9 billion), was granted the first government investment incentive. The company employs 250 people. Siemens Automobilova Technika opened a plant for the production of electrical components for the car industry in Frenstat pod Radhostem, North Moravia, in May 2000, worth €22 million (CZK806 million) and employing 200 people. In 2001, Aisan, one of Japan‘s largest producers of components for the car industry, was attracted to the industrial zone in Louny, North Bohemia. The company will be making fuel pumps for diesel engines and the plant will cost US$17.5 million (CZK700 million) to build. It is expected to employ 170 people.

Automotive components

Many foreign component suppliers have chosen to establish operations in the Czech Republic, initially often by entering into joint ventures or purchasing an existing Czech company but increasingly by building greenfield facilities. Many of these suppliers invested in the country to be close to Skoda. However, many others chose the Czech Republic due to its proximity to markets in neighbouring countries. There are some 100 foreign-owned automotive component suppliers with operations in the Czech Republic, including Bosch, Continental, Hayes-Lemmerz, Invensys, Johnson Controls, Siemens, TRW and Mannesmann.

The overwhelming market presence of Skoda is undoubtedly a primary reason for many of these foreign suppliers to operate in the Czech Republic, and Skoda alone is responsible for 10 per cent of the country's entire volume of export trade. Skoda has some 1200 suppliers at present, 340 of whom are located in the Czech Republic and supply 69 per cent of all components. Skoda currently has some 120 Tier 1 suppliers, of which 92 have foreign capital (of which a further 41 are greenfield investors with the remainder having formed joint ventures). Skoda has two main assembly facilities, in Mlada Boleslav and Kvasiny (one hour's drive north-east of Prague) with an engine production facility due for completion in 2003. There are also small kit assembly operations in Poland, India and Turkey. The company has an annual production of some 450,000 vehicles.

Skoda is always happy to consider new suppliers. However, in common with other OEMs, they set rigorous standards. In particular, it is necessary to demonstrate the ability to deliver highquality product in high volumes on time and at a competitive price. Traditionally, this has meant that companies wishing to supply Skoda have increasingly had to invest in the Czech Republic. However, Skoda has of late been at the forefront of companies calling for action to stop the relentless appreciation of the Czech crown. It is known to be considering sourcing more of its components overseas. Suppliers do not need to have an existing relationship with the VW Group to supply Skoda, but they must be able to demonstrate that they do supply other leading automotive companies. Senior Skoda management has indicated its interest in innovative new products and techniques. One area of particular interest is recycling, given the need for Skoda's cars to conform with EU regulation in this area.

The other vehicle manufacturer of significance in the Czech Republic, however, is Karosa, an enterprise that is part of the Irisbus holding, based in Vysoke Myto (two hours' drive east of Prague). Renault is the majority shareholder in the enterprise, holding more than 90 per cent of shares. Karosa boasts annual production of 1250 buses, with over half of production destined for public authority bus companies in the Czech Republic. Karosa is generally said to be always open to new suppliers and has recently invested in a new paint shop.

The Czech after-market is relatively underdeveloped. At present, consumers seeking service and repairs either use a franchise dealer or one of the many small entrepreneurs who often operate from their own home. There is a gradual move towards offering a more comprehensive service (eg tyres and exhausts), but there is no chain that, for example, compares with KwikFit in the United Kingdom. As the range of cars increases, smaller outfits are finding it increasingly difficult to stock the full range of parts needed to service all cars quickly and reliably. At the same time, however, cost-conscious Czechs are not always ready to use the relatively expensive dealer networks.

The after-market is likely to further develop as consumers switch to newer and more expensive cars. At the end of 2000, there were some 3.4 million cars in the Czech Republic (for a population of 10.3 million), with the average age of a car being 13.5 years. Over half of these are cars produced by Skoda. New-car sales in 2001

(January-November) increased by 3.1 per cent to 139,185. Over half of all new sales are small cars. Car ownership in 2006 is estimated to reach 4.3 million. Car parts are sold mainly through well-established original parts/spare parts dealers. The majority of them have a network of contracted garages across the whole country. Smaller companies tend to have one large warehouse and deliver parts on request. Given the size of the country, they can still supply on a same day/next day delivery basis.

Car accessories and car care products are sold in most garages/repair shops, petrol stations and also in supermarket/ hypermarket chains such as Tesco or Ahold. These chains do not import themselves, but are supplied by local wholesalers/distributors. They will directly import extremely price-competitive or attractive products, but only if they do not have to be tested or otherwise certified. The type of products that are sold through supermarket chains tends to fall into the middle/lower price and quality range.

International comparison and competitiveness

The car industry as a whole is among the key sectors of industry in the Czech Republic. This can be confirmed through both the absolute as well as the relative results of production and sales activities, including their share in overall industrial production and foreign trade of the Czech Republic. It is obvious that Czech producers (of final products in particular) are searching for export opportunities on new markets, on which lower price and comparable level of quality are still good trading arguments. Examples can be found in Skoda Auto (in Poland, China, Russia and India), Karosa (in France), but also Tatra Koprivnice and others.

The competitiveness of the sector has also been determined recently by a number of comparative advantages such as the still not fully liberalized market in material and energy inputs and skilled labour with lower wage costs (in particular when compared with EU countries). These advantages will eventually vanish through the course of the association period—restructuring of the industry will be decisive for maintaining the position of Czech producers on global markets.

The importance of the R&D basis for the car industry is indisputable, although no major changes took place in this field in 1999. Many firms are incorporated into the supranational system of R&D of their foreign partners, which thus strengthen its overall capacity. These activities are also influenced by globalization, and the participation of Czech firms in the process improves their chances on the road vehicle market. Two-thirds of firms in the car industry have their own R&D facilities or other activities connected with this field. Looking at the distribution of R&D among the main sub-groups of producers, it can be seen that 80 per cent of firms producing final products have their own R&D facilities, while for the producers of accessories it is only 58 per cent. Among the firms with foreign capital participation, 46 per cent have their own R&D capacities. The amounts invested into R&D activities reach as much as 12 per cent of income from sales of own production. Legislation in the field of motor vehicle production has been largely harmonized with EU Directives. The prepared amendments in this field, such as the amendments to Act No.38/1995 Coll. and the Directive of Ministry of Transport and Communications No.102/1995 Coll. are already fully based on EU legislation.

Prospects for the sector

The Czech car industry is under tremendous pressure in the field of quality, range of products and prices and needs to respond flexibly to the changing situation in the sale of its products. Any change in production requires large-scale investments and all innovative steps have to be considered carefully. The strong competition on the domestic market forces Czech producers to respond flexibly to the demands of customers and to fulfil their individual requirements. Problems are in the sphere of order financing (in particular in production of trucks, vans and utility vehicles) where Czech producers are often unable to offer similar financing conditions as their foreign competitors.

The prospects of the sector stress a common strategy for all the firms operating in Sector 34 (NACE): to fully maintain their competitiveness. In the period of globalization it will be increasingly difficult to distinguish between domestic and foreign markets. The investments flowing into the car industry will be of multinational character. They have to find well-prepared local firms to which the individual countries will create an optimum framework. The response to the incorporation of the Czech Republic into EU structures has to be similar. When compared with other sectors of Czech industry, the car industry is somewhat ahead. The relatively high foreign capital participation has also led, among other things, to a levelling of labour productivity, quality and input prices to the level reached by similar firms in the European Union. It can be expected that the car industry will also cope well with the approaching liberalization of energy prices and wage costs. A problem still lying ahead is how to restructure and recover van and truck production. Improvement of demand on the domestic market is expected in the context of revival of industrial production and construction activities.

Table 4.8.1 Sales of new motor vehicles

New Cars (kat. M1) Period: **January to December 2001**

	Make		*Domestic Sales (pcs)*	*Market share (only OFI* +TUZV**)*	*Sales same period year ago (pcs)*	*Change of Domestic Sales*	*Change of Market share new OFI*+ TUZV***
1	Skoda	TUZV	79,944	52.55%	78,187	2.25%	-0.04%
2	Volkswagen	OFI	9,517	6.26%	7,836	21.45%	0.99%
3	Renault	OFI	8,838	5.81%	7,509	17.70%	0.76%
4	Opel/GM	OFI	8,369	5.50%	8,879	-5.74%	-0.47%
5	Peugeot	OFI	8,344	5.48%	6,836	22.06%	0.89%
6	Ford	OFI	4,609	3.03%	4,378	5.28%	0.08%
7	Citroën	OFI	4,259	2.80%	2,989	42.49%	0.79%
8	Toyota	OFI	3,750	2.46%	3,666	2.29%	0.00%
9	Seat	OFI	2,793	1.84%	3,549	-21.30%	-0.55%
10	Fiat	OFI	2,773	1.82%	3,374	-17.81%	-0.45%
11	Nissan	OFI	2,546	1.67%	2,552	-0.24%	-0.04%
12	Mazda	OFI	2,358	1.55%	2,796	-15.67%	-0.33%
13	Daewoo	OFI	1,995	1.31%	4,665	-57.23%	-1.83%
14	Suzuki	OFI	1,767	1.16%	1,441	22.62%	0.19%
15	Hyundai	OFI	1,463	0.96%	1,210	20.91%	0.15%

New Light CVs (kat. N1) Period: **January to December 2001**

1	Ford	OFI	2,551	17.01%	2,379	7.23%	1.18%
2	Skoda	TUZV	2,461	16.41%	2,695	-8.68%	-1.53%
3	Volkswagen	OFI	2,171	14.47%	2,109	2.94%	0.44%
4	Mercedes Benz	OFI	1,311	8.74%	1,275	2.82%	0.26%
5	Peugeot	OFI	1,150	7.67%	1,192	-3.52%	-0.26%
6	Renault	OFI	816	5.44%	961	-15.09%	-0.95%

Table 4.8.1 continued
New Light CVs (kat. N1) Period: **January to December 2001**

Make			*Domestic Sales (pcs)*	*Market share (only OFI* +TUZV**)*	*Sales same period year ago (pcs)*	*Change of Domestic Sales*	*Change of Market share new OFI*+ TUZV***
7	Citroën	OFI	762	5.08%	664	14.76%	0.66%
8	Fiat	OFI	456	3.04%	541	-15.71%	-0.56%
9	Open/GM	OFI	414	2.76%	263	57.41%	1.01%
10	Nissan	OFI	376	2.51%	424	-11.32%	-0.31%
11	Kia	OFI	350	2.33%	436	-19.72%	-0.57%
12	Mazda	OFI	346	2.31%	424	-18.40%	-0.51%
13	Dacia	OFI	322	2.15%	163	97.55%	1.06%
14	Iveco	OFI	302	2.01%	299	1.00%	0.02%
15	Hyundai	OFI	273	1.82%	132	106.82%	0.94%
Total first 15 makes:			14,061	93.74%	13,957	0.75%	0.87%
Other 14 makes:			939				

Market OFI+TUZV TOTAL: -0.19%		—
Year 2001 (TUZV+OFI total pcs):		15,000
Year 2000 (TUZV+OFI total pcs):		15,029
Change (pcs):	-29	
incl: TUZV (ks)	-227	
OFI (ks)	198	

**TUZV—Sales of Czech Makes
*OFI—Sales of Officially Imported Vehicles
Source: Automotive Industry Association

4.9

Engineering Industry Products: Machining and Forming Equipment[1]

Jiri Langer, Head of the Engineering Department of the Ministry of Industry and Trade, and Zdenek Hruby, Executive Director, Union of Machinery Manufacturers and Suppliers

Overview

The engineering sector (ie general engineering, the metalworking industry and transport engineering) supplies production equipment to the entire economy. The Czech Republic's engineering production has a broad range and embraces everything from individual components to complete plant equipment. The base of the Czech industry is the engineering and electrical engineering complex, which forms one-third of the processing industry. It includes the branches of general and transport engineering, the metalworking industry and electrical engineering.

These branches form a segment of the processing industry and account for 30 per cent of its revenues, 31 per cent of its value added and approximately 37 per cent of its exports. It employs about 31 per cent of the total number of processing industry employees. An important branch of the complex is general engineering, accounting for approximately 28 per cent of its total

---

[1] This chapter is based on material supplied by the PP Agency in Prague.

production. The present trends indicate greatly diversified competitiveness of the products of this branch. General engineering also includes machine tools and forming machines.

The main branches of general engineering are the production of machines for the generation and use of mechanical energy, the production of machinery and equipment for general uses, machine tool manufacture, and the production of special machines. General engineering production is concentrated in the regions of Brno, Pardubice, Ostrava and Olomouc, and the Central Bohemia region including Prague. On the one hand, the present location of production has historical roots, and on the other the location is the result of extensive investments into the development of the engineering branches in the last few decades.

Machine tools and forming equipment

Machine tools and metal-forming machines are central to the engineering industry in the Czech Republic and have a notable impact on the results and standards of the entire processing industry in the country. This sub-sector of the engineering industry has always been export driven, since the scope of production offered by the sector has generally been of greater significance than demand in the domestic market. Metal-cutting machines have the largest share in Czech production of machine tools and forming machines, accounting for between 85 per cent and 90 per cent of total production. More than 80 per cent of products turned out in the branch are exported.

After 1990, Czech producers in the sector lost most of their eastern markets due to the insolvency of their partners from these countries. However, major innovation of products paved their way into the markets of the advanced industrial states, particularly the EU countries and North America during the 1990s. In recent years, the Czech Republic has advanced to 14th position in global machine tool and forming machine production (Japan, Germany and the United States are the leading countries in the sector), as well as seventh position in Europe in their manufacture and export. Germany, Italy and Switzerland have been the top European producers for many years.

The production of machine tools and forming machines, including accessories, spare parts and general repairs, and their exports rose annually by 12–44 per cent and 23–28 per cent respectively between the mid-1990s and the end of the decade. The world-wide recession in the machine tools and forming machines industry in 1999 hit Czech manufacturers hard, however, since over 80 per cent of their production is exported. Sales by Czech producers decreased significantly in Western Europe, and demand for their products also declined in North America. The overall result of the recession was a 5 per cent decrease in domestic production of machine tools and forming machines as compared to 1998. However, the recession did not affect all enterprises in the sector, with some Czech producers actually increasing production despite the recession. Furthermore, a number of industry sources suggest that the impact of recession should not be long lasting, and that both the volumes of sales and production of Czech enterprises in the sector is set to increase, especially in connection with the expected boom in the automobile industry.

The sector's potential in foreign trade

Tradition and quality have always placed Czech producers among the best even among the industrially advanced states. The export performance of the sector has been rising since 1994, and the rate of export expansion is good. Data on the worldwide machine tool production and demand show that demand exceeds production in North America, Africa and parts of South America. Exports from the Czech Republic have risen markedly since 1990, particularly to North American states, which applied mainly to the export machining units to the United States and Canada. In the machine tool sector, the Czech Republic has a distinct surplus in the balance of trade with territories in which demand exceeds production. A larger share on the market can be reached in some Middle East countries with transition economies and also the former Soviet Union. The general foreign trade performance of the sector is illustrated in Table 4.9.1.

The products in Sector 29.4 are machine tools and forming machines, namely for the machining of all materials, machining by lasers, luminous or photon beams and ultrasound, machining units, lathes, boring machines, milling and grinding machines, forming machines, and woodworking machines. This group also includes machines and equipment for soldering and welding, surface malleablizing and hot spraying, pneumatic or motor-driven hand-operated tools, index heads, and other special accessories of machine tools.

Table 4.9.1 **Exports and imports for the second half of the 1990s**

CZK million	*1995*	*1996*	*1997*	*1998*	*1999*	*96/95*	*97/96*	*98/97*	*99/98*
Exports in current prices									
NACE 29.1	13,954	15,416	19,013	23,824	25,000	110.5	123.3	125.3	104.9
NACE 29.2	10,648	13,316	17,806	21,538	24,500	125.1	133.7	121.0	113.8
NACE 29.3	5425	5542	6853	7555	6000	102.1	123.7	110.2	79.4
NACE 29.4	9209	11,092	13,593	15,518	17,000	120.4	122.6	114.2	109.5
NACE 29.5	19,723	21,025	25,321	29,967	31,000	106.6	120.4	118.3	103.4
NACE 29.6	2396	2036	2102	2494	2800	84.9	103.3	118.6	112.3
NACE 29.7	3473	3893	4241	4815	5000	112.1	108.9	113.6	103.8
NACE 29	64,829	72,319	88,931	105,712	111,300	111.6	123.0	118.9	105.3
Imports in current prices									
NACE 29.1	18,502	20,231	22,778	26,154	26,000	109.3	112.6	114.8	99.4
NACE 29.2	23,151	26,588	27,489	26,734	26,000	114.8	103.4	97.3	97.3
NACE 29.3	5755	7670	6820	4845	3500	133.3	88.9	71.0	72.2
NACE 29.4	11,528	12,140	13,177	15,585	15,000	105.3	108.5	118.3	96.2
NACE 29.5	32,510	29,964	31,358	33,514	35,000	92.2	104.7	106.9	104.4
NACE 29.6	874	421	621	536	700	48.1	147.6	86.4	130.5
NACE 29.7	9108	11,512	11,770	11,479	10,000	126.4	102.2	97.5	87.1
NACE 29	101,428	108,525	114,013	118,847	116,200	107.0	105.1	104.2	97.8
Balance of trade									
NACE 29.1	-4548	-4816	-3764	-2330	-1000	X	x	X	x
NACE 29.2	-12,504	-13,271	-9683	-5196	-1500	X	x	X	x
NACE 29.3	-330	-2128	33	2710	2500	X	x	X	x
NACE 29.4	-2318	-1048	416	-66	2000	X	x	X	x
NACE 29.5	-12,787	-8939	-6037	-3,547	-4000	X	x	X	x
NACE 29.6	1522	1615	1482	1958	2100	X	x	X	x
NACE 29.7	-5635	-7619	-7529	-6663	-5000	X	x	X	x
NACE 29	-36,600	-36,206	-25,083	-13,136	-4900	X	x	X	x

Source: Czech Statistical Office

Summary

In all branches of the engineering industry, machine tools and forming machines rank among the limiting factors of the level of their capability to turn out high-quality, precise and competitive products. The technical parameters and quality of machine tools and forming machines going from the Czech Republic are at least comparable to foreign products. In view of the increasing competition and demand for faultless and safe operation, the placing of this commodity on the domestic and foreign markets is not without its problems. Czech manufacturers are facing strong pressure from imports, thus inducing them to increase the competitiveness of their products. Competitiveness will now have to rest mainly on factors other than price, such as technical parameters at high-tech level, quality, prompt delivery, meeting of customers' requirements, and service. Many enterprises are gradually adapting themselves to these internal factors.

Export performance figures in the group of machine tools and forming machines indicates their sound competitiveness. However, it must be noted that Czech engineering has so far been capable of price competition, but this will soon cease to be sufficient. The preservation of the rate of growth and its desirable increase requires far larger investment, especially into new technologies and machinery. The main factor of success will be permanent growth in productivity, which must be triggered by consistent restructuring of engineering enterprises. Machine tools and forming machines have good prerequisites for being increasingly supplied to advanced markets. Czech engineering products, including machine tools and forming machines, have their weight on the domestic and foreign markets, as they are important commodities exported to the industrially advanced countries.

With recession overcome, countries throughout the world are giving preference to investments. Investments will have to be markedly increased in the Czech Republic in view of the restructuring of industry and securing economic growth. Thus, the promising sales potential of the advanced Czech engineering rests on foreign and domestic capital construction and the accelerating integration and globalization of production. This affords the conclusion that one can be optimistic about the further development of this important branch, but the decisive role in the development of its production will be played by the gaining of markets and the competitiveness of supplies.

4.10

Production of Electronic Components and Equipment

Pavel Ríha Ing., Ministerial Counsellor, Ministry of Industry and Trade of the Czech Republic

Introduction

In 2000, the production of electronic components, telecommunication equipment and consumer electronics (branch 32 according to branch classification of economic activities—OKEČ) in the Czech Republic was worth CZK42,379.2 million, with added value amounting to CZK10,111.6 million. In total, 31,289 people were employed in the sector. Important producers and suppliers of electronic components include AVX CZ, with divisions at Lanškroun and Uherské Hradiště , Tesla Sezam and Terosil Rožnov pod Radhoště m, Tesla Lanškroun, TCT Rožnov pod Radhoště m, Unit Expert Př elouč , PCB Benešov u Prahy, Tesla Vršovice, Tesla Jihlava, Tesla Blatná, Trimex Rožnov pod Radhoště m, Elektronické souč ástky Ostrava, Krystaly Hradec Králové and Polovodič e Praha. During the transformation of the Czech economy, the production base of electronic parts became diversified from a technological perspective as well as in terms of competitiveness.

Electronic components

AVX Czech Republic launched the production of tantalum capacitors in Lanškroun in 1993, and in only a few years became one of the Czech Republic's two largest tantalum capacitor producers. The company is owned by AVX Corporation (United States), whose majority shareholder is Kyocera Corporation (Japan). The Lanškroun division is currently the world's largest plant making tantalum capacitors. In 1999, AVX CZ invested massively in the construction of a new production plant and new technological lines. In addition to its capacitor programme at Lanškroun, the company developed another investment project at Uherské Hradiště , where it manufactures connectors and ceramic capacitors. AVX CZ exports 100 per cent of its output and covers an important part of world consumption.

The production of bipolar integrated circuit chips and the assembly of diode, transistor and integrated structures by Tesla Sezam in cooperation with Motorola at Rožnov pod Radhoště m is another project concerning a producer of worldwide significance. At Rožnov, they also use facilities for the assembly of bipolar power transistors and power MOS FETs for TO 220 packages. They use the same packages for integrated circuits made by Tesla Sezam. A line has been installed for the assembly of special automobile diodes, which are exported to US and European markets. Production has undergone a QS 9000 customer audit conducted by DELCO. In addition to raising chip production, the plan is to increase the capacity of the assembly plant. The chips, which are not packaged in the firm's own assembly plant, are supplied to Motorola's divisions in other countries. Over time, Motorola has undergone restructuring, during which its SCG division became an independent company, ON Semiconductor. This firm is now a partner to Tesla Sezam, Terosil and the SCG Design Centre at Rožnov pod Radhoště m. The core of Terosil's current programme is the production of silicon monocrystals and polished boards. Another project is the manufacture of epitaxy boards.

The modernized production of flat TV screens at TCT Rožnov pod Radhoště m has also found its way to market. The firm also makes good-quality printed circuit boards at a relatively low cost. The disadvantage of the production base in comparison with rival firms is its small production series. In addition, in 1997, Matsushita Television Central Europe (MTE) built a plant for the assembly of colour monophony television sets at Borské Pole in Plzeň . It is the largest foreign investment project in the sphere of consumer electronics. Currently, a massive enlargement of the company making Panasonic colour TV sets in the Czech Republic is under way to include stereo and digital sets.

Telecommunication equipment

The largest Czech producer of digital telecommunication equipment is TTC Tesla Telekomunikace, s.r.o. TTC Marconi is a joint venture of TTC Tesla Telekomunikace and Marconi Communications. Its position on the telecommunication market indicates the necessity of linking the domestic producer with a strong supranational partner, which will enable the firm to meet customer demand in a comprehensive way and help it penetrate foreign markets. TTC Marconi is a supplier of technologies and a network integrator in the area of telephone, data and radio signal transfer, videoconferences, etc. TTC Marconi uses the technologies of both TTC Telecommunications and Marconi Communications. The multinational Marconi Communications came into being through the merger of two leading world suppliers of communication technologies, Marconi SpA from Italy and GEC Marconi from the United Kingdom.

The Sagem Group terminals and telecommunication division has decided to build a new plant to assemble mobile telephones from disassembled components in the Czech Republic. It selected the Kladno industrial zone as the most suitable locality for this project. The assembly of 250,000 mobile telephones per year has created new jobs for 300 specialists. The realization of the next stage of the project will make it possible to produce and assemble two million mobile telephones a year, creating job opportunities for 700 people.

Foreign trade

In the long term, it is evident that the Czech Republic's imports of electronic components, telecommunication equipment and consumer electronics are higher than its exports. In 2000, imports totalled CZK89,976.2 million, of which imports for active improvement amounted to CZK37,015 million. Exports of electronic components, telecommunication equipment and consumer electronics in the same year were worth CZK35,386.1 million. The average per kilogram export price was CZK812. The share of supranational companies in the production of electronic components and equipment in the Czech Republic keeps increasing. The growth of exports after active improvement helps improve the country's balance of trade.

Czech exports of electronic components in 2000 accounted for 62 per cent of the sector's total exports, amounting to CZK33,564 million. The largest export item in the group of electronic components was HS/CN 85322100 'Electric fixed tantalum capacitors'. Exports of this item to the United Kingdom, the United States, Singapore and Japan account for 85 per cent of total exports. Altogether, 5873 million pieces were exported priced at CZK16,798 per kilogram. Another important export item was HS/CN 85322400 'Firm electric capacitors'. Its export fetched CZK5255 million. The United Kingdom, Malaysia and Germany account for 90 per cent of the total export of this item. Altogether, 16,294 million pieces of this item were exported priced at CZK7799 per kilogram. HS/CN 85401115 'Colour TV screens' was also an important export item. Its exports were worth CZK1434 million, comprising 684,000 pieces, which were sold at a price of CZK139 per kilogram. The export of HS/CN 85340090 'Printed circuit boards and other passive elements' was worth CZK1374 million. The export price was CZK4259 per kilogram.

The largest import item in the electronic components group in 2000, totalling CZK43,610 million, was HS/CN 8532900 'Parts of electric fixed rotary capacitors', worth CZK4672 million. Seventy-seven per cent of these imports come from the United Kingdom. The per-kilogram price of these imports was CZK2767. Another large import item is HS/CN 85322400 'Electric fixed ceramic capacitors', totalling CZK4502 million. Seventy per cent of these imports come from the United Kingdom. The import price was CZK11,446 per kilogram. Also significant was the import of HS/CN 85421200 'Integrated circuit cards (smart cards)', amounting to CZK4197 million. Eighty-six per cent of these imports come from Germany and France. The item was imported at the price of CZK14,722 per kilogram. Yet another important import item was HS/CN 85423090 'Monolithic integrated circuits'. Its import was worth CZK3864 million. Seventy-four per cent of the goods came from the United Kingdom and Belgium, at an import price of CZK14,701 per kilogram.

A large import item in the sphere of telecommunication equipment in 2000 was HS/CN 85252091 'Transmitter receivers for cellular networks'. Its import was worth CZK12,328 million. Eighty-four per cent of imports came from Germany, followed by France, Estonia and the United Kingdom. Altogether, 2.7 million pieces of this equipment were imported and priced at CZK6619 per kilogram. Another significant import item was HS/CN 85252099 'Other transmitter receivers'. The total sum of these imports was CZK6106 million. Seventy-four per cent of these goods came from Sweden, Italy and Germany. Altogether, 226,000 pieces were imported and priced at CZK4889 per kilogram.

An important part of Czech exports of telecommunication equipment in 2000, totalling CZK6035 million, was accounted for by the export of item HS/CN 85252091 'Transmitter receivers for the cellular network', which fetched CZK3637 million. Sixty-six per cent of these exports went to France, Poland, Taiwan and Turkey. Altogether, 1.2 million pieces of this equipment were exported at a price of CZK7410 per kilogram. In the sphere of consumer electronics, the export of item HS/CN 85281256 'Colour TV sets' in 2000 was worth CZK6313 million. Ninety per cent of these exports went to Germany, the United Kingdom, Poland and Austria. The price for the export of 910,325 sets was CZK258 per kilogram.

The item figuring highest on the list of consumer electronics imports in 2000 was HS/CN 85281256 'Colour TV sets'. The import of this item was worth CZK18,461 million. Seventy-seven per cent of these imports came from Poland, France, Slovakia, Turkey, Spain and Slovenia. The imports were worth CZK1579 million. Altogether, 403,978 items were imported at a price of CZK264 per kilogram.

Prospects for development

The common feature of technological processes in the manufacture of electronic components and equipment, where the production technologies become obsolete more quickly than in the conventional sectors of the manufacturing industry, is investment intensiveness. There is a good opportunity for multinational companies interested in transferring a part of their production to areas with a highly skilled labour force and a country with an advantageous geographical position to cooperate. Through Act No. 72/2000 Coll. on Investment Incentives, the Czech government has advocated its interest in the technological restructuring of the country's industry. A priority is the import of a set of equipment forming technological lines and making possible the production, assembly and diagnosing of high-technology equipment, such as electronic components and digital communication systems. The interest of foreign investors in investing capital especially in new greenfield projects creates prerequisites for accelerating technological restructuring and raising the competitiveness of products for the support of telecommunication technologies.

Koninklijke Philips Electronics, Philips Display Components division has begun realizing a project to build the world's largest enterprise to make conventional colour TV screens. The location of this vast project is Hranice na Moravě . As part of the project, the latest types of super-flat screens will be made there at a later stage, More than 3000 new jobs will be created at Hranice over the next seven years. The company's output will be eight million TV screens per year. More than 90 per cent of the output will go for export to EU countries.

The Philips investment project is the largest direct foreign investment in the construction of a greenfield venture in the Czech Republic. The location of the Philips project in the Czech Republic will facilitate the placing of new development centres for the electronic industry in the Czech Republic. For example, in Prague a specialized developmental centre, S3, already exists. It is formed by a team of developmental workers concerned with top-standard technologies and the design of new chips for mobile telephones, not only for the use of its parent firm, but also for other customers.

The Matsushita Communication Industrial division of the Japanese concern Matsushita Electric Industrial has started building a plant in Pardubice for the production and assembly of mobile telephones. The company will invest more than CZK3200 million in the project, which will employ 550 people. The new plant will start production in October 2002. The investor assumes that the first investment stage will be followed by a second one. The company hopes that the new investment will help it raise its share of the world mobile telephone market.

4.11

Chemicals[1]

Blanka Ksandrova, Director of the Department of Industry, Ministry of Industry and Trade; and František Stránský, Economist

Background

The Czech chemical industry has a long-established tradition and belongs among the essential sectors of the processing industry. The economic transformation that commenced in the country in 1990 and the break-up of Czechoslovakia at the end of 1992 did not, by and large, have such negative effects on the chemical industry in the country relative to other processing sectors. Since 1993–1994, however, when the Czech Republic began its gradual recovery from the preceding decline, the chemical industry has been developing with far higher dynamics than other processing sectors.

According to the Branch Classification of Economic Activities (BCEA) and the Standard Classification of Production (SCP), the Czech chemical industry is defined as a sum of aggregations: Refinery Oil Processing Including Carbonization (BCEA 23), Chemical and Pharmaceutical Industry (BCEA 24) and the Rubber and Plastics Industry (BCEA 25). Since 1996, the organizational structure has changed and businesses involved in petrochemistry and the related manufacture of primary plastics (Chemopetrol a.s. and Kaucuk a.s.) are now grouped within BCEA 24.

Its volume of sales and share in exports ranks the chemical industry among the leading sectors of the processing industry of the Czech Republic. The industry's production base at the end of the 1990s was made up of 449 organizations with 20-plus employees of which 140 organizations were in the chemical and pharmaceutical industry and 303 in the rubber and plastics industry. In total, there are over 1100 businesses involved in the chemical industry, of which approximately 67 per cent are in the rubber and plastics industry, approximately one-third in the chemical and

[1] This chapter is based on materials supplied by the PP Agency in Prague.

pharmaceutical industry and the remainder in refinery production (including carbonization), which together employ approximately 93,000 people. The total number of entities includes almost 88 per cent of organizations having 1–99 employees, which evidences the considerable diversification and origin of a wide spectrum ranging from small firms to companies with their number of employees exceeding 1000. However, the decisive part of the sales of the chemical industry, almost three-quarters, is made up from companies having 100-plus employees.

Position and function of the chemical industry in the economy

The Czech chemical industry contributes approximately 3.9 per cent to the national GDP. The chemical industry produces semi-finished goods for further processing and final products with a wide range of further uses in all industrial and non-industrial sectors, eg in agriculture (fertilizers, pesticides, veterinary products etc), in health care (medicaments, pure chemicals), in construction (plastic products, paints etc.), in the power and heat industry (heating oils, transformer oils, lubricants, coagulants for water treatment etc.), transport (petrol, diesel, lubricants, car cosmetics etc). Chemical products are closely connected with the everyday life of every person (cosmetics, detergents, soaps).

Contrary to the experience of a number of other sectors of the processing industry, the chemical industry did not record a significant decline in production during the first years of economic transformation at the start of the 1990s, with the same also applying to domestic demand. From 1993, when the economic revival stage started, both production and demand began to develop significantly, with the trend continuing in 1997. However, as production failed to keep pace with the structure of domestic demand, primarily in products with higher added value, the share of imports to satisfy domestic demand gradually grew in both the chemical industry itself and other processing sectors. Domestic demand has maintained a constantly growing trend. It should be noted that in the mid-1990s there was an absolute decline of demand for BCEA 23, while in contrast there was considerable growth in demand for BCEA 24 as a result of the aforementioned organizational changes from 1 January 1996. As a result of the change to calculation methods, the annual growth rate of demand increased by 2 per cent relative to the original methods.

Offer of products and services

Due to insufficient restructuring, the Czech chemical industry is not currently able to offer a product range to satisfy the growth in domestic demand. Interest primarily in sophisticated products endures and therefore this demand must be covered mainly by imports, which have recently had a negative impact on the deteriorating balance of foreign trade.

Chemical industry and the environment

With regard to the environment, the chemical industry is perceived by the public as a problematic processing sector. However, it exceeds most other sectors in its permanent efforts to improve health and environmental effects and safety. This is documented by costly ecological investments by most companies (in recent years, on average 50 per cent of total investments were set aside for these purposes) and implementation of environment-oriented management. The most important companies in the chemical industry joined the voluntary programme of the world chemical industry named 'Responsible Care—Responsible Business in Chemistry'. The certificate for use of the 'RC' logo has already been granted to a number of representatives of the industry, eg to Chemicke Zavody Sokolov, Deza, Chemopetrol, Kaucuk, Precheza, Spolek pro Chemickou a Hutni Vyrobu, Spolana, Synthesia, among others. A number of companies, primarily members of the Union of Chemical Industry, are preparing for implementation of the EN ISO 14001 standard and in most cases already have experience with EN ISO 9000. Chemicke Zavody Sokolov, a.s. was first to acquire an ecological management system certificate under the requirements of EN ISO 14001 and British Standard 7750/94.

The sector is also very actively involved in the World Business Council for Sustainable Development, whose conference was held in Prague in late 2001. In October 1996, a joint project of the Union of the Chemical Industry and the Ministry of Environment called 'Sustainable Development of the Czech Chemical Industry' was established to identify the key problems arising in the chemical industry as a result of adoption of EU environmental legislation. Through the Ministry of Industry and Trade, the Czech Republic is involved in a pilot project of decontamination of environmental burdens in selected locations polluted by chemical toxins, which is undertaken with the European Economic Commission and the

United Nations. Out of 40 proposed projects in transition economy countries, the highest priority was given to a decontamination project by Synthesia, a.s. Besides the European Economic Commission and the company itself, the project will be 50 per cent (approximately US$40 million) co-financed by the European Union.

Businesses on the capital market

The situation for chemical joint-stock companies on the capital market is not favourable and prices of their shares have mostly fallen gradually since their introduction to the market. It is generally thought that the main causes for this decline are changes in ownership in companies and non-transparent ownership relations. Although in the mid-1990s shares were owned mainly by investment funds and small shareholders, the most important companies in the industry at present are owned by majority shareholders. For this reason, the volume of shares freely negotiable on the market has declined, as has their liquidity. In addition, small shareholders began to sell their shares due to the zero-dividend policy of the owners.

Employment in the industry

The number of employees in the chemical industry has undergone a constant reduction in recent years, on average decreasing by 2 per cent–2.4 per cent annually. This trend will undoubtedly continue as part of the further restructuring and rationalization of companies. An up-to-date example is the Chemapol Group, which, with regard to the establishment of a new entity called Aliachem, announced that it intends to reduce its workforce in the chemical companies Synthesia, Fatra, Technoplast and Moravske Chemicke Zavody by 3000.

Foreign trade

Following the break-up of the Eastern bloc, ie the former COMECON, the territorial structure of foreign trade in chemical products of the Czech Republic has changed radically. From the former planned economy, the Czech chemical industry inherited an unfavourable product structure with respect to international competitiveness, which is dominated by bulk products with low added value. As a result of opening up the Czech economy to the world, this industry was exposed to the growing pressures of the competitive environment of the global market in chemical products, both at home and abroad.

Relatively low prices matched with quality comparable to international standards allowed domestic manufacturers to place a considerable part of their production on advanced Western European markets, with the result that the rapidly growing export market gradually compensated for the decline in consumption brought about by the temporary reduction of domestic demand primarily, in addition to the loss of traditional COMECON markets. A significant reversal occurred in 1991 and the industry returned a positive balance over CZK2 billion. In the ensuing years, however, the dynamics of imports into the Czech Republic began to advance the rate of growth of exports of chemical products. There were several reasons for this reversal, including:

- the unfavourable structure of domestic production was insufficient to cover the growing demand for special products of qualified chemistry and pharmacy, plastic products and other commodities to the required quality and product range.
- there was a disintegration of markets in Eastern Europe, primarily the former Soviet Union where a considerable portion of the exports went;
- customs barriers were removed, creating vast openness of the market for chemical products;
- there was a revival in demand for chemical products brought about by relative favourable domestic economic development from 1993–1995;
- there was high consumption of imported medicaments;
- the free convertibility of the Czech crown.

In Czech foreign trade at present, chemical products occupy a relatively important position, and the fact that their role in foreign trade is increasing alludes to one of the most complicated structural problems of the Czech economy in general and in Czech industry in particular. This fact is illustrated by Table 4.11.1, which gives export and import figures for recent years.

The export and import of chemicals plays an important role in the country's overall economic development, and it is appropriate to point out that the existing trends are showing great inertia and reproduction capacity. From a global perspective it is clear that:

Table 4.11.1 **Imports and exports of chemicals, 1994–2000**

	1994	*1995*	*1996*	*1997*	*1998*	*1999*	*2000 first half*	*1994 1999 index*
(in current prices, CZK billion)								
Total Czech exports	458.8	566.2	610.1	7225.0	850.3	929.5	539.5	202
of which: chemicals	42.4	52.9	54.3	63.5	65.5	66.9	39.5	158
Total Czech imports	498.4	665.7	759.0	8707.0	928.9	995.9	582.9	200
of which: chemicals	59.4	78.6	89.1	105.4	112.6	119.8	67.5	202
Overall trade balance	-39.5	-99.6	-148.9	-148.2	-78.6	-66.0	-43.4	177
of which: chemicals	-17.0	-25.8	-34.8	-41.9	-47.1	-52.9	-27.9	312

- chemical exports are considerably lagging behind overall Czech exports and their position in the commodity structure of Czech exports is weakening. In 1994, chemicals accounted for 9.2 per cent of Czech exports, in 1997 their share dropped to 8.8 per cent and in 1999 to only 7.2 per cent;
- in Czech imports, chemicals have maintained their structural position on a long-term basis (11.9 per cent in 1994, 12 per cent in 1999).

Chemical trade strongly influences the overall imbalance of the Czech Republic's foreign trade, which is particularly true of recent years, when chemicals have been most responsible for the overall deficit of the country's balance of trade. This development is most evident through the geographic orientation of chemical trade,

Table 4.11.2 **The proportion of chemicals within total imports and exports (from and to developed countries), 1996–2000**

	1996	*1 997*	*1998*	*1999*	*2000 first half*
Czech exports to developed market economies, CZK billion	398.8	474.2	591.2	694.3	409.4
of which: chemicals (SITC 5)	26.7	32.3	33.5	35.1	22.7
equivalent to (%)	7.1	6.9	5.7	5.1	5.5
Czech imports from developed market economies, CZK billion	533.9	613.1	672.5	732.3	426.0
of which: chemicals (SITC 5)	68.5	82.0	89.9	97.3	54.6
equivalent to (%)	12.8	13.4	13.4	13.3	12.9
Balance of trade of the Czech Republic with developed market economies, CZK billion	-140.1	-138.9	-81.4	-38.0	-16.7
of which: chemicals (SITC 5)	-41.8	-49.7	-56.4	-62.2	-32.1
equivalent to (%)	30	36	69	164	192

which is apparent through the dominant role of trade relations with advanced countries, as can be seen in Table 4.11.2.

In terms of its standing with advanced market economies, the Czech Republic is the weaker partner as a result of a number of factors (scientific, technical, capital, qualitative and productive). The most advanced countries occupy a dominant position in chemical trade with the rest of the world, including the Czech Republic. The result is the widening gap between Czech exports and imports (accelerated by the progressive development of modernization trends in industry with chemicals occupying an increasingly important role not only in the material and construction base, but also in services, eg in new packaging technologies) and the aggressive supply of a wide range of a practically universal range of chemical products. Under these conditions, the Czech chemical industry can succeed by specialization and the use of different forms of cooperation and its own scientific and research base.

In this respect, it is also appropriate to mention the development of Czech chemical trade with other regions, in particular the states in transition and developing countries. Global characteristics are provided by figures shown in Table 4.11.3.

In relation to these countries, the Czech Republic appears as economically more advanced with a favourable partial balance of trade. In contrast, its trade with advanced countries is not sufficiently intensive, resulting in a weakening on the part of Czech exports and imports as well as the partial balance. As a consequence, the surplus of chemical trade with transition and developing countries cannot significantly offset the Czech Republic's overall deficit in chemical trade.

An analysis of the internal structure of Czech export and import trade in chemicals clearly reveals the determining factors of the

Table 4.11.3 **The proportion of chemical imports and exports (from and to transition states and developing countries), 1996–2000**

	1996	*1999*	*2000 first half*
Percentage share of states in transition and developing countries of the total value of			
—Czech chemical exports	51	48	43
—Czech chemical imports	23	19	19
Balance of chemical trade in relation to transitional and developing countries, in CZK billion	+7.0	-9.4	-4.2

unfavourable situation and trends in chemical trade. The dynamic growth of Czech imports is determined by Pharmaceuticals, plastics, plastics in non-primary form and the 'other chemicals' group, where the gap between imports and exports is continually widening. These products account for as much as 90 per cent of the CZK18.1 billion increase in the balance of trade deficit in the chemicals sector in the second half of the 1990s. In the case of other chemicals, the gap between exports and imports is less pronounced and the deficit is increasing only slowly. In general, however, in all groups of chemical products (except organic chemicals) imports predominate over exports, with no signs of improvement.

Important aspects of the problems accompanying and influencing the Czech Republic's trade in general and its trade in chemicals in particular are prices. Prices, whether in export or import transactions, are one of the key conditions of effective trade. In the case of the Czech Republic, a more detailed analysis reveals that chemical production is characterized by very low added value in the processing of input materials, which differs dramatically from the situation in Czech imports of chemicals. While there are a large number of complicated causes in operation, the Czech economy, with its limited raw material resources and inadequate structure, can find a solution in the maximum valorization of input materials and the wide-ranging use of the scientific and research base in finalization.

This development is strongly influenced by medicaments and Pharmaceuticals, which in 1999 accounted for 23 per cent of the overall value of Czech chemical imports (and for only 10 per cent of overall chemical imports). The relationship between average export and import prices is worsening, the proportion in 1999 being only 44 per cent. The position and role of chemical production constitutes a permanent problem in the Czech economy, which affects both the balance of trade and the structure of the incorporation of Czech industry into world trade. In the current internal and external conditions this is leaving the problem of restructuring open, all the more so as the trend is worsening.

Foreign trade therefore reflects, in an amplified form, the problems of the further development of the Czech chemical industry, including its position in the structure of industry and its position in the structure of supply on the Czech market, as regards both consumer goods and modern construction materials, packaging and building materials etc. Opportunities on the domestic as well as foreign markets are very open, particularly in the perspective of future development, and finding outlets in those markets in the face of growing competition from the world chemical giants is one of the key problems of the process of restructuring.

Preparation for accession to the European Union

The chemical industry belongs among the processing sectors where the economic effects of the Czech Republic's accession to the European Union will be considerable and will most significantly affect the business sector, less so the government budget and the population. These effects will concern the following areas:

- costs connected with achievement of conformity in environmental legislation;
- integrated conception of safe operation of technological processes;
- chemical legislation;
- restructuring of manufacturing sectors, modernization and expansion of production.

In order to keep pace with Western European chemistry, it will be necessary, according to expert estimates, to invest a minimum of CZK25 billion–CZK35 billion annually in the medium term. This is also connected with the necessity to increase investments in science and research, which have been insufficient up until now. The most important tasks of the Czech Republic until its entry into the European Union in this area will be to solve issues of price creation transparency and medicament policy in general.

Characteristics of the chemical industry

It can generally be said about the chemical industry that the global demand for its products grows faster then demand for industrial products in total, primarily in the most developed countries. This is shown in the level of development of the industry as well as in the dynamics of its development and competitiveness. The level of development in the advanced countries is characterized by the following:

- high degree of concentration of production;
- need for highly qualified personnel;
- flexibility and readiness to restructure;
- ability to innovate;
- increased sense of responsibility towards the environment.

The following are the decisive moves taken towards the global development of the chemical industry:

- deepening globalization and integration of the world market (resulting in high dynamics of international exchange);
- 'ecologization' of products and manufacturing processes;
- continuing internationalization of production linked to increased specialization, primarily on the international market (primarily chemical specialities);
- growing concentration of the production base linked to constant growth in demand for fast innovations of higher importance.

Czech industry has a number of weak points in this respect, including:

- insufficient product range dominated by less sophisticated products with lower added value (negatively affecting balance of trade);
- low level of dynamics of innovation activity (products and technology) closely related to restriction of R&D and to insufficient investment activity;
- insufficient territorial diversification of foreign trade, primarily in exports;
- environmental burdens from the past, which draw considerable funds (a minimum of 50 per cent of annual investment);
- low degree of concentration and specialization of production.

In contrast, there are certain positive factors affecting the branch in the Czech Republic to some degree outweighing its weak points:

- domestic demand is growing (12 per cent–15 per cent annually), which is naturally accompanied by growing requirements for product range and quality and growing demand for imports;
- qualified and experienced workforce in production and research is still obtainable at substantially very low cost compared to economically advanced countries;
- the quality of most commodities is comparable with common foreign equivalent products, primarily in bulk products but also in a certain amount of production of qualified and processing production.

In the interests of approximation to European and world levels, it will thus be necessary to focus on structural and modernization investments linked to the strengthening of manufacturing specialization and an improvement of factors which decisively contribute to enhancing competitiveness.

Apart from quality and product range, the most important competitive factor is price, and successful price competition is based on the total costs of the manufacturer. Detailed analysis of the cost items in the chemical industry indicates that the cause of deterioration of efficiency is primarily the growth of other costs (particularly interest rates). Relative to the developed world, the cost structure has too high a share in manufacturing consumption, due primarily to a low level of finality, high energy requirements and low concentration of the production base. Surprisingly, there is a higher share of depreciation in the total costs in the Czech Republic than in Germany. This can be explained by lower efficiency of fixed assets, which is probably a result of insufficiently high production capacities—economies of scale. Increasing the efficiency of fixed assets is therefore one of the key directions in strengthening competitiveness in both the medium and long term. Another is the need to considerably increase labour productivity.

Business policy and strategy

A significant handicap to most business entities in this sector is often an insufficiently prepared business strategy (both at home and abroad), and the need for experienced personnel for marketing, promotion, servicing etc. In the period of growth in demand and overall boom, Czech chemical products—mainly raw materials and semi-finished goods—were successfully sold on international markets. However, as soon as stagnation occurred, Czech exports fell much faster than the total imports of chemical products from the relevant countries. Business policy and strategy is even more important in sophisticated products where success on the market is determined by high-quality business and technical services and overall customer comfort.

Thus, the Czech chemical industry has to preferentially focus on solving the above-mentioned problems in the coming years. Only then will it have a chance to gradually achieve the level of industrially developed countries of the European Union in performance and competitiveness, to adapt its production base for entry to the European Union and to fully integrate itself into the framework of the world's chemical industry.

4.12

Plastics[1]

Miroslav Maň as, Head of the Rubber and Plastics Technology Department of the Zlín-based Technological Faculty

Background

Polymer production and processing has always been a relatively important branch of industry and its tradition in the Czech Republic is very long, with the rubber industry and plastics processing undergoing successful development over time. Annual plastics production in the Czech Republic amounts to 450,000 tonnes, which totals approximately 45 kilograms per capita of plastics consumption. The plastics industry accounts for nearly 8 per cent of the Czech Republic's total industrial production.

The basis of plastics production is formed by raw materials. At the start the 21st century, world consumption of thermoplastics was approximately 125 million tonnes per year. The largest share was accounted for by standard plastics, mainly due to the favourable property/price ratio. Czech firms contributed a small share to the world plastics production (approximately 0.5 per cent), supplying the market mainly with standard thermoplastics comprising PE and PP (Chemopetrol Litvínov), PS (Kaucuk Kralupy), PVC (Spolana Neratovice), PES and PA (Silon Planá nad Lužnicí), PA (Tanex Jaromer) and polyester and epoxy resins (Spolek). Part of the output is processed in the Czech Republic and the remainder is exported. The rubber and plastics industries are among the few branches of industry in the Czech Republic that have been showing a steady year-on-year growth in production, exceeding average growth levels by a sizeable margin. Production

[1] This chapter is based on material supplied by the PP Agency in Prague.

in nearly all areas of the plastics sector was increasing during the 1990s, including during the later years of the decade when industrial production in the country was in recession. This trend continued in the plastics industry during 2000–2001, and the sector held its own even in comparison to the highly prosperous branches of the Czech economy.

The largest production plants in the Czech Republic produce polyethylene and polypropylene, and as a result of large investments in Litvínov their capacity is expected to increase further. Large amounts of raw materials are imported, to include construction plastics in particular.

Plastics processing is a very diversified sector as it comprises the production of a huge number of plastic products for different applications. Polymer products and polymeric matrix composites are widely used in industry. Polymers are used to make products for everyday use, sports equipment and household appliances, packaging materials for industrial products and foodstuffs, with them being increasingly used in construction, electrical engineering and electronics, general engineering and the automobile industry. One particular use is that of plastics in medical care.

Production base

There are more than 350 firms in the Czech Republic engaged in plastics production and processing. They include companies with only a few workers, in addition to firms with more than 1000 employees. Plastics processing currently employs some 45,000 people.

The largest and most successful firms in the Czech Republic are (in alphabetical order):

- Aliachem, a.s., the Fatra factory in Napajedla, which turns out a broad range of products in a programme aptly named 'From the Floor to the Roof', and the Technoplast factory in Chropyne, making mainly foils.
- Granitol, a.s. in Moravsky Beroun, manufacturing numerous types of wrapping material.
- Gumotex, a.s. in Breclav, known to the public mainly for its manufacture of soft polyurethane foams (under the Molitan trademark).
- Lisovny Plastovych Hmot, a.s. in Vrbno pod Pradedem, traditionally processing reactoplasts.

- Plastimat, a.s. in Liberec, and Strojplast, a.s. in Tachov, known mainly for injected thermoplast products.
- Silon, a.s. in Plana nad Luznici, a traditional manufacturer of polyamide and polyester fibres, in recent years also recycling polyethylene terephtalate bottles into fibres and non-woven textiles.
- Tanex Plasty, a.s. in Jaromer, specializing in products from construction polyamide.

Despite the very successful development of the sector, plastics-making firms in the Czech Republic are unable to cover domestic demand fully. This creates conditions for the further development of the industry, especially for domestic consumption, but also for export in order to attain a more favourable balance in this branch of foreign trade. This, however, will require further investment in modern technologies and materials, as well as in the education of specialists.

Processing technologies

Most processing technologies are used in the Czech plastics industry. Rolling is employed mainly in the production of foils, flooring and artificial leather. Existing facilities are sufficient to allow further growth in production. Considering the high investment costs required, any further enlargement of the facilities is unlikely. Extrusion is mainly used in the production of pipes, sections, fibres, blow-out foils and conductor sheathing. Production equipment which has become obsolete is being gradually replaced or at least modernized. The aim is to introduce modern production technologies to allow economic production based on both standard and new materials.

Injection moulding technologies have witnessed a rapid development recently. There are some 5500 injection moulding machines currently in use. It is encouraging to note that the proportion of new injection moulding machines of advanced design in Czech plastics manufacturing plants is continuously increasing. As there is no major producer of injection moulding machines in the Czech Republic (with the exception of Invera Rakovník, whose share of the market, however, is negligible), most of the machines are imported. The predominant makes are Mannesmann Demag, Arburg and Engel. The significant development of injection moulding technologies is mainly due to increasing demand on the part of the automobile industry, electrical engineering, electronics and other engineering-related sectors. Deliveries for these industry sectors has significantly changed the product ranges. The trend is towards technically demanding products made from high-quality construction plastics. The production of such parts requires high-quality injection moulding machines and excellent injection moulds, in addition to well-trained personnel. Indeed, in addition to investment incentives, skill is a very important factor influencing foreign firms' decisions to invest in the Czech Republic.

Research and development

The production of tools needed in plastic processing is developing just as dramatically as the processing technologies themselves. An extremely important requirement for their development, however, is the availability of highly skilled specialists in this area. The only university-level workplace in the Czech Republic concerned with the training of experts for polymer processing, including the construction of plastic products and tools, particularly injection moulds, is the Zlín-based Technological Faculty of the Technical University in Brno. The faculty is well equipped with the necessary instrumentation and computers. It has a number of unique instruments, such as one for measuring the thermodynamic quantities of polymers and their melts pvT 100, and an instrument for measuring the thermal conductivity of polymers and their melts and other equipment. It possesses modern computer equipment with simulation software facilitating the solution of demanding tasks.

The Faculty cooperates with a number of firms in the Czech Republic and organizes educational programmes for specialists concerned with polymer processing. More than 100 workers employed by different plastics processing firms have so far attended its courses. The steadily growing interest in the Faculty's graduates has prompted its management to introduce additional courses for students. Other institutes concerned with research in the area of polymer materials include the Polymers Institute of the Chemical Technology College in Prague, the Chemical Faculty of the Technical University in Brno and the Chemical Technology Faculty of Pardubice University. Besides the Academy of Sciences of the Czech Republic (particularly the Macromolecular Chemistry Institute of the Academy of Sciences), the only places that carry out basic research and partly applied research in the area of polymer materials and technologies are the universities. Only a few research workplaces have remained from the relatively extensive research base—in Brno, Prague, Kralupy nad Vltavou, Pardubice and Litvínov. Cooperation between industry and universities is therefore a necessity, which will also enable the further development of this prosperous sector into the future.

4.13

Textile, Clothing and Leather Industry[1]

Václav Haas, Consumer Industry Department of the Ministry of Industry and Trade

Since the textile, clothing and leather industry depends to a great extent on human labour, this industry is highly important to employment despite a continuing decline in the size of its workforce. The sector is focused on exports and its foreign currency collection is rapid. Heavy competition in world markets, along with the special rules for international trading in textile and clothing products, rank this sector among the most sensitive and to which many countries are paying increased attention. Privatization and the organizational changes made since 1992 have increased the number of SMEs, and changes in market orientation have brought about the recognition of the need for restructuring production and its base.

However, the rate of restructuring and improvements in the competitiveness of products have been slow, and the sector is not yet responding fully to new market conditions and requirements of consumers. Most enterprises are equipped with obsolete machines and have limited possibilities for financing the new technologies which would accelerate this response. Although the privatization of the production base has been completed, changes in ownership often take place—particularly in the textile industry—due to mergers of similar firms and the integration of investment funds. Production is being concentrated in enterprises having modern and less worn-out equipment used on a shiftwork basis. Restructuring also involves increases in the share of products with higher value added and specific use. Due to their inadequate equipment and low availability of fibres of a higher generation, most enterprises are prevented, however, from introducing products with a higher utility value.

[1] This chapter was supplied by the PP Agency in Prague.

Textiles

The largest branch of the textile, clothing and leather industry is the textile sector. Its 1999 revenues from sale of products and services accounted for approximately 65.2 per cent of the total revenues of the industry. In the NACE classification of economic activities, textile products are included in Section 17. Textile products consist of the following groups:

17.1 Preparation and spinning of textile fibres
17.2 Textile weaving
17.3 Finishing of textiles
17.4 Manufacture of made-up textile articles, except clothing
17.5 Manufacture of other textiles
17.6 Manufacture of knitted and crocheted fabrics
17.7 Manufacture of knitted and crocheted articles.

All branches of the textile, clothing and leather industry are dependent on imports of raw and other basic materials. The 1999 requirement of textile raw materials was some 170,200 tonnes, of which 70 per cent were imported. In the clothing sector, materials imported for processing were worth approximately CZK11 billion, including CZK7.3 billion for fabrics. The share of imported material in the total use of material for clothing production was about 53.9 per cent. In the leather sector, the share of imported raw material (oxhide and hogskin) ranged around 75 per cent. Raw material prices are rising as a result of exchange rate influences—and in some cases due to a shortage on world markets (viscose-based fibres and oxhide). Good news in the last period has been the rising number of production units under foreign control and a greater inclination towards mergers, particularly of textile companies, which have taken place in connection with restructuring. Also beneficial have been changes in the structure of production, such as increased manufacture of textile products for technical purposes and products for non-textile use.

The interest of foreign investors has been focused on the textile industry, which has the largest share of enterprises under foreign control, and a large share of direct investments. Some 29 enterprises in the industry (with 100 and more employees) were under foreign control in 1999. They employed about 11 per cent of the total workforce in enterprises of similar size, and accounted for almost 21.5 per cent of total performance, which was an increase of 23.8 per cent on 1998. In 1999, value added per employee in the textile industry among enterprises under foreign control was 53.1 per cent higher than in all enterprises with 100 and more employees in the industry, and 25.1 per cent higher than in 1998. The number of foreign-controlled textile enterprises increased to 32 in 2000, and their share in the mentioned indicators is growing. Three firms in the textile industry (Pegas a.s. Znojmo, Schöller Litvínov k.s., and Toray Textiles Central Europe Prostejov s.r.o.) have made use of Act No. 72/2000 Coll. on Investment Incentives. The textile industry ranks fourth in terms of financial investment, after the production of electrical and optical equipment, transport, and rubber and plastics.

The restructuring of production is reflected in changes in the production base. This was highly apparent in the productivity of labour from value added in constant prices, which rose by 43.9 per cent in the period 1994–1999, amid which the size of the workforce shrank by more than 33,000. The highest productivity of labour from value added is being achieved in other textile production (NACE 17.5), weaving, and final treatment of textiles (NACE 17.2, 17.3). The section of other textile production has the lowest energy consumption.

Clothes

A specific feature of the clothing industry is its high degree of cooperation with external customers, mainly in EU countries. Piecework, including the value of material, held a share of some 75.2 per cent in 1999 exports. This was reflected in diminishing operations on the sophisticated parts of production, in model creation and in the preparation of production. Only a few enterprises can ensure complete production, including model creation, and flexibly respond to the requirements of clients. These are primarily large clothing companies.

In the clothing industry, enterprises with foreign capital involvement (with 100 and more employees) had a share of some 20.5 per cent in the total number of enterprises of the branch. They employed almost 13.6 per cent of the total workforce and accounted for 16.1 per cent of the total 1999 revenues of enterprises with 100 and more employees, which was 1.3 per cent more than in 1998. The 1999 book value added per employee was 10.3 per cent higher in companies with foreign capital involvement than the average value in clothing industry enterprises with 100 and more employees.

In the leather industry, primary production—the tanning and treatment of skins—accounted for some 11.7 per cent of total 1999 revenues from the sale of products and services. The remaining revenues came from secondary production, including about 66.2 per cent from footwear manufacture.

The sections have the following specific features:

- primary production (tanning)—need for large investments into environmental protection (sewage water treatment plants and waste processing);
- secondary production (manufacture of footwear, bags and saddles)—high material requirement, low investments into machinery and technological equipment, large share of labour in production and consequent important influence on regional employment.

Most firms operating in the leather industry are now involved in enterprise restructuring, particularly in the areas of production, products and staff. Over the past six years, the number of employees in the footwear sector has been reduced by approximately 12,500, a decline of some 43.5 per cent compared with 1994. This reduced production is accompanied by a radical restructuring of the range of products to the benefit of more sophisticated products, and also by an increased share of piecework in exports, which was 69 per cent in the period January–September 2000. The manufacture of briefcases and suitcases from textile materials instead of leather has increased (easier handling and affordable prices).

Foreign capital involvement has minimum influence on production. The share of foreign-controlled firms with 100 and more employees in the total workforce in this group of enterprises was about 3.8 per cent in 1998. The number of firms under foreign control rose from four in 1998 to five in 1999, and value added from CZK151 million to CZK239 million in the same comparison. The share of leather industry firms under foreign control in total value added in enterprises with 100 and more employees in the first half of 2000 was about 8.7 per cent, ie 1.3 per cent up on 1999.

Revenues and production figures of firms in the industry

The textile industry revenues from the sale of products and services between 1994 and 1999 increased by 16.4 per cent in current prices, and declined by 9.3 per cent in constant prices. The 1999 revenues in constant prices on the 1994 basis were about CZK39.2 billion. Of the different sectors of the textile industry, divided according to the raw materials they process, the highest rise in revenues from the sale of products and services in 1999 compared to 1998 was recorded by the flax sector (6.1 per cent) and the wool sector (0.5 per cent). A decline was recorded by the sectors of cotton (11.4 per cent) and knitwear (0.5 per cent). The revenues were influenced by the year-on-year decline in the manufacture of cotton yarn (15.2 per cent) and cotton fabrics (18.6 per cent). Important increases in production in 1999 were recorded in the following commodities: synthetic silk and rayon fabrics (14.3 per cent), linen yarn (8.9 per cent) and hosiery (1.3 per cent).

The revenues of enterprises with 20 and more employees from the sale of their products and services rose by 10.8 per cent in the first half of 2000 against the same period in 1999. The increase in these revenues in constant prices was 10.4 per cent in the same comparison.

Revenues from the sale of the products and services of the clothing industry went into decline in both current and constant prices from 1997 to 1999. 1999 revenues in constant prices were just below CZK12.4 billion. The year 2000 saw a year-on-year increase in revenues from the sale of products and services in both current and constant prices, at 3.1 per cent and 2.4 per cent respectively. The largest increase was in NACE 18.2 'Manufacture of clothing and accessories', while, in contrast, there was a decline of 6.7 per cent in NACE 18.1 'Production of leather clothing'.

The adverse trend in the leather industry revenues was due to increased competitiveness of products and complications of sale on foreign markets. This trend was most apparent in the footwear industry, which had been accounting for 66 per cent of branch revenues. In contrast, development has been good in the leather goods sector, which found customers on foreign markets due to good quality and reasonable prices. Revenues in 1999 from both the sale of products and services of the leather industry amounted to almost CZK7 billion. Revenues of the footwear sector dropped to some 44 per cent of 1994 revenues, whereas the revenues of the leather goods sector rose by more than 11 per cent in constant prices. However, revenues of the leather industry did not increase in 2000.

Foreign trade

Of the combined textile, clothing and leather industry, the textile industry has the best performance in foreign trade. Textile products to a total value of CZK39.8 billion were exported in 1999 and, deducting the cost of materials imported for cooperation in the clothing industry, the surplus in the balance of trade was almost CZK10 billion. Furthermore, this figure rose by more than 10 per cent in 2000. In the structure of exports, the share of fabrics is 37.9 per cent, off-the-peg textile products 21.5 per cent, and other textile products, mainly for technical purposes, 19.3 per cent. A total of CZK34.9 billion in textile products were exported in the period January–September 2000, ie a rise of some 19 per cent against the same period in 1999. Of these exports, 69.6 per cent went to EU countries, followed by East European countries and Slovakia.

Items with the largest share in exports to EU countries include cotton fabrics weighing up to 200 g/m^2, combed woollen yarn, pile fabrics, bed clothes, linens of all kinds, non-woven and upholstery textiles, and items for technical purposes. The importance of imports for processing and exports of processed products is increasing in the textile industry and its branches. The share of these imports and exports rose from 35.2 per cent in 1998 to 36.4 per cent in 1999. The 1999 share of off-the-peg textile products was 59 per cent, and knitwear 53.4 per cent. The clothing industry exported some 58 per cent of its products in 1999, ie 6.2 per cent more than in 1998. These exports have been on the rise since 1995 and amounted to approximately CZK20.7 billion in 1999.

The 1998–2000 balance of foreign trade, adjusted by material transfers between the sectors, has been showing a slightly upward trend. The adjusted balance was CZK497 million in 1999, and continued to rise in 2000. Also favourable is the increasing export share of piecework from materials of domestic origin. Results in the January–September 2000 period show a decline in the share of piecework in exports, to 72.9 per cent as compared with 76.1 per cent in the same period of 1999. The share of imports for processing and exports of processed products in the turnover of overall trade shows their importance to the branch or sector. The influences stemming from the transfer of materials for processing were taken into consideration in the two calculations. These imports and exports accounted for 65 per cent of the clothing industry turnover in both 1998 and 1999. A decline took place in 2000 and was due to the mentioned rise in the processing of domestic materials, which reached CZK1 billion.

The EU countries account for the largest share in foreign trade of the clothing industry; they accounted for 85.1 per cent in 1999, ie 3.1 per cent more than in 1998. Direct exports of clothing products to EU countries increased from some CZK2.8 billion in 1998 to CZK 2.94 billion in 1999, a rise of some 6 per cent, with the trend continuing in 2000. The value of direct exports to EU countries was

CZK2.68 billion in the first three quarters of 2000, ie 21 per cent more than in the same period of 1999. The cost of labour is decisive in the competitiveness of clothing production. Although the per minute cost of labour increased from CZK4.028 in 1995 to CZK4.978 in 1999, the Czech Republic remains a very interesting territory for clothing manufacturers in the European Union, particularly for the neighbouring countries of Germany and Austria. This is due not only to the short distance, but also and in particular to the reliability and quality of products, and the observance of deadlines. The per-minute cost of labour in the Czech Republic is one-third of the cost in Germany.

Exports of leather products have been on the decline since 1996 with the exception of a slight revival in 1999 due to an increase in the share of piecework. The share of imports for processing and exports of processed products rose from 45.9 per cent in 1998 to 48.4 per cent in 1999, with the rise continuing in 2000. Of the different sectors, footwear had the highest share in 1999, at 53.7 per cent. The total export of leather commodities was worth some CZK9.8 billion in 1999, CZK2.5 billion less than in 1996. There has been a deficit in the balance of trade since 1997, one of the reasons being increasing imports from Asia, particularly of footwear.

For many years, Germany has been the Czech Republic's most important partner in leather commodity exchange, which accounted for about one-quarter of Czech trade in leather products in 1999. The Czech surplus in the balance of this trade is healthy, but its structure is poor (a large share of piecework). The Czech Republic registers a deficit in this trade with China, which, of the 30 million pairs of shoes on the Czech market, supplied some 17.8 million. In addition to the traditional textile footwear, there was an increase in the import of leather footwear (3.2 million pairs). The Czech textile, clothing, and leather industry accounts for 13 per cent of Central European Free Trade Agreement (CEFTA) exports to the European Union. The textile industry has the largest share, 28.9 per cent in 1999, with the clothing industry registering the lowest share at 7.5 per cent.

Industry trends

The industry's prospects are influenced by consumer policy in Europe and the domestic market, particularly with regard to the involvement of producers in the distribution network. Prerequisites for the preservation of the competitiveness of the industry are the introduction of new information technologies and the availability of these technologies to SMEs to enable a rapid response to demands in the market. These electronic networks are important for offering collections of products, transferring production technologies, and trading.

Development will continue to be influenced by the globalization of industry in Europe, and adaptation to the policy of the unified European market. There will be constant increases in the competition of producers who have their own raw material resources, mainly in Asia.

Competitiveness in the different branches of production will be influenced by the capability of enterprises to establish higher forms of partnership with mutually balanced advantages.

In addition, favourable conditions must be created for business, mainly by supporting SMEs, assistance in economically weak regions, support for exports, and creation of prerequisites for support to immaterial factors of production for the achievement of higher competitiveness of the industry and an increase in the share of products with a higher utility value.

4.14

The Printing Industry[1]

Milada Vlasakova, Deputy Minister of Industry and Trade

Introduction

The printing and publishing industry in the regions of Bohemia, Moravia and Silesia has a long tradition going back to the early last century and building on the tradition of home printing. Between the two World Wars, the printing industry abandoned the predominantly mechanical and metallurgical printing technologies and went over to plain printing, letterpress printing and offset. Today's technologies include flexoprinting and other electrographic and digital printing technologies, which have reduced or completely eliminated the inter-operating wet chemical processes. The printing and publishing industry has been growing not only in terms of volume, but also in terms of the range of production and the use of different printing techniques.

The printing industry in the Czech Republic comprises three branches: the printing industry proper, publishing, and reproduction of recordings. The first two branches are comparable internationally as they are covered by international statistics. The reproduction of recordings and electronically published products is not monitored statistically.

Chief characteristics

A characteristic feature of the Czech printing industry over the past five years has been the dynamic growth of all its production indicators. For example, the productivity of labour increased more than 3.25-fold between the mid to late 1990s, while the workforce in the industry fell by more than 1200 during this period. The

[1] This chapter was supplied by the PP Agency in Prague.

industry's other characteristics are rapid automation, electronification and digitalization, involving massive investment costs, which are higher than wage costs. The investment costs are particularly high in the printing industry proper, where the price of printing machines rises with their higher performance, electronification and computerization, and the cost of putting them into operation. This is accompanied by growing demand for skilled labour, both with regards to apprenticed printers and to personnel with secondary and university education. Employing workers with only little training is practically excluded, as the final quality of the product strongly depends on the skill of the personnel.

Also characteristic is the wider use of imported raw materials (dyestuffs, paper, chemicals, films, diskettes, etc) and machinery. The industry is therefore considerably affected by the movement of the foreign prices of these products. On the other hand, the printing industry's exports are not so closely tied to eastern markets as are, for example, the textiles, clothing and leather industries. The position of the printing industry within the manufacturing industry remains stable on a long-term basis, accounting for 2.83 per cent-2.89 per cent in terms of income from the sale of own products and services and for 2.38–2.52 per cent in terms of the number of people employed in this branch of industry in the period under review.

The printing industry has gradually lost some of its previous comparative advantages, which it could utilize for strengthening its position on the domestic and foreign markets (eg low-cost skilled labour, lower input costs, etc). The input prices have reached the level of world prices and printing facilities are being gradually incorporated in the publishing sector. Independent printing production, which existed before privatization, has been consigned to history. Privatized print firms linked to foreign publishing and printing houses have provided a number of large printing units with imported machinery, which is much more efficient than that used before privatization. Today's print firms have equipment and skill meeting even the most demanding requirements of publishers.

Significance of foreign capital

Foreign competition is putting pressure on the productivity of labour and quality and the qualification of managers and attendant personnel. Some Czech companies are trying to solve this problem, or have already solved it, by merging with a strategic foreign partner. This applies to both printing and publishing houses. It is estimated that foreign capital has privatized, owns and controls about 80 per cent of print firms and some 60 per cent of printing houses in the Czech Republic. Only small printing houses, particularly of regional importance, have remained in Czech hands.

Foreign firms with a decisive interest in companies publishing the country's largest dailies include:

- Rheinisch-Bergische Verlagsgesellschaft (FRG), publishing the largest Czech daily *Mlada Fronta Dnes,* the Moravian newspaper *Rovnost,* the Moravian-Silesian paper *Svoboda, Lidove noviny,* among others;
- Ringier-Springer (FRG), publishing the daily *BLESK,* the weeklies *TYDEN, Reflex, Profit,* among others;
- Mittelrhein-Verlag MRV-Beteiligungs GmbH (FRG), publishing the dailies *Zemske noviny, Slovo, Ostravsky den,* among others;
- the German publishing group PoL Print KG (Passauer Neue Presse controls more than 40 regional dailies);
- HB-DOW Jones, S.A. (Belgium) owns 44.5 per cent of the Economia a.s. publishing house and publishes the *Hospodarske noviny* daily, the *Ekonom* magazine, among others.

Development

The period after 1990 saw the emergence of new entities, such as the Ueberreuther Print, s.r.o. printing house in Pohorelice u Brna (affiliation of the Austrian concern Salzer Veberreuther) and the Amulet publishing house (publishing books for children and young people). This publishing house, which grew up practically on a green field site not far from Brno, specializes in book production (capacity 8 million books per year), with some 70 per cent of its output going to the markets of German-speaking countries.

Medium-sized printing houses include Svoboda, Graficke Zavody, a.s., Ceska Typografie, a.s, all of these being located in Prague. The most important firms concerned with publishing in the area of audiovisual recordings are Gramofonove Zavody, a.s., Lodenice, Fermata, s.r.o, Celakovice and Bohemia Video Arts, a.s., Brno.

As is the case with other branches of the economy, the printing industry must also adjust to the impact of the recent recession in the Czech economy. From the mid-to-late 1990s, the revenues of companies engaged in the printing industry (firms employing more than 20 people) dropped by approximately 20 per cent. This does not apply to publishing, however, where revenues in this period increased by approximately 45 per cent (in the case of companies employing more than 20 people, the increase was 58.7 per cent), although in other sectors a number of economic factors were showing negative trends. The growth in this area was boosted by revenues for advertising and mercantile goods (packings, labels, postcards, calendars, etc). Revenues for the publishing of periodicals and magazines also showed massive growth. In both cases, the growth of revenue was supported by wider advertising of domestic firms and the launching of new kinds of advertising, such as direct mailing. Adding to the wider use of advertising are advertising supplements and the pasting of trade samples in technical magazines.

In the near future, the prospects of the Czech printing industry will be closely tied to the development of this industry in a broader context, particularly with regard to developments in EU countries. For the time being, however, the export efficiency of the Czech printing industry is low in comparison with the European Union. While the balance of trade has been favourable for EU countries vis á vis the Czech Republic in the long term (eg in 1994, total EU exports were nearly 2.3 times higher than total EU imports in terms of value), the current trade balance is generally running against the Czech Republic. The latter's trade deficit is slowly showing signs of decreasing however.

The media market

The current structure of the Czech media market also differs strongly from that prevailing in the world, where companies operating in the branch under review own both electronic media (television, cable television, video studios, film and radio broadcasting companies) and printed media (newspapers, magazines). The structure of the Czech media market is similar to that in neighbouring Germany and other EU countries. Only less than one per cent of printing houses employ more than 500 people (according to Intergraf data), while 85 per cent of the firms have fewer employees. From the point of view of the technical standard of fixed assets, which has improved significantly over the past few years, the standard of the Czech printing industry is approaching the level of advanced countries.

Differences still remain, however, for example in the use of printing techniques, with offset continuing to prevail (accounting for approximately 85 per cent and deep print for approximately 10 per cent, according to the Association of Master Printers), while the proportion of other techniques (flexoprint, letterpress printing and other techniques) is much lower in comparison with Western Europe, the United States and Japan. Modernization may proceed with the help of domestic investments backed by loans or foreign capital. Considering the lower share of the printing industry within manufacturing industry in comparison with the world as a whole, it can be expected that the Czech printing industry will undergo a dynamic rate of development, for which the prerequisites are gradually being created.

4.15

Telecommunications: An Overview

Tomas Studenik, BT Ignite Czech Republic

The association between the Czech Republic and the European Union and its member states was established by the Europe Agreement, which came into effect in February 1995. The Czech Republic is actively pursuing its aim of becoming a fully fledged EU member by 2004 and thereby enhancing its prosperity. The country supports recent EU initiatives to strengthen competition by means of the extensive application of modern information and communication technologies. The European Union has positively evaluated the process of alignment of the Czech telecommunications sector with EU common practice, as stated, for example, in the 2000 Regular Report from the European Commission on the Czech Republic's Progress Towards Accession. In the framework of negotiation between the Czech Republic and the European Union, the chapter dealing with telecommunications and information technologies was provisionally closed in 1999 as one of the first chapters.

During recent years, the telecommunication networks and telecommunication services in the Czech Republic have reached a relatively good level. Practically only digital technologies are used within the networks, and the scope of services offered approaches that provided by telecommunication operators in the European Union. New networks for mobile communication (HSDC, GPRS, 3G) are being developed rapidly and cover the whole country. In addition to public networks, the number and extent of private networks for voice and data communications and for interconnection of management and commercial systems are growing quickly. At the level of telecommunication infrastructure and in the exploitation of telecommunication services, the Czech Republic is ranked first (in 2001) among Central and Eastern European (CEE) countries. Pursuant to the legislation in force, the telecommunication sector in the Czech Republic is liberalized. No entrepreneurial subject is precluded from the operation of telecommunication networks and from providing telecommunication services. On the other hand, political pressures exist to dwarf competition with the aim of increasing value for potential buyers of the former incumbent operator, Ceský Telecom. Yet officially, no exclusive rights exist and the level of the competitive environment in telecommunications in the Czech Republic is, with the exception of some postponements (introduction of carrier selection, number portability and local loop unbundling), practically the same as for the European Union. Individual licences are issued for the establishment and operation of public telecommunication networks, for the provision of telephone services and for radio transmission. The regulation of all other activities is performed by means of general licences. The government telecommunication sector falls under the control of the Czech Ministry of Transport and Communications. The Act on Telecommunications and on Amendments to other Acts No. 151/2000 Coll. specifies in detail further authorities for this Ministry, such as legislation, telecommunication policy, determination of principles and the main rules of state regulation in telecommunications, the Czech Republic's integration into the European Union in the sphere of telecommunications, international relations and fulfilment of international agreements. The Ministry also approves the plan for frequency band allocations. The independent regulatory authority for telecommunications is the Czech Telecommunication Office, which performs, in addition to its regulatory functions, the common administrative activities associated with the implementation of the Acts.

The Office for the Protection of Competition intervenes where necessary into entrepreneurial activities in the telecommunication sector, supervises the application of legal regulations and regulates general economic competition.

Privatization

During the first half of the 1990s, the privatization of all former state enterprises in the telecommunication sector took place. The State retained a share of approximately 51 per cent in the joint-stock companies Ceský Telecom and Ceské Radiokomunikace via the National Property Fund. In 1999, the Czech government declared its intention to sell the shares owned by the National Property Fund to private entities and subsequently determined the form of privatization as the sale of the whole shareholding to one investor only by tender procedures. The sale of the National Property Fund's share in Ceské

Radiokomunikace was realized before the end of 2001. Privatization of Ceský Telecom still continues; the tender in process (as of 18 April 2002) will probably fail due to a lack of investor interest. Therefore, the principle of the State enforcing its influence on all entrepreneurial subjects in the telecommunication sector through the use of regulations and by the regulating bodies performing their functions will be in force only after the privatization of Ceský Telecom, which is expected either at the end of 2002 or during 2003.

National telecommunication policy

In 1999, the Ministry of Transport and Communications developed the National Telecommunications Policy to determine state policy in the telecommunication sector for the next five years. The policy originates from European trends towards implementing reforms in the telecommunication sector and calls for the establishment of a transparent regulatory network, refers to the main issues in this sector, determines tasks and indicates their solution according to requirements resulting from Czech Republic NATO membership and from the eventual accession of the Czech Republic to the European Union. The Czech government took formal note of this document in April 1999. In the liberalized market, simultaneous access to the defined set of basic telecommunication services (universal service) should be assured for each user. Progress in realizing the National Telecommunication Policy and promoting its principles was evaluated by the Ministry of Transport and Communications at the beginning of 2001 as being satisfactory. The report was submitted to the government for information. In the context of dynamic telecommunication development in the Czech Republic and in the European Union, it is anticipated that updates and additions to this basic strategy document will be made during 2002.

Liberalization and faster telecommunication development in the Czech Republic began in 1992 with amendment of the Act on Telecommunications No. 150/1992 Coll. Except for incomplete liberalization and demonopolization of the telecommunication sector, this amendment also permitted a rapid convergence of the Czech Republic telecommunication policy with that of the European Union in the area of telecommunications. This enabled providers to offer services such as the provision of long distance and international telephone services (including local telephone services outside the delimited local network areas) and the establishment and operation of telecommunication equipment and a fixed network for provision of these services. The new legal norm—the Act on Telecommunications and on Amendment to other Acts No. 151/2000 Coll. took effect on 1 July 2000 after approval by the Czech parliament. In order to support competition, the Act clarifies the legal position of the business entities in the market and provides them with absolute certainty that they are doing business in a fair and predictable environment. Simultaneously, the rights of users to quality services and to the protection of their communications and privacy are protected by legal measures. The Act defines clear rules for granting licences and special obligations assigned to licence holders with a significant market share for the desired competition development of the telecommunication market. The Act further determines conditions for ensuring universal service provision in terms of access to basic telecommunication services for all citizens. The Act also safeguards open access to public telecommunication networks and defines conditions for the interconnectivity of networks and interaction of services under reasonable conditions for all market participants. The provisions of the Act also provide for fair and transparent procedures for the allocation of scarce resources, such as frequencies and numbers, for their optimum exploitation.

An analysis of legal regulations and of the regulatory system for telecommunications in the Czech Republic will be made during 2002 in relation to the extensive revision of the legal and regulatory framework for electronic communication being carried out currently in the European Union and reflecting the obvious trends towards convergence of communication, information and media technologies.

Developments

Telecommunications in the Czech Republic have undergone dynamic development since 1992. A relatively outdated telecommunication network, still based overwhelmingly at the beginning of the 1990s on analogue transmission systems and exchanges with mechanical switching, was continuously expanded and rebuilt by digital technology. At the present time, the network is almost fully digital. Within the core network, but also largely in regional and local networks, optical cables are used. New networks for mobile communication have been established covering the whole state territory. In addition to the public network, the number and extent of private networks for voice and data communication and for the interconnection of management and business networks are growing rapidly.

Telephone services on public telecommunication networks will also predominate in the future but the market shares of data transmissions – and particularly of Internet access services – are growing rapidly. During recent years, mobile services and the Internet have developed most rapidly in terms of user numbers. Table 4.15.1 gives an overview of selected indicators of telecommunication services development within the period 1994–2001.

The number of subscribers to the fixed public telecommunication network increased rapidly up to 1998, but since 1999 this sector of the market has in fact stagnated. Figure 4.15.1 shows the development of the total number of subscribers and the number of subscribers per 1000 inhabitants.

Ceský Telecom continues to be the most important fixed public telecommunication network operator and provider of telephone services within this network even after privatization. Other companies that were granted territorially delimited licences in 1995 and 1996 hold no significant share in the total volume of telephone services. However, these 'alternative' operators (British Telecom, GTS, Aliatel, Contactel, eTel, Nextra) have focused solely on large and SME enterprise clients, where their combined share is higher than that of Ceský Telecom. On the basis of the new Act on Telecommunications, the Czech Telecommunication Office is granting

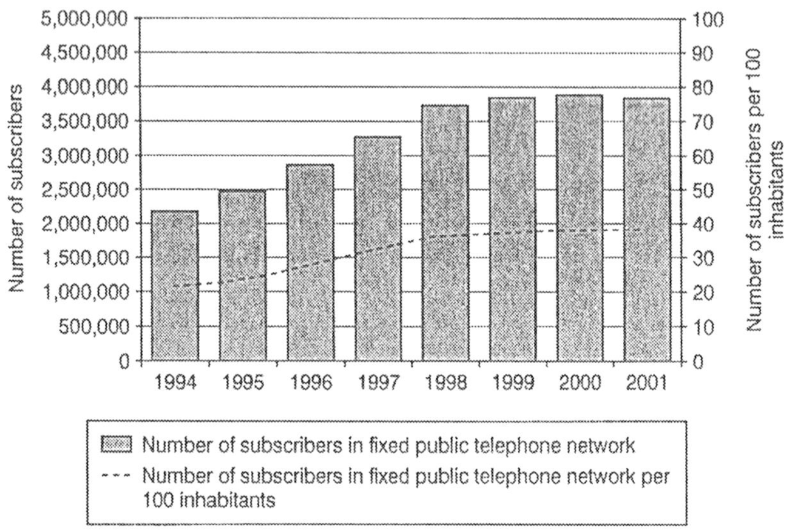

Figure 4.15.1 Subscribers and fixed network market penetration

Table 4.15.1 Telecommunications market development, Czech Republic—1994 to 2001

Indicator	*1994*	*1995*	*1996*	*1997*	*1998*	*1999*	*2000*	*2001*
Number of subscribers in fixed public tlph. network per 100 inhabitants	20.89	23.24	27.34	31.78	36.29	36.96	37.67	37.51
Average waiting time for MTS establishment (months)	47.95	71.55	17.23	7.15	1.89	1.23	0.95	0.83
Number of residence telephone stations in fixed network per 100 flats	38.76	42.19	50.09	59.95	69.74	72.51	71.86	68.73
Share of fixed network subscribers connected to digital exchanges (%)	15.06	17.89	31.70	48.49	64.02	74.43	85.72	93.85
Number of public pay telephones per 100 inhabitants	0.18	0.20	0.26	0.28	0.29	0.29	0.29	0.28
Total number of ISDN subscribers	—	—	—	196	2,753	11,394	26,194	276,010
Number of subscribers in public mobile networks per 100 inhabitants	0.26	0.44	1.94	5.05	9.36	18.88	42.28	68.20
Number of registered Internet domain hosts	10,397	21,856	40,846	56,869	86,482	122,253	160,000	215,525

Telecommunication Office is granting further licences for fixed networks operation and for provision of services throughout the country.

Mobile communications

The first mobile network of the NMT 450 type offered mobile services to the public from 1992, but a strong increase in networks and services began with the granting of two licences for GSM networks in 1996. In 2000, the number of mobile network subscribers exceeded four million and surpassed the number of fixed network subscribers. By the end of 2001, a density of 68 mobile stations per 100 inhabitants had been mobile stations per 100 inhabitants had been achieved. At the present time, three companies in the Czech Republic are operating mobile networks and providing mobile services. With the dynamics of the rapid increase in numbers, the services of mobile network operators show strong innovatory activity supported by the growing potential of electronic communications, which the Act on Digital Signature No. 227/2000 Coll. has facilitated. The market shares of the three service network operators are defined in Figure 4.15.2 and the growth in the number of network subscribers and market penetration is recorded in Figure 4.15.3

Internet usage

There are no official figures for the number of Internet users in the Czech Republic, but current estimates are that there are two million Internet users in the country. Both the number of users and the extent of Internet usage are increasing rapidly. In spite of growing take-up of Internet use and increasing competition among Internet access providers, there are a number of factors working against the expansion of Internet usage. These include the relatively high price of personal computers, the present limited possibilities of electronic communication with bodies of the state administration, and high charges for Internet access during the daytime while charges in periods of low traffic are quite acceptable. Favourable developments in these areas also are expected in the

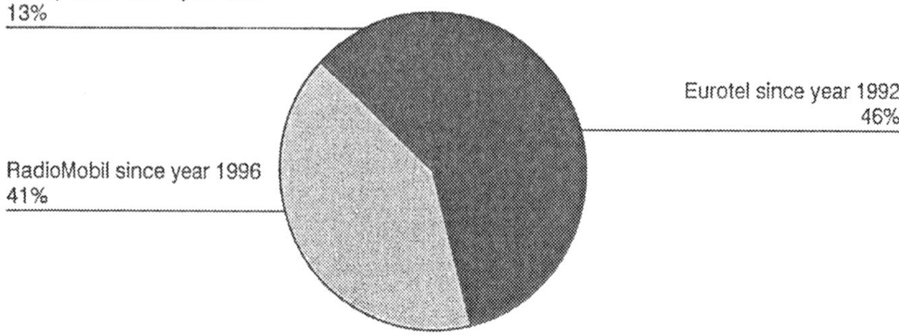

Figure 4.15.2 Service network operators' market share

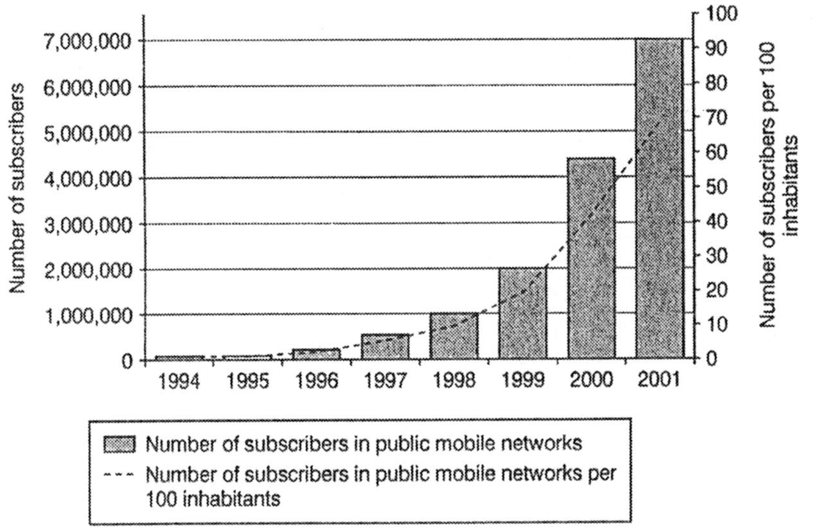

Figure 4.15.3 Subscribers and mobile network penetration

short term. The following factors are expected to contribute to a substantial decrease in access costs for Internet services:

- increased competition from new telecommunication networks;
- obligatory sharing of subscriber access networks;
- extended usage of alternative wireless access networks.

Reference sources

1. Press releases of the Czech Telecommunication Office 2000 – 2002
2. Czech Telecom website: www.ct.cz
3. Act on Telecommunication, 2000
4. Lupa, a server about Internet in the Czech Republic: www.lupa.cz
5. Mobil Server, a server about mobile communications in the Czech Republic, www.mobil.cz

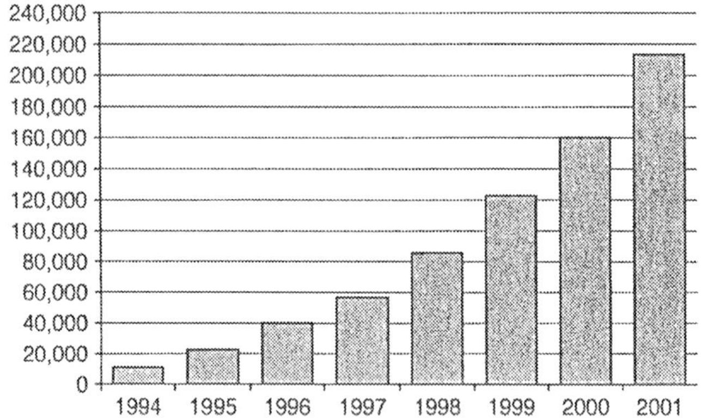

Figure 4.15.4 Growth in the number of registered Internet hosts, from 1994

4.16

State Policy for the Development of Transport and Communications[1]

Josef Zatloukal, Director, Department of Transport Policy, International Relations and the Environment, Ministry of Transport and Communications

Introduction

In European countries, within the public policy sphere, apart from agriculture, transport and telecommunications policy is the most widely discussed subject. In the same way as other Central and Eastern European (CEE) countries, the Czech Republic has had to tackle a number of issues recently relating not only to the changed economic system, but also to the need for the adjustment of its transport and communications policy to prevailing European standards. This has not been an easy task to achieve and the process is ongoing. The government has adopted the basic documents on the country's transport policy, the national telecommunications policy and the development of transport networks in the medium-term period, including a number of other partial documents.

Legislation in the area of transport, telecommunications and postal services has in large part already been harmonized with EU legislation and intensive preparations are in progress for the country's accession to the European Union. A number of new acts and amendments dealing with the most acute problems of transport, telecommunications and

[1] The content for this chapter was supplied by the PP Agency in Prague.

postal services have been enacted in the last two years, in accordance with the Acquis Communautaire of the European Union. In this area, the Czech Republic demands no transitional periods and is ready to meet all the conditions that the European Union requests it to comply with at the moment of admission. Rather than the legislation itself, the problem in this area will instead be the practical implementation and enforceability of the laws.

Recent developments in legislation in support of transport and communications

Within this context it has to be pointed out that, from the point of view of transport, important acts have been passed recently in the road transport sector: the act on acquiring and improving professional qualification to drive motor vehicles (Act No. 247/2000) and the Road Traffic Act (Act No. 361/2000). These acts became effective on 1 January 2001. Further acts on the conditions of road traffic have more recently gradually superceded Act No. 38/1995, to which implementation decrees No. 102/1995 (on the approval of vehicles and the conditions of road traffic) and No. 103/1995 (on technical control stations and exhaust fumes measuring stations) relate.

These acts are being very sensitively commented upon by the public in connection with the transfer of transport administration from the Ministry of the Interior to the District Councils and the Ministry of Transport and Communications. The registration of drivers, the issue of driving licences and traffic offence proceedings were transferred to District Councils in early 2001. New driving licences will be issued and the work of driving schools will be subject to new rules. Before this, important amendments were passed, such as the Road Transport Act Amendment (Act No. 150/2000) and the Road Traffic Act Amendment (Act No. 102/2000), which became effective on 1 July 2000.

In the railway sector, a very important amendment to the Railways Act (Act No. 23/2000) became effective on 1 April 2000, which fully accords with the requirements of the Acquis Communautaire not only as regards access to the transport market, but also from the point of view of the requirements of a public service. One relatively important act which is yet to be passed is the controversial act on the transformation of Czech Railways. Work on it is still continuing and the proposed act is expected to be passed to parliament later in 2002. The act is to transform Czech

Railways into an efficient trading company and to solve the problem of railway debt. The passage of this act is being closely observed by the European Commission, although Czech opinion is that the existence of this act is not an essential requirement of the Acquis Communautaire, but rather a substitute problem.

With respect to the air transport sector, an amendment to the Aviation Act (Act No. 146/2000) became effective on 12 June 2000, and is already being superceded by further legislation harmonizing Czech standards with those of the EU. In sea transport, a new act (Act No. 61/2000) became effective on 1 July 2000. Although there are currently no sea-going vessels flying the Czech flag, the act is supplemented by important implementing decrees, which also cover the operation and ownership of sea-going sporting yachts, where the number of Czech owners is continuously increasing. The amendment to the act on river transport became effective even before this, on 14 January 2000 (Act No. 358/1999).

Act No. 104/2000, on the State Fund for the Transport Infrastructure, entered into force on 1 July 2000 and the fund's total capital amounts to CZK34.8 billion. The Labour Code Amendment, effective from 1 January 2001, made it necessary for the government to issue a new regulation concerning employees working irregular hours and to make new arrangements for the organization of labour.

In the telecommunications sector, a new Telecommunications Act (Act No. 151/2000) entered into force on 1 July 2000, which is an essential document in this sector, in addition to the National Telecommunications Policy document. In accordance with the act, the telecommunications market is now fully open to both domestic and foreign businessmen. In postal services, a new act (Act No. 29/2000), fully compatible with the Acquis Communautaire, entered into force on 1 July 2000. The application of this act ensures the opening up of postal services to competition and the necessary regulation of the postal sector.

Further state support for the creation of modern transport infrastructure

In common with other countries, the Czech Republic has launched an ambitious investment programme for the modernization of its transport infrastructure, and is keeping up with the schedules required by European integration. As part of this programme, 503 kilometres of motorway and

335 kilometres of highway had been built by the end of 2000, Prague Airport has been modernized and the modernization of key rail routes is continuing; more than three-quarters of the length of the so-called fourth pan-European corridor (Děčín–Prague–Břeclav) and two-fifths of the length of the sixth pan-European corridor (Břeclav–Petrovice u Karviné) have been modernized or commenced. Still, this is only about half of the government's strategic plan, and the modernization of the waterways is continually being postponed.

In 1999, the Czech government approved (by Resolution No. 741 of 21 July) a draft plan for the development of transport networks up to 2010. The draft envisages that, in addition to the D1 Prague–Brno–Lipník nad Bečvou motorway, the basic motorway network will comprise the ring road around Prague, the D5 motorway with the completed Plzeň bypass, the D47 motorway linking up with D1 and connecting Brno with Ostrava, and continuing to the Polish border. Also part of the network will be the D8 motorway connecting Prague with Ústí nad Labem and continuing to the German border in the direction of Dresden.

Other links envisaged by the draft are the D3 motorway to connect Prague with Dolní Dvořiště and Austria. Up to České Budějovice the link is designed as a motorway, and the section from Ceské Budejovice to the Austrian border as highway R3. The D11 road from Prague via Hradec Králové to Poland will take the form of a motorway as far as Jaroměř, and the section up to the border will take the form of highway R11. More roads will be built after the plans have been discussed with regional authorities.

In rail transport, the plan provides for the completion of the first rail corridor by 2002, and for the completion of the second rail corridor by 2005. The government also approved the priority construction of the fourth transit corridor from Prague, via Horní Dvořiště, to Linz, Austria (to be completed in 2008), and after that the modernization of the third transit rail corridor from Prague to Nuremberg (starting in 2004). The lower reaches of the Labe (Elbe) will be adjusted to improve navigation in that section of the river. The construction of two low stages is envisaged.

The country's attention is presently focused on the following projects within the context of its support for the development of modern transport infrastructure in the Czech Republic.

Road infrastructure

- Completing the missing sections of the D8 motorway to Saxony by 2005.
- Completing the Plzeň bypass on the D5 motorway as soon as possible.
- Building the D47 motorway Lipník nad Bečvou–Ostrava.
- Early continuation of the construction of the D11 motorway in the direction of Hradec Králové and Jaroměř.
- Building the D1 motorway from Vyškov to Kroměříž and Lipník nad Bečvou.
- Preparing and commencing construction of the D3 motorway first in the area of the Tábor agglomeration.
- Continuing the construction of the ring road round Prague, including radial connections with priority connections in a northwesterly direction.
- Completion of the four-lane Prague–Liberec highway.
- Construction of the R35 highway passing by Hradec Králové and linking up with the D11.
- Construction of the R35 highway passing by Olomouc and the R48 by Bělotín and in the section Frýdek–Místek–Český Těšín.
- Continuing the construction of the R52 highway linking up with the motorway from Vienna now under construction.
- Finding a solution to capacity problems, defective areas, bridges, the construction of bypasses and approach roads to border crossings.

Railway infrastructure

- Completion of the reconstruction and modernization of railway transit corridors: Děčín–Prague–Břeclav, Bohumín–Přerov–Břeclav.
- Preparation and modernization of other sections of transit corridors: Praha–Veselí n. Luž.–Horní Dvořiště /České Velenice, Česká Třebová–Olomouc–Petrovice u Kar.–Mosty u Jablunkova, Cheb–Plzeň–Praha.
- Completion of electrification of lines: České Budějovice–Horní Dvořiště and Kadaň–Karlovy Vary, Letohrad–Lichkov, and further electrification programmes after 2005.
- Reconstruction and modernization of several railway stations, with the priority of ensuring passage along modernized corridors.
- Reconstruction of the Prague–Kladno railway link, with a connection to the Prague Ruzyne Airport.

Inland waterway infrastructure

- Improving navigation conditions on the Labe-Vltava waterway in the Ústí n. Lab.–Czech/German state border section.
- Making the Labe navigable up to Pardubice by linking up the navigable sections between Chvaletice and Př elouč and constructing a port in Pardubice.

Air transport infrastructure

- Reconstruction and modernization of the Prague Ruzyne Airport, with the construction of a new terminal and application of Schengen Convention standards.
- Implementation of a programme for transformation of the airport traffic management, security and control systems.
- Linkage with other transport systems.

The transport infrastructure for combined transport and public city transport, including the Prague Underground and bus transport, will also undergo development. In this area the State will invest in development and reconstruction, or will participate directly in the development of the infrastructure.

In the telecommunications sector, development will continue to be the exclusive responsibility of the different telecommunication operators, which will provide the funds from private resources within the principle of self-financing. Free access of businessmen to the telecommunication market is guaranteed. In 2000, three licences were accorded for fixed wireless access (FWA) in the range of 26 GHz. In 2001, four nationwide licences were further accorded for the operation of third-generation universal mobile telecom systems (UMTS). Their operation is expected to start in 2002, in accordance with the EU time schedule.

In the postal services sector, the appropriate implementing regulations have been issued in connection with the new Postal Services Act. For the time being, competition in express services, where multinational postal monopolies also operate, is minimal. However, it can be expected that preparations will have to begin soon for changing the status of Czech Post from a state corporation into a trading company, in accordance with EU standards. Within this transformation, it will be necessary to separate the performance of ownership rights to the new company from material and price regulation.

Sources of finance for the development of transport infrastructure

One of the most vital factors in the implementation of transport policy is locating sufficient resources for financing the maintenance of, and investments into, the transport infrastructure and the public transport rolling stock. In the case of the Czech Republic, most frequently used sources for modernization and reconstruction in the area of transport have been public budgets and bank loans, primarily offered by the likes of the World Bank, the European Bank for Reconstruction and Development (EBRD), the European Investment Bank (EIB), and similar institutions. There is also the possibility of conventional credits, grants and EU structural assistance (PHARE, ISPA programmes), as well as the use of private capital and PPPs.

Since 1993, the EIB has offered credits to the Czech Republic totalling €2.1 billion. More than half of this amount has gone on transport projects. The last two loans granted, in 1999, were allocated for the improvement of the condition of international motorways and a programme for road maintenance and repair. The programme for the modernization of the transport infrastructure was also supported by grants from the PHARE National Programme, the PHARE Cross-border Cooperation Programme (CBC) and the PHARE Multinational Programme for transport. Since 1994, approximately €40 million has been invested in or allocated to transport through the CBC Programme; through the National Programme, approximately €60 million has been made available since 1995; and the sum received between 1991 and 1997 through the Multinational Programme totalled €12.7 million.

In 2001, the budgetary rules were changed, and from now on parliamentary consent will be needed for guarantees on public and private projects. By the end of 2000, overall state guarantees reached some CZK136 billion, which is about one-fifth of the Czech Republic's state budget for one year.

An important instrument for financing the development of transport networks in the coming period will be ISPA, a structural fund of assistance in the area of transport and environmental protection, from which the Czech Republic can obtain up to CZK1.3 billion annually as part of EU assistance for transport infrastructure projects. Before that, however, it must meet the conditions set by the European Union, which also include co-financing, but which is not a simple matter. After admission to the European Union, it will also be possible to use financial contributions from the EU Cohesion Fund. In 1999, the first eight transport projects were submitted to the European Commission for assessment. In the autumn of 2000, the ISPA Management Committee approved the first three transport projects for the Czech Republic, including two railway projects: the modernization of the Záboř í n. Lab.–Př elouč section, with financing of €39.9 million, and the modernization of the Ústí n. Orl.–Česká Tř ebová section, with financing of €14.3 million, on the first transit corridor of Czech Railways. The third is the Frýdek-Místek—Dobrá road project, with financing of €20.4 million. To date, therefore, the total financial contribution from the ISPA Programme has been approximately €65.6 million.

4.17

Transport Logistics[1]

Bohumil Řezníč k, Pavel Šaradín and Jan Perner, Transport Faculty, University of Pardubice

Introduction

The main concern of transport logistics is the application of the logistic approach to the management of the movement of consignments within the transport network, from taking them over from the sender to their eventual handing over to the recipient. This process comprises a number of partial operations requiring a comprehensive solution. One such solution is conventional transport, which links up with other partial operations such as storage, handling, grouping and separation of consignments, packing and possibly other services (customs clearance, marketing, insuring and financial, information and consulting services). Logistic transport, on the other hand, is a set of the mentioned operations provided in the transport of a consignment by one or more transport systems. Transport and logistics should be seen as a system of operations closely linked together. Although the cost of these operations in practice necessitates considerable willingness to compromise, decisions must be made within the framework of the system in its entirety. The starting point for the creation of such a system is an analysis of what clients need and what they are offered by competitors. In general, it can be assumed that clients expect timely delivery, flexibility in meeting urgent requirements, safe transportation and handling of consignments, comprehensive services, sensitivity and credibility of the forwarder's employees, and obliging and fair behaviour in the case of damage to or loss of a consignment.

In comprehensive transport logistics, the interlinking of the computer systems of the client and the forwarder has become

[1] The content for this chapter was provided by the PP Agency in Prague.

increasingly common and operations between them are generally automated. For example, the client's supply and distribution system is directly linked to the system of the forwarder, who can respond quickly and flexibly to the client's needs. Logistic processes in transport can be characterized thus:

- they must be oriented to the final product of transport, ie conveyance;
- they must be focused on the coordination, synchronization and overall optimization of the movement of consignments in the transport network;
- the transportation of consignments must be connected to the processes of handling, storage and packaging, and possibly other related activities;
- non-material processes (flow of information) are part of the logistic processes;
- the decisive element in the overall logistic process is the client.

The world logistic service market is undergoing important change, the result of which is the overall globalization of trade and the comprehensive provision of logistic services by one provider, ie the creation of so-called logistic firms (transport and forwarding logistics). This chapter focuses on transport logistics in the Czech Republic and covers the different methods of transport currently available in the country, including rail transport, road, air freight, water and combined transport.

Logistic forwarding in rail transport

The last decade has seen a noticeable degree of liberalization introduced into the system of Czech Railways, and a number of external forwarders have subsequently broken up the State's former monopoly in this sector. For the time being, the operation of external forwarders is restricted to domestic firms, whose share of the overall freight carried by the railway is continually increasing. External forwarders transport goods for their own use or for the use of others, which mainly include bulk cargoes such as coal, gravel sand and limestone. Important external forwarders in the Czech Republic include OKD Doprava, a.s., Ostrava, Viamont, a.s., Ústí nad Labem, Škoda Doprava, a.s., Plzeň and Sokolovská Uhelní Společ nost, a.s., Sokolov.

There is presently a surplus of forwarding capacity in railway freight transport in the Czech Republic. In the process of optimization and use of capacity it is important to take advantage of the technical and technological benefits of this form of transport. An instrument suitable for solving this problem is the application of logistical processes. Here the position of rail transport on the domestic market must first of all be considered, not only in the context of the Czech Republic, but also on a European scale. Rail transport still has the following strong points:

- an unequivocal advantage in transporting bulk materials, dangerous goods and special consignments;
- advantage of transport over long distances;
- the large number of sidings facilitate transport right to the client;
- network character;
- higher degree of safety;
- linkage with other transport systems (multimodal transport);
- greater resistance to exposure (especially in winter).
- cleaner impact on the environment;
- shorter time needed for the clearance of consignments at border crossing stations in interstate transport;
- prospects for using transit corridors.

To increase the competitiveness of rail transport in 'door-to-door' and 'hub-and-spoke' transport, it is particularly necessary to cope with final forwarding. This can be done:

- by using the forwarders' sidings, if available (currently there are about 3500 sidings in the Czech Republic);
- if the client is not directly within the reach of a rail line, the rail forwarder must:
  - cooperate with haulage contractors in collecting the consignments and delivering them to the required destinations; in this case the entire transport operation should be carried out on a single delivery document; or
  - carry out all operations with its own road vehicles directly, or through its affiliated companies.

The railway freight transport market can be divided into import, export, domestic transport and transit. The first three groups cater particularly for the following three commodity groups:

- solid fuels (bituminous coal, brown coal and coke);
- liquid and gaseous materials (petrol, motor oil, liquid and gaseous fuels, chemicals);
- metallurgical raw materials and products (ores, slag, iron and iron scrap, steel and iron products);

- building materials (cement, sand, gravel, crushed material, gravel sand, other building materials);
- wood and wood products;
- foodstuffs and farm produce;
- combined transport (large-size containers, ROLA road semi-trailers and other combined transport);
- other goods (mineral fertilizers, paper and paper products, mechanical and electrical machines and instruments, surface transport vehicles, non-ferrous metals and products).

Transit deliveries are not classified by transported material. The volume of this transport has been stable on a long-term basis, with a slightly rising trend, which will continue with the expected finalization of the rail corridors. In connection with the approved forecasts of freight transport trends in the Czech Republic up to 2015, large rail forwarders have prepared their own business strategies based on the trends and the expected changes in the structure of transported commodities.

Logistics in road transport

Road haulage is the dominant feature of the European transport market and the Czech market is rapidly reaching European standards. The reasons for the positive developments in the Czech market are clear: speed, accuracy, reliability, and easy availability and flexibility of road transport. These are ideal characteristics for participation in the logistic chains. Haulage contractors are beginning to use these advantages as best they can. In connection with growing competition in this branch of transport, a number of larger firms have changed the range of their services. Conventional lorry transport is no longer the dominant form, although it is by no means in decline. The greater part of overall performance, however, has shifted to other activities, such as the sale of fuel, spare parts, services and, naturally, logistics. In the future, haulage operators will be using and broadening logistic services in the following areas in particular:

- foodstuffs;
- raw materials and products for the chemical industry, metalworking, the electrical engineering and electronics industry, metallurgy and the automobile industry;
- express transport of piece deliveries (mail, parcels and courier deliveries).

Air freight transport

Air transport is predetermined for the fast conveyance of mail and goods particularly in international transport. This is where logistic systems are most widely used. Today's air transport is developing so as to meet the steadily growing demands of clients regarding speed, timely delivery, global networking, collecting and delivering consignments at the client's end, and low costs. The cycle of logistic operations in transport from sender to recipient is continuously accelerating as a result of the efforts of air forwarders and handling agents and forwarding companies. Air companies are continuously broadening the range of their products with the addition of time-definite regimes, whereby they guarantee forwarding within prearranged time limits of 24, 48 and 72 hours. Handling companies help towards the shortening of logistic operations by accelerating clearance with the use of new information technologies (electronic transfer of data, bar codes etc).

Forwarding firms use network data in the framework of their interstate partner connections and global networks. For the time being, the greatest obstacles to the further acceleration of the transport cycle in air transport are the customs procedures. To ensure that the customer is satisfied with the entire transport cycle, the mutual cooperation of all parties involved (ie the air carrier, the handling company, the forwarder and the customer) is essential. The further expansion of express transport of piece deliveries requires the creation of express and postal centres at air junctions, which will play the role of logistic junctions. An important trend in air-freight transport is the growing demand for forwarding consignments weighing more than a tonne. Over the next 20 years this will require growth to more than double the existing capacity of the air-freight fleet on the world scale.

Water transport

The transportation of goods by water in the Czech Republic can be divided into river (continental) transport and sea transport. In general, it applies that water transport is one of the cheapest and ecologically most friendly forms of transport. At the same time, however, it is slower and unreliable throughout the year. River transport in the Czech Republic is used for both inland and international freight transport. Inland transport is operated on the Labe (Elbe) and the navigable section of the Vltava. The most frequent cargoes are building materials and coal. With the declining consumption of these materials, however, the volume of this form of transport is also being reduced. International river transport is used for the transportation of goods between the Czech Republic and countries of Western Europe and between the Czech Republic and the sea ports. The main cargoes are building materials, coal, chemicals, extra large and heavy items, feed and grain.

Sea transport is the decisive form of transport ensuring freight transport between the Czech Republic and countries of other continents. It facilitates the export of various traditional products of Czech industry and the import of cheap consumer goods from Asia, production technologies, and a number of important raw materials, manure, fruit etc. The position of sea transport in the Czech economy has remained unchanged for a number of years. From the point of view of the development of transport technologies, however, a great future is being forecast for container transport. Reloading operations at sea ports have changed radically as a result of the use of containers. With the continuously increasing size of ocean-going vessels there will be growing demand for pan-European transport logistics.

Combined transport

In the past few decades, Europe has witnessed a rapid development of inter-modal transport in the form of combined transport (ie the interlinking of at least two different forms of transport to ship goods from one place to another). Combined transport is inter-modal transport ensuring the transport of goods in one and the same transport unit or road set without handling the cargo. The longest part of the route is by rail, inland waterway or sea, and the opening or closing part is realized by road and must be as short as possible. The importance of combined transport stands out particularly in connection with the general effort to regulate the excessive growth of long-distance road transport, the effort to reduce the impact of road transport on the environment and the need to accelerate reloading operations between different kinds of transport. Combined transport must also be promoted in connection with the liberalization of the transport market.

The long-term plan for the introduction and development of combined transport in the Czech Republic is to attain the abovementioned aims. Participating in the development of combined transport, besides forwarders and state administration, are indi vidual contractors, and recently also combined transport operators. The development of combined transport will be influenced by conditions in the country's legislation, the technical base and the technology and management of combined transport. The technical base of combined transport is formed by combined transport terminals, reloading units, road vehicles and reloading facilities, rail vehicles and transport units. An important condition of promoting combined transport is a sufficient supply of suitable transport units. In the near future, such units will be containers and exchangeable superstructures.

Container transport is particularly suitable for the transport of palleted goods, goods requiring special packing, all consumer goods and goods involving transportation risks (computers, cigarettes and alcohol). Specific containers are used to transport loose, granular, powdery and liquid materials and consignments sensitive to temperature change. Containerization plays an important role not only in inland but also in international transport of materials. Besides containers, exchangeable superstructures are the most efficient means for creating logistic transport chains in combined transport. Sometimes they are referred to as cargo-boxes and combi-boxes. Another new system in combined transport is the Abroll Container Transport System (ACTS), offering a smooth and reliable transport service in the road–rail and rail–road chain. The operator of this system in the Czech Republic is OKD Doprava, a.s., Ostrava. Other forward-looking combined transport systems are Kombirail and Road Railer. These are bimodal systems, using a double semitrailer, which is a specially adjusted road semitrailer. This adjustment makes it possible to push a bogie underneath, allowing the semitrailer to be transported by rail. In the logistic transport chain, this system allows a reduction in the number of used means of transport in comparison with ordinary combined transport systems. A part of modern combined transport is logistic centres, which are of basic importance for the future tasks awaiting this type of transport. These centres are important links in logistic transport chains, providing comprehensive logistic services, ie transport, reloading, warehousing, classification, grouping and separation of the consignments, dispatching the consignment, and carrying out the related intangible transactions. There are presently plans to build six or seven such logistic centres in the Czech Republic.

4.18

Tourism[1]

Commercial Section of the British Embassy, Prague

Introduction

The tourism industry developed dynamically in the Czech Republic after the collapse of communism in 1989. The development of the industry was driven by the nature of tourist destinations in the country which long held a reputation in Europe as worthy places for cultural, ecological and health-associated forms of relaxation. The collapse of the Iron Curtain in Eastern Europe, however, was the catalyst allowing mass tourism from the former excluded countries of Western Europe and North America to visit the Czech Republic, many of whom were driven by the mystical nature of the Bohemian culture of this formerly closed-off country of high appeal. It should be noted that many visitors were not particularly focused on the quality of services and infrastructure provided in the Czech Republic, but instead were motivated by an interest to explore a new, largely unknown tourist destination. At present, however, the novelty of Czech tourism in the earlier 1990s has largely been exhausted, and the country belongs among standard tourism destinations of a high appeal.

Tourism is one of the most important sectors of the Czech economy, since tourism and related supporting services presently contribute between 9 per cent and 11 per cent to Czech GDP, and around 10 per cent of total employment. During the late 1990s, foreign exchange reserves generated from tourism represented around 14 per cent of the export equivalence and over half of the income of the services sector. It is possible to summarize the development of the tourism industry in the Czech Republic during the 1990s thus:

---

[1] This chapter is based on re-worked extracts of a report by Trade Partners UK, entitled 'Tourism and Spa Industry in the Czech Republic'.

- The number of foreigners visiting the Czech Republic increased threefold, and the average term of their stay increased.
- The Czech Republic's share of the world tourism market grew to total almost 3 per cent.
- The country's share of the EU tourism market also expanded, now totalling around 7 per cent.
- The annual development rate of incoming tourism is high, however, due to the minimal base resulting from the political situation before 1990.

Tourism in Prague and the regions

The material and technical facilities of tourism experienced significant quantitative change during the 1990s. In 1989, for example, Czechoslovakia had 2863 accommodation facilities with a total of 342,246 beds. At the end of the 1990s, the number of accommodation facilities in the country had increased more than four-fold, to 13,124, and the number of beds increased by more than 90 per cent to 654,031. Almost two fifths of the accommodation facilities are hotels, motels, boatels and pensions. Individual accommodation or private accommodation facilities represent more than 7 per cent (4.3 per cent in 1989).

More than 15 per cent of the country's bed capacity is concentrated in Prague, whereas the figure was around 23.8 per cent in the mid-1990s. This alludes to the fact that accommodation capacity is gradually spreading to other parts of the country—a positive sign with regards to the importance of tourism for regional development. In 1999, the average annual utilization of the accommodation capacity in hotels and pensions (as monitored by statistics) amounted to 33.6 per cent, with Prague (43.7 per cent) and Western Bohemia (38.5 per cent) reporting coefficients above the national average.

The distribution of accommodation facilities in different divisions of the tourism sector in the Czech Republic can be summarized as follows:

- City and cultural tourism (32.2 per cent of total bed capacity).
- Mountain tourism (24.2 per cent of total bed capacity).
- Tourism at water areas (13.7 per cent of beds).
- Spa tourism (8.5 per cent of beds).
- Not specified (around 21.4 per cent of beds).

It is now axiomatic that Prague has become an international tourist centre and the Czech Republic's tourism hub. However, Prague is presently dominant in the county's distribution of accommodation facilities primarily due to the lack of good regional tourism products despite the fact that almost all of the area of the Czech Republic is available for recreation purposes. The country has numerous historical, cultural and technical monuments, including monuments stated in the UNESCO list. There is a dense and well-marked network of interconnected tourist paths and routes, maintained by the Czech Tourist Club. Moreover, the Czech Republic has a unique chance to succeed in tourism markets with an offer of new products such as city, convention and incentive tourism as well as sport tourism, cultural tourism, country tourism and particularly its sub-products, agro-tourism and eco-tourism, for which the country has ideal conditions. There is the possibility of further development of the traditional spa industry.

The new definition of government administration and local government powers and considerable limitation of state involvement in matters of economic development affected tourism positively on the one hand (ie rapid privatization and development of private business), and negatively on the other (dissolution of information flows and a slow adaptation of regional and local governments to new tasks related to the economic development of the administered areas). The development of tourism services in the regions dealt with the following barriers:

- Insufficient and unsuitable tourism infrastructure.
- Lack of experts to manage development of facilities.
- Absence of marketing development concepts.
- Unsuitable legislation and tax system.
- Limited financial resources for business development.
- Lack of funds for maintenance and reconstruction of cultural heritage.

The removal of these barriers will require the cooperation of all involved bodies and social partners. The space for this work is provided by the implementation of the measures contained in the Czech Republic's concept of tourism policy in the legislation sphere (ie the amended Trade Act, VAT Act and Taxes and Charges Administration Act, creation of a Support Fund for the Development of Tourism in the Czech Republic, adoption of the Act of Terms of Tourist Business—the operation of travel agencies and protection of their customers etc), as well as by the elaboration and implementation of the priorities (eg HR development, tourism information system, creation of new tourism products and regional tourism products) in regional operation plans.

New tourism products

In addition to traditional tourism products (spas, city tourism, cultural tourism, sport tourism and hiking etc), the Czech Republic has ideal conditions for almost all the modern products of tourism—particularly for the development of country tourism. This new product may revive economically the problematic districts of Northern Moravia (Bruntál, Jesenik, Šumperk, Vsetín), the area of Českomoravská Vysocina and in particular the former military area along the German and Austrian borders (Šumava, Novohradské mountains etc). Country tourism, with its sub-products (agro-tourism, eco-tourism etc), as a product of a permanently sustainable development of tourism, may also be applied more or less generally to protected landscape areas of national parks. The Czech Republic has optimal conditions for the development of cycle tourism (particularly the development of international cycle routes), convention and religious tourism and new products of cultural tourism (heritage paths, industrial open-air museums and monuments etc).

Strengths and weaknesses

Strengths

- The country enjoys an advantageous geographical location (centre of Europe, morphology, above sea level, climate).
- There are a wealth of cultural, historic and technical monuments and other cultural and folklore attractions, spa tradition, nature attractions (protected landscape areas and national parks), sport premises, and Prague itself, as a worldwide tourism attraction.
- There is a dense and well-marketed network of interconnected tourist paths and routes throughout the entire Czech Republic.
- There is sufficient accommodation capacity and a flexible labour force.

Weaknesses

- There are low-quality basic and supplementary tourism services.
- There is insufficient maintenance and reconstruction of historical buildings and of the cultural heritage sites (particularly some of those listed by UNESCO).

- There is an absence of marketing studies for the development of potential tourist regions.
- There is insufficient promotion of the Czech Republic and the regions of the country both at home and abroad.
- There is still insufficient tourism infrastructure (particularly insufficient information system, transport and communications).
- There is an imbalance in the demand and supply of qualified labour.
- There is a high concentration of visitors to the Czech Republic in Prague (almost 70 per cent).

Opportunities and threats

Opportunities

- Improvement of the position of the Czech Republic worldwide and particularly in the European tourism market.
- Wider cooperation of border regions (Šumava, Southern Moravia, Nisa, Labe, Krušné mountains) and other regions and municipalities with their respective foreign partners in the sphere of tourism.
- Development of the traditional spa industry.
- Development of new modern tourism products (country and ecological tourism, cycle tourism, city, convention and incentive tourism, cultural tourism etc), including accompanying programmes.

Threats

- Disregard of the significance of the legislative framework concerning business and service quality control, including consumer protection.
- Lack of funds for the stabilization and further development of tourism business.
- Disregard of the significance of the coordination of joint actions of government bodies, local governments, regional development agencies, regional tourism associations and industry-led tourism associations.
- Disregard of the significance of tourism activities for the development of SMEs and for the creation of new jobs in the regions.
- Disregard of human factor and professional preparation of experts in the sphere of tourism, including consultancy and education for start-up entrepreneurs (adult education).

State support

State funds played a minimal role in the dynamic expansion of the tourism sector during the 1990s (in 1997, for example, state funds represented a contribution amounting to only 0.6 per cent of the total generated foreign exchange income). In 2000, however, the Czech government created an official state programme in support of the tourism industry, facilitated on the basis of Government Resolution No. 1075/2000 on 1 November 2000. In coordination with several Czech state bodies (primarily the Czech Centre for Tourism, the Ministry of Regional Development and the Higher Self-governing Territorial Units) and technical assistance programmes from the European Union, the programme will focus on the development of the spa industry and the improvement of its material and technical facilities, including the development of new alternatives of spa tourism for specific client groups. The goal of the programme in subsequent years is to support—via its sub-programmes—an increasing quality and competitiveness of tourism products and services on domestic as well as international markets.

The government programme will provide for a systematic solution of tourism support as well as support of SMEs in the tourism sector primarily employing state subsidies, including:

- subsidies to companies and municipalities for business projects (eg the construction and reconstruction of accommodation and boarding facilities);
- subsidies to municipalities for investment activity related to the development of the tourism infrastructure;
- subsidies to legal and physical persons for tourism development activities (programmes related to the preparation and provision of new tourism products—marketing studies, projects, consultancy and information services, education and training.

Concerning implementation, the state programme in support of tourism will provide the Sectoral Operating Programme with funds for national programmes (around 60 per cent of funds) as well as regional programmes (around 40 per cent of funds). The state programme will depend largely on funds from the state budget and some CZK185 million was made available for its development during 2001. Similar annual amounts should be available for subsequent years of the programme, assuming that the implemented sub-programmes operating under its auspices have been successful. It is hence envisaged that some of the benefits achieved under the State's systematic support for the industry will include:

- An annual 100,000 increase in tourists visiting the Czech Republic, with an average expense of US$38 per day, working on an average visit of 3.6 days. This would result in a forecasted increase of foreign exchange revenues by almost US$14 million.
- An increase in the average expense of each foreign visitor in the Czech Republic by US$5 per day (taking into consideration the lower limit of the estimated number of tourists of seven million, this would mean a further increase in foreign exchange revenues by almost US$130 million).

4.19

Operating through Agencies, Distributorships and Franchises

Jan Grozdanovic and Barbara Stankevová, Seddons Solicitors

Introduction

Since 1989, there has been a boom in business in the Czech Republic accompanied by numerous investments made by foreign companies. Many of these foreign firms have established branches or subsidiaries in the Czech Republic. However, the establishment of a branch or a subsidiary remains a rather time-consuming and costly business. As a result, some foreign producers prefer to enter the Czech market through selected local agents or distributors. The business environment has changed during the past seven years following the end of the state monopoly on trade with foreign companies; the appointment of agents is thus long established. There are now many private companies in the market searching for foreign expertise and goods in order to set up their own businesses. For the local entrepreneur, cooperation with a well-established foreign company, taking advantage of its good reputation, long history and sophisticated advertising and marketing techniques, is seen as a guarantee of success. However, despite the fact that many agreements have been concluded on an agency, distributorship or franchise basis, the Czech post-1989 law (including Act No.513/1991 Coll., the Commercial Code) still does not contain any direct provisions on distributorship franchises. For a foreign entrepreneur, it is deemed necessary to conclude an 'innominate contract' (ie a contract not falling within the specific categories governed by the Commercial Code), thus using the general provisions of the Commercial Code. In addition, the general principles to be applied are those of the Civil Code, the Act on Economic Competition and all special laws relevant to the area of business in which their participants wish to operate.

Commercial representation

The relevant provisions of the Commercial Code are paragraph 652 and the following:

- There is a requirement that the contract shall be concluded in a written form. Under the contract, the representative undertakes either to perform long-term activities for the principal focused on the conclusion of specified types of contracts or to negotiate and to conclude contracts on behalf of and in the name of the principal.
- Commission shall accrue to the representative upon fulfilment of the principal's obligations under the concluded agreement, or on the day of prescribed fulfilment of the principal's obligations under the agreement, or upon fulfilment of a third party's obligations under the agreement, or upon expiry of a six-month period in the event that the third party has not fulfilled its obligations under the concluded agreement within such period.
- The representative is obliged to assist the principal when concluding such an agreement with a third party, and he guarantees to the principal the fulfilment of the obligations of such third party if this formed part of his agreement with the principal.
- The representative is expected to report to the principal on market developments and to provide all other data relevant to the principal's interests. He is obliged to follow the instructions of the principal. If he is empowered to sign agreements on behalf of the principal, he is entitled to do so only under the commercial conditions given to him by the principal.
- Czech law does recognize exclusive and non-exclusive representation. If an exclusive representation agreement is concluded, the principal is required to pay a commission to the representative even for contracts he has signed without the representative's cooperation, unless otherwise agreed.
- The representative's contract may be concluded either for limited or unlimited periods of time. After the expiration of the agreement, the

representative has a right to compensation in cases where it has acquired new customers or substantially developed business with the current customers and such compensation is fair in view of all applicable circumstances. The compensation must not exceed annual commission based on the average annual commissions received by the representative within the last five years.

Agency

The relevant provisions of the Commercial Code governing framework agency agreements are paragraph 566 and the following:

- The difference between commercial representation and an agency agreement is that a representative acts for a principal for the purpose of arranging certain kinds of agreements, whereas the agent is primarily appointed to arrange one agreement or another matter for the principal.
- The agent is obliged to act in accordance with the instructions of the principal and advise him of any circumstances which may necessitate a change in the instructions to him. The agreement does not have to be in a written form. However, if the principal requires the agent to conclude any legal transactions on his behalf, he has to furnish the agent with a written power of attorney.
- Unless agreed otherwise, commission accrues to the agent after the successful conclusion of the matter on the principal's behalf. However, unlike a representation agreement, the agent is not liable and does not guarantee fulfilment of the obligations of a third party unless he undertook to do so.

Distributorship

Goods are supplied to the local market by sale of the goods from a foreign manufacturer to a local distributorship who, at his own expense, distributes the goods to the local market. This seems to provide very little risk for the foreign manufacturer. However, what has to be considered is the strength of the local partner and whether lack of professionalism, capital and experience may adversely affect the goodwill of the manufacturer.

The agreement between the manufacturer and the distributor may be governed by the Commercial Code if the parties do not select the law of the country of the manufacturer as the governing law for their agreement. Their relationship implies certain obligations on the manufacturer to supply non-defective goods, to bear responsibility for defective goods, warranties, delivery obligations, and damage to the goods up until the time they are delivered to the purchaser. However, it seems most important to secure the intellectual property rights of the manufacturer in the area where the goods will be distributed, and also to establish a good service and to set a certain standard for future distribution, thereby avoiding subsequent loss of goodwill and any deterioration in the quality of goods caused by bad storage, service and repair. Thus it seems feasible to include in the agreement extra provisos which imply the right of the manufacturer to control the quality of sale of his goods and to impose certain standards or marketing tools which are to be maintained with assistance and guidance from the manufacturer. As a result of choosing the wrong distributor, a manufacturer may lose the market even though there may be a demand for his high-quality goods.

Before concluding such an agreement, a search of the necessary import licences, import duty and technical standards should be carried out. If required by Czech law, the goods may have to be submitted to the Czech authorities for testing. It is up to the contracting parties to agree on the law that will govern their relationship (as in the case of commercial representative and agency agreements) and also to decide the way in which subsequent disputes may be resolved. Under the new law on arbitration, it is now possible to choose an arbitration court or an arbitrator to resolve a dispute.

Franchising

Although growing substantially in recent years, no specific rules for franchising have been adopted by Czech legislative bodies, despite general announcement of such intention.

Franchise agreements are concluded as innominate contracts and therefore it is most important to cover in detail every aspect of the prospective relationship—otherwise, there may be no protection from the law if the rules are not expressly defined in the agreement.

In addition, franchising represents a relatively low capital risk for the manufacturer or a service provider who wishes to expand into the local market. However, certain tolls for control of the goods and services provided need to be maintained as well as the provision of in-depth training on the company philosophy and expertise. The choice of a strong local partner is very important as failure by the local franchisee to provide the foreign products or services to a high standard could damage irreparably the company's image and goodwill, leading potentially to a loss of the whole market.

It is very important to provide the local franchisee with all relevant technical data as Czech law imposes stringent rules on workshops and shops maintenance with regard to environmental protection, hygiene, static and fire safety regulations and so forth. The franchiser should ensure that all his intellectual property rights are protected under local law in the relevant market and that appropriate licences are given to the franchisee. All information and training provided to the franchisee should be protected under the Commercial Code's provisions on unfair competition and breach of business secrecy. Agreement should be reached with the franchisee on the form that the standard employment contracts should take to secure quality of work, to maintain confidence and to restrain employees from using the company's expertise to set up businesses in competition with that of the franchisee and franchiser. Possible rulings by the Constitutional Court should be carefully considered since there are limits to preventing employees from carrying out certain activities after their employment has been terminated. Becoming a co-partner in the local company of the franchisee may be recommended in order to maintain good control over the franchise business. It may also help to build up a strong capital base for the franchisee, for example, by improving the possibility of obtaining bank loans.

4.20

Real Estate Development

Anders Hall, Managing Director, and Ludek Schmidt, Head of Project Development, Skanska Property Czech Republic, s.r.o.

Evolution of the market

After developing gradually for about eight years, the Czech real estate market is finally showing clear signs of stability. The significant volume of good quality properties, stabilized rents in all sectors, some potential for rental growth, further development opportunities and relatively high yields are attractive to both developers and final investors. Moreover, lasting economic growth has had a positive effect on the market mood, although a relatively limited take-up, particularly in the office sector, during 2001 was not very encouraging. The recent very rapidly strengthening Czech currency has raised concerns for many developers who fix their cash flows in euros due to the negative effect on the return of capital and overall profitability of their investments. The Czech economy and continuing inflow of foreign capital to the country currently give no signals that the strength of the Czech crown is only temporary; however, in the short to mid term the less favourable return should be compensated by a gradual rental growth combined with decreasing investment yields.

Rules for foreign ownership

The Foreign Exchange Act was amended in 2001 enabling foreign companies with branches and representation in the Czech Republic to buy real estate other than forestry and agricultural land without limitations. Acquisition of real estate with this limitation is thus possible through the formation of a Czech legal entity or by a locally registered branch office of the foreign company. Foreign citizens remain excluded from real estate transactions; however, this restriction can be avoided by simply setting up a company.

Market values

The Prague market has recently seen increasing activity among institutional investors, who have acquired several new properties and have continued to search intensively for further opportunities. The local product is undoubtedly interesting to investors, due to the fact that the prime market yields in all property sectors remain about 2 per cent–3 per cent above those achieved in the Western European markets. This makes Prague properties still relatively cheap to acquire and in 2002 the investment market is predicted to perform well. As the rent levels are stabilized, most leases have rents denominated in Deutschemarks or euros and the standard of many buildings is high, the remaining issues to be resolved are the quality and length of the leases and the quality of the covenant. It is expected that investment activity will increase over the coming years, which will put prime yields under pressure.

Role of the property developer

The property developer's role is very similar to that in other European countries. Good knowledge of the market together with the ability to find good quality consultants in all related branches is crucial to success. Particularly in the case of Prague, it is very important to understand the zoning and planning rules well and to fulfil all the requirements set by the authorities involved in the planning consent procedures.

Construction costs

Construction costs vary from € 300 to € 500 per square metre of gross area for warehouse buildings and from €500 to €900 per square metre of gross area for retail premises to € 800 to €1,000 per square metre of gross area for office premises. Over recent years the gradual growth of construction costs has followed average price inflation in the market.

Lease terms

Typical lease terms are:

- Lease length: generally 5–10 years depending on the market sector. Retail leases tend to be fixed for longer periods (usually around 10 years) than those for office and industrial space.

- Rental terms: rent payable in quarterly advance instalments and denominated in euros (previously Deutschemarks), but mostly payable in Czech crowns according to the rates valid at the date of invoicing. In the case of retail leasing practice, a variable rent pro rata to turnover is often set by the landlord alongside the base rent, whereby the tenant is obliged to pay the higher of those two sums.
- Security deposits: minimum 3–6 months' rent deposit or an equivalent bank guarantee. Corporate guarantees are also an alternative in the case of large and financially stable companies.
- Rental growth: annual indexation according to the CPI of the Euro zone (previously Germany).
- Service charges: covering all the costs of the tenant occupancy and building operation inclusive of all charges such as utilities, facility management and insurance. In the case of retail units, the utilities are often measured by separate meters and charged to the tenant directly by the suppliers.

Freehold versus leasehold

Most developers have a strong preference for a freehold as opposed to a leasehold interest in the property. The main reason is security of tenure, and the consequent availability of funding for the development and, in the final stage, market values and liquidity in the investment market.

Skanska's market entry and developments

Skanska Property Czech Republic, s.r.o. is a member of the Swedish-based Skanska group. Skanska is one of the largest companies in the world in construction-related services and project development. Its aim is to develop substantial commercial projects in good locations. Skanska has operations in some 60 countries. Among its most significant markets are the home market of Sweden and then Denmark, Finland, Central European countries and the United States.

Since 1997, Skanska Property Czech Republic, s.r.o. has been operating as a real estate developer in the Czech Republic. Its office is located in Prague. Skanska is further represented by IPS Skanska, a.s., which is the largest construction company on the

Czech market with a number of successfully completed construction projects.

Skanska Property has recently finalized a new commercial project—Bredovský Dvur—situated in Prague city centre, which provides approximately 10,000 square metres of high-quality office space. The many amenities within this project include two open courtyards, underground parking and an atrium with central reception, as well as a new restaurant called Bredovský Dvur within the building.

Skanska is currently developing two new commercial schemes: Vysocanská Brána, Prague 9 and Budejovická Alej, Prague 4, each of which offers approximately 10,000 square metres of office space. The construction materials utilized—steel, light materials and glass—as well as a complete package of technical equipment are typical of 21st-century buildings.

Following these office projects, Skanska commenced construction in March 2002 of the Retail Park in Cestlice. The new shopping centre, which will be situated in the current commercial zone, will offer predominantly all consumer electronics by Dixons, the largest retailer in this field in Europe, together with shoes by Humanic, lamps by Rendl and carpets by Topwert. This development of more than 9,000 square metres of commercial space and a car park will start serving its first customers at the end of November 2002. Construction of a similar retail park in Cerný Most, Prague 14 will start in the near future. These projects are the first retail schemes for Skanska Property in the Czech Republic and also the first in a series of similar projects for Skanska in Central Europe.

Skanska Property's long-term goal is to become one of the leading developers in the Czech Republic's real estate market and to cooperate as an independent partner for companies looking for modern office premises and attractive locations.

4.21

Czech Media Market

Marian Rasik, Head of Telecom, Media and Technology Group, ABN Amro Bank NV

2002 is likely to be very interesting but fairly difficult to predict in terms of investment in the media. On the one hand, the market will be affected by a number of negative impacts such as the economic recession in Europe and the worldwide slump in advertising expenditure; it must not be forgotten that the advertising market in the Czech Republic is mainly dependent upon large multinationals who may cut down their advertising budgets within their global strategies because of the worldwide recession, although a slump on the world markets may not affect the Czech economy directly. On the other hand, a number of positive aspects can also be seen. In particular, the 2002 parliamentary elections are supposed to be associated with additional investments in mainly outdoor advertising; also important are big sports events, such as the Olympic Games, the ice hockey world championship and the football World Cup. In addition, the privatization of a number of large Czech companies may be a positive factor influencing the total advertising spend. The forecasts of ARBOmedia and OMD for investment in media advertising in 2002 are summarized in Table 4.21.1.

Table 4.21.1 Estimated investments in media advertising in 2002 (Media Net, CZK billion)

	ARBOmedia	*OMD*
TV	7.350	7.850
Press	5.850	5.900
Outdoor	1.135	1.420
Radio	1.095	1.190
Internet	0.190	0.205
Other	0.235	0.200
Total	15.855	16.765

Comparing the local situation with the latest developments in Europe or the United States, the Czech Republic seems to be surprisingly well off. The commotion in the US and European markets caused by the economic recession and the impact of other negative factors resulted in a year-on-year slump in media investments. Therefore, many experts were quite logically concerned when and to what degree the economic recession in Western countries would affect the Czech market. However, current forecasts are optimistic. As Table 4.21.2 demonstrates, ARBO Media expects that investments in media advertising space will grow nearly 7 per cent. OMD Czech is less optimistic; its investments-related forecast being for only a 3.1 per cent year-on-year growth.

TV's major share of advertising

Analysing the respective media mix components, ABN Amro expects TV stations to have the biggest share of advertising, just as in previous years. Advertising clients are expected to invest as much as CZK7.85 billion in TV advertising, representing a 4.1 per cent growth. That would mean that of the total companies' spend on advertising in the Czech Republic, TV stations would get 46.8 per cent and their share would grow 0.4 per cent. The biggest portion of this cake will go to TV NOVA, whose long-term viewing figures are about 48 per cent. It is expected that TV NOVA will earn about CZK5.2 billion in advertising, with ET1 finishing second and TV PRIMA third.

A very important breakthrough in the Czech advertising market, in particular in TV advertising, was the introduction of a new 'peoplemeter' survey by Mediasearch in April 2002, which will replace the existing TNS survey. The change in the surveying method is likely to affect the

Table 4.21.2 Expected year-on-year growth in 2002 (%)

	OMD	*ARBOmedia*
TV	4.1	8.9
Press	0.7	4.5
Outdoor	5.2	6.1
Radio	3.5	5.3
Internet	28.1	18.8
Other	0.0	6.8
Total	3.1	6.8

results, as the second-tier data will provide a more accurate evaluation of the viewing figures relating to the respective spots than the existing data that are based on minutes.

Press

In the printed media, ABN Amro expects the advertising spend to grow and to total CZK5.9 billion (ie 36.5 per cent of the total advertising market). Nationwide and regional dailies will receive the largest share of the spend, earning about CZK680 billion in advertising. The market leader is *MF Dnes*.

The Czech dailies market went through a number of changes in 2001, including changes in content, design (colour) and massive reader contests. The nationwide dailies market was mainly affected by three events: two nationwide dailies went under and *Super*, a new nationwide tabloid, made its debut. The dailies competing for first place in terms of their average circulation in the Czech Republic are *Blesk* and *MF Dnes*. In January 2002 *Blesk* finished first with 331,516 and *MF Dnes* second with 324,159 copies sold.

Sales of nationwide dailies in the Czech Republic are expected to slump 2–5 per cent, while the sales of regional newspapers will continue to grow. In December 2001, the average number of copies sold by seven nationwide dailies was 1,199,806, which is 0.12 copies sold per capita in the entire Czech Republic. The average circulation of seven regional dailies in the same month was 442,290, ie 0.04 copies sold per capita. The number of readers per one copy sold was 2.51 for nationwide dailies and 3.31 for regional dailies. The individual readership of nationwide dailies is registered in Table 4.21.3.

Subscriptions account for 20–25 per cent of the total sold circulation of nationwide dailies and about 50–55 per cent of regional dailies. The subscription-versus-free sales proportions will not change dramatically during 2002. ABN Amro expects most dailies to increase their prices soon in response to growing input costs. *Super* increased its price at the end of 2001; a number of other dailies are also considering the possibility of increasing their prices.

Internet share of advertising

Internet advertising turnovers are growing rapidly. According to surveys conducted by the Internet Title Publishers Section of the Publishers Union (SVIT), the Internet market earnings in advertising may grow by

Table 4.21.3 Number of readers of nationwide dailies, 2000–2001 ('000)

	2001	*2000*
Mladá fronta Dnes	1171	1242
Blesk	1076	1099
Právo	656	684
Lidové noviny	325	306
Sport	216	289
Hospodář ské noviny	166	199

Source: Media Projekt

as much as 50 per cent in 2002. Internet advertising turnover for 2000 was estimated by SVIT to total CZK120 million; in 2001, advertising sales were CZK240 million and are expected to total as much as CZK330 million in 2002. However, it is very difficult to estimate the Internet advertising spend, as no trustworthy evaluation method is in place so far—for example, ARBO Media estimates that turnover has grown from CZK170 million to just CZK210 million. Nevertheless, the expected growth reinforces the Internet's estimated share in the advertising cake.

Outdoor advertising

Prospects for the owners of outdoor advertising carriers for 2002 are fairly positive. The upcoming parliamentary elections, privatization and important sporting events are arousing optimism mainly among billboard owners. Outdoor advertising is therefore expected to see some revitalization during 2002. OMD Czech estimates the outdoor advertising spend at CZK1.42 billion, while ARBO Media's estimate is just 1.14 billion. Statistics show that outdoor advertising is mainly used by tobacco companies, producers of alcoholic drinks, car manufacturers, car dealers and mobile network operators, closely followed by food companies. The frequency of charity campaigns is growing. While tobacco companies and car manufacturers tend to use traditional billboards, mobile network operators seem to prefer untypical carriers.

The problem with Czech outdoor advertising is the absence of market research. However, this problem should be resolved during 2002, as the Association for Outdoor Advertising and the Association of Advertising Agencies has started negotiations on the introduction of unified outdoor advertising research in the Czech Republic.

Advertising clients

The most important clients are FMCG companies dealing in food and beverages, cosmetics and body care products. Their contributions have been growing steadily over the monitored period. According to AC Nielsen's survey, the most important clients in 2001 were telecommunications companies: Eurotel, RadioMobil, Cesky Mobil and Ceský Telecom, and Procter & Gamble, Opavia-LU, Danone, Unilever, Kraft Foods International and Henkel. The average annual advertising spend totalled between CZK6 billion and CZK8 billion in the food and beverages sector and between CZK4 billion and CZK5 billion in cosmetics and body care. TV advertising spends are stable in the sector of financial institutions and lotteries (approximately CZK1 billion per year). Also stable is the auto-manufacturing sector (approximately CZK700 million per year). Declines are expected in health care and pharmaceuticals (approximately 500 million per year) and 'teleshopping and other' (approximately CZK100 million per year).

Latest developments in media market legislation

The Czech parliament passed a new Media Act in June 2001, which is intended to liberalize the media business. Adversaries of the new Act state that the amendment complicates market entry for companies wishing to operate nationwide radio and TV networks. Pursuant to the amendment, a TV licence may be extended by 12 years and a radio licence by eight years. The Act also offers greater opportunities for establishing media owners' alliances, although proprietary mergers by

Table 4.21.4 Top 10 advertising clients in 2001

	Spend (CZK '000)
Procter & Gamble	1,031,596
Eurotel	897,565
Opavia-LU	779,523
Danone Benešov	777,773
RadioMobil	732,923
Cesky Mobil	576,051
Unilever	562,992
Kraft Foods International	478,120
Henkel	403,992
Ceský Telcom	391,824

two nationwide TV or radio stations remain prohibited. The Act has also introduced quotas for European production, ie the obligation to ensure that more than 50 per cent of the respective TV programmes are produced in Europe.

The Advertising Act has also been amended. The amendment was expected to be enacted in June 2002; although it is extensive, it has not introduced any dramatic changes in terms of content. Instead, it explains and specifies the existing items of legislation. The main objective of the amendment is to harmonize this part of Czech legislation with that of the European Community. The most important items specified relate to the spread of unsolicited advertising (junk mail), advertising for children and adolescents and advertising promoting tobacco products and alcohol. However, the most significant changes and specifications are those relating to advertising in the health care sector.

4.22

Human Resources[1]

Oliver Schmitt, Managing Partner, Teamconsult

Introduction

Since the Velvet Revolution of 1989, the Czech Republic has been moving towards a market economy. Among other things, this has resulted in constantly increasing foreign direct investment (FDI) inflows, amounting to €4 billion–€5 billion annually for the last three years. Universities have started to teach modern know-how and international scholarships make it possible for students to study abroad. As the post-revolution generation of managers is growing into power, so the 'old-boys network' is losing in importance and real skills are becoming the essential criteria for success. Expatriates are being replaced by local management. All of these factors have led to dynamic changes on the labour market, bringing it closer to a modern market economy.

Education

Age structure in the Czech Republic is as follows:

0–14 years	17%
15–64 years	69%
65+years	14%

Secondary education

School attendance is compulsory until the age of 15. However, in the case of people in their mid-20s, over 90 per cent have attained secondary

[1] Teamconsult has endeavoured to present its view of the current situation of HR in the Czech Republic. All the information and estimates provided are based on Teamconsult's 10 years' experience with executive search in the Czech Republic.

education (EU average: 69 per cent). The curriculum includes one compulsory foreign language, and today 95 per cent of students learn English.

Universities/MBAs

There are 24 universities with a total of 111 faculties in the Czech Republic. University graduates represent 11 per cent of the labour force. Approximately 27,000 students graduate from the university every year. The best-known universities are Charles University (one of the oldest universities in Europe) and the University of Economics (VSE) in Prague. The title awarded to economics and science graduates is 'bakalář ' (abbreviated 'B.c.', after three years of study) or 'inženýr' ('ing.', after five years of study); social sciences graduates receive 'Magistr' ('Mgr.'). About 10 per cent of the population is computer literate.

Recently, the MBA has been gaining in popularity. It is usually taken by young professionals with two or three years' work experience or by people who graduated before the revolution.

Salary levels

In 2000, the average monthly salary was €450 (€570 in Prague). However, these figures may be misleading in that they do not reflect the significant difference in salary levels between the countryside and large cities. People with foreign language skills have substantially higher salaries. With regard to the type of candidates that foreign investors compete for, the salary levels in the following paragraphs are more relevant.

Table 4.22.1 Numbers of university students and graduates, 2000/2001

University	*Students*	*Graduates*
Total	199,840	27,443
Natural Sciences	15,987	1695
Technology	57,542	5882
Agriculture, Forestry	7946	1068
Medicine, Pharmacy	13,289	1831
Social Sciences	100,251	16,378
Culture, Art	4825	589

Manual workers

Manual workers usually do not have substantial language skills. There are several relatively large areas with high unemployment (eg the North Bohemia and North Moravia regions) due to the restructuring of the old steel and coal industry. Gross salaries in these regions average between €400 and €500 per month.

However, there are regions where manual workers are in short supply, such as industrial parks and regions with large foreign investments (eg Mlada Boleslav/Skoda and suppliers, Hranice na Morave, 50 kilometres from the city of Olomouc/Phillips). The same situation will occur in Kolín after the car factory—a joint venture of Peugeot, Citroën and Toyota Motors—is built.

It is interesting to note that construction companies rely heavily on workers from the Ukraine, Slovakia and former Yugoslavia. Salary dumping is a problem in the Czech Republic as well as in the West.

University graduates

Economics graduates with one foreign language achieve a starting income of around €600 per month in Prague and other major cities, rising to about €1000 after two years of work experience. For technical positions, salaries are more or less comparable. The average age of graduates is relatively low at 23–24 years.

Secretaries

Salaries range from €400 to €1000, depending on the person‘s language skills and range of duties. Top office managers achieve up to €2500 per month.

Bookkeepers, credit controllers, finance specialists

Good language skills are hard to find among bookkeepers and credit controllers. The average salary for people without a degree and with two years of experience is in the region of €800. Controllers with a university degree, one foreign language and five years of experience average €2000–€3000 per month.

Middle management

Most managers in middle management are relatively young. This is mainly due to the fact that most companies prefer managers who completed their studies after 1990. It is not uncommon for people with five years of professional experience to take on managerial functions. Depending on the size of the department and business field, salaries range from €2500 to €6000. The head of finance for a Prague-based company with a turnover of €30 million can expect between €3000 and €4500 per month plus bonuses.

Top management

As in other countries, the salary range for top managers is very broad. Board members of the leading companies in the Czech Republic achieve annual incomes of up to €500,000. Salaries of local partners in international law, tax or management consulting companies are in the region of €150,000–€200,000 per year. The CEO of a sales company with a turnover of €30 million is likely to have a salary of between €4500 and €6000 per month. It is almost impossible to find a qualified CEO under €3000, even for a smaller company, at least in the Prague region.

Regional differences

The Czech Republic is a relatively centralized country, with Prague as its economic, political and cultural centre. Prague is home to the best-qualified people from a wide range of educational and training facilities. With low unemployment, good knowledge of foreign languages and strong competition among employers, the average salary level is the highest in the Czech Republic.

Outside Prague, salaries are lower by 10 per cent-20 per cent (Brno, Plzen), 20 per cent-30 per cent in other large cities (Budweis, Zlin, Liberec) and up to 50 per cent lower if you stay far enough from the investment hot spots. On the other hand, it is much harder to find the right people outside the regional centres.

Labour mobility is very low in the Czech Republic. State flats are very valuable because of low regulated rents. Moving to another part of the country means substantially higher rents on the deregulated housing market. As a consequence, people often do not move, even if they are unemployed.

Unemployment

The average rate of unemployment in 2000 was 8.79 per cent, with a mere 4 per cent in Prague and as much as 16.6 per cent in Ostrava. The highest unemployment is in North Bohemia, the centre of the old centre of the old mining and steel industry where a modern infrastructure is missing. The national unemployment trend and regional unemployment profiles are identified in Figures 4.22.1 and 4.22.2.

Recruiting the best – how to attract good staff

There is high demand for a skilled workforce. This is partly due to the fact that on middle and higher management levels local

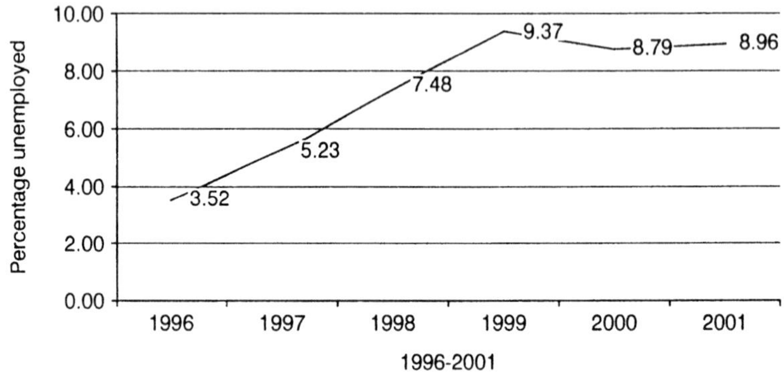

Figure 4.22.1 Czech Republic unemployment trends, 1996–2000

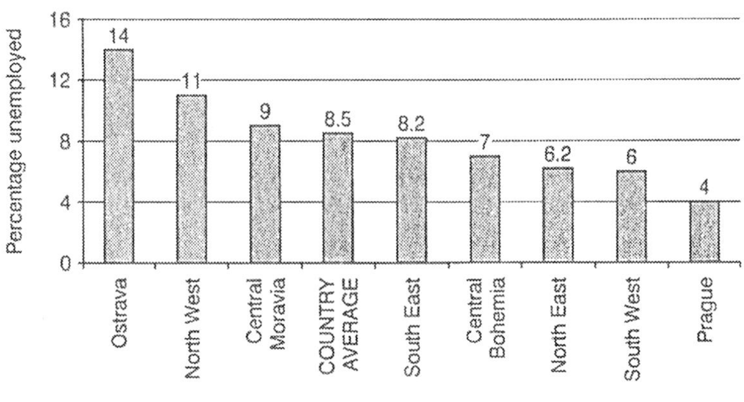

Figure 4.22.2 Regional unemployment, 2001

gradually replacing ex-pats. For this reason, the 1990s have been the golden years for young professionals.

Online recruitment

There are several online recruitment companies in the Czech Republic. However, it is good to bear in mind that Internet penetration has not yet reached Western levels and the motivation of job seekers on the Internet is often low. This search method works best for IT or telecom positions.

Job advertisements

Most companies use job advertisements on a regular basis. The two most popular dailies are *Mlada Fronta Dnes* (MFD) and *Hospodarske Noviny* (HN). The cost of a 10×15 cm advertisement is about €1000 in HN and €1500 in MFD. However, even more than in other Western countries, job advertisements for managerial positions attract only poor results, both in terms of quantity and quality. Therefore, these advertisements are recommended for recruiting junior and support staff only.

Employment agencies

There are dozens, if not hundreds of employment agencies on the market. They mostly rely on their databases, not necessarily interviewing candidates before recommending them. The fees are about two monthly salaries. Employment agencies are best used to hire support staff.

Executive search

Executive search is mostly used to hire professionals for senior and managerial positions. There are both local and international search companies operating in the Czech Republic. Several prominent market players recently closed their Prague offices due to low market

Table 4.22.2 Czech employment profile by sector

Sector	*Employment (%)*	
	1998	*1999*
Agriculture	7.1	6.6
Industry+Construction	39.7	39.3
Services	53.2	54.1
Total	100.0	100.0

potential. At present, most companies cover all fields as the market is too small for specialization.

There is no association of executive search companies that would guarantee certain market standards. Fees are in the range of 35 per cent of the candidate's annual income. Some consultants work on retainer fees, others on a success-fee basis.

Application documents

Do not expect much. A CV and maybe a motivation letter is all you get, unless you ask clearly for more. Photos on CVs are not common. Candidates do not usually include their school transcripts/certificates in the application. References from previous employers are not very common as most candidates do not have any. There are no standard reference forms.

Retaining good staff

In the past, staff turnover has been rather high, often reaching up to 15 per cent–20 per cent. This was mainly due to very low wages after 1990, to the wish to try new things and to the traditionally low employee loyalty under communism.

Regarding compensation, the common practice is 12 salary months plus one to two months' bonus salary (usually before holidays and at Christmas). The bonus structure depends on the position: 8 per cent–15 per cent of annual income for junior positions and support staff, 15 per cent–25 per cent for middle management and other senior positions, and around 30 per cent–40 per cent for top management. Manager packages usually include a company car, a mobile phone and a notebook computer.

With regard to holiday, the legal minimum is 20 days per year; however, most companies offer five extra days a year. Increasingly more companies offer full salary during sick leave for up to six weeks. In addition, pension plans, insurance or stock options can be seen but are not necessarily the standard. Some companies also offer loans to selected employees for the purchase of a flat or a house to increase employee loyalty

With the general increase in salaries, other conditions become increasingly important also:

- Stable and professional work environment.
- Opportunities for training.
- Career prospects.
- Cooperation and acceptance in international teams.

Outlook

As the Czech Republic prepares for EU accession in 2004, FDI inflows are expected to increase. However, no significant large-scale migration from the Czech Republic into the European Union is expected. If there is any, it will be well-trained young professionals going abroad to gain more experience, only to return later to the Czech Republic. People are slowly adjusting themselves to an international work style.

Salaries are likely to continue rising, albeit not as dynamically as in the past. Good managers will continue to be scarce and their salaries will reach Western levels. On the other hand, career progression in hierarchies will become more difficult because of the relatively low average age at practically all management levels.

Looking for professionals ?

4.23

Executive Search

Lubomir Ochotnicky, Egon Zehnder International

It has been slightly over a decade since monumental political changes shook Central and Eastern Europe, including the Czech Republic. The most significant business changes have resulted from foreign direct investment (FDI), which laid down the foundations for improvements in competitiveness and workforce qualifications. Over the last 10 years, many of the Czech Republic's most successful companies—which, not coincidentally, are those with the foreign strategic investors—have made important investments in educating and training all their staff, from assembly workers to top managers. They have fostered ethical business practices among their existing employees and encouraged quality, creativity and initiative. In some cases, their approach has been nothing short of revolutionary.

From the labour market's perspective, doing business with the Czech Republic predominantly means two things: changing the attitudes formed under the old communist regime and utilizing the investment opportunities that remain in abundance.

Legacies of the old regime

Changing old habits has proved to be a bigger challenge than many had previously thought. Under communism, the state mechanism was set with one goal: to control citizens. Therefore, ordinary people rightly assumed the position of 'state versus us'. Formerly, all companies were state owned and, in the mind of ordinary people, the rules of enterprises were simply linked to the oppressive rules of state vehicles such as the government, municipalities, police, army, etc. While in any society there is a perceived difference between managers and line employees, the managers in communist Czechoslovakia personified one small part of the whole system of oppression. Now that many things in society have changed and some are still changing, the mental block of many ordinary citizens has adjusted only partially. Because the old attitude of 'us against them' persists, the single biggest challenge facing any foreign investor in the Czech Republic is in the area of the proactive involvement of workers in the daily operations of the company. It is difficult to explain that participating in and contributing to the enterprise's results is not simply another management ploy. However, as with any challenge at hand, those company owners and managers able to cross this mental barrier enjoy extraordinary commitment and a more than satisfactory return on their investments.

Another old habit lies in each individual's involvement in the operational decision-making process. Openly stating your opinion, particularly while strongly supporting one of the choices, means taking individual responsibility. Under Big Brother, the survival skill to be learned by each individual and then passed through generations was not to stand out from the crowd. While this skill of avoiding the spotlight takes many different forms, most prevalent in the corporate environment is the avoidance of accountability. Middle-level managers in 'the old times' mastered the expertise of pushing acts of decision making on to their superiors. Therefore, if you are an investor expecting each employee to display initiative, you may find that one of your first challenges will be to instil confidence and a sense of accountability in all managers and workers. You might reward individuality and ingenuity in order to encourage them to stand out of the line.

Top management competencies in demand

It is no wonder that the competencies required by investors for their CEO or the top management team, regardless of the nature of the business and industry sector, are change management, service orientation, a Western mindset with a sensitivity to local conditions and, finally, communication skills.

The lack of resources and the existence of oppression stimulated the creativity and implementation skills of those individuals with the desire to improve or be different. Therefore, many in the Czech Republic have such skills to some degree. However, when searching for a managing director with change management capabilities, we find that his industry-specific knowledge becomes critical for success. It is more often a question of defining the end result than the change process itself, for which there are many qualified personnel. The full understanding of the task ahead, by a search consultant and subsequently by the candidate chosen for the change task, is the key success factor.

From such a perspective, it is a realistic expectation to find local managers who can ensure that the change project will stay on track until the end. What is absolutely essential is to assign a key managerial position to a professional with 'problem' specific expertise, such as a financial guru for the financial restructuring of the steel mill or an automobile industry expert for the task of preparing an auto-parts supplier for acquisition by a multinational conglomerate.

Successful search experience

Search results are always subject to what is available in the markets, either local or global. Even with a very systematic approach, there are occasions when the ideal candidate simply does not exist or is not available. In such cases, the next best and proven solution is a manager whose personal values and attitudes are almost identical to those expected in the whole company after the turnaround. Such individuals have a track record in change management projects and are able to learn about the industry or company specifics as they go. This is the reason why a major portion of turnaround successes in the Czech Republic are executed by professionals from different industries and the majority of investors have to adjust their expectations regarding industry-specific knowledge. (Indeed, it seems fair to say that the same flexibility needed for success is expected also from investors.) There are many cases in practice which prove that this is a worthwhile approach.

The situation in the service sector has improved, in some instances such as professional services even dramatically, although there remains room for further improvement. Those managers striving to improve their service departments or service-related enterprises face their biggest challenge in finding employees capable of correctly assessing the rapidly changing needs of their customers. The combination of customer orientation and service attitude necessary to translate the understanding of one's customer into professional and profitable service is in high demand and among the most sought after competencies.

A standard role for any managing director in a foreign country is to provide a bridge between foreign owners and local employees.

Although many clients present it in different ways, for example as 'cultural sensitivity', they all mean the same thing: to understand how profitable business is done in the West and to import this into the Czech Republic. Given the first part of the condition, the role of expatriates is still important and well evidenced by their number in the country. While in the beginning of the 1990s being a Western executive was enough to secure an interesting assignment, Egon Zehnder clients currently indicate a preference for local managers or foreigners with a mastery of the Czech language. The number of the latter has grown significantly over the past decade. While investors with less courage and higher risk aversion prefer foreign managers with long-term residence in the Czech Republic, the most successful business stories tend to be written by local managers with Western experience, especially when adaptability to local conditions is among the critical success factors.

Many investors' most desired option is to find a Czech expatriate in Western Europe. The number of these remains small and, although Egon Zehnder has solved some assignments with such hirings, few of those still abroad are interested in returning to the local market yet. Such situations are very case and position specific. The overall trend is still in the opposite direction: to become an expatriate is a chance which many Czech managers would immediately snap up.

The most significant group of managers able to bridge 'West and East' is the one with MBA degrees. Over the last 10 years, the number of schools offering MBA programmes, either solely in the Czech Republic or with assignments in the West, has grown. Moreover, the number of Czechs participating in business training programmes abroad has also increased. Therefore, possession of an accredited training in business management is no longer something spectacular in this market. The most significant change in this group, when compared with the situation just five to six years ago, is in experience gained. An increasing proportion of managers with MBA degrees has already had relevant experience and, therefore, a track record in successful projects. As they have gone through the 'reality check' and have learned about their own capabilities and limits, they have become very realistic in their assessment of anticipated projects and their own contribution to their success. They have evolved from project implementers to valuable business partners; many of them are open to new opportunities.

Communication

With regard to communication, the latest and most interesting shift is in the use of foreign languages. Mostly due to the influence of business schools, the English language has gradually become as prevalent among the foreign languages of top executives as the once dominant German language. The appropriate and adjustable communication style needed for effective collaboration with all external and internal stakeholders in the business is a skill that has received more attention and demand but also gained a reasonable supply among locally active managers. This specific competence is the single most sought after skill regardless of the industry sector or task specification, and in Egon Zehnder's experience there are enough fully qualified Czech managers.

After 11 years of executive search assignments in the Czech Republic and Slovakia, the most challenging and rewarding experience for Egon Zehnder is meeting an executive with top function-specific skills combined with a holistic view of business.

It is not so unusual to find a manager with a strong strategic competency or with a great overview of the competition and business trends, including those outside the Czech Republic. Equally, there are Czech managers with top functional knowledge and skills, such as in law or indirect channel management. There are also a fair number of sales and marketing executives who are both wise and experienced. Good finance-related professionals are less abundant and a search for a strategically thinking human resources director is akin to seeking a needle in a haystack. What is almost impossible to find is a combination of top functional knowledge, strong business understanding and clear understanding where those functional skills will contribute to business in the future. There are plenty of high-quality professionals across a variety of functions throughout Central Europe. The biggest gap between investors' expectations from a top executive and market supply is in the area of a proactive blend of functional expertise with business needs on the part of the executive. Those human resources managers, financial professionals, sales executives or production experts with the ability to become a valuable strategic partner and contributor to the CEO are still very scarce. The mindset of proactively seeking, identifying and seizing the function-related opportunity in order to contribute to the overall business strategy and performance on the part of functional managers is unfortunately not yet present.

The bad habits are dying out, some more slowly than others. The Czech Republic is on an irreversible march towards the European Union. Functional expertise has been improving and the number of successful business stories grows constantly. All of us in the Czech Republic are participants in the ordinary but ever so exciting process of improving professionalism.

4.24

Insurance Industry

Petr Knebl and Jitka Bendova, Aon Czech Republic

History

Insurance in the Czech Republic dates from the nineteenth century when Joseph Matyas, Count of Thun and Hohenstein and Frantisek Joseph, Count of Vrba established the first Czech insurance company in 1827. In 1945, there were 733 insurance companies and mutual insurance companies licensed in Czechoslovakia. All of them were closed down in the 1950s and only the one state-owned insurance company remained.

After the Velvet Revolution of 1989, the political and economic situation in Czechoslovakia changed completely. The next milestone in the country's history came on 1 January 1993 when Czechoslovakia was split into two countries: the Czech Republic and Slovakia. These changes also influenced the development of insurance activity. The new Act No. 185/1991 Coll. on Insurance, opened the way for construction of the insurance market, its liberalization, the development of competition and for its links to European and global insurance markets.

The establishment of the insurance industry's two key institutions, the State Supervisory Body and the Czech-Slovak Insurance Association (CSAP) founded in 1991, was a necessary part of this development. From the beginning, CSAP together with the Czech Insurance Association (CAP), founded in 1993, have been collecting and processing statistical data covering their members' activities. Most of the data covers the activities of CAP members, whose long-term market share has exceeded 99 per cent.

The economic transformation of the Czech Republic since 1989 also included abolition of the state-owned insurance company monopoly, the birth of new insurance undertakings including the establishment of foreign insurance companies' branch offices, and the development of numerous modern insurance products. All of these changes were prerequisites for establishing the profession of insurance broker on the Czech insurance market.

The Association of Czech Insurance Brokers (ACIB) was established in March 1994. ACIB has been clearly constituted as a professional body promoting absolutely correct relations among competitors and full harmonization between their business interests and the interests of their customers, insurance companies and the State Supervisory Body. ACIB became a member of the Bureau International des Producteurs d'Assurance et de Reassurances (BIPAR) in October 1998 and participates in its activities. ACIB also cooperates in the preparation of standards, which stipulate conditions for the activities of insurance intermediaries in the part of Europe from which the Czech Republic would like to be considered inseparable.

Czech insurance market

The Finance Ministry of the Czech Republic is responsible for control of the insurance industry. The Ministry issues licences to insurers, registers insurance brokers, provides supervision and makes the rules for reserve funding.

A 'broker of record' letter is the necessary written authority to enable a broker to negotiate with insurers. The local broker of record letter has to be issued for the local broker and signed by the executive stated in the local company Trade Registration List. Some international underwriters accept an international broker of record letter.

Most policies are issued for a one-year period. Some underwriters use an automatic renewal clause. Insurers sometimes agree to arrange longer period policies (mostly three years) with rebates on premiums. Advance notice of cancellation has to be sent at least six weeks before the end of the insurance period; some insurers require three months' notice instead of six weeks.

Czech law does not allow non-admitted insurance. Insurance may only be written by a locally established company or branch licensed by the Ministry of Finance. If business is to be placed by a broker with the branch of a foreign company, the intermediary itself must also have obtained a licence from the supervisory authority.

Insurers can develop their own general insurance conditions. All general insurance conditions must be issued in Czech and adapted to

Czech law. The policy must be written in Czech; no translation has legal validity.

Any policy has to be signed by both the insured and the insurer to be valid. A copy of the Insured Trade Registration, which becomes part of the policy, has to be provided to the insurer.

No tariffs are given, with the exception of automobile third-party liability and fully compulsory insurances, which have centrally regulated rates. For other types of risk, each insurance company works within its own framework of rates.

There are no taxes and stamp duties on insurance contracts in the Czech Republic.

There are no legal restrictions for reinsurance. Reinsurance may be arranged for large risks in the event that the client requests the use of a leading insurer for a global insurance programme. Since there are no taxes and the reinsurance can be 100 per cent, it is easy to arrange cover which conforms to Czech law and saves money on taxes.

The evolution of insurance premiums paid as a proportion of GDP from 1991 to 2000 is reported in Figure 4.24.1.

Types of insurance

The following types of insurance are available on the Czech insurance market.

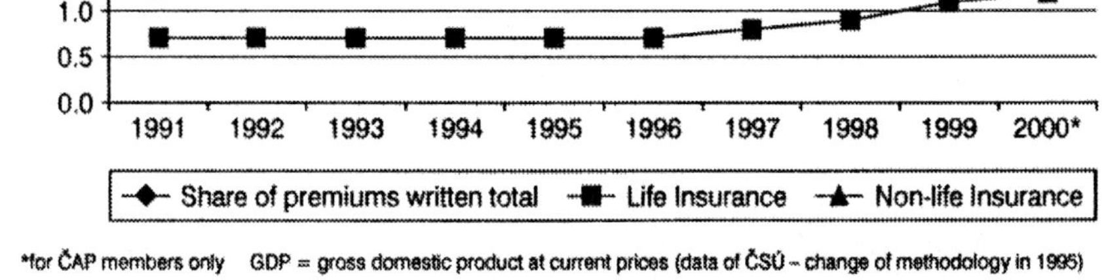

Figure 4.24.1 Premiums paid as a proportion of GDP, 1991–2000

Compulsory cover

There are two types of compulsory insurance in the Czech Republic:

- Fully compulsory insurance, for which everything, such as conditions, scope of cover and premium, is determined by the law.
- Compulsory insurance, where there is a duty written in the law to be insured for named specific activities, but policy conditions and premiums are freely determined in the market.

Fully compulsory insurance includes workers' compensation/ employer's liability cover. Brokers are not allowed to be involved in fully compulsory insurance.

Compulsory insurance comprises cover for:

- private hospital liability;
- tax advisers and auditors' liability;
- legal aid bureau liability;
- liability of architects, designers, engineers in construction;
- automobile third-party liability.

Mainly optional cover

- fire and special perils insurance;
- insurance against vandalism;
- insurance against theft and burglary;
- deterioration of goods insurance;
- all risks insurance;
- machinery breakdown insurance;
- electronics insurance;
- CAR/EAR (Contractors All Risks/Erections All Risks);
- motor hull insurance (automobile physical damage and theft);
- insurance against damage to railway vehicles, vessels and aircraft;
- transport insurance;
- auto liability insurance;
- liability insurance for an owner of a railway vehicle, vessel and aircraft;
- liability insurance for a carrier;
- general liability and product liability insurance;
- liability insurance against product contamination;

- liability insurance for members of board of directors and executive directors;
- professional liability insurance;
- liability insurance of an employee towards an employer;
- liability insurance for environmental damage;
- loss of profit insurance;
- insurance of bank and customs' risks;
- insurance of receivables;
- credit insurance;
- financial loss insurance;
- guarantee insurance;
- agricultural insurance;
- insurance of travel offices;
- insurance of films, entertainment and sport;
- capital life insurance and pension insurance;
- accident insurance;
- travel insurance;
- insurance of legal representation (defence costs);
- insurance of daily amount during work disablement and during a stay in a hospital;
- pensions supplementary insurance.

Property damage and business interruption

Property damage and business interruption is a basic type of insurance. In many companies it represents the principal insurance risk covered. This type of insurance covers the property of a company (mainly buildings, equipment and stock) against damages caused by natural hazards. It can be either all risks or named perils insurance. The sums insured are based on new (replacement) values. Business interruption insurance covers the loss of profit and fixed costs arising from business interruption following the claims caused by a natural hazard. These types of insurance are similar to those insurance products available in the European Union.

General liability insurance

General liability insurance is another type of basic insurance. Czech law does not impose a duty to have such insurance cover, but it should be in each legal subject's interest to arrange this type of policy. This insurance product covers the liability of a legal subject towards third parties arising in connection with its activities registered in the Czech Trade Register against the third parties. The insurance conditions are usually written on a 'claims basis'.

Automobile insurance

Automobile liability insurance is compulsory in the Czech Republic. Owners of vehicles with Czech licence plates pay an annual premium based on engine volume (cm^3). The cover is provided according to Czech law for physical damage or injury to third parties with minimum limits stated by the law. The minimum cover requirements are CZK5 million for motor liability due to physical damage and CZK18 million for personal injury. Brokers are allowed to be involved in arranging policies. Non-residents must show evidence of liability insurance cover in their home country before entering the Czech Republic. The Czech Republic is a member of the European Green Card Agreement.

Supplementary pension insurance

During the first half of 1999, the Czech parliament approved a legislative update of Act 42/1994, Coll. on State-subsidized Supplementary Pension Insurance. Under this Act, the following kinds of supplementary pension can be provided:

- old-age pension;
- disability pension;
- length-of-insurance pension;
- survivor's pension.

In addition, the Czech parliament has also amended tax legislation on supplementary pension insurance, which came into force on 1 January 2000, and which grants considerable tax advantages to employers who provide supplementary pension group insurance to employees. The following is a summary of all the already approved and upcoming tax breaks:

- An employer's contribution to the employee's supplementary pension insurance is exempted from the tax base used for the calculation of mandatory health and social security insurance premium payments; this exemption applies regardless of other deductions.
- An employer's contribution to the employees' supplementary pension insurance, amounting to 3 per cent of the employee's tax base for the

calculation of the security insurance premium, is a tax-deductible amount to the employer.

- An employer's contribution to supplementary pension insurance, of up to 5 per cent of the employee's tax base, is not part of the employee's personal taxable income.
- Subsidy of actual employees' contributions ranging from CZK100 to CZK500 in the form of a state contribution shall continue.
- Contributions of citizens, such as employees or entrepreneurs, exceeding CZK500 are deductible from the tax base of personal taxable income, up to a maximum of CZK12,000 each year.

Life insurance

With effect from 1 January 2001, several types of life assurance are tax advantaged for both an employee and an employer. In order to take advantage of the tax break, the law states that the insurance must be arranged for a minimum insurance period of 60 calendar months, ie five years. At the same time, a policy must provide that a first compensation payment in the event of living to a certain age will be made in the year when an insured will be 60.

Tax breaks for private entities

An insured who is also an insurance policy holder can, according to an insurance policy concluded between him and an insurance company, deduct from his income tax basis for a tax year (a calendar year) a paid premium for private life insurance up to a total maximum sum of CZK12,000.

Tax breaks for employees

A premium for the private life insurance that is paid by an employer for employees, according to an insurance policy concluded between an employee as a policy holder and an insurance company, is exempt from the employee's income tax up to the amount of CZK12,000 from the same employer.

From this premium paid by an employer for employees' private life insurance, an employee does not pay a premium for the mandatory social security insurance and State's employment policy contribution nor a premium for the mandatory health insurance.

Tax breaks for employers

A premium for private life insurance that is paid by an employer for employees, according to an insurance policy concluded between an employee as a policy holder and an insurance company, is regarded as deductible business expenditure spent in order to achieve, secure and maintain a taxable income up to the maximum amount of CZK8000 per tax year or any part thereof. From this premium paid by an employer for employees' private life insurance, an employer is not liable to pay a premium for the mandatory social security insurance and State's employment policy contribution nor a premium for the mandatory health insurance.

4.25

Prague Office Market

Omar Sattar, Joint Managing Director, DTZ Zadelhoff Tie Leung

Introduction

2001 saw a realignment of the office market after the development boom of 1999–2000. The over-supply situation that arose in 1999 and 2000 eased further during 2001 as little new space came to the market. The overall market vacancy rate fell from around 13 per cent at end-2000 to approximately 11 per cent 12 months later.

New completions (both refurbishments and new builds) for the year amounted to just under 55,000 square metres, a large fall from over 200,000 square metres and 150,000 square metres in 1999 and 2000 respectively. Only 31,000 square metres of new-build supply were released. In particular, there has been a brake on new-build supply in the central districts of Prague 1 and Prague 2. New development is focusing on out-of-centre locations.

Letting activity also slowed relative to the record level recorded in 2000, particularly in the third quarter, but with signs of resurgence in the last quarter of 2001, occupier confidence appears to be returning. In total, almost 130,000 square metres of space were transacted in 2001, conforming to an upward underlying growth path. Q1 2002 figures show a 30 per cent decrease year on year, which is slightly worrying given the new supply coming on stream by the end of the year.

Telecoms take-up, which was the demand driver in 2000, has fallen significantly, although demand from the financial services and IT sectors remained steady. The auditing sector was an engine of demand during 2001, with three of the international firms being involved in large moves. KPMG's 7500 square metres pre-lease at IBC Square was the largest transaction of the year.

Rents have stabilized as the over-supply situation has eased. Prime rents for central space have fallen below €20 since the begin ning of ning of 2000, but have remained largely stable during 2001 at €18–€19. €20 has been achieved in only a very small number of transactions.

Supply

Total lettable modern office stock at the end of Q4 2001, including new-build offices and quality refurbished office space, totalled approximately 1,086,000 square metres, comprising 611,000 square metres new build and 475,000 square metres of refurbished space. This compares with approximately 1,577,000 square metres in Warsaw and 1,144,000 square metres in Budapest.[1]

Approximately 55,000 square metres of Class A supply were delivered during 2001, of which around 31,000 square metres were new-build and 20,000 square metres refurbished. This was the lowest annual addition to supply since 1994 and a drop of over 75 per cent from the peak of 1999. 2002 will see a rise in new completions with a forecast 120,000 square metres scheduled for delivery, including approximately 100,000 square metres of new-build space.

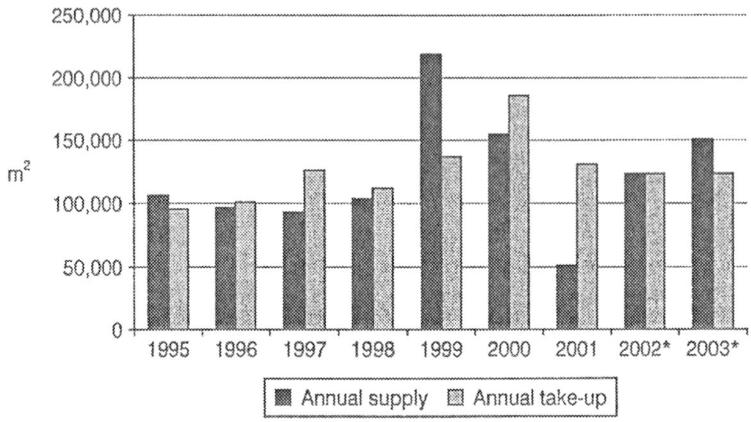

*Forecast
Source: DTZ Research, Prague Research Forum[2]

Figure 4.25.1 Supply and take-up, 1995–2003

[1] Source: Warsaw Research Forum, Budapest Research Forum.
[2] The Prague Research Forum is a group of market researchers from leading property consultancy companies comprising CB Richard Ellis, DTZ Zadelhoff Tie Leung, Healey & Baker and Jones Lang LaSalle, which have agreed to jointly coordinate some of their data collection activities in the Czech market.

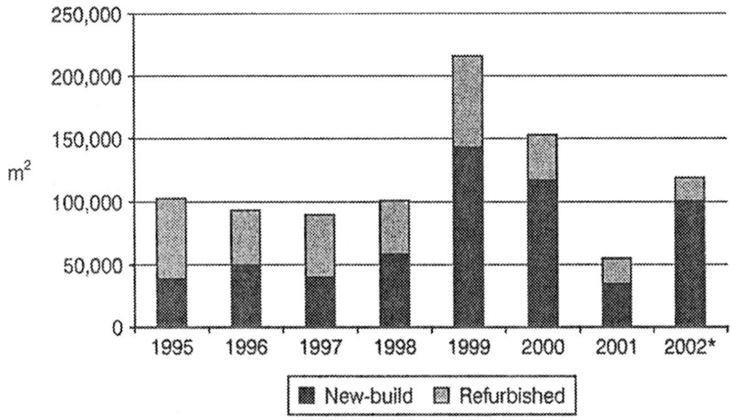

* Forecast
Source: DTZ Research

Figure 4.25.2 New supply, 1995–2002, new-build and refurbished

Part of the reason for a drop of supply can be attributed to planning delays caused by the lengthy and often complex Czech planning system. Bank financing of office developments is also influential, as many of the lending banks will insist on a 30 per cent–40 per cent pre-lease requirement prior to releasing funds.

Another trend is that of the smaller niche players (usually Austrian), which are being increasingly replaced by well-known international developers such as Skanska, AIG Lincoln, Golub, ING, Doughty Hanson and MDC. Developers that were present on the market in the early 1990s and are still active include Orco, Real Estate Karlin, Vanguard and Karimpol.

In the long term, due to the low ratio of office space per head of population in Prague, it is believed that there is still room for new-build space.

The trend of decentralization continued in 2001. The figures below illustrate the shift in development since 1999 away from the central Prague 1 and 2 districts and into suburban locations, particularly the Prague 4, 5 and 8 districts.

2001 saw the completion of just three major schemes in Prague 1: Slovanský dum, Bredovsky Dvur and Stara Celnice. No large schemes are scheduled for completion in Prague 1 before 2003.

There are three large projects that can be realized in the city centre, including the Na Florenci project with a potential 60,000 square metres of development potential, located at the former

Table 4.25.1 Major office schemes pre-2001

Building	*Year*	*District*	*m²*	*Owner*
IBC Building	1993	8	24,000	CDC Ixis
IPB Vinice	1999	10	22,000	IBP Real
Praha City Center	1995	1	17,000	EPD
Myslbek	1996	1	17,000	CDC Ixis
BB Centrum B	2000	4	15,000	Passerinvest
Zlaty Andel	2000	5	13,000	ING
Hadovka Office Park A, B	1999	6	12,500	Europolis
Hadovka Office Park C, D	2000	6	12,500	Europolis
BB Centrum C	1998	4	12,400	Passerinvest
Millennium Plaza	1999	1	12,000	Strabag
Sokolovska 84–86	1997	8	10,500	MAIL
Katerř inskaá	2000	2	8000	Irelandia
Longin Business Centre	2000	2	7500	ECM
SAP Building	1997	5	7400	Saller
OMG Panorama	2000	2	6500	OMG
Office Park Nove Butovice A	2000	5	6100	PDP/Doughty Hanson

Source: DTZ Research

Typographie Building. However, these three are all at very early stages.

Between 135,000 square metres and 157,000 square metres are scheduled for completion in 2002, depending on whether there are any construction delays. The majority of the floor space will not reach the market until the second half of 2002. DTZ estimates that 40 per cent of the supply upper estimate is already pre-leased.

The Prague 4 corridor and Prague 5 remain the two most popular suburban locations. Approximately 100,000 square metres of modern space are currently being developed in Prague 4 alone. Larger schemes include the Kommerzzentrum development (Proinvest), the latest phase

Table 4.25.2 Prague 2001, major office schemes

Building	*Location*	*m²*	*Developer*
Slovanský Dum	1	11,000	COPA
Bredovský Dvur	1	9500	Skanska
Corso Karlin	8	9200	REK
Stara Celnice	1	6500	Ikano
Nagano II	3	3500	Pobrezni 46
Javor Office Centre	8	3300	DCRC
Namesti Hrdinu	4	2200	Glockner
Vitkov	3	1730	Raiffeisen
Holeckova	5	1200	NK*
Pankrac Bus. Center III	4	1050	Plan & Bau

*Not known

Source: DTZ Research

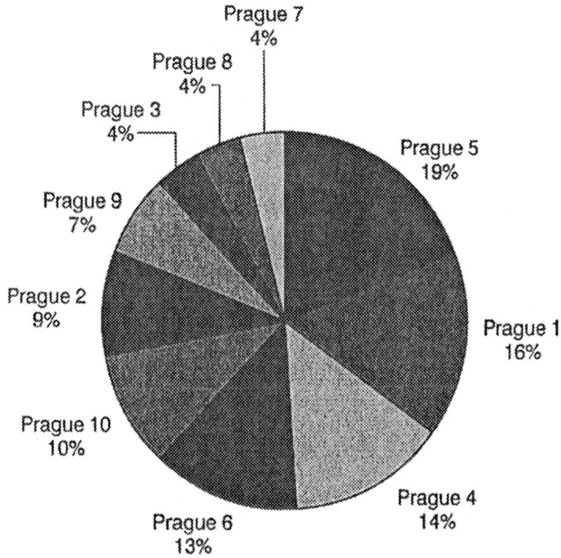

Source: DTZ Research

Figure 4.25.3 New supply by district, 1999–2000

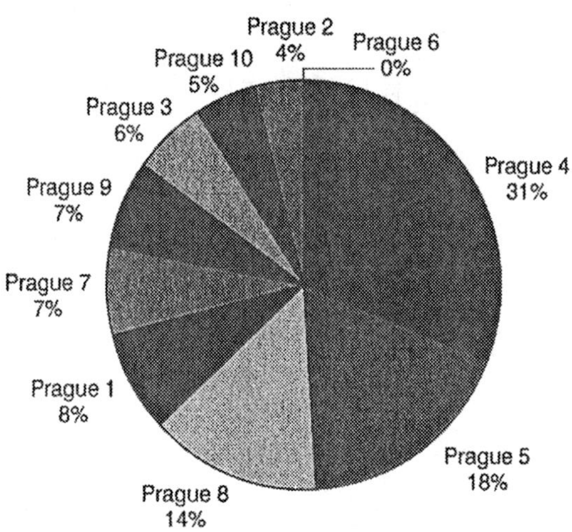

Source: DTZ Research

Figure 4.25.4 Pipeline supply by district, 2002–2003

at BB Centrum (PasserInvest), The Park (AIG), and Prague Gate (Mayfield).

The addition of IBC Square (AIG Lincoln) at Florenc and Danube House (Europolis) along the river will further strengthen the popularity of Prague 8 as a commercial centre. The proximity of the city centre and good public transport links are two of the main advantages of this part of Prague

Table 4.25.3 Prague 2002, major pipeline office schemes

Building	*Location*	*m²*	*Developer*
Danube House	8	22,000	Europolis
BB Centrum A	4	21,000	Passer Invest
Flora Plaza	3	18,000	SEN
Raiffeisen Cetrim	4	16,000	ProInvest
Prague Gate	4	12,000	Mayfield
Office Park Nové Butovice D	5	11,200	Doughty Hanson/PDP
Charles Square Center	2	10,000	Golub
Andě l City	5	9000	UBM

Source: DTZ Research

Slightly over 100,000 square metres are scheduled for completion in 2003.

Table 4.25.4 Prague 2003, major pipeline office schemes

Building	*Location*	*m²*	*Developer*
Luxembourg Plaza	3	20,000	Orco
West Gate	5	20,000	Golub
Zlicin Business Park	5	18,000	Portland
The Park	4	10,000	AIG
Jungmannova	1	10,000	Lordship
U Hajku II	1	9500	AS Immobilia
South Point	4	6500	AMA

Source: DTZ Research

Several large tracts of land at Karlin in Prague 8 along the river are earmarked for development. There are also plans to develop along the river in Prague 7 at the harbour.

Demand

Following a record gross office take-up in 2000, lettings activity slowed in 2001, particularly in the third quarter of the year. Apart from Komercni Bank's (Slovanský Dum) and KPMG (IBC Square), no other deal was transacted for more than 4000 square metres. After a slow middle year, demand recovered in Q4, with business sentiment improving, and a gross take-up of 128,000 square metres was recorded for 2001. There is a positive upside to this result for 2002 should confidence and performance in the global and EU economy rebound strongly from a sluggish 2001.

Letting activity in the first quarter of 2002 has shown a year-on-year drop of about. 30 per cent, with 26,000 square metres of office space being transacted. Although a slowdown was anticipated, the hangover from the atrocities of 11 September and the general world economic slowdown has not been as bad as many had predicted. DTZ are at present tracking in the region of 135,000 square metres of demand in the market, which means that, despite a slow start in 2002, the worst could be over.

Table 4.25.5 Major office transactions (above 1000 m^2), 2001

Building	*District*	*m^2*	*Tenant*	*Sector*
IBC Square	8	7500	KPMG	Prof. Servs
Slovanský Dům	1	4000	Komercni Banka[(3)]	Fin. servs
IBC	8	4000[(2)]	Astra Zeneca	Pharma
Podiobradska	9	4000	Auto Cont	FMCG
Corso Karlin	8	3500	Red Bus Interhouse	IT
Corso Karlin	8	3000	Czech Telecom	Telecoms
BB Centrum	4	2400	APP	IT
Javor Office Centre	8	2200	J&T Banka	Fin. servs
Off. Park Nove Butovice	5	2200[(1)]	Accenture	Fin. servs
Arbes	5	2100	Merlin	IT
Praha City Centre	1	1630[(2)]	Motorola	Tech
Hvezda	6	1600	Logica	IT
Ckalova	6	1480	Prague 6 District Court	Public
IBC Building	8	1360[(2)]	Renault	Man./ind[(1)]
Benesovska	10	1300	DAS	Man./ind[(1)]
Italska 25	2	1240	Unisys	IT
Stara Celnice	1	1230	AIG	Fin. servs
Zlicin Business Park	5	1200	Expert & Partners	
Corso Karlin	8	1200	Volksbank	Fin. servs
Velvarska 1652/7		1200	Universal Music	FMCG
Stara Celnice	1	1100	Allen & Overy	Prof. servs
Myslbek	1	1100	Haarman Hemerath & Co.	Prof. servs
Paramount	7	1100	Avon	FMCG
Corso Karlin	8	1000	Panasonic	Man./ind[(1)]

Notes: [(1)] Pre-leases, [(2)] Lease renewals, [(3)] A further 3750 m^2 were signed for in 2000
Source: DTZ Research

Average transaction size increased from around 400 square metres in 1995 to approximately 1000 square metres in 2001. The average requirement currently monitored by DTZ for occupation between now and the first half of 2002 measures 1400 square metres.

Overall office demand between 1998 and 2002 is tracked quarter by quarter in Figure 4.25.5.

Although Prague 1 was a sought-after location in 2001, with over a third of all transactions in the market occurring there, early indications show a trend of companies relocating to edge of city developments. The Kommercni Bank transaction at Slovanský Dům, which was the largest of 2001 in Prague 1, helped the central district to account for approximately 24 per cent of let space although the average transaction was below 400 square metres. Other large transactions were concluded at the new Stara Celnice, Myslbek and Praha City Centre. However, available quality space is becoming scarce with Bredovský Dvůr being the only new property to come online in 2001.

In 2002, Prague 2 has seen the major share of transactions to date, as companies look to relocate to better and more efficient accommodation with higher specification and a more pleasant all-round working environment. In particular, two large deals have been signed in Prague 2, at the Vinohradska Office Center (Allianz, 3800 square metres) and the Charles Square Center (Ernst & Young, 3065 square metres).

Prague 8 accounted for the highest share of take-up in 2001 at almost 25 per cent of the total or over 30,000 square metres, of

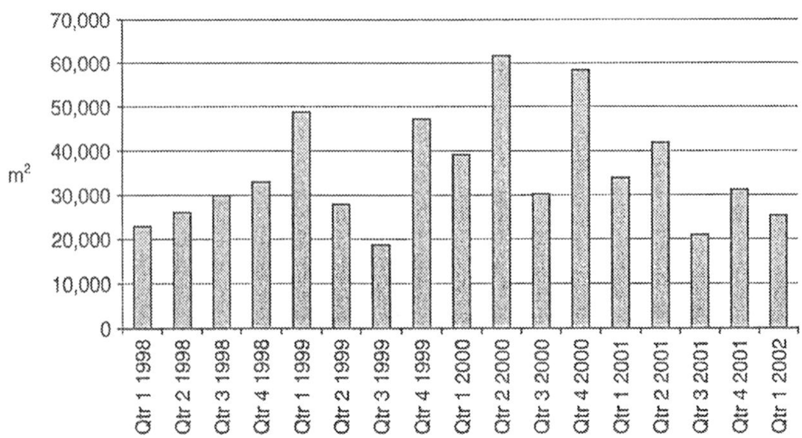

Figure 4.25.5 Office demand by quarter, 1998–2002

which lettings in Corso Karlin represent almost a third. Other large lettings were signed at IBC Square (KPMG) and Javor Office Centre (J&T Banka), while Astra Zeneca extended their approximately 4000 square metres lease at IBC. Only three transactions were completed there up to end-April 2002, totalling just over 1000 square metres, but with around 8000 square metres becoming available in Q3 DTZ expects take-up to improve later in the year.

Due to the small number of lettings at BB Centrum (Prague 4) and Zlicin Centrum and Office Park Nové Butovice (Prague 5) – now fully leased – taking place during the year, 2001 was a quiet period for Prague 4 and 5. However, these popular suburban locations saw a high proportion of demand for office space in Q1 2002, enjoying market shares of 21 per cent and 18 per cent respectively. As predicted, the letting activity there is rising due to the large supply of new developments. Schemes such as Zlatý Anděl and Anděl City are beginning to draw demand across the river into Prague 5 and the latest edition to Office Park Nové Butovice scheme, an 18-storey tower, is expected to be complete in early August 2002.

Take-up by sector

Demand is mainly from companies already present in the market, upgrading or expanding their offices.

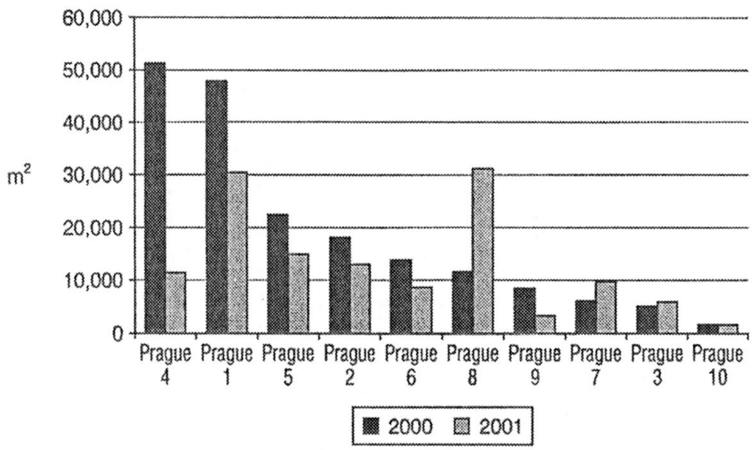

Source: DTZ Research

Figure 4.25.6 Take-up by district, 2000–2001

The slowdown in global and EU economic activity in 2001 was felt in Prague as take-up from the traditional demand drivers – the financial services and IT sectors – fell by 33 per cent and 26 per cent respectively. However, both sectors managed to increase their share of total take-up. Demand from legal and auditing companies has been particularly strong, with three major auditors having recently moved or in the process of moving. Local bank Komercni Banka accounted for the year's largest transaction.

Overall, take-up was bolstered by demand from emerging private sectors such as industrial, manufacturing and distribution companies, and the public sector as well as professional services.

The telehousing or communications sector has had a disappointing year, due largely to the financial difficulties faced globally by the telecoms industry. Only a few deals had been concluded to end-April 2002, such as Red Bus at Corso Karlin. The sector is not expected to account for significant take-up in 2002.

Vacancy

The overall market vacancy rate at the end of 2001 was approximately 11 per cent, down from around 16 per cent in 1999 and 13 per cent in 2000. A significant part of this vacancy is due to the relocation of firms to newer properties. The large number of moves has

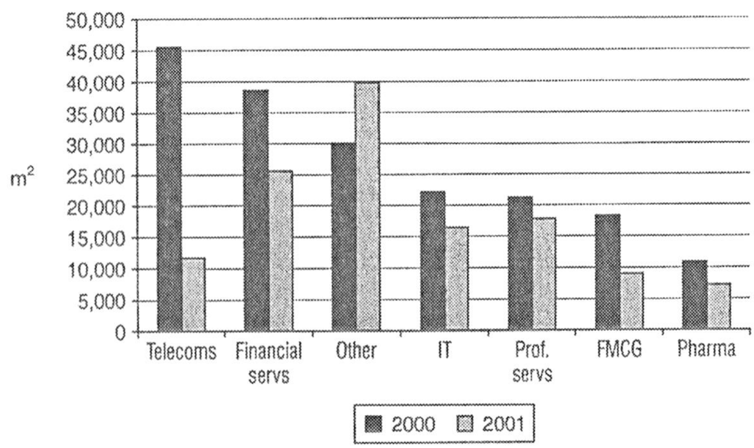

Source: DTZ Research

Figure 4.25.7 Total take-up by sector, 2000–end-2001

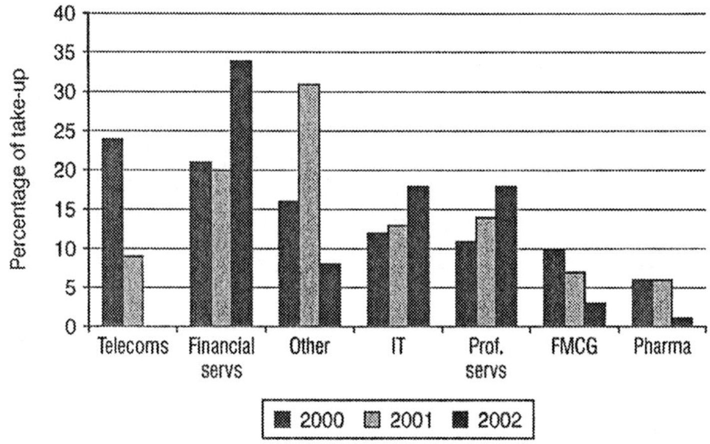

Source: DTZ Research

Figure 4.25.8 Share of total take-up by sector, 2000–2002

meant that a significant amount of Class B space has become available in the city centre districts.

Given the limited supply in the historic city centre and the low overall stock level of quality compared to Western cities, it is felt there is little risk of market saturation. In addition, some 25 per cent of the realistic supply pipeline to the end of 2003 is either prelet or purpose-built.

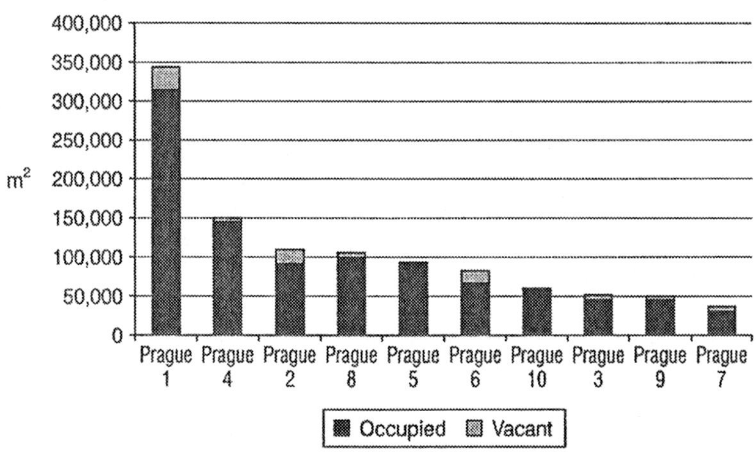

Source: DTZ Research

Figure 4.25.9 Vacancy by district, end-2001

Rental levels

Prime rents in city centre locations for Class A offices have been stable during 2001 at€18–€20 per square metre per month. A small number of buildings are able to achieve higher rents, but in general,€20 is only really achieved on the most attractive floors in the best office locations. There remains a shortage of quality stock, particularly in Prague 1, where the supply pipeline is limited. The high vacancy rate for refurbished space has led to downward pressure on rents. Prague 1 asking rents are now in the €14–€ 16 range, as opposed to 20 in 1995–1997. Top rents in edge of centre locations are in the €15– €16 range, while suburban locations rent in the €13–€15 range.

Investment market

Despite strong investor interest, the lack of institutional grade buildings held back investment activity in Prague during 2001, with just over €80 million completed compared with over€160 million in the previous year. However, the 2000 figure includes the acquisition by a Heitman-managed fund of the 28,500 square metre BB Centrum buildings B and C with a total lot value in excess of€50 million and Rodamco's approximately €45 million acquisition of the Cerny Most shopping centre.

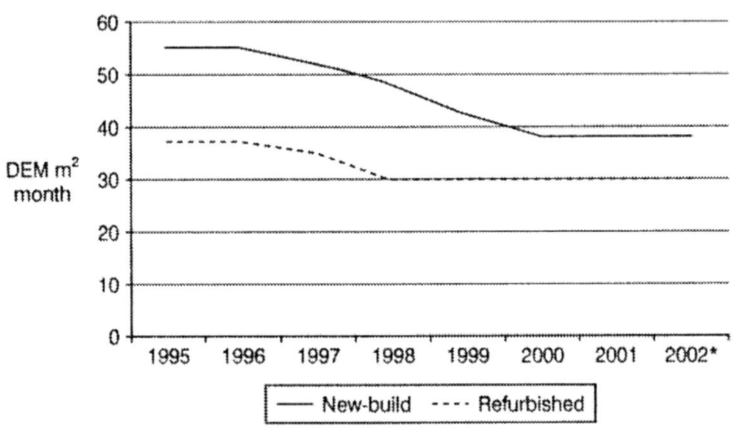

Source: DTZ Research

Figure 4.25.10 Modern office rental levels

In reality, Prague has witnessed a total number of deals similar to Warsaw and only a few less than Budapest, but with significantly smaller lot values, an average of €20 million compared with in excess of €30 million found in both Budapest and Warsaw.

Office yields have hardened slightly to around 10 per cent since the first transactions of 1998 and 1999, although Prague has still to see a prime city centre sale; if sold on the open market, a yield of about 9 per cent would be anticipated.

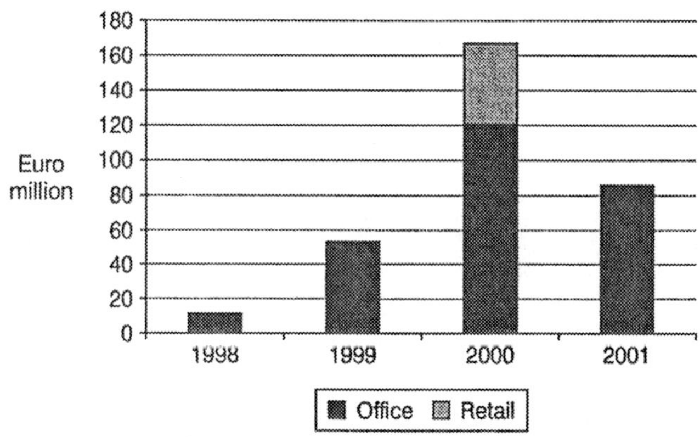

Source: DTZ Research

Figure 4.25.11 Institutional investment in Prague, 1998–2001

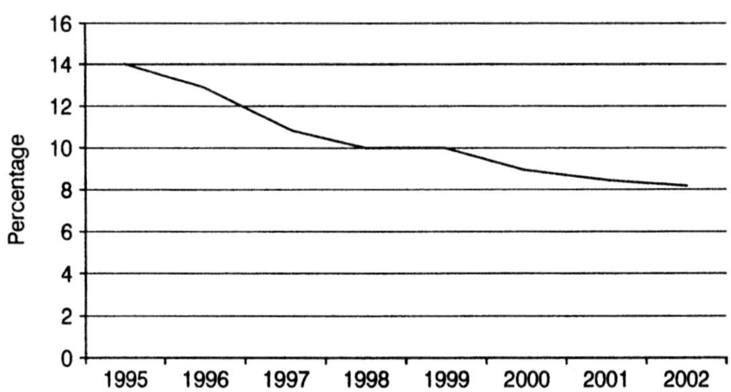

Source: DTZ Research

Figure 4.25.12 Prime office yields

Table 4.25.6 Major office investment transactions to date

Property	*District*	*Year*	*Initial yield %*	*Lot size (€million)*	*Buyer*
Palac Kodanska	10	2002	15	12.6	BSR
IP Pavlova 5	2	2002	n/a	15–16	DGI
Katerinska (PWC)	2	2001	9–10	20–21	Irelandia
Karlin Palac	8	2001	11	28–30	Immorent
Rubin Building	9	2001	10	23–24	MAIL
Dvorana	9	2001	10–11	3–4	MAIL
Pankrac Metro	4	2001	12	2–3	Smaller investors
Rodop Airport Centre	6	2001	10	8–9	Smaller investors
Ericsson Palace	1	2000	10	5.1	Flow East
BB Centrum (B & C)	4	2000	10–10.5	58–60	GE Capital/Heitman
Sokolovska 84–86	9	2000	10–11	22–23	MAIL
Sokolovska 855 (Vysocanska Point)	9	2000	17	10.75	Czech Property Partners (HVB)
Longin Business Centre	2	2000	10	24–25	Czech Property Partners (HVB)
Hadovka Office Park	6	1999	10–10.5	40–42	Europolis
Karlin Administration Centre	8	1999	11	11–12	Czech Property Partners (HVB)
Mediatel	8	1998	10.5–11	9–10	Czech Property Partners (HVB)

Source: DTZ Research

Part Five

Case Studies

5.1

Tesco in the Czech Republic

Ian Hutchins, International Corporate Affairs Manager, Tesco Plc

Tesco Plc is the United Kingdom's largest retailer, with 1000 stores in 11 countries. Established in 1932, for the first 70 years of its history Tesco focused almost exclusively on the UK grocery market. By 1995, Tesco had become the number one UK supermarket and systematically overhauled its strategy to expand from its traditional UK base into new products, services and countries.

Today Tesco operates in 11 countries with a clear strategy comprising four key elements:

- Strong UK core business: focused on becoming cheaper, offering better value and providing more choice for customers in the domestic UK market.
- Non-foods: developing the Tesco general merchandise offer, with the long-term goal to be as strong in non-food retailing as in food retailing.
- Retail services: following the customer into new areas of demand and delivering innovative services such as Tesco.com (the world's largest Internet-based home shopping operation) and Tesco Personal Finance.
- International growth: expanding beyond the United Kingdom in order to access additional growth.

The addition of international growth to the Tesco strategy has led it to look for new opportunities outside its traditional UK base and to date it has focused on two regions: Central Europe and South East Asia.

Reasons for choosing the Czech Republic

Tesco made its first venture into Central Europe with the acquisition of two small supermarket chains in Hungary and Poland in 1995. This was followed by the decision to target the Czech Republic as a logical next step.

In assessing the suitability of the Czech Republic as a potential location for investment, Tesco considered four main factors:

- Growth: in order to accelerate growth, Tesco sought markets offering the opportunity of potential growth rates at a higher level than those predicted for its traditional UK base.
- Market size: any potential overseas market needed to be of sufficient size to allow Tesco to achieve critical mass. Rising consumer incomes and increasing car ownership pointed to a promising opportunity for future spend on both food and non-food products. The opportunity to build a leading position within a market was also critical if Tesco was to attract the staff and suppliers it needed to deliver for customers and to achieve its growth targets.
- Environmental factors: the political and legal situations were examined carefully to ensure that barriers to entry did not exist which would prevent Tesco from opening stores and serving customers.
- Opportunity to apply strengths: rather than venture into completely new areas, Tesco sought opportunities to apply the core retail strengths it had successfully developed within the home UK business.

On each of the above counts the Czech Republic met fully with Tesco's criteria and, in 1996, the company acquired six existing department stores across the Czech Republic from US retailer, K-Mart.

Post acquisition

Pre-acquisition research showed a clear opportunity for retailers offering a wide range of food and non-food products at the right price—and all under one roof. In order to maximize the opportunity, efficiency and low operating costs would be crucial.

As a result, Tesco decided to focus on the development of a hypermarket business to complement the existing department stores (a hypermarket being a single-level store of around 100,000 square feet, offering a range of 50,000 products and devoting equal space to both food and non-food items). It also decided to look for opportunities across the Czech Republic for potential sites and set in motion an ambitious hypermarket-opening plan focused on achieving sufficient scale Tesco Stores CR to trade efficiently.

The acquisition of the department stores gave Tesco immediate access to a team of experienced retail staff upon whom it was able to draw as an initial pool of local talent. It also provided Tesco Stores CR with an existing base of suppliers, property and customers. To maximize the benefits, the decision was taken to re-brand all existing department stores under the Tesco name.

How Tesco operates in the Czech Republic

Pre-entry research convinced Tesco that it could not simply export the model it operates in the United Kingdom to the Czech Republic. Instead, Tesco has developed a unique approach based on a combination of world-class skills, local focus and a framework of common values.

World-class skills, systems and ways of working

All hypermarkets operated by Tesco in the Czech Republic are based on a blueprint of state-of-the-art systems and ways of working which help the local management team manage people, customers, finance and operations in a manner consistent with Tesco best practice.

In addition to the framework of retail operations, a concerted effort has been made to transfer core skills built up within the UK support functions such as site research, supply chain, marketing and HR.

Czech managers, staff, range, suppliers, marketing

Tesco realized that local cultural differences meant that it needed to truly understand Czech customers if it was to meet its ambitious goals. Tesco understood that the most effective way of achieving this would be to recruit and develop a pool of Czech managers to run the local business.

As a result, 100 per cent of Tesco hypermarket and department store directors in the Czech Republic are Czech nationals, as are the heads of the majority of head office support functions in Prague. This approach has enabled Tesco to understand the reality of Czech seasonality, range requirements and shopping patterns.

Tesco Values

Underpinning the operations and local focus are a set of Tesco Values, as detailed in Table 5.1.1 below. While many organizations have mission statements, the Tesco Values are more than just a statement of intent and manifest themselves in a number of ways throughout the business, helping to take decisions and assess performance. They also act as a reference point which guards the integrity of the Tesco brand and ensures that customers and staff in the Czech Republic receive a standard of shopping experience equal to that offered by Tesco in its other markets

Listening to customers and adding value

The combination of world-class ways of working, local focus and the Tesco Values has led Tesco Stores CR to focus on areas where additional value for customers could be created in order to increase loyalty. This has led Tesco to introduce a number of innovations to the Czech retail market:

- 24-hour opening: as lifestyles have changed in the Czech Republic over the last 10 years Czech customers increasingly want to shop at a time that is convenient to them. The result has been the introduction of 24-hour non-stop opening in eight out of the nine hypermarkets across the Czech Republic.
- Price cuts: customer feedback has highlighted the importance of price to Czech customers. As Tesco has grown, it has undertaken a number of programmes aimed at increasing productivity within the business. When combined with growing scale and efficiencies, this has enabled Tesco to make substantial savings in operational costs, which it has then been able to invest in reducing prices.
- Own label development: as trust has grown in relation to a previously unknown brand, Tesco has introduced a wide range of own-brand products. Not only has this benefited Czech customers, but it has also provided opportunities for smaller Czech suppliers to work with Tesco and use the strength of the Tesco brand for the benefit of their own businesses.

- Buying better: local sourcing is popular with customers and for a company focused on maximizing efficiency makes good business sense. Tesco has worked closely with Czech suppliers through the sharing of technical and marketing support, which has led to an increase in the quality and attractiveness of products offered through Tesco stores.

Over 90 per cent of all products stocked within the Czech hypermarkets are sourced from suppliers based within the Czech Republic.

A further benefit of this approach is that supplier standards have increased, which in turn has increased supplier competitiveness and their export potential (both to Tesco and to other retailers). Tesco has also provided Czech suppliers with access to Internet-based auctions for supply to Tesco stores outside of the Czech Republic and a regional Non-Food Sourcing Office has also been established in Prague to act as a hub for the whole of the Central European region.

Achievements to date

The increasing scale and internationalization of Tesco sales and purchasing operations have made a significant contribution to efficiency, long-term profitability and growth of the whole of the Tesco group. The input of the Czech business has been an increase in turnover in four years of over 235 per cent (December 1997 versus December 2001) and a direct contribution to profit.

Tesco has also learned a huge amount from operating in the Czech Republic with an increasing amount of learning being shared not only regionally (eg from the Czech Republic to other countries in Central Europe) but also back to the United Kingdom, with the layout, merchandising and operation of the newer Tesco Extra stores in the UK being based on the hypermarkets developed by Tesco in Central Europe and South East Asia.

Table 5.1.1 Tesco Stores CR key facts

Hypermarkets	9	No. of Czech suppliers:	1,500
Department stores:	6	No. of own-brand lines:	300
Employees:	7,000	Customers per week:	800,000+
% of Czech store directors:	100	End 2001 retail floor space	1.2 m. sq. ft.

5.2

Czech Technology Park, Brno

Roderick Barker, General Manager

Structure of the joint venture

The Czech Technology Park in Brno is a joint venture between the UK P&O Group and the city of Brno. The company, Technology Park Brno, a.s., has a formal cooperation agreement with the Brno University of Technology (BUT) and the project is being developed adjacent to the university campus. Founded in 1993, the Park was the brainchild of the chairman of the Bovis Group, Sir Frank Lampl. Bovis was formerly a wholly owned subsidiary of P&O and Lampl, who studied at the Technical University, recognized the advantages that the scheme could offer following the political and economic changes that were taking place throughout the region.

P&O and the city of Brno each hold 50 per cent of the shares in the joint-venture company, with the university holding a single 'priority share'. The local authority contributed long leasehold land within the first phase, with the commercial partner matching the long leasehold value with cash equity. The city of Brno provides general support and assists with major infrastructure and traffic connections. P&O provides development management expertise and a finance guarantee, which enables the joint-venture company to secure development funding.

Business philosophy

The Technology Park's philosophy is to combine commerce and academia in a business park environment, providing modern commercial premises for high-tech companies. The Park's proximity to and relationship with BUT is a major attraction for locating companies. Founded in 1899, BUT has excellent faculties for mechanical, civil, electronics, informatics and chemical engineering as well as architecture, and has almost 14,000 students and 2500 staff. The institution, along with Brno's five other universities, provides a highly qualified graduate workforce. BUT regularly undertakes project work with commercial applications in collaboration with a range of companies and is actively pursuing further research links with quality foreign and domestic organizations and welcomes opportunities to foster cooperation.

Brno, the Czech Republic's second city, is strategically located at the heart of Europe and has been an important centre of trade for generations. With a population of 400,000, Brno itself has a long-established tradition in engineering and electronics and provides a highly skilled workforce coupled with low employment costs. With the development of the new economy, the city has become a centre for high-tech electronics, IT and computing; it is also home to Brno Exhibitions and Fairs, BVV, a major exhibition and trade fair site, which draws over one million people annually from all over the world, reinforcing the city's importance as a centre of commerce.

Construction and development

The master plan for the entire Technology Park covers 120 hectares of land, including the BUT campus, and will provide a total of 190,000 square metres of mixed commercial accommodation for office, research and light industry, together with associated retail, leisure and services facilities. The original master plan was developed by Building Design Partnership (BDP), one of the largest multi-disciplinary architectural design practices in Europe. The master plan was formally adopted as the land use strategy for the site and approved by the city of Brno within the city's regulation development plan, designated as a special zone in 1993. The first office zone providing 28,000 square metres was launched by way of an architectural competition. Peter Foggo International submitted the winning phase design and the first building, the 3600-square metre Kaplan Building, was completed in the summer of 1995. This building provided some of the most advanced office space in the Czech Republic at that time. With flexible open-plan floor plates, fully accessible raised floors and internal environment control systems, the building helped to attract the first tenant to the Park, Siemens Communication Systems.

The Technology Park is currently developing the remainder of phase one of the scheme concentrated on two zones providing office and high-tech production space. Five buildings have been completed to date in addition to an on-site restaurant. Planning permission is in place for the whole first phase and building permits exist for standard offices and production buildings. Individual building permits require to be negotiated with the local construction department where changes are required to the existing specification, although usually these changes can be agreed during the construction period negating any delay in the development programme. The developer has just commenced work on site for construction of a new 8600-square metre production unit to be occupied by FEI Company for the development and manufacture of electron microscopes.

Occupants

Other tenants at the Park in addition to Siemens include SGI, Lexmark International, Invensys, GTS, Honeywell, Cesky Mobil, Control Techniques, Tranza and IBM. The project is now home to 16 companies, which undertake various activities on the Park from high-tech manufacturing to more office-based functions. The majority of these companies are regional Czech subsidiaries of US, British, German and Dutch multinationals although some companies are wholly Czech owned. Invensys Sensor Systems manufacture and assemble a sensor unit used for the control of air conditioning in cars, which involves combining a small electrical printed circuit board with an ASIC silicon chip linked to a pressure sensor. This technology and assembly operation typifies the manufacturing undertaken on site. The university provides the capability for product development and has an excellent reputation in the fields of materials research. Torrington, the US precision engineering company, recently opened a large bearings manufacturing plant in the town of Olomouc some 70 kilometres from Brno. While such a large manufacturing facility is unsuitable for the Technology Park, the company has established a technical development centre at the Park in cooperation with the university. Other sectors include telecommunications, computing and IT, engineering, electronics, optics and regulation and control systems.

Czech government support

The Technology Park works closely in cooperation with CzechInvest, the Czech government agency for promoting foreign investment, and has completed several successful projects to date. The decision by IBM to choose the Technology Park as the location for a new Information Technology Service Centre was important for both the project and the city. As we explained at the time, such a decision by the world's largest information technology company was significant for the project and also the city of Brno. IBM, which was drawn to Central and Eastern Europe in their site location deliberations, weighed the pros and cons of locating their investment in either one of the Czech Republic, Slovakia, Hungary or Estonia. As with many such investment decisions, government incentives played a part, and the project was used as a pilot scheme for expanding the existing investment incentive package offered by the Czech government into the so-called 'strategic services' sector. In the Czech Republic, IBM first considered Prague and Brno and, after in-depth comparative analysis, the company recognized the cost advantages that the Technology Park and city offered compared to the capital location.

The developer also received a contribution towards the cost of primary infrastructure installation under a government scheme for assisting the establishment of industrial zones throughout the country. This has enabled the project to react quickly to manufacturers' requirements for new buildings and allows the developer to offer a more competitive rental level. Such flexibility is important in the competition to attract foreign investors seeking a Central European manufacturing location. Often such projects need to be in operation very quickly from receipt of final approval. Reaction time is critical as well as future expansion possibilities. Sometimes an interim solution is necessary while a new facility is constructed. The development team at the Technology Park have experience in handling such enquiries and are able to offer a complete turnkey solution to satisfy locating companies' property requirements.

Quality environment

High-tech production and assembly operations often involve technical installations within the building, which control the internal environment and supply the production process. Clean rooms, humidity-controlled areas, anti-static floors, compressed air networks and liquid nitrogen distribution are often a requirement. Since these installations can form an integral part of the building, it is complicated to divide the specification between the developer's specification and the occupier company's fit-out. This is straightforward where the investing company is constructing its own building for occupation. The matter is more complicated when the building is constructed by a developer and leased by the occupier. Nevertheless, many investors seek the flexibility of the leasing solution at the Technology Park, which is not available at alternative locations.

The Technology Park should also provide conditions for technology transfer and business incubation. This process has moved forward with the university recently securing funding to develop a business incubator. Start-up companies whose projects are approved will be able to receive beneficial conditions and business support services through the incubator management structure. The proximity of multinational companies in the Technology Park will provide excellent opportunities for cooperation and the injection of new ideas and processes. This is an important ingredient of any technology park and it will provide a route for the commercialization of university research.

Future prospects

The Technology Park has secured its position as one of the most important business developments in Central Europe. It believes that the founding principles were sound. It has reached critical mass and is 100 per cent leased with a good tenant profile at a time when others are embarking on such schemes. It was a considerable task to launch such a progressive scheme in Brno when most of the focus was on Prague in the early-to-mid-1990s. However, the Park is certainly the better option in the medium to long term. The cost and availability of staff is very important and, in this respect, Brno certainly has a distinct advantage over the capital. Occupancy costs are also a consideration and relative leasing rates are lower outside the capital. As the economy develops farther, both factors will combine to become increasingly important. The Technology Park approach of attracting a number of high-profile investors has created a solid foundation on which to base future development. Business incubation and technology transfer are equally important but easier to achieve if the Technology Park is underpinned with a strong cash flow from its commercial tenants. There are many so-called technology parks registered in the country but the Brno Technology Park is by far the most developed. Potential clients visiting the Technology Park can see that it actually exists physically and is not just a vision on paper.

The Brno Technology Park welcomes enquiries and interested parties should contact the address below:

Technology Park Brno a.s.
Technicka 15
616 00 Brno
Czech Republic
Tel.+420 5 4119 1112
Fax.+420 5 4119 1133
http://www.technologypark.cz
email: tpb@technologypark.cz

Part Six

Appendices

Appendix 1

Sources of Further Information

In the Czech Republic

Ministry of Finance
Letenská 15
118 10 Praha 1
Tel: +420 2 5704 1111
Fax: +420 2 5704 2788
E-mail: WebMaster@mfcr.cz
Website: www.mfcr.cz

Ministry of Foreign Affairs
Loretánské náméstí 5
118 00 Praha1
Tel: +420 2 2418 1111
Fax: +420 2 2418 2068
E-mail: info@mzv.cz
Website: www.mzv.cz

Ministry of Industry and Trade
Na Františku 32
110 15 Praha 1
Tel: +420 2 2485 1111
Fax: +420 2 2311 970
Website: www.mpo.cz

Confederation of Industry of the Czech Republic (SPCR)
Mikulandska 7
113 61 Praha 1
Tel: +420 2 2491 8037
Fax: +420 2 2491 5253
E-mail: dkuchtova@spcr.cz
Website: www.spcr.cz
Contact: Ms. Dagmar Kuchtova, Director of External Relation Department

Economic Chamber of the Czech Republic
Seifertova 22
130 00 Praha 3—Zizkov
Tel: +420 2 2409 6111
Fax: +420 2 2409 6222
E-mail: info@hkcr.cz
Website: www.komora.cz

British Chamber of Commerce in the Czech Republic
IBC, Pobřežni 3
180 00 Praha 8
Tel: +420 2 2483 5161
Fax: +420 2 2483 5162
E-mail: britcham@gts.cz

Czech Statistics Office
Sokolovska 142
186 04 Praha 8
Tel: +420 2 7405 2451
Fax: +420 2 6631 0429
E-mail: bondyova@gw.czso.cz
Website: www.czso.cz
Contact: Mrs. Jana Bondyova, Director of Inf. Department

Union of Professional Unions
Skretova 6
120 59 Praha 2
Tel: +420 2 2423 6322, 4689
Fax: +420 2 2423 0606
E-mail: irena.vlckova@socr.cz or socr@socr.cz
Contact: Mrs Ing. Irena Vlckova, Director

Association of Czech Entrepreneurs
Skretova 6
120 59 Praha 2
Tel: +420 2 2423 0580
Fax: +420 2 2421 0434
Website: www.sp-cr.cz

National Property Fund
Rasinovo nabrezi 42
128 00 Praha 2
Tel: +420 2 2499 1111
Fax: +420 2 2499 1555
Website: www.fnm.cz

Czech Venture Capital Association
c/o Fond rizikového kapitálu, s.r.o.
Na Šťáhlavce 2,160 00 Praha 6
Tel: +420 2 3332 6340
Fax: +420 2 3332 6295
E-mail: info@cvca.cz
Website: www.cvca.cz

Czech National Bank
Na Př ikopě 28
115 03 Praha 1
Tel: +420 2 2441 1111
Fax: +420 2 2421 8522, 7865
Website: www.cnb.cz

Czech Banking Association
Vodickova 30
110 00 Praha
Tel: +420 2 2422 5926
Fax: +420 2 2422 5957
E-mail: bank.asociace@mbox.vol.cz
Website: www.bankovni-asociace.cz

Society of Science and Technology Parks
Novotneho lavka 5
116 68 Praha 1
Tel: +420 2 2108 2275
Fax: +420 2 2108 2276
E-mail: icitt@aiecr.cz
Website: www.aiecr.cz
Contact: Mr. Pavel Svejda, Secretary

General Customs Office
Budejovicka 7
140 96 Praha 4
Tel: +420 2 6133 1111
Fax: +420 2 6133 2000
Website: www.cs.mfcr.cz

CzechTrade (Trade Promotion Agency)
Dittrichova 21
PO Box 76
128 02 Praha 1
Tel: +420 2 2490 7500
Fax: +420 2 2490 7503
Website: www.czechtrade.cz

Czech Export Bank
Vodickova 34/701
110 00 Praha 1
Tel: +420 2 2284 3111
Fax: +420 2 2422 6162
Website: www.ceb.cz

Association of Real Estate Agencies
Na Chodovci 2880/3
141 00 Praha 4—Sporilov
Tel: +420 2 771 642
Fax: +420 2 766 401
E-mail: sekretariat@arkcms.cz
Website: www.arkcms.cz

Prague Stock Exchange
Rybna 14, PO.BOX 49
110 05 Praha 1
Tel: +420 2 2183 1111
Fax: +420 2 2183 3040
Website: www.pse.cz

EGAP (Export Guarantee and Insurance Corporation)
Vodickova 34/701
111 21 Praha 1
Tel: +420 2 2284 1111
Fax: +420 2 2284 4001
Website: www.egap.cz

European Bank for Reconstruction and Development (EBRD)
Karlova 27
110 00 Praha 1
Tel: +420 2 2423 9070
Fax: +420 2 2423 3077
Website: www.ebrd.org

Embassy of the United Kingdom and Northern Ireland
Thunovská 14
118 00 Praha 1
Czech Republic
Tel: +420 2 5740 2111
Fax: +420 2 5740 2296
E-mail: info@britain.cz

British Embassy Commercial Section
Palác Myslbek
Na Př íkopé 21
117 19 Prague 1
E-mail: commerce@fco.gov.uk
Tel: +420 2 2224 0021/3
Fax: +420 2 2224 3625
Website: www.britain.cz

Outside the Czech Republic

Embassy of the Czech Republic in the UK
26, Kensington Palace Gardens
London W8 4QY
UK
Tel: +44 20 7243 1115
Fax: +44 20 7727 9654

Czech Republic Unit
Trade Partners UK
Bay 749, Kingsgate House
66–74 Victoria Street
London SW1E 6SW
UK
Tel: +44 20 7215 4775
Fax: +44 20 7215 4743
Website: www.tradepartners.gov.uk

Trade Partners Information Centre
Room 134
66–74 Victoria Street
London SW1E 6SW
Tel: +44 20 7215 5445
Fax: +44 20 7215 4231

Confederation of British Industry
Centre Point
103 New Oxford Street
London WC1A 1DU
Tel: +44 20 7379 7400
Fax: +44 20 7240 1578
Website: cbi.org.uk

British Council
Export Promotion Unit
10 Spring Gardens
London SW1A 2BN
Tel: +44 20 7389 4818
Fax: +44 20 7389 4885
Website: www.britishcouncil.org/promotion

Export Market Research Scheme (EMRS)
British Chamber of Commerce
4 Westwood House
Westwood Business Park
Coventry CV4 8HS
Tel: +44 24 7669 4484
Fax: +44 24 7669 5844
Website: www.britishchambers.org.uk/exportzone/emrs

EBRD
One Exchange Square
London EC2 2JN
Tel: +44 20 7338 6000
Fax: +44 20 7338 6100
Website: www.ebrd.com

European Investment Bank
100 Boulevard Konrad Adenauer
L-2950 Luxembourg
Tel: +35 2 43791
Fax: +35 2 437704
E-mail: info@eib.org
Website: www.eib.org

International Finance Corporation (IFC)
European Office
4 Millbank
London SW1P 3JA
Tel: +44 20 7222 7711
Fax: +44 20 7976 8323
Website: www.ifc.org

Representation of the European Commission in the UK
8 Storey's Gate
London SW1P 3AT
Tel: +44 20 7973 1992
Fax: +44 20 7973 1900
Website: www.cec.org.uk

European Commission
Rue de la Loi/Wetstraat 200
1049 Brussels
Belgium
Tel: +32 2 295 8266
Fax: +32 2 295 8094

Permanent Missions, Consulates and Honorary Consulates of the Czech Republic

Australia
Consulate General of the Czech Republic
169 Military Road
Dover Heights
NSW 2030, Sydney
Australia
Tel: +61 2 9371 0860
Fax: +61 2 9371 9635

Austria
Permanent Mission of the CR to the United Nations, OSCE and other International Organizations in Vienna
Penzingerstrasse 11–13
A-1140 Wien
Austria
Tel: +43 1 894 21 256
Fax: +43 1 894 57 98

Belgium
Permanent Delegation of the Czech Republic to NATO and WEU
Boulevard Léopold III., NATO HQ
1110 Brussels
Belgium
Tel: +32 2 707 17 27/707 13 52
Fax: +32 2 707 17 03

Canada
Consulat Général de la République Tcheque
1305 Ave. des Pins, Quest Montreal
Quebec H3G 1B2
Canada
Tel: +1 514 849 44 95
Fax: +1 514 849 41 17

Denmark
Honorary Consulate of the Czech Republic
Priorslokkevej 1
Postbox: 169
DK-8700 Horsens
Denmark
Tel: +45 7562 5111
Fax: +45 7561 8091

Finland
Honorary Consulate of the Czech Republic
Newspaper Kaleva
PO Box 70
901 01 Oulu
Finland
Tel: +358 8 537 72 00
Fax: +358 8 537 72 06

France
Délégation Permanente de la Rt Aupres du Conseil de l'Europe
53, allée de la Robertsau
67000 Strasbourg
France
Tel: +33 3 8825 7677
Fax: +33 3 8837 3362

Germany
Generalkonsulat der Tschechischen Republik
Siedlerstrasse 2
85774 Unterföhring b. München
Germany
Tel: +49 89 950 124 6
Fax: +49 89 950 36 88

Hungary
Czech Köztársaság Nagykövetsége
Szegfü utca 4
1064 Budapest VI
Hungary
Tel: +361 352 18 23
Fax: +361 321 26 42

Israel
Honorary General Consulate of the Czech Republic
Leah Str. 7
Ramat Gan
Tel Aviv
Israel
Tel: +9720 672 50 41

Italy
Consolato Generale della Repubblica Ceca
G.B. Morgagni 20
20129, Milano
Italy
Tel: +39 02 29403007
Fax: +39 02 29404401

Japan
Honorary Consulate of the Czech Republic
4–2–12, Isobe-dori, Chuo-ku
Kobe 651 0084
Japan
Tel: +81 78 252 28 20
Fax: +81 78 252 28 10

Luxembourg
Consulat Honoraire de la République Tcheque
3, boulevard Prince Henri
L-1724 Luxembourg
Luxembourg
Tel: +352 227 341
Fax: +352 227 341

The Netherlands
Consulaat van de Tsjechische Republik
Weena 340
3012 NJ Rotterdam
The Netherlands
Phone/Fax: +31 10 414 18 35

Norway
Honorary Consulate of the Czech Republic
Fortunen 1
5013 Bergen
Norway
Tel: +47 55 232 200
Fax: +47 55 232 199

Poland
Konsulat Generalny Republiki Czeskiej
ul. Pawla Stalmacha 21
40–058 Katowice,
OEÁ-ul. Rózana 5
40–045 Katowice
Poland
Tel: +48 32 518 576 7
Fax: +48 32 515 567
OEÁ Tel/Fax: +4832 251 15 09,

Portugal
Consulado Honorário da RepŁblica Checa
Rua Senhora de Porto 930
4200–453 Porto
Portugal
Tel: +351 22 834 25 45
Fax: +351 22 834 26 11

Russia
General'noje Konsulstvo ň keskoj Respubliki
Tverskaja ul. 5
193 015 Sankt Peterburg
Russia
Tel: +7 812 271 04 59, 271 46 12
Fax: +7 812 271 46 15

Slovakia
Generálny Konzulát Českej Republiky
Rázusova 13, P.O. Box E-10, 042 40 Koice
Slovakia
Tel: +42 195 623 18 01 2
Fax: +42 195 623 17 99

Slovenia
Konzulat Česke Republike
Vilfanova 9
66 000 Portorož
Slovenia
Tel/Fax: +386 66 747 270

Spain
Consulado Honorario de la República Checa
Provenza 273 pral.
08008 Barcelona
Spain
Tel: +34 932 720 432
Fax: +34 932 720 433

Sweden
Honorary Consulate of the Czech Republic
Västergatan 22
211 21 Malmo
Sweden
Tel: +46 40 973 698
Fax: +46 40 120 382

Switzerland
Mission Permanente de la Rt Aupres de l'Office des Nations
Unies et des Autres Organ. Inter. a Geneve
17, ch. Louis-Dunant
Case postale 109
1211 Geneva 20
Switzerland
Tel: +41 22 740 38 88
Fax: +41 22 740 36 62

Konsulat der Tschechischen Republik
Zihlackerstrasse 13
4153 Reinach
Switzerland
Tel: +41 61 712 00 70/462 00 11
Fax: +41 61 462 00 03

UK
Honorary Consulate of the Czech Republic in Manchester
26 Church Street
Altrincham
Cheshire
WAA 14 4DW
Tel: +44 161 928 9988
Fax: +44 161 926 8726

Honorary Consulate of the Czech Republic
12A Riselaw Crescent
Edinburgh EH10 6HL
Scotland
Tel: +44 131 447 95 09/447 55 28
Fax: +44 131 447 55 28

USA

Permanent Mission of the Czech Republic to the United Nations
1109–1111 Madison Avenue
New York.
NY 100 28
USA
Tel: +1 212 535 88 14–5
Fax: +1 212 772 05 86

Appendix 2

Contributor Contact Details

ABN AMRO
Lazanska 3
PO Box 773
111 21 Praha 1
Czech Republic
Tel: +420 2 4405 2338
Fax: +420 2 4405 2885
Contact: Ms Sarka Sankova, PR and Marketing Manager

AON Czech Republic
Karlova namesti 28
120 00 Praha 2
Tel: +420 2 2223 2220
Fax: +420 2 2223 0077
E-mail: aon@aon.cz
Website: www.aon.cz
Contact: Ms Jitka Bendova, GBU Manager

AWS Structured Finance
Tel: +44 1892 667891
Fax: +44 1892 610891
E-mail: kevin.r.smith@awsconsult.co.uk
Website: www.awsconsult.co.uk
Contact: Kevin Smith

Bank Austria Creditanstalt
Dr. Karl Lueger-Ring 10,1010 Wien
Tel: +43 1 53131–41964
Fax:+43 1 53131–41050
E-mail: bernhard.sinhuber@ba-ca.com
Contact: Bernhard Sinhuber

CA IB
nam. Kinskych 2/602
150 00 Prague 5
Czech Republic
Tel: +420 2 5701 6111
Fax: +420 2 5701 6550
E-mail: sec.prg@ca-ib.com
Website: www.ca-ib.cz
Contacts: Mr. Michal Srb, Associate, Research Department
Mrs. Martina Lambert, PR Manager

CMS Cameron McKenna
Karoliny Svetle 25
110 00 Prague 1
Czech Republic
Tel: +420 2 2109 8888
Fax: +420 2 2109 8000
E-mail: cmck.com@mbox.vol.cz
Website: www.law-now.com

CzechInvest
Stepanska 15
120 00 Praha 2
Czech Republic
Tel: +420 2 9634 2581
Fax: +420 2 9634 2502
Website: www.czechinvest.org
Contact: Robert Hejzak, Director of Marketing

The Czech Association of the Petroleum Industry and Trade
E-mail: cappo@asmnet.cz
Contact: Miloš Podrazil, General Manager

Deloitte & Touche Czech Republic
Tyn 641/4
110 00 Prague 1
Czech Republic
Tel: +420 2 2489 5500
Fax: +420 2 2489 5555
Website: www.deloittece.com

DTZ Prague spol. s.r.o.
IBC Building
Pobrezni 3
18600 Prague 8
Czech Republic
Tel: +420 2 2232 2086
Fax: +420 2 2232 2134
E-mail: Omar.Sattar@dtz.com
Contact: Omar Sattar

Egon Zehnder International
Kaunický Palác, Panská 7
110 00 Prague 1
Czech Republic
Tel: +420 2 2423 4400
Fax: +420 2 2423 4030
E-mail: eziprague@ezi.net
Website: www.zehnder.com
Contact: Lubomir Ochotnicky

Healey & Baker
Melantrichova 17b–19
110 01 Praha 1
Czech Republic
Tel: +420 2 2163 2424
Fax: +420 2 2163 2425
E-mail: Andrew_Thompson@healey-baker.com
Contact: Andrew Thompson

Ministry of Industry and Trade of the Czech Republic
Ing. Pavel Říha, Ministerial Counsellor
E-mail: rihapa@mpo.cz
Department of Mechanical Engineering and Electrical Industry
Viktor Danielis, Director
E-mail: danielis@mpo.cz
Engineering Department
Jiri Langer, Head of Department
E-mail: langer@mpo.cz
Consumer Industry Department
Václav Haas
E-mail: haas@mpo.cz

Ministry of Transport and Communications
Department of Transport Policy, International Relations and the Environment
E-mail: zatloukal@mdcr.cz
Contact: Josef Zatloukal, Director

PP Agency, s.r.o.
Myslíkova 25,
110 00 Praha 1
Czech Republic
Tel:: +420 2 2140 6601
Fax: +420 2 2493 4236
Website: www.ppagency.cz
Contact: Mrs Romana Slaninova

Seddons
Rybna 1
110 00 Praha 1
The Czech Republic
Tel: +420 2 2231 6522, +420 2 2177 1711
Fax: +420 2 2231 6805
E-mail: seddons@seddons.cz
Website: www.seddons.cz
Contact: Mr. Jan Grozdanovic

Skanska Property
Olivova 4
110 00 Prague 1
Czech Republic
Tel: +420 2 2450 6111
Fax: +42 2 2450 6112
Contact: Radka Jiraskova, Marketing Manager

Teamconsult s.r.o.
Italska 2
120 00 Praha 2
Czech Republic
Tel: +420 2 2251 0251
Fax: +420 2 2425 3123
E-mail: teamconsult@telecom.cz
Contact: Oliver Schmitt

Technology Park Brno a.s.
Technicka 15
616 00 Brno
Czech Republic
Tel:+420 5 4119 1112
Fax:+420 5 4119 1133
E-mail: tpb@technologypark.cz
Website: www.technologypark.cz

Trade Partners UK
Website: www.tradepartners.gov.uk

Union of Machinery Manufacturers and Suppliers
Website: www.sst.cz
Zdenek Hruby, Executive Director,

University of Pardubice
Transport Faculty
Bohumil Řezníč ek
E-mail: bohumil.reznicek@upce.cz
Pavel Šaradín
E-mail: pavel.saradin@upce.cz

Volvo Auto Czech sro
V Oblouku 731
Pruhonice
Czech Republic,
Telephone: +420 2967 87111
Fax: +420 2967 87222
Website: www.volvocars.cz
E-mail: dklocurk@volvocars.com

Appendix 3

Bank Austria Creditanstalt Contact List

Economics Department

Marianne Kager, Chief Economist
Gigergasse 1, A-1030 Vienna
Tel: (+43 1) 711 91 ext.51952
E-mail: matianne.kager@ba-ca.com

Stefan Bruckbauer, Deputy Department Head
Dr.-Karl-Lueger-Ring 10, A-1010 Vienna
Tel. +43 (0) 505 05 ext. 41951
E-mail: stefan.bruckbauer@ba-ca.com

Kurt Fesselhofer
Gigergasse 1, A-1010 Vienna
Tel: (+43 1) 711 91 ext. 1953
E-mail: kurt.fesselhofer@ba-ca.com

Hans Holzhacker
Dr.-Karl-Lueger-Ring 10, A-1010 Vienna
Tel. +43 (0) 505 05 ext. 41965

Walter Pudschedl
Dr.-Karl-Lueger-Ring 10, A-1010 Vienna
Tel. +43 (0) 505 05 ext. 41957

Manfred Weidmann
Dr.-Karl-Lueger-Ring 10, A-1010 Vienna
Tel. +43 (0) 505 05 ext. 41962
E-mail: manfred.weidmann@ba-ca.com

Brussels Representative Office

Peter Rieger
Avenue de Cortenbergh 89
Tel: (+32 2) 735 41 22
E-mail: peter.rieger@pophost.eunet.be

International Export and Trade Finance

Robert Fleischmann, Department Head
Am Hof 2, A-110110 Vienna
Tel: (+43 1) 711 91 ext. 56901
E-mail: robert.fleischmann@ba-ca.com

Florence Werdisheim, Deputy Head
Am Hof 2, A-1010 Vienna
Tel: (+43 1) 71191 ext. 50330
E-mail: florence.werdisheim@ba-ca.com

Margit Slezak, Deputy head
Am Hof 2, A-1010 Vienna
Tel: (+43 1) 711 91 ext. 87320
E-mail: margit.slezak@ba-ca.com

Brigitte Elmecker
Am Hof 2, A-1010 Vienna
Tel: (+43 1) 71191 ext. 50320
E-mail: brigitte.eolmecker@ba-ca.com

Commodity Trade Finance/Structured Trade Finance

Michael Heger, Head
Am Hof 2, A-1010 Vienna
Tel: (+43 1) 711 91 ext. 53390
E-mail: michael.heger@ba-ca.com

Corporate and Project Finance

Martin Frank, Department Head
Schottengaasse 6, A-1010 Vienna
Tel: (+43 1) 531 31 ext. 44202
E-mail: martin.frank@ba-ca.com

EU Finance

Otto Giebneer
Landstrasser Hauptstrasse 1, A-1030 Vienna
Tel: (+43 1) 711 91 ext. 52546
E-mail: otto.giebner@ba-ca.com

Karin Heiling
Landstrasser Hauptstrasse 1, A-1030 Vienna
Tel: (+43 1) 711 91 ext. 5434
E-mail: karin.heiling@baa-ca.com

Corporate Customer Advice and Export & Investment Promotion Finance

Tel: (+43 1) 531 31 ext. 44405, 44424
E-mail: 8844_EXIN@ba-ca.com

Index

References in *italic* indicate figures or tables

The *Doing Business with…* Series

Originally launched in 1992, this highly regarded series provides advice on the risks and rewards of business engagement in key emerging and established markets around the world. Each individual country title looks at the economic prospects, the climate for foreign investment and at commercial opportunities in key industry sectors. It combines this with up-to-date advice on the rules of engagement for foreign investors and trading partners. Contributors to the series include some of the very top international firms in their field, such as: AON, Baker & McKenzie, Bank Austria, CMS Cameron McKenna, Deloitte & Touche, Ernst & Young, Eversheds, Herbert Smith, KPMG, HSBC, Standard & Poor's and PricewaterhouseCoopers.

Doing Business with Bahrain
Doing Business with China
Doing Business with Croatia
Doing Business with the Czech Republic
Doing Business with the Republic of Cyprus
Doing Business with Hungary
Doing Business with Jordan
Doing Business with Kazakhstan
Doing Business with Kuwait
Doing Business with Latvia
Doing Business with Libya
Doing Business with Lithuania
Doing Business with Malta
Doing Business with Poland
Doing Business with Qatar
Doing Business with Russia
Doing Business with Saudi Arabia
Doing Business with Serbia
Doing Business with Slovakia
Doing Business with Slovenia
Doing Business with Turkey
Doing Business with Ukraine
Doing Business with United Arab Emirates

For details on these and other titles from GMB publishing Ltd. please visit **www.globalmarketbriefings.com**

Printed in the United Kingdom
by Lightning Source UK Ltd.
118381UK00001BA/2

9 781905 050215